ALL
ANY
EVERY
NO
OTHER
SOME
LITTLE
MUCH
SUCH
THAT
THIS
I
HE
YOU
WHO
AND
BECAUSE
BUT
OR
IF
THOUGH
WHILE
HOW
WHEN
WHERE
WHY
AGAIN
EVER
FAR
FORWARD
HERE
NEAR
NOW
OUT
STILL
THEN
THERE
TOGETHER
WELL
ALMOST
ENOUGH
EVEN
NOT
ONLY
QUITE
SO
VERY
TOMORROW
YESTERDAY
NORTH
SOUTH
EAST
WEST
PLEASE
YES

CHANGE
CLOTH
COAL
COLOUR
COMFORT
COMMITTEE
COMPANY
COMPARISON
COMPETITION
CONDITION
CONNECTION
CONTROL
COOK
COPPER
COPY
CORK
COTTON
COUGH
COUNTRY
COVER
CRACK
CREDIT
CRIME
CRUSH
CRY
CURRENT
CURVE
DAMAGE
DANGER
DAUGHTER
DAY
DEATH
DEBT
DECISION
DEGREE
DESIGN
DESIRE
DESTRUCTION
DETAIL
DEVELOPMENT
DIGESTION
DIRECTION
DISCOVERY
DISCUSSION
DISEASE
DISGUST
DISTANCE
DISTRIBUTION
DIVISION
DOUBT
DRINK
DRIVING
DUST
EARTH
EDGE

HELP
HISTORY
HOLE
HOPE
HOUR
HUMOUR
ICE
IDEA
IMPULSE
INCREASE
INDUSTRY
INK
INSECT
INSTRUMENT
INSURANCE
INTEREST
INVENTION
IRON
JELLY
JOIN
JOURNEY
JUDGE
JUMP
KICK
KISS
KNOWLEDGE
LAND
LANGUAGE
LAUGH
LAW
LEAD
LEARNING
LEATHER
LETTER
LEVEL
LIFT
LIGHT
LIMIT
LINEN
LIQUID
LIST
LOOK
LOSS
LOVE
MACHINE
MAN
MANAGER
MARK
MARKET
MASS
MEAL
MEASURE
MEAT
MEETING
MEMORY

POINT
POISON
POLISH
PORTER
POSITION
POWDER
POWER
PRICE
PRINT
PROCESS
PRODUCE
PROFIT
PROPERTY
PROSE
PROTEST
PULL
PUNISHMENT
PURPOSE
PUSH
QUALITY
QUESTION
RAIN
RANGE
RATE
RAY
REACTION
READING
REASON
RECORD
REGRET
RELATION
RELIGION
REPRESENTATIVE
REQUEST
RESPECT
REST
REWARD
RHYTHM
RICE
RIVER
ROAD
ROLL
ROOM
RUB
RULE
RUN
SALT
SAND
SCALE
SCIENCE
SEA
SEAT
SECRETARY
SELECTION
SELF

SUGGESTION
SUMMER
SUPPORT
SURPRISE
SWIM
SYSTEM
TALK
TASTE
TAX
TEACHING
TENDENCY
TEST
THEORY
THING
THOUGHT
THUNDER
TIME
TIN
TOP
TOUCH
TRADE
TRANSPORT
TRICK
TROUBLE
TURN
TWIST
UNIT
USE
VALUE
VERSE
VESSEL
VIEW
VOICE
WALK
WAR
WASH
WASTE
WATER
WAVE
WAX
WAY
WEATHER
WEEK
WEIGHT
WIND
WINE
WINTER
WOMAN
WOOD
WOOL
WORD
WORK
WOUND
WRITING
YEAR

CHIN
CHURCH
CIRCLE
CLOCK
CLOUD
COAT
COLLAR
COMB
CORD
COW
CUP
CURTAIN
CUSHION
DOG
DOOR
DRAIN
DRAWER
DRESS
DROP
EAR
EGG
ENGINE
EYE
FACE
FARM
FEATHER
FINGER
FISH
FLAG
FLOOR
FLY
FOOT
FORK
FOWL
FRAME
GARDEN
GIRL
GLOVE
GOAT
GUN
HAIR
HAMMER
HAND
HAT
HEAD
HEART
HOOK
HORN
HORSE
HOSPITAL
HOUSE
ISLAND
JEWEL
KETTLE
KEY

ROOF
ROOT
SAIL
SCHOOL
SCISSORS
SCREW
SEED
SHEEP
SHELF
SHIP
SHIRT
SHOE
SKIN
SKIRT
SNAKE
SOCK
SPADE
SPONGE
SPOON
SPRING
SQUARE
STAMP
STAR
STATION
STEM
STICK
STOCKING
STOMACH
STORE
STREET
SUN
TABLE
TAIL
THREAD
THROAT
THUMB
TICKET
TOE
TONGUE
TOOTH
TOWN
TRAIN
TRAY
TREE
TROUSERS
UMBRELLA
WALL
WATCH
WHEEL
WHIP
WHISTLE
WINDOW
WING
WIRE
WORM

LIKE
LIVING
LONG
MALE
MARRIED
MATERIAL
MEDICAL
MILITARY
NATURAL
NECESSARY
NEW
NORMAL
OPEN
PARALLEL
PAST
PHYSICAL
POLITICAL
POOR
POSSIBLE
PRESENT
PRIVATE
PROBABLE
QUICK
QUIET
READY
RED
REGULAR
RESPONSIBLE
RIGHT
ROUND
SAME
SECOND
SEPARATE
SERIOUS
SHARP
SMOOTH
STICKY
STIFF
STRAIGHT
STRONG
SUDDEN
SWEET
TALL
THICK
TIGHT
TIRED
TRUE
VIOLENT
WAITING
WARM
WET
WIDE
WISE
YELLOW
YOUNG

SPECIAL
STRANGE
THIN
WHITE
WRONG

NO 'VERBS'

IT IS POSSIBLE TO GET ALL THESE WORDS ON THE BACK OF A BIT OF NOTEPAPER BECAUSE THERE ARE NO 'VERBS' IN BASIC ENGLISH

A WEEK OR TWO WITH THE RULES AND THE SPECIAL RECORDS GIVES COMPLETE KNOWLEDGE OF THE SYSTEM FOR READING OR WRITING

RULES

ADDITION OF 'S' TO THINGS WHEN THERE IS MORE THAN ONE

ENDINGS IN 'ER,' 'ING,' 'ED' FROM 300 NAMES OF THINGS

'LY' FORMS FROM QUALITIES

DEGREE WITH 'MORE' AND 'MOST'

QUESTIONS BY CHANGE OF ORDER, AND 'DO'

FORM-CHANGES IN NAMES OF ACTS, AND 'THAT,' 'THIS,' 'I,' 'HE,' 'YOU,' 'WHO,' AS IN NORMAL ENGLISH

MEASURES NUMBERS DAYS, MONTHS AND THE INTERNATIONAL WORDS IN ENGLISH FORM

THE
ORTHOLOGICAL
INSTITUTE
LONDON

Reproduced with the consent of the Orthological Institute and The Basic English Foundation.

Basic English:
International Second Language

"Basic English has two chief purposes:
(1) To serve as an international auxiliary
language; that is to say, a second language
for use throughout the world in general
communication, commerce, and science.
(2) To provide a rational introduction to
normal English; both as a first step, complete in
itself, for those whose national language is not
English, and as a grammatical introduction,
encouraging clarity of thought and expression,
for English-speaking peoples at any stage of
proficiency."

C. K. OGDEN.

Basic English
International Second
Language

A revised and expanded version of
The System of Basic English
by

C. K. Ogden

Authorized by the Orthological Institute
and prepared by
E. C. Graham
Editor of *The Basic Dictionary of Science*

With a Foreword by
L. W. Lockhart
Former Assistant Director, Orthological Institute

Harcourt, Brace & World, Inc., New York

For permission to reprint copyrighted material, grateful acknowledgment is
made to the following publishers, authors, and agents:

Basic English Foundation and Orthological Institute: *The Word List and
System.*

Cambridge University Press in association with Evans Brothers Limited:
From *The Bible in Basic English.*

Cassell and Company Ltd., and the Canadian publishers, McClelland and
Stewart Limited, Toronto: From *Onwards to Victory* by Winston S.
Churchill.

Duell, Sloan & Pearce, affiliate of Meredith Press, and George C. Harrap &
Company Limited: From *F.D.R. His Personal Papers* (*1928–1945*), Vol.
II, copyright 1950 by Elliott Roosevelt.

Harper & Row, Publishers, Incorporated, Chatto & Windus Ltd., and Dr.
Helen Spurway: "On Scales" from *Possible Worlds* by J. B. S. Haldane,
copyright 1928 by Harper & Brothers, renewed 1956 by J. B. S. Haldane.
Put into Basic English by W. Empson, 1935.

Houghton Mifflin Company and Cassell and Company Ltd.: From *The
Second World War*, Vol. V, by Winston S. Churchill.

The Macmillan Company and Evans Brothers Limited: From *The Basic
Dictionary of Science*, edited by E. C. Graham, copyright © 1964 Orthological Institute, Lot Gates, and F. K. Ogden. Published in England under
the title *The Science Dictionary in Basic English.*

Orthological Institute: "The Rights of Man" by H. G. Wells from *Psyche,*
Vol. XVIII, 1938–1952. Put into Basic English by C. K. Ogden, 1941.

The Royal Society of Arts: "Basic English—Its Present Position and Plans"
by J. A. Lauwerys from the *Journal of the Royal Society of Arts,* July
1966.

The Society of Authors: Act I of *Arms and the Man* by George Bernard
Shaw. Put into Basic English by L. W. Lockhart, 1936.

Foreword

Basic English: International Second Language is a revised and expanded version of *The System of Basic English,* which has long been out of print. Its reappearance in a revised edition some ten years after C. K. Ogden's death is a welcome event which will give a new generation of English-speaking students an opportunity to make their own assessment of the merits of Basic. The book will be of special interest to all who teach English as a foreign language by methods which owe a great deal to Ogden's ideas but who have no firsthand knowledge of the Basic system itself.

The present volume differs from its predecessor in two respects. The general account of Basic which formed Section One of the book in previous editions has been replaced by an adapted version of *Basic English,* Ogden's original introduction to the system, and Section Two has been expanded by the inclusion of *The Basic Words,* a comprehensive guide to the permitted senses and uses of the Basic Vocabulary. It is a fitting tribute to Ogden that *Basic English, The ABC of Basic English,* and *The Basic Words,* the classic trilogy with which he laid the foundations of his system, should now be presented for the first time in a single volume. Together they provide the intelligent reader with all he needs to make himself proficient in the use of Basic. The selection of examples of Basic writing in Section Three has at the same time been revised and strengthened by the addition of new material, taken for the most part from Basic publications but including various items of special interest, such as the original text, with the Basic English version opposite, of the pronouncement by the

British Government following Churchill's celebrated speech at Harvard in 1943 in favor of Basic English. An extract from the latter appears elsewhere in the book.

Readers familiar with Basic may observe that certain minor changes in usage have been incorporated in *The Basic Words*. All these changes were sanctioned by Ogden, and it was his intention to introduce them into the authorized teaching material as and when the opportunity offered; a few of them have in fact already been adopted in *The Basic Teacher* and its translations. The present revision is, accordingly, in the nature of, a "tidying up" operation. The use of -er, -ing, and -ed endings with adjectives has been extended a little and the reclassification of a number of quasi-idioms which are more properly extensions of sense has enabled further useful idiomatic phrases to be included in the list of permitted uses, but the essential framework of Basic remains unchanged. It must be emphasized that the modifications in question, while increasing the resources of Basic, in no way invalidate existing Basic texts since virtually nothing has been discarded.

The hopes that were raised for the future of Basic as a world language by the powerful support it received from Churchill and others (see pages 97–114) have unfortunately not been realized. Its lack of progress in the last two decades has not surprisingly led some to assume that the system would not work. In a paper read to the Royal Society of Arts in London in April 1966, Professor J. A. Lauwerys, Chairman of the Basic English Foundation, corrected this impression by disclosing that the failure of Ogden's carefully laid plans for the promotion of Basic on a worldwide scale was due almost entirely to the obstructions and difficulties he had to contend with when he became involved with officialdom. By kind permission of the Royal Society of Arts, this paper by Professor Lauwerys is reproduced as an Appendix to Section One.

The decision of the publishers of *The System* to make it available again in a more comprehensive form and the recent publication of *The Science Dictionary in Basic English,* in both England and the United States [1] is an encouraging sign that Basic is attracting increasing interest. Professor Lauwerys outlined in his paper some of the projects that the Basic English Foundation would like to put in hand if funds were available. He also pointed out that there is a growing demand for English in the newly emerging countries. Is it too much to hope that the invaluable part that Basic could play in facilitating programs of scientific and technological aid to these countries will soon be fully recognized?

L. W. LOCKHART

London,
March 1968

[1] Under the title *The Basic Dictionary of Science.*

Contents

ix

S E C T I O N   T W O

The System in Detail

Basic English

A General Introduction with Rules
and Grammar

with Appendices

A. Basic English—Its Present Position and Plans,
a paper by Professor J. A. Lauwerys

B. Churchill and Roosevelt on Basic English

Editor's Note

The account of Basic English in this book is designed to give a general introduction to the system. Written by C. K. Ogden in 1930, and last revised by him for the Ninth Edition of 1944, it has now been re-edited to bring it up to date. This has been done mainly by the addition of two Appendices covering the war and post-war developments, and by footnotes and editorial insertions making adjustments which the passing of time has rendered necessary. Apart from these additions, the book has been left as C. K. Ogden wrote it, except for the omission of certain portions of the third section of Part One, which duplicated material more fully presented in *The ABC of Basic English* and available in Section Two of this omnibus volume. References and other passages in square brackets are editorial.

E. C. G.

Editor's Note

1. Introductory

It is clear that the problem of a universal language would have been solved if it were possible to say all that we normally desire to say with no more words than can be made easily legible to the naked eye, in column form, on the back of a sheet of notepaper. The fact, therefore, that it is possible to say almost everything we normally desire to say with the 850 words on the endpapers, which occupy about three-quarters of the space on the back of an ordinary sheet of business notepaper, makes Basic English something more than a mere educational experiment.

In brief, the words in question have been scientifically selected to form an International Auxiliary Language, i.e., a universal second language, for general communication and science; but in accordance with the second purpose of Basic, they also provide the best first step, complete in itself, to any form of wider English, and an educational instrument (see pages 58–61) of great value.

English, in some form, has long served as the second language of the East. It is, therefore, not surprising that the adoption of Basic English is being advocated by publicists and international organizations throughout the world. Its vocabulary is designed to deal with two distinct levels:

1. The 850 words reproduced on the endpapers are sufficient

for ordinary communication in idiomatic English. (For the convenience of the learner, a selection of 600—forming a first stage at which a wide range of simple reading matter can be provided—is presented with explanatory notes in the first twenty lessons of *Basic Step by Step*.)

2. By the addition of 100 words required for general science, and 50 for any particular science, a total of 1,000 enables any scientific congress or periodical to achieve internationalism.

The 850 are equal in efficiency to approximately 3,000 words in any previous attempt at simplification. They do all the essential work of 20,000. The *effect* will be that of idiomatic English with no literary pretensions, but clear and precise at the level for which it is designed. The difficulties being known, they can be given special attention from the very start; and if it is desired to proceed at a later stage to normal English, the intermediate steps are all provided.

The number of general nouns is 400, of adjectives 100, of verb-forms ('operation-words'), particles, etc., 100. To avoid awkward periphrases, a judicious selection of 200 names of picturable objects (common things such as the auctioneer handles daily, parts of the body, etc.), and 50 adjectival opposites brings the general total here exhibited to 850. With this vocabulary the style and brevity of the Basic translations of Swift, Tolstoi, Stevenson, and Franklin can be attained.

Below the minimum 600, only Pidgin English or travelers' inquiries can emerge; above the scientific total, we are at the level of international standardization and notation, with which the 1,000 word maximum has been systematically linked.

It is perhaps desirable to explain in parenthesis that *all* grammatical instructions can readily be given in terms with which the teacher is familiar. Such novelties of expression or method as are introduced in what follows will not necessarily reappear in the elementary graded textbooks designed for the orthodox beginner. On the other hand, there are those who may welcome an opportunity of escaping from current grammatical formulae.

The Basic vocabulary dispenses with practically all phonetic ambiguities; and when a machine for typing from dictation is invented Basic will prove an ideal language for the purpose. When once the functions of the different parts of speech are understood and the senses of the 850 words have been memorized, it only remains to learn the conjugates of the operation-words [Section Two, verb-forms, page 169] and pronouns [page 170], and the five simple rules covering the formation of plurals, compounds, derivatives, comparatives, and adverbs. The mechanism of normal word-order is explained by a special educational device (a sentence-builder, the Panopticon [1]), illustrating the essential parts of speech and their relations to one another by means of concentric circles on which the words are printed. All necessary idioms (see page 212) are listed in *The ABC* and illustrated by examples.

If it be asked: why 600 words, why 850 words, why 1,000 words; why not 750 or 1,100, or even 1,234, since there is no magic in numbers?—the answer is that Basic is severely practical. Inasmuch as there are limits set (a) by the number of words which can be legibly printed on the back of a single sheet of notepaper, (b) by the capacity of humans to assimilate symbols in thirty to fifty hours, (c) by the minimum first stage that is complete in itself, certain definite frames are indicated to which the linguistic material of a universal language must endeavor to adapt itself. Partly by good fortune, partly by dexterous manipulation, these spatial and mnemonic exigencies have been met without undue sacrifice.

From one standpoint, that of technology and of writers like James Joyce, the 500,000 words of the lexicologist are too few; from another, that of the occidentalizing Oriental, the 10,000 words of the man in the street are too many. Perhaps, in time, both can be satisfied. Standard English may be enriched and cosmopolitanized as the world contracts through the expansion of modern science; and Basic may meet the universal demand for a compact and efficient technological medium. If so, English will

[1] See p. 40.

become not only the international auxiliary language, but the
universal language of the world.

To have succeeded in getting on the back of a sheet of notepaper, in legible form, all the words actually needed to com-
municate idiomatically most of the requirements of international
correspondence, science, and commerce, is, then, the claim of
those who have spent a decade in compiling the Basic vocabulary.

To read an ordinary issue of the *Times* newspaper with profit,
a vocabulary of over 50,000 words is implied. Actually, many
readers get along with 25,000 or less. A conscientious foreigner
is apt to have to memorize about 15,000 by way of insurance,
before he can understand a particular 1,000—even if he will never
have occasion to speak or write English himself. Let us suppose
that this requires from two to four years' hard labor; the problem
of an auxiliary language is to reduce his labor to, at most, two
months.

The artificial languages which contrive, with varying degrees
of plausibility, to make similar claims, cannot attain this minimum; they are all based on a limited group of languages, quite
unfamiliar in type to the millions of Orientals who must chiefly
be kept in view, and their adherents have not yet studied the
problem of simplification systematically.

Moreover, when learned, an artificial language still awaits a
millennium in which conversion shall cease to be confined to a
few thousand enthusiasts; and here the importance of accurate
statistics is once more apparent. It is often stated that English
is the language of 200,000,000 people, and this figure is then
compared with the figures for French, German, Spanish, etc., with
the implication that it would be invidious to be influenced by so
small a lead, when the tide of national prejudice is running so
high. Actually, however, English is the expanding administrative
(or auxiliary) language of over 600,000,000 people, and financial
reasons alone should convince even those who take statistics
seriously that it is bound to expand more rapidly in the near
future.

The "normal vocabulary of the average man" hovers between the alleged 300 words of the Somersetshire farmer, the 4,000 of President Wilson's State Papers, the 7,000 of the Japanese diplomat, the 12,000 of the Eskimo fisherman or the average undergraduate, the 30,000 of Sir Vade Mecum, C.V.O. at Geneva, and the 250,000 of a James Joyce. It is therefore of little value to us in assessing the needs of the Riga merchant endeavoring to establish friendly relations with Pernambuco, or the endocrinologist of Ispahan anxious to convey the significance of his latest adrenal catalyst to the Mayo clinician.

How many words are necessary to meet the needs of the latter pair? We must bear in mind (a) that the sciences have already internationalized so large a part of their notations that they require only the veriest interstitial mortar at the untechnical level of general communication; (b) that the commercial world also has its international background of trade terms, formulae, etc. The entomologists start with more than 10,000 names of ants alone; and in any particular science or trade a small *ad hoc* supplementary vocabulary will double the efficiency of the panoptic minimum. Fifty extra words on the back of the notepaper of the chemist, the geologist, the banker, the printer, or the engineer still leave room for 100 further technical terms in the same type as that here adopted.

The special supplementary vocabularies for chemistry, physics, and biology are printed (together with model translations) in *Basic for Science.*[2]

The preparation of these special supplementary vocabularies, which have little general utility apart from their particular purpose, is now in active progress, and side by side with this goes the reinstatement in graduated installments, for educational purposes, of the words rejected on the panoptic diagrams in the first process of elimination.

In view of the fact that nearly a quarter of the human race already knows *some* English, it is important to observe that

[2] And also in Section Three of this book, pp. 391–93. ED.

the 300,000,000 [3] who can use it fairly fluently need not trouble to learn the grammatical rules which will at first limit the idiom of the foreigner. Provided they keep approximately to the vocabulary, they will be *understood*.

Those, however, who devote a few weeks to this *Auxiliary* medium—of the 1,500,000,000 who are at present linguistically isolated—will be able to make the most of the smallest possible *phonetic* outfit for any international purpose, scientific, commercial, or conversational, and will also have laid the soundest possible foundation for further attainment in the world's most widespread literary idiom.

Take, for instance, Japan, where, after decades of compromise on orthodox lines, the teaching of standard literary English is a failure—and even in danger of being abandoned.[4] The present vocabulary provides the practical and theoretical foundation for a reform movement such as that envisaged by Professor Okakura; and any serious Japanese student should be able, with the assistance of radio, to find his way about the system in less than a month. The 4,000 English words which have already been adopted [5] haphazard into the Japanese language might *then* be fitted into a teaching system whose further stages, in the direction of literature, the student could approach with assurance.

The reader who is prepared to devise practical tests of the claim here made can, of course, take the theoretical background

[3] Presumably this figure was arrived at by adding to the number of those owning English as their native language, the number, all over the world, estimated to have attained some proficiency in it. ED.

[4] This danger is nonexistent today, though the average quality of the teaching remains disappointing. See Colin Simpson, *Picture of Japan* (Angus & Robertson, Sydney, 1957) and an unsigned article, "Teaching English in Japan," in the London *Times Educational Supplement*, March 29, 1963. ED.

[5] See *Japanized English*, by S. Arakawa, Tokyo, 1931. The present number of Japanized English words far exceeds 4,000. But their phonetic form, or their sense, or both, are often so far from their English originals that they are a doubtful boon to Japanese learning English. Ogden may have underestimated the difficulty of fitting these words into English teaching, though he was quite right in suggesting that they need to be dealt with in that teaching, and not ignored, as they largely are today. ED.

largely on trust.[6] For all practical purposes, there are the *objects* which we wish to talk about, the *operations* which we perform on them, and the *directions* in which we operate. When the most necessary *names*, the most fundamental '*operation-words*,' and the essential *directives* have been determined, it can be shown that a verb is primarily a symbolic device for telescoping an operation and an object or a direction ('enter' for *go into*).[7] Sometimes an operation-word, a directive, *and* a name are thus telescoped, as in the odd word 'disembark' (*get, off*, a *ship*); Latin goes so far as to throw in a pronoun, and a tense auxiliary (which would be illustrated on the device described below, page 40, by the collapsing of five concentric annuli). The fundamental operations of physics—the displacements or motions due to pushes and pulls—when caused by the human organism as a whole, can be covered, in English, by ten of the sixteen operational symbols in the Basic vocabulary. The directives proper reduce to the twenty whose definitions are obvious with the aid of a diagram (page 30).

So long as the essentially contractive nature of the verb was concealed by the existing grammatical definitions, there could be no reduction in the vocabulary sufficiently radical to affect the problem of a universal language, *nor is this now possible in any language other than English;* and it is the continuous approximation of East and West, as a result of the analytic character of Chinese and English (especially in its latest American developments), which makes this particular form of English *basic* for the whole world.

---

[6] The theorist will note (what the purely practical may safely ignore) that the five chief principles for which novelty may be claimed, in the sense that their application has made so radical a reduction feasible, are: the elimination of verbs, the analysis of the ten main operation-words and twenty spatial directives which replace them in universal grammar, the use of panoptic conjugation in systematic definition, the projectional interpretation of emotive adjectives, and the development of Bentham's theory of Fictions in the treatment of metaphor. See pp. 52–53.

[7] See pp. 25–26.

Many special captions or trademarks for the system were suggested, but **B A S I C**—British American Scientific International Commercial (English)—has been finally adopted. The term *panoptic* [8] serves to emphasize that in its written or printed form it can (on the back of a sheet of notepaper), as it were, be seen at a glance.

A chief obstacle to the spread of English has hitherto been its phonetic irregularity, the frequency with which the same symbols are used to represent different sounds, and the uncertainties of stress. There is the fact that the word *fish*, as Sir Richard Paget has noted, might appear as *ghoti* (*gh* as in *enough*, etc.); and if dealt with in the same way *foolish* might be spelled in 613,975 different ways.

To master such details in a vocabulary of 20,000 words, or even 2,000, necessitates an amount of drudgery which has given phoneticians and advocates of synthetic languages their opportunity. With the Basic vocabulary, however, such irregularities are reduced to a minimum [9] in which, by treating each word as an individual, the learner can even profit by its peculiar appearance in written form as an aid to memory, and historical continuity can thus be preserved. The 850 sounds being fixed by the gramophone records, their written forms can be memorized as individual entities, with no special emphasis on any principle but that of stress.

Phonetic (spelling) reform can thus be left to pursue its separate path. It may find Basic a useful ally, and Basic may later profit by its progress. Hence the importance of Basic for educational work which cannot allow itself to be involved in controversies such as any violent departure from the habits of centuries must always engender. [10]

[8] 'Seen at a glance.' Cf. p. 40.
[9] See *The Sounds and Forms of Basic English*, by J. Rantz [and *Word-Stress and Sentence-Stress*, by J. C. Catford (1950). ED.].
[10] Although Ogden refused to associate Basic with any movement for spelling reform, he was, of course, prepared to accept whatever could be ac-

It is significant that the initiative in promoting inquiries into the International Language problem has usually come from the natural scientists, as the chief prospective users of an auxiliary language who are organized internationally. Unfortunately they have not realized that the solution lay so near at hand, and have supposed that they must rely on the linguists to whom they have turned for help. But where there is a pipe, the aqueduct becomes unnecessary, and the study of principles for the erection of elaborate structures to get ideas across the linguistic valley is equally unnecessary, when once the notion that all ideas can flow freely through the medium of Basic, at a convenient level, is fully grasped.

How far matters have moved in the twenty years [preceding 1944] may be gathered from the Report of the Committee appointed by the American Association for the Advancement of Science (1921),[11] where two essentials are emphasized, preliminary to any further step on the part of the scientists.

The first concerns the need for "a searching fundamental study of the principles involved and experimental data available."

Such an inquiry was reasonable in 1921, when the British Association also published a Report in which the possibilities of the various artificial languages were seriously considered. But in 1942 a further Report was able to point to Basic English as the most promising solution,[12] so that the only experiments now required would be consequent on the actual adoption of Basic itself.

The second essential of the American report can also, happily, be circumvented; for it demands "authoritative international

complished, and he recommended that "wherever possible without arousing prejudice, the changes already achieved in America should be extended to the rest of the English-speaking world." Accordingly, in *The Basic Words* as here printed in Section Two, the American spellings, *behavior, color, harbor, humor,* and *plow* will be found. ED.

[11] *Science,* February 17, 1922.

[12] *The Advancement of Science,* October 1942, p. 246. [See, for a more recent demonstration of interest by the British Association, p. 81. ED.]

agreement, both as to linguistic details and as to the practical measures to be taken."

The capacity of mankind to secure authoritative international agreement about any subject lags far behind both its more urgent needs and its power of appreciating and adopting the means of satisfying them. Whether as individuals, nations, or commercial and scientific organizations, men can still achieve many of their ends without prior international agreement; and this particular reform is likely to be achieved in practice long before any international committee has succeeded in overcoming the objections of its more intransigent members, preparatory to some further interim recommendation—in Portuguese, in Armenian, and in Greek.

Suggestions for concentration on political action are therefore to be viewed with suspicion. They are likely to lead to the shelving for a decade or a generation of any problem which is ripe for solution outside the political sphere. Any official or political sanction must of course be welcomed, but it is often harder to convert Pharaoh or enthuse Pilate than to induce the people to enter a promised land.

On the other hand, this same American Committee, under the Chairmanship of the Director of the United States Bureau of Standards, by referring to the movement for an international auxiliary language as "heretofore relatively neglected" and "deserving of support and encouragement," showed its awareness of the *impasse*. The achievements of science in the right direction are also usefully summarized, with respect to

> The system of numbers.
> The metric system.
> The measurement of latitude and longitude.
> Mathematical symbols.
> Chemical formulae.
> Time and the calendar.
> Notation in music.[13]

[13] See also *International Picture Language* (in Basic) by Dr. Otto Neurath.

The two main reasons for making English the basis of a universal language are (1) the statistical considerations set forth above, and (2) the fact that English is the only major language in which the analytic tendency has gone far enough for purposes of simplification.

Inflected systems are highly resistant to simplification, and their Latin origin is still only too evident in all the Romance languages of today. In the course of centuries, however, most of the European speech systems have progressed considerably in the right direction, and the analytic tendency, as we know from a passage in Suetonius, may even have been accelerated by the Emperor Augustus himself, who broke away from the ancient habits of literary elegance and obscurity by inserting directives before his nouns; thereby creating an analytic link with such inscriptions as we find already in 57 B.C.—"Si pecunia ad id templum data erit." [14]

English, both in its Anglo-Saxon and its Latin derivatives, has carried the process of simplification to a point where the final step was possible; and by the selection of its vocabulary from the word groups most adapted for universal purposes, irregularities of form and idiom in the Basic nucleus have been reduced to negligible dimensions. The 'operation-words' ['verbs'] still preserve some of their inflections, the pronouns are still infected by case anomalies, a few special plurals and comparatives mar the grammatical picture, and there are certain established idioms which cannot conveniently be circumvented.

The memorization of these irregularities is fortunately only a matter of days, or even hours; but since we have to admit them temporarily into Basic (i.e., until such time as Standard English, with its growing tendency to simplification, shall have progressed far enough to allow us to dispense with them if we so desire), what justification can be offered for their existence, which may at the same time account for their actual preservation?

There is an analogy here with the numbering of streets and

[14] C.I.L., IX, 3513; *apud* Bréal, *Semantics*, p. 19.

houses in a modern city. By anyone who has driven around the
suburbs in search of The Laurels, 13A, Aspidistra Court Gardens—
peering from a taxi through the darkness at No. 8, at Catspaw
Mansions, at The Chestnuts, at No. 41, and at a variety of in-
discernibles, before finally turning the corner of an unsuspected
mews, known locally as Smith's Passage—the advantages of living
in No. 123 West 456th Street will hardly be disputed. Yet even
the best regulated system can conveniently retain certain
mnemonic survivals, whether they be Madison Avenue and River-
side Drive, or *do* and *did*, *he* and *him*, *trousers* and *scissors*,
better and *best*. Provided the exceptions are not too numerous,
and have a significant historical background, they may even
assist the memory. This does not mean that every anomaly which
Basic includes can be excused or justified—many will doubtless
pass away gradually, as linguistic analogy completes its inevitable
work—but it serves to emphasize the negligible character of those
irregularities which need give rise to real regret.

The practical analytic tendency which has made Basic possible
is one which has had various causes at various times in the history of language, but in two respects at least has reflected modern
scientific developments (a) away from the word-magic which
induced a reverence for linguistic forms and rituals; (b) away
from specific and toward general names.

The passage from classical Latin to the Romance languages
was an important step in the right direction. The inheritors of
the language of Cicero and Caesar found a complicated in-
flexional system too laborious for their practical needs.[15] Subtleties were discarded in everyday speech by people of a
simpler mentality, and the learned classes retained the language
of an earlier age for literary purposes.[16] A society which lays

[15] The evidence has been studied from two very different angles by Tap-
polet (*Germ.-Rom. Monatsschrift*, July 1926), and Vossler, *The Spirit of
Language in Civilization*, Chapter IV.
[16] Cf. the Welsh use of a compact, laconic, classical style of serious literature, as contrasted with the looser, analytic prolixity of the business world
(Collinson, *Litteris*, September 1927, p. 102).

stress on verbal niceties in ordinary communication has either succumbed to word-magic, or been victimized by literary pedantry in its educational system. Humanity has not proved sufficiently capable, or it may be, sufficiently long-lived, to profit by a meticulous verbal training. Where the first two decades of life are occupied chiefly with the acquisition of symbolic conventions, scientific and practical considerations almost inevitably suffer; nor has the average proficiency of the victims of the system been such as to justify their sacrifice in the interests of a few master stylists.

It is from America, however, that the chief impetus to profit by this tendency of language in daily speech has come. Although developments of this sort are thus of supreme significance in any systematic approach to language improvement, they naturally tend to be regarded with misgiving in conservative and literary circles.

When Henry James remarked that the American people were romping amid the ruins of the English language, he left it an open question whether they were there to destroy or to fulfill. From the psychological point of view, at any rate, a linguistic romp may be a highly creditable performance. The antic haverings of a pedantic pedestrianism in quest of Pure English are rapidly producing a new form of Addison's disease—for Addison was the first to complain that "the late war has adulterated our tongue with strange words."

But if we are agreed that they are ruins, the case for a newer edifice is all the stronger. If, however, we can build on the old site, so much the better. We may even be able to preserve the old bricks, so that our children's children may say, "This was known to Johnson, to Webster," or "Here Bentham, here Runyon fought and won." The strength of Basic English lies in its determination to discard nothing that is essential from the standpoint of continuity.

2. The Basic Approach [17]

In presenting Basic English as a universal auxiliary language, there are two distinct needs to be met, that of the foreign learner and that of the translator able to make full use of the material at his disposal. A man of letters might correctly ascribe an excruciating noise in the street to gear-changing operations, without being able to distinguish the gearbox from the cylinder if confronted by those objects. On the one occasion his use of the words would commend itself even to experts; on the other he would be dismissed as totally ignorant of their meaning. Similarly, it is possible for a foreigner to know a language satisfactorily in the sense that he can read it and understand it as written by a native, and yet be quite incapable of writing it or speaking it himself; and this fact—that a vocabulary may be 'known' in the sense that it can be interpreted, though not 'known' in the sense that it can be used—has an important bearing on the teaching of Basic English.

Speakers and writers familiar with Standard English can be allowed more freedom in their use of the Basic words than those who employ them *only* in accordance with the rulings laid down for their convenience. These avoid the minor irregularities and idioms of Standard English, which are, however, readily intelligible to the reader or listener, and would be as much trouble to

[17] This section combines, under a new title, two sections of the original book called "The System" and "Grammatical Principles." The reason for this is that the first of these was largely, and the second partly, concerned with giving, in more summary form, the details of the system which are more fully set forth in *The ABC of Basic English*. Those parts judged to be unnecessarily repetitious in this volume have, accordingly, been omitted. The omissions have sometimes been indicated in the text, but since a consequence of them was to necessitate some rearrangement of the material that was left, this has not always been possible. Nothing has been sacrificed to the desire to weed out repetitions. Wherever a point has been made in a new way, with a new emphasis, and so on, it has been left in even though it may be encountered again. ED.

exclude when learned as to learn when not already known. . . .

The question of intelligibility is one which has generally been neglected by an undue insistence on correctness. An idiom, to those who do not use it, may be no more unintelligible than any other dialectal variant; and a little practice with the examples in the *ABC* will take the learner a very long way.

1. NOUNS

Basic English, as may be seen from the vocabulary, in which 600 out of the 850 words are noun-forms, is a system in which the noun plays a predominant part. Much space has been wasted on the barren controversy between noun and verb advocates, with their claims that one or other of these forms was historically the first speech-unit to appear. Both sides seem to have supposed that by stressing such a claim the adjective 'natural' would receive additional justification if applied to their system.

One important advantage of any system which features the noun is the assistance to be derived from the pictorial method, and particularly from the pictorial dictionary to which the various Larousse compilations are already pointing the way. In addition, therefore, to a copiously illustrated dictionary, a volume entitled *Basic by Pictures* will eventually be available; [18] and the compilers of the dictionary of the future will doubtless see the wisdom of combining the pictorial method with the various panoptic [19] diagrams devised for the teaching of Basic.

The nouns cover a very wide range. The list of 200 pictured things (i.e., words *best* taught by pictures) refers, apart from geometrical shapes, to objects which can be touched, seen, and isolated from other things. Some of the things referred to by the 400 necessary names, such as an *animal,* or a *vessel,* are of a

---

[18] *Basic Picture Talks* (1942), by L. W. Lockhart, and *Basic by Picture Stamps* (1941) provide examples of this extensive material. [*Basic by Pictures* has never, in fact, materialized. ED.]

[19] See above, p. 12, also *The Panoptic Method* (in preparation). [This projected work, too, was never completed for publication. ED.]

similar character but much less suitable for pictorial presentation. Others, such as a *mine,* or a *road,* can be touched and seen, but not, as a rule, detached from their surroundings. Others again, such as *ink, oil,* or *tin,* are names of liquids or materials which cannot be treated either as movable or as fixed material objects, but are yet concrete, and can be isolated in definite amounts. The names of these last do not take 'a' in front of them or form plurals except when the unit thus indicated is a class (e.g., *a paint* = a kind of paint, *paints* = kinds of paint). The same limitation applies to the use of the plural form.

In addition to these names there are a number of nouns (for example, *harmony, quality*) which do not stand for anything concrete, though all languages by a convenient make-believe have treated them as though they did. These are names of fictions.[20] They present no special problems from a grammatical point of view, but the distinction is important if we are to understand what language is communicating.

There are two main ways in which the scope of a noun, or of any other word in the vocabulary, may be expanded: extension and specialization.

Expansion is the use of a symbol, devised for one thing or group of things, to refer to some related thing or group. The relation may be that of part to whole, as in the derivation of *letter* (epistle) from *letter* (of the alphabet); of cause to effect, as in the use of *bite* for the act of biting and the wound made by it; of performer to performance, as in the derivation of *lift* (elevator) from the act of lifting, and so on.[21]

[20] The nature of linguistic fictions is perhaps made clearer if they are recognized as a branch of metaphor. Metaphor as commonly understood is the analogical use of a word: a fiction may be loosely described as the analogical use of a word-function (noun). Thus *force of circumstance* is an analogy borrowed from the world of the physicist, but *force* itself, even as the physicist uses it, is a name for which no corresponding object can be found in the universe. For a detailed treatment, see *Bentham's Theory of Fictions* (1932), in the International Library of Psychology.

[21] Metaphor is a particular form of extension, whereby a symbol devised for one group of things between which a given relation holds is applied to an-

Specialization is the differentiated use of an undifferentiated word. A man who 'sends in an account' is understood to have sent in a bill. When we read in the papers of 'the death of a famous Judge' we do not speculate as to whether he was a judge of horses, wine, or pictures; we know at once that he was a legal judge. Specialization is in one sense a limiting factor, but it enlarges the scope of a general vocabulary by enabling it to dispense with words having only a very particularized usage.

From any Basic word it is legitimate to form one specialization, and as many recognized extensions as are simple and convenient. Details of these derived uses of the vocabulary will be found in *The Basic Words*.[22]

Noun-forms can generate four derivatives: two nouns (*-er* and *-ing* suffixes) and two adjectives (*-ing* and *-ed* suffixes), where these are in use in Standard English.

In addition to these, all action nouns ending in *-ing* may be used as qualifiers, and form the *-er* derivative (as do the *-ing* adjectives) by substituting the *-er* suffix for their *-ing* ending, e.g., *building, builder*.

The active sense of the *-ing* form makes it natural for it to be followed by the name of the thing acted on. (*I am printing. What? A book.*) This, for Basic, is not a concession to verb usage, and the traditional account of the "direct object in the accusative," etc., would clearly be out of place. It is, however, a stylistic convenience, and, for beginners, substitutes present no difficulty:

other group of things, in order to display an analogous relationship. Thus we may talk of 'the grip of a disease' or 'designs for the future' in order to avoid including words like *tenacity* and *scheme* in the vocabulary.

[22] Another means of extending the vocabulary is to use one word as more than one part of speech. The most important of these transferences are:

Back, as an adverb, having the sense of the opposite of *forward;*

Light as an adjective (to cover 'pale');

Round as a directive (preposition);

The use of certain adjectives, such as *acid, male,* as nouns. [For the list of these, see Section Two, Part One, p. 189. ED.]

acting a play = getting a play acted; doing a play; putting a play
                on the stage.
airing dresses = giving dresses an airing; getting dresses aired.
answering letters = giving answers to letters; getting letters answered;
                writing in answer to letters.
attacking a town = making an attack on a town.

The *-ed* ending, being purely adjectival (a *printed book, a
book printed in London*), must not be used as a past tense form.
The learner cannot say "I have yellow the printed book,"
and "I have printed the yellow book" would involve the whole
verb technique.

A distinction must, of course, be made between the two *-ing*
derivatives, one of which is a noun and the other an adjective.
The adjective is used of the active participant in an action, e.g.,
the moving train; the noun may be used of something connected
with the action but not performing it, e.g., *walking-stick, jump-
ing-place.* To avoid confusion, it is wisest always to put a hyphen
after the noun-derivative when it is being used as a qualifier.

There is, however, a further difficulty, that of distinguishing
between the transitive and intransitive uses of the adjective
where the sense permits of two uses. Some adjectives are only
used before the name transitively (e.g., *loving*), some only in-
transitively (e.g., *folding*), but others may be used in either sense.
Thus a 'moving song' is a song which, figuratively, moves the
listener, but a 'moving animal' is an animal which moves itself.
Here context rather than any grammatical rule must be the
learner's guide, for experience shows that no serious embarrass-
ment is likely to arise.

About a quarter of the 300 *-ing* derivatives are never used, in
good Standard English, before the noun they qualify, e.g., *requesting, viewing.*[23] The reason for this is that these qualifiers

[23] The 'viewing public' of this television age may need reminding that
Ogden was writing before the need for such a term had been created.
Clearly, however, it would have been no surprise to him to find develop-
ments falsifying his example within a very few years. ED.

have not yet become dissociated from the present participle forms from which they are derived. This explanation, though it serves for the teacher, cannot of course be given to the learner, and the foreigner need not be restrained in this respect. Minor solecisms are a lesser evil here than an extra rule, and in practice the slips would probably be negligible. Many of the derivatives in question are seldom used. The others would almost always appear with a direct object, and in this case the natural impulse would be to place them after the noun.

Although the -er, -ing, and -ed endings may be used, as desired, with any of the 300 nouns which are listed as forming derivatives, there are some words to which one or other of the endings would seldom or never apply. Thus *rained* and *snowed* are only used in such sentences as *This has been rained (snowed) on,* while *judger,* and *guider* are redundant. Note the -or variant with *act, sail,* and *credit.* The derivatives, however, will be learned by practice rather than by deliberate memorizing. [The complete list is given in Section Two, Part One, pages 180–81. ED.]

2. ADJECTIVES

Adjectives are of two kinds: qualifiers, which ascribe qualities to objects; and quantifiers, which indicate the quantities of objects. These last are never preceded by *a* or *the* and do not form comparatives.[24] They are listed in the column of 'operations, etc.'

[24] *A* and *the* are the only adjectives of the nonsymbolic type which are not, strictly speaking, quantifiers:

> *A* indicates an individual of a class, without emphasizing its being a particular member of a class. From this it follows that *a* cannot be used for quantities of substances having no individual form, but only for kinds of substances as distinct from other kinds.
>
> For euphony, *a* becomes *an* before all the vowels, except 'u' when pronounced as in *unit.*

> *The* indicates a particular individual or group of individuals in a class, or a unique individual. It is also used with the singular form to indicate the representative of a class. For a further account of *a* and *the,* adapted for learners, see *The ABC.* [Section Two, Part One, 1, p. 128.]

because, unlike the qualifiers, they are mere linguistic accessories
and have no referential function.

In the rules printed on the Word List it is indicated that the
comparative and superlative are formed with *more* and *most*
respectively. But the alternative forms made by the addition of
-er and *-est* to the adjective are also allowed. The general rule is
that qualifiers of one syllable form comparatives in *-er* and *-est*,
while those of more than one syllable do so with *more* and *most*.
It is, however, subject to a few exceptions: *bent, like, wrong*
compare with *more* and *most; early* takes *-er, -est*.

There are 50 qualifiers which may form negatives, coinciding
in many cases with the opposites, by adding the prefix *un-*. [For
example, *able, certain, natural*. For the complete list, see Section
Two, Part One, 2, page 131.]

A few of these formations, such as *unnormal*, are departures
from Standard English. All, however, can readily be avoided by
the use of *not*, and the beginner who desires not to disturb the
susceptibilities of the purist during the next few years can thus
always attain his desire—while, for others, *improbable*, etc., will
cause no trouble.[25] The justification for these optional innova-
tions would be that they may develop a salutary tendency in
the language and are not unduly offensive.

The qualifiers form derivatives in a manner similar to the
nouns, but the range is more circumscribed; 6 out of the 150
take the suffixes *-er* and *-ing*. They are as follows: *clean, cut, dry,
open, separate, shut.*[26]

3. OPERATION-WORDS

One of the main principles of simplification in Basic is the use
of 'operation-words' combined with prepositions in their ad-

[25] Other permissible variants include *never* [Section Two, p. 139] for *not
ever, further (furthest)* [Section Two, pp. 174–75], and *don't*, etc. [Section
Two, p. 139].
[26] This list was later increased by the addition of the adjectives *clear, smooth,
complete, free, dirty*, and *wet*, making 12 in all; and of these all but *cut* and
shut were allowed to take the *-ed* ending as well. See Section Two, Part
One, p. 180. ED.

verbial form to take the place of verbs. This construction has been gaining ground in Standard English since the fifteenth century, and the language now possesses a host of respectable idioms constructed in this way which offer alternatives, within the scope of the 'operation-words,' for all the important verb utterances.

It is with a view to eliminating word waste that Basic has introduced a very considerable modification in the verb-system by developing the use of these alternatives.

The verb-form has hitherto been one of the great barriers to all attempts at simplification, and as a linguistic device it is not in universal use. For some, therefore, it raises difficulties too great to be mastered at the outset, while even for those who are familiar with the intricacies of the system, irregularities of form in a foreign language overload the memory. Another objection is that verbs involve a wasteful vocabulary in the preliminary stage; by using the 'operation-words' to the fullest possible extent, nouns and adjectives can be made to do double work. Finally, and this is an even more fundamental consideration, verbs, like all stylistic contractions, may lead to confusion of thought at any stage of symbolization.

The operation-words, as may be seen from the picture on page 27, are ten in number, if *be, seem,* and *have* are treated for convenience with the two auxiliaries *may* and *will.* In addition to these there are three analogical extras, *say, see,* and *send*—included in the vocabulary because they lend facility to communication and provide a useful link between the operation-words and the verb-system proper.

The combination of the ten operation-words and the three operator-auxiliaries with the twenty directives immediately gives us equivalents of roughly 200 simple English verbs. Thus, *put in* = 'insert.' But since the ordinary English vocabulary is chiefly composed of synonyms distinguished by subtleties which are not relevant in more than 10 percent of their uses, *put in* is actually the equivalent of many other verbs in particular situations. Thus,

put (a word) *in* = 'interject,' *put* (an account) *in* = 'render,'
put (the tea) *in* = 'infuse,' *put* (the sheep) *in* = 'fold,' *put* (a
request) *in* = 'file,' *put* (a seed) *in* (the earth) = 'plant,' *put*
(the baby) *in* (the bath) = 'immerse,' *put* (things) *in* (a house)
= 'install,' and so forth. Let us suppose that twenty of these lie
on the surface for the average translator, and we have in fact
not 200 but 4,000 fresh 'words,' i.e., self-evident, bipartite analytic equivalents for what in ordinary English usually involves
an extra word, all without adding a single 'idiom' proper (see
page 31), or increasing in any way the phonetic difficulty of
the foreigner.

By an operation is meant not only the fundamental operations
of physics, but the simplest and most familiar actions of everyday life in so far as they are performed by one thing on another,
or by the human organism as a whole on some other thing.

Actually, the most general operation is to 'move'; to 'push' and
to 'pull' are a little more specific.

In the case of human beings, the most general operations are
likewise moving, pushing, and pulling; together with *put* and
take. Slightly more specific are *give* and *get;* and for movements
of the organism, *come* and *go*. Then we have *make* (creative
change), *keep* (continuity), *let* (acquiescence), and *do* (gen-
eralized activity). Fortunately it is possible to cover the first
group, in Basic, with the help of nouns:

> move = give (a thing) a move, or put (a thing) in motion.
> push = give a push to (a thing).
> pull = give a pull to (a thing).

So ten operation-words, supplemented by the operational uses of
be (existence), *seem* (oppositional accessory to *be*), and *have*
(possession), achieve all that is required.

The relation of the operation-words both to one another and
to the human form, and their constructional possibilities, are illustrated in the diagram on the opposite page. Its hero is de-
picted with the paper hat ('this') which he has *made,* and *has,*

and is *keeping* where it is at the moment. He says: "I *make* (*keep, have*) this"; and the various lines indicate the ways or directions in which he would *put, take, give,* or *get* (this), etc. Any child can do the same. The oppositional factor gives us *seem* as a sort of mirror-image of *be;* while, as opposed to *come* (here) and *keep,* we have *go* (away) and *let,* etc.

OPERATIONS

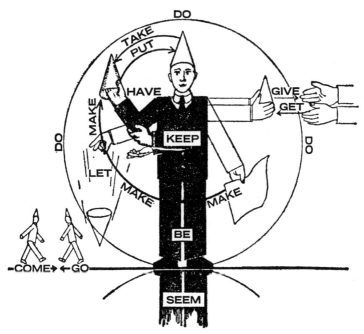

MAKE the paper into a hat.	GIVE the hat to someone.
HAVE the hat.	GET the hat from someone.
PUT the hat on the head.	GO from this place.
TAKE the hat from the head.	COME to this place.
KEEP the hat here.	BE doing.
LET the hat go.	SEEM to be (doing).

DO any act.

The 'auxiliaries' are used as in Standard English—*may* to express possibility or permission, *will* and *have* to form compound tenses, *be* for the passive voice. But the fact that Basic has only *will* as the auxiliary of futurity raises certain points to which it will be well to give attention here.

Basic English makes no distinction between *shall* and *will*, and the insensitiveness of most speakers of Standard English on this point ensures that on almost all occasions the substitution will go undetected. In questions, however, where *shall* = 'Is it your desire that,' 'Am I wise to,' 'Is it necessary,' etc. (as in 'Shall I go?'), it may be preferable, stylistically, to use these alternative phrases.

The distinction between *shall* and *will* having been discarded, that between *should* and *would* can also be neglected in so far as it coincides with the former.

There are, however, three uses of *should* which have no counterpart in the uses of *shall*, and for these it is necessary to find substitute phrases.

1. *Duty*   FOR *You should do your best* SUBSTITUTE
                   'It is right for you to do your best.'

2. *Plan*   FOR *The order was that I (or he) should go*
                   SUBSTITUTE 'The order was that I (he) was
                   to go, for me (him) to go'
                   OR 'My (His) order was to go.'

3. *Subjunctive*   FOR *If he should come,* SUBSTITUTE
   Future   'If he came.'

It has been explained that the main auxiliary use of *may* is to indicate possibility. The permissive operator-form arises out of this auxiliary use. Where the possibility is due to the will of the speaker or of some other person, then *may* becomes permissive, so that *You may go* is really a contraction for *I will let you go* or *You have a right to go.* There are also two subsidiary auxiliary uses of *may* for which substitute phrases can easily be found. The subjunctive form, *Do this that you may be strong,* is rendered in Basic as *Do this so that you will be strong;* and the exclamatory form, *May they do well!* becomes *It is my desire (or hope) that they will do well.* See also *The ABC*, pages 137–38.

Given the word-order and the function of each auxiliary, there should be no difficulty in forming the compound tenses. Familiarity with the expressions *I will go* and *I have gone* generates the more complex *I will have gone,* and so on.

The sequence of tenses is also, in the main, a matter for the exercise of common sense. A present or future tense in the principal sentence may be followed by any tense appropriate to the sense in the dependent clauses; a past tense is followed by a past tense except where a comparison is introduced, in which case the present may be required, e.g., *I was more tired than you are,* or where the statement in the clause applies to the present or the future as well as to the past, e.g., *It was his view that in another hundred years Britain will be a second-rate power.*

The present participles, in addition to their use for the formation of the tenses of the operation-words, have a noun and adjective function on the lines of the *-ing* derivatives.

4. PREPOSITIONS

Each of the 'directives' is spatially definable without ambiguity in its root use. These root definitions are set out in the diagram on the next page; but the movements of a fish in a tank would be equally applicable for the first stages of teaching by dumb-show.

By trying out each operation-word in turn with each directive it will readily be discovered in a general way which combinations conform to the nature of the physical universe, and which phrases, therefore, are free from idiomatic difficulty. *Out* is included as a borderline example between an adverb and a directive. Grammatically, it is an adverb, but its significance is directional; and as its opposite *in* is a directive, the diagram would be incomplete if *out* were omitted.

DIRECTIONS

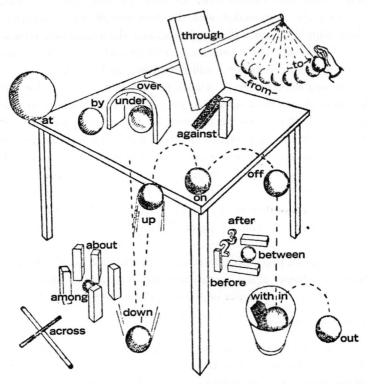

AT	The ball is **at** the edge of the table.	**WITH**	The black brick is **with** the ball.
FROM	The ball is going **from** the hand.	**AGAINST**	The black brick is **against** the white brick.
TO	The ball is going **to** the hand.	**ACROSS**	The black rod is **across** the white rod.
AFTER	3 is **after** 2.	**AMONG**	The ball is **among** the bricks.
BEFORE	1 is **before** 2.		
THROUGH	The rod is **through** the board.	**ABOUT**	The bricks are **about** the ball.
BETWEEN	The ball is **between** the bricks.	**DOWN**	The ball is **down.**
UNDER	The ball is **under** the arch.	**UP**	The ball is **up.**
OVER	The arch is **over** the ball.	**ON**	The ball is **on** the table.
BY	The ball is **by** the arch.	**OFF**	The ball is **off** the table.
		IN	The ball is **in** the bucket.

OUT   The ball is **out** of the bucket.

Expansion and metaphor play an important part in the use of directives, for it is in this way that they are made to signify other than directional relations, but there is less possibility of associational expansion than in the case of noun-forms. Expansions with directives frequently take the form of fictional analogies; that is to say, they arise through the use of a directive in a phrase where fictions occur, e.g., *Thoughts come into the mind, Get at the details.* These fictional analogies present no problem as regards intelligibility; in almost all cases their meaning is self-evident when once the root use has been mastered. Another unambiguous form of metaphor is the temporal analogy, giving such uses as *Get ready at six, Knowledge before the event.*

There are, however, a number of metaphorical uses of the directive depending on less straightforward analogies than these, e.g., *Go against a friend* (antagonism from opposition of force), *Painted by Leonardo* (instrumentality from proximity), *Do it through a representative* (agency from transition). It is here that the teacher must be careful to distinguish natural and legitimate combinations from more capricious usage.

In *The ABC of Basic English,* all the necessary idioms which would not be clear to, for example, a Japanese learner who had mastered the sense of the single words are listed in examples— 250 in all. Of these about 50 require special attention at an early stage; and in *The Basic Words* a further 250 are illustrated for the benefit of those who wish to acquire a more idiomatic style than the simpler forms of communication demand.

In addition to the directives shown on the diagram, *for, of,* and *till* are used on the same analogy, as nondirectional prepositions:

i. *For,* which is of doubtful spatial origin (possibly derived from *fore*), is a sort of pro-preposition, covering substitution, exchange, or purpose. In relation to purpose, *for* generally takes the place of the infinitive in such phrases as *desire for* (= to have) *food, ornaments,* etc.

ii. *Of,* the preposition signifying possession or close connection, is derived from *off.* If *x* is *off y,* it must have once been *on* it, that is to say, in close proximity or belonging to it. By a slight semantic twist all things which are in the *y* context are said to be *of/off* it irrespective of whether they are now apart from it or not.

iii. *Till* is a contraction of 'to the time that.'

The directives can always be used in combination where the sense demands it, making *into, upon, down from,* etc.

5. ADVERBS

The adverb exists as a separate part of speech only through a process of linguistic abbreviation. Any statement made by means of an adverb can be translated intelligibly, though perhaps clumsily, into terms of other parts of speech. Adverbs of degree are 'to some extent'; of place, 'in some place'; of time, 'at some time'; of manner, 'in some way or manner.' It is only by representing the adverb as a 'potted' form of symbolization that the student unfamiliar with adverbs can be made to grasp their nature.

6. PRONOUNS

Except for the '*s,* which is required as an alternative method of indicating possession, there are no so-called case inflections among the nouns. In the Basic system, therefore, these inflections may be treated as forms peculiar to pronouns. Since pronouns are themselves grammatical accessories, any elaboration of grammar is more appropriate to them than to the nouns.

The alternative possessive inflection for use when the pronoun comes after the noun which it qualifies is convenient rather than necessary. Details of this sort should not be introduced to the learner till he is completely fluent.

7. CONJUNCTIONS

Conjunctions, like quantifiers, are not simple referential words, but accessories in the machinery of linguistic communication. It is the function of the conjunction to link groups of words to one another so that they conform to a pattern of thought.

8. WORD-ORDER

MODEL SENTENCES:

(1) *I will give simple rules to the boy slowly.*

(2) *The camera man who made an attempt to take a moving picture of the society women, before they got their hats off, did not get off the ship till he was questioned by the police.*

A sentence is any arrangement of words intended as a formal unit of communication.

Although word-order is dealt with at some length, both here and in *The ABC*, it is obviously not an essential part of the course to a student who desires no more than a reader's acquaintance with Basic English. Nor is it a first-level necessity, even for the speaker. Anyone who has learned the Basic Vocabulary with its nearest equivalents in his own language can proceed to put the words together in sentences; he will usually be understood both by English hearers and by all who know the words, provided the main sequence of thing-operation-direction is followed.

The model sentences, however, are so easy to learn, as a framework into which the whole vocabulary may be fitted *as it is learned,* that probably few will risk the oddities of expression which any word-for-word translation must involve.

It is, therefore, recommended that the vocabulary be learned both as a series of word-pairs (the single word with its nearest equivalent in a foreign language), and also with each word fitted into model sentences—as in *Basic by Examples.*

The rules which cover the essentials of word-order will enable almost any sentence to be given a correct equivalent in Basic. If relatively simple sentences only are attempted, both fluency and intelligibility are assured on all occasions. Anything more ambitious, whether in the direction of style or complication, can best be attained by a study of the specimen translations.

It would be foolish to take exception to the placing of the
preposition at the end of a sentence. This word-order is sanctioned by old-established English idiom.[27] The gradual return
to the prepositional ending is encouraged by the increasing use
of the verb-preposition combinations. When the directive is
combined with the verb adverbially, it naturally comes at the
end of the sentence, and so accustoms the eye to the word-order,
e.g.,

> *He is getting on.*
> *This is the horse which he is getting on.*

The intelligent student will no doubt seek for an explanation
of the introduction of the auxiliary *do* to supplement the Simple
Present and the Simple Past in interrogation. The normal
sequence in English, as in most European languages, is that of
subject—verb—object. A variation of this order suggested itself
as a simple device to indicate the interrogative. But the habit
of the normal order (as observed by Jespersen) was so strong
that a compromise between the two principles resulted. By
placing the subject after the auxiliary, the formal inversion is
effected; by placing it before the principal verb, the reality of
the normal word-order is preserved. A similar evasion is to be
found in Danish and in French.

9. INTERNATIONAL TERMS, MEASUREMENT, ETC.

Words which are internationally understood are available for
use. For the 101 international words so far recognized by Basic,
see *The ABC of Basic English* [in this volume, page 234], where
12 names of sciences and 15 'international names' (i.e., words
used in titles, etc.) are also accepted. If such words have local
variations, the English form should be employed. The Interna-

---

[27] The prejudice against it dates from the time of the Renaissance when
English was painfully adjusted to the stylistic models of Greece and Rome.
Where *that* is the relative pronoun employed, the preposition is forced to
the end of the sentence even in Standard English; e.g., *This is the flag
that you gave your life for.*

tional vocabulary covers measurement terms, including numerals, and the currency systems of the various countries of the world. Knowledge is assumed of the English form of the Calendar.

The pronunciation of the general international terms will, of course, be included in the gramophone records which will cover the whole phonetic and grammatical side of the system, but it is unnecessary to load the printed Vocabulary with anything that is not a mnemonic essential. The number of such terms to be accepted is still the subject of various questionnaires. There is a long list of candidates which have a *prima facie* claim to internationality in the West and have already obtained considerable currency in Japan. The advice of Radio Committees in different countries is now being sought, and their rulings will be sifted by those who are collaborating in the forthcoming Basic translations. Here is a selection:

academic, academy, accumulator, adieu, alpha, alphabet, ampère, apostrophe, aristocracy, atlas, atmosphere, atom, baby, bacillus, balcony, banana, banjo, barbarism, baritone, bayonet, benzol, bicycle, billiards, blonde, blouse, Bolshevik, bonbon, boss, boulevard, bouquet, bourgeois, bravo, bridge, buffet, bull-dog, bulletin, cable, cadet, cafeteria, calico, camouflage, caravan, card, carnival, catastrophe, caviar, center, chaos, civilization, cocoa, condenser, contralto, cosmopolitan, crepe, cricket, crochet, dahlia, decadent, demagogue, dessert, diarrhea, dictionary, dilettante, dynamo, dyspepsia, economic, electric, electron, element, energy, ensemble, erotic, eucalyptus, eugenics, facade, feminism, film, flirt, freemason, fresco, frieze, garage, gazette, gentleman, golf, gondola, grammar, graph, guillotine, gymnastics, hockey, hors d'oeuvres, hyacinth, imperial, impromptu, intelligentsia, interest, iodine, kangaroo, kodak, laboratory, lacquer, lady, lamp, lancet, lavatory, league, legal, lemon, lion, lunch, lynch, machine, mademoiselle, magnet, mannequin, manuscript, mask, maximum, memo, menthol, minimum, minus, modern, monopoly, monsieur, moral, morphia, motif, motor, music, muslin, narcissus, nature, Negro, nuance, oasis, obelisk, octave, optimism, option, oracle, palace, palette, panic, panorama, paradox, parallel, parasol, parody, pathos, pessimism, philosophy, phonetics, picnic, photograph, pince-nez, ping-pong, pistol, plus, polo, porridge, pragmatism, press, prima-donna, professor, profile, proletariat, promenade, public, pudding, realism, register, rendezvous, republic, revue, rhetoric, rhythm, robot, rotor, roulette, rucksack, sabotage, sago, salon, saloon, sapphire, satyr, saxophone, scenario, schema, scout, serenade, sextant, shampoo, shellac, silhouette, ski, socialism, soirée, solo, soprano, soufflé, souvenir, spectrum, sphinx, staccato, stadium, station, steppe, student, symbolism, symmetry, symphony, synchronization, syndicalism, syntax, syringe, system, tango, technique, technology, tempo, tennis, tenor, text, theory, thermometer, toilet, tomato, tournament, tragedy, tramway, transformer, turban, turbine, typhoon, tzar, unicorn, universe, utopia, vaudeville, verandah, vermouth, waffle, waltz, whist, xylophone, zig-zag.

Standard English has hitherto adapted foreign names with a certain amount of arbitrary phonetic distortion. There is already a growing tendency to admit the native use, even where a distortion is part of the language. Exceptions like *Germany* and *Rome* are few. Basic English adopts the native name as far as possible, until the improvement of international communications makes standardization more practicable.

There are lists of International words supplementing the scientific and special technical vocabularies as well as the general vocabulary, but these unfortunately cannot be annexed for general purposes as their standard of internationality is different. Since all advanced scientific work has been Occidental in inspiration, an Easterner interested in science is compelled to learn one or other of the main European languages before he can pursue his studies seriously. A scientific word can therefore be regarded as international if it is common to English, French, German, Russian, Italian, and Spanish. But for the general reader, a word is not international unless it is familiar to the East as well as to the West, and hence the popular list is considerably more circumscribed. With the internationalization of science, notation and measurement must soon also be internationalized, and with the spread of scientific knowledge, scientific terms will gradually permeate the ordinary vocabulary.

10. SLANG, ONOMATOPOEIA

Slang terms are introduced into Basic English in inverted commas, as also are technical terms which are not covered by any special vocabulary when they are introduced into the text with explanatory matter.

It is also worth taking advantage of onomatopoeia. A very large number of English monosyllables, for which equivalents are hard to find, just because of their peculiar appropriateness, are conventionally onomatopoeic in character and therefore universally intelligible in many simple contexts. Some of these [28] are therefore available for a Universal Language in their simple noun form, together with other purely onomatopoeic symbols such as *cuckoo, hiccup,* and *tom-tom.* Examples are *buzz, cluck, crash, croak, flap, miaou, pop, splash, tick,* and possibly even *wheeze.*

To sum up for English translators:

(i) Use all Nouns, Adjectives, and Particles as in Standard English, avoiding obscure idioms, far-fetched metaphors, and intricate word order. Nouns must not, of course, be used as verbs.

(ii) The usual variants from the sixteen Operation-Words (Verb-forms) and the seven Pronouns in the vocabulary are available; also plurals, comparatives, adjectives used as nouns, adverbs formed from adjectives by the addition of *-ly,* and the prefix *un-*.

(iii) Noun forms can generate four derivatives: two nouns (*-er* and *-ing* suffixes) and two adjectives (*-ing* and *-ed* suffixes), where these are in use in Standard English.

(iv) Proper names, mathematical and metric systems, and international terms (*q.v.*) may be incorporated at discretion.

---

[28] The reasons for the rejection of any more general use of onomatopoeia in Basic are given in *Progress,* Vol. III, No. 1, and in *Counter-Offensive,* pp. 48–55.

NOTE. An idiomatic use of the Vocabulary with less attention to detail than uniformity would demand may (though less frequently than the majority of existing dialects) necessitate occasional reference to a Standard Dictionary on the part of those whose knowledge is confined to Basic. Where a word has two or more widely different senses in Standard English, the Basic use is given in *The Basic Words*—in which all necessary and legitimate extensions and idioms have been fully covered. Some acquaintance with *The ABC of Basic English* is also desirable, if *The Basic Dictionary* (for translators) is to be used effectively. [*The Basic Dictionary* is not now in print. *The General Basic English Dictionary*, which is, was not designed for the same purpose. Its aim is to furnish learners of English with definitions in Basic of non-Basic words, not to give the translator suggestions for rendering non-Basic words in Basic. Nevertheless, it inevitably frequently does this, and so translators will be well advised to consult it until a new translators' dictionary can be got out. ED.]

3. Teaching and Learning

As an auxiliary language constructed to meet the needs of persons of all ages and as a first step to any form of wider English or as an educational instrument, Basic English has to offer not one but several methods of presentation.

It is obvious that a different approach must be adopted in teaching adults with a knowledge of a Western European language, and those with a knowledge only of non-European languages; and there is a further difference between the methods applicable to children who are learning English in English schools [29] by the method of Basic, and those who are learning Basic in the first instance as an end in itself.

[29] As an antidote to the prevailing word magic encouraged by the echo ("correct usage") method; as a substitute for the older forms of grammati-

The three key volumes, on which all other teaching material is based, are

(1) *The ABC of Basic English.* A graded explanation in Basic, providing a structural outline of the system, for translation into other languages.

(2) *Basic Step by Step.* The 850 words in 30 illustrated lessons, graded in relation to structure and for adaptation to class requirements.

(3) *The Basic Words.* The senses and uses of the 850 words, with the compounds and internationals, in alphabetical order.

A general introductory course for schools was prepared in 1937 (see page 74), and a number of adaptations, in various languages, have now been published or are in preparation. *Basic in a Month,*[30] for adults with a knowledge of a European language, will complete this preliminary educational material.

In due time, the child of tomorrow will gradually absorb Basic by an ideal technique in four stages beginning in the cradle with phonetic exercises not directly related to the symbolic side of the vocabulary, followed by the alphabet [31] and the simpler words at the age of significant speech; a first attempt on the vocabulary as a whole; and finally, at the school-leaving age, a few weeks of intensive study to consolidate the system.

In addition, there would be five brief courses for those who speak English as a native tongue; for children, for adults, for typists, for translators, and for teachers.

All these approaches, however much they may differ in detail, will have one underlying principle in common: the fullest pos-

cal training; as a nucleus in terms of which the vocabulary may be extended; as a medium for the simplification of scientific knowledge; as a technique for the study of poetry and literature; and as an apparatus for the development of clarity in thought and expression. See *Basic in Teaching,* by I. A. Richards, and *Statement and Suggestion,* by A. P. Rossiter.

30 This book, which it was hoped to get out in 1944, was never completed in its original form. The same ground was covered, in greater detail, in *The Basic Teacher* (1950). ED.

31 See *From Pictures to Letters* (1937), by Ellen Walpole.

sible exploitation of the gestural (concrete), and visual factors in learning.

A series of gramophone records, giving the pronunciation of the 850 words, with an account of the sounds of Basic English, has been made by Professor Lloyd James.[32] Later records will deal with the grammatical rules, and provide specimen conversations—a complete radio series.

The value of a gramophone course to the self-taught student must be obvious to all, but less generally recognized is the value of such a course in supplementing the work of a trained teacher. A record obviates the fatigue of reiteration and may be played over and over again till its matter has been assimilated by even the dullest members of a class.

The phonetic advantages of language records are twofold. They create a standard pronunciation, and by reproducing different types of voice they make it possible to show how pronunciation is affected by variations of tone and pitch. Between male and female voices these variations are so considerable that where teacher and class are of opposite sexes, a gramophone is invaluable for the purpose of demonstrating the necessary adjustment of pronunciation when the vocal noises made by the teacher are transposed by the class.[33]

The visual memory is appealed to by various 'panoptic' devices: the presentation of the vocabulary as a visual unit, the diagrams of operations and directions, and above all the Panopticon. This word wheel is a contrivance for teaching sentence-formation, and consists of a series of concentric revolving disks, on each of which is printed a list of words belonging to one of the Basic categories (name, operation-word, directive, qualifier, or modifier). These classes of words are so arranged as to compare with the order of the different classes of words in typically constructed sentences, and when the disks

[32] Since replaced by others made by Professor J. C. Catford. ED.
[33] It needs to be kept in mind, here and elsewhere, that Ogden was writing before the days of language laboratories and tape-recorders. ED.

are revolved, sentences of different types are automatically formed.

By means of this simple mechanical device every exegetic need can be appropriately met. It is a matter only of how much is to be attempted above the minimum; the seven disks required to illustrate the primary sentence-model, viz. *"(I) will give simple rule(s) to (the) boy slowly"* can readily be expanded to the normal twelve of a complex sentence, even after a few hours' practice.

The invention lends itself to demonstrations of various kinds. For example, the experiment of readily discovering which directives can be combined with which operation-words may be carried out most satisfactorily (and most dramatically from the standpoint of the teacher), by rotating the second of the concentric disks (operation-words) against the fifth (directives). Every combination which gives a reference physically possible in common experience may be used in Basic English, and is also used in ordinary English. At this point those familiar with Indo-European languages can be shown how each fresh combination of operation-word and directive exhibited by the rotation enables them to dispense with one or more of the common verbs— which will afford a convenient opportunity to introduce the important features of analysis and substitution which have made Basic English possible.

Any systematic method of teaching a language must grade its lessons in some ordered manner, so that the simplest and most concrete requirements are mastered first, forming in turn a basis for the more difficult words and structures. On the same principle, the Panopticon first teaches the beginner how he may form sentences on the model of uniform word-order, restricting his use of the operation-words to the present tense, and then leads him by gradual stages to the use of the full range of operation-word conjugates in the numerous variations of order sanctioned by the conventions of English style.

On the vocabulary side, the graded school course, with illustrations, is already available—*The Basic Way* (see page 74) in which a certain number of words are introduced in each lesson, the words becoming more difficult as the lessons proceed. In grading material on this principle, it must, however, be remembered that the unique character of Basic makes it a law unto itself, and for this reason its gradations are bound to diverge very considerably from even the most competently constructed gradations in a system which neither eliminates verbs nor reduces its vocabulary to the point at which substitution technique becomes really important.

The 850 words may best be memorized in groups related to the chief interests of everyday life, and put together in model sentences which may be operated with the help of the sentence-builder. It is recommended that the adult should frame such groups for himself. The complete vocabulary takes a quarter of an hour to repeat on the gramophone records. The average learner can memorize 30 words per hour (maximum 100). Assuming that 3 hours a day for a month are to be devoted to the system, and that 28 hours in all will be necessary to memorize the entire vocabulary, two hours a day will be available for the rules and for sentence practice. This practice will, of course, be largely concerned with the form-changes of operation-words and directives on pages 169 and 170.

As a guide for teaching purposes, a companion volume to *The ABC of Basic English* and *Basic Step by Step* has been prepared —entitled *Basic by Examples*.

Anyone with a knowledge of one of the Indo-European languages will naturally find the learning of the vocabulary a comparatively simple matter. More than 35 percent of the words will be recognized by a Frenchman, and a slightly lower percentage by a German.[34] So that for some 300,000,000 foreign learners the time required might be reduced by approximately one quarter (apart from the advantage of familiarity with the sentence structure).

---

[34] Cf. Eddy, M. H., "The French Element in English," *Mod. Lang. Journal.*

The needs of foreigners with language structures differing greatly from our own must receive special treatment, since the rate of 30 words per hour is based on the learning of word-pairs (i.e., one Basic word with its foreign equivalent), which is not possible in all languages. For children, graded picture courses will supplement the material in *Basic Step by Step.*

Finally, in addition to these various treatments of Basic as a system complete in itself for all classes of learners, there is the problem of providing the necessary links with Standard English for those who desire to supplement their knowledge by degrees.[35] With this purpose in view, the next 150 words (making a total of 1,000), the subsequent 350, increased to 500 and thereafter to 1,000 or (incorporating the essentials of the verb-manipulation) to 2,000, as well as a series of special vocabularies, have all been selected on the same principles as the Basic words themselves. At no point will the learner have anything to *un*learn; and when the entire material is available for orthodox educational requirements it will be found that Basic itself constitutes a unique foundation for all further language study.

One special point deserves mention here. It is obvious that the majority of the 850 words in the list are capable of other uses than those which Basic, as a universal medium, permits; and at some stage in the acquisition of Standard English these further uses, treating the words themselves as roots, will clearly find a place in the expanded system. At first, however, the nucleus must be kept intact until the graded additions have provided the necessary analogies for new derivatives and inflections. Confusion is otherwise inevitable; and, in particular, the introduction of 50 characteristic (strong) verbs at an appropriate stage (preferably *after* a total of 1,500 has been passed) is essential to the desired transition.

The first supplement consists therefore of the 150 names of animals, plants, and foods, which have no international distribu-

---

[35] One such linking course, *From Basic to Wider English,* has now been on the market since 1944. A completely revised edition is just being published. ED.

tion. This extension of the list of picturables may then be followed by the 350 first-level addenda, and so on; at the same time
the special vocabularies which have been prepared for the application of Basic to trade and economics, and for *The Basic
Bible,* are available for gradual incorporation in the general list
at the 2,000 level. Meanwhile the following provisional list of
350 early candidates may be suggestive to our collaborators.

*absence, accident, address, adventure, advice, age, agent, ago,
along, also, always, ambition, anchor, ankle, arrangement, ash, awkward, balcony, barrel, beard, beat, behind, belt, bet, blame, blanket,
both, bottom, brave, breakfast, breast, bubble, bud, bunch, burial,
busy, calculation, call, capital, carpet, case, ceremony, chair, character,
child, chimney, china, choice, civilization, clay, clever, collection,
column, communication, concert, concrete, convenient, cool, corner,
cost, crop, cross, cunning, date, demand, department, dew, difficulty,
dinner, disgrace, dislike, ditch, dive, divorce, doll, dreadful, dream,
dull, duty, each, easy, economy, effort, either, employer, empty,
enemy, envelope, envy, evening, exact, excitement, exercise, explanation, explosion, expression, eyebrow, eyelash, failure, fair, famous,
fan, fastening, fever, figure, financial, flash, flesh, flood, flour, forecast,
forehead, foreign, forgiveness, fresh, frost, frozen, funny, fur, furni-
ture, gate, generation, germ, god, grand, grateful, grease, grief,
grocery, ground, guard, guess, gum, habit, handkerchief, handle, heavy,
hedge, hill, holiday, home, honest, honey, human, hunt, hurry, hurt,
husband, imagination, innocent, institution, intelligent, invitation,
jam, jaw, jealous, jerk, joint, jug, juice, jury, justice, kennel, kidney,
kitchen, knock, lace, lame, lamp, large, lawyer, lazy, lecture, legal,
lesson, lever, licence, lid, life, lime, liver, load, local, loop, luck, lump,
lunch, lung, magic, manner, many, marble, marriage, mast, mattress,
mean, meaning, medicine, member, mess, message, mill, mineral,
model, modern, modest, mood, moral, mud, murder, mustache, nasty,
nature, navy, neat, neglect, neighbor, nest, next, nice, nostril, nurse,
obedient, officer, orchestra, organ, origin, oval, own, pad, pair, pan,
paragraph, party, passage, patience, pedal, people, perfect, plaster,
poetry, pool, practice, praise, prayer, prick, priest, progress, promise,
proof, proud, pupil, pure, race, real, reference, remark, remedy, repair,
result, revenge, rich, rise, rival, rude, rust, sale, satisfaction, saucer,*

scratch, screen, search, selfish, sentence, set, shave, sheet, shell, shoulder, show, sight, since, sleeve, social, soldier, sorry, spark, spirit, spit, splash, spot, stable, stair, steady, storm, strain, straw, stream, string, study, subject, success, sum, supply, surface, surgeon, suspicious, swing, sympathetic, tailor, tame, tap, tear, tent, thief, thimble, threat, tie, too, towel, tower, traffic, tragedy, trap, travel, treatment, truck, tube, tune, tunnel, twin, typist, ugly, understanding, universe, valley, vegetable, victim, victory, vote, weak, welcome, whether, widow, wife, wild, world, wreck, wrist, yawn.

The psychological value of synthetic language experiments has been emphasized, and their interest in regard to statistics of learning is also considerable. Hitherto, of course, advocates of these experiments have been able to contrast the regularity of their own constructions with the complexity and eccentricity of English. Thus the experience of foreigners is said to be "well illustrated by the remarks of a German bank official sent over here to polish up his English. 'English—seven years hard study. I would have committed suicide rather than learn it, had I known what it meant. Esperanto—seven months and at the end a knowledge of the language such as I can never hope to have of English.'"[36] Foreign businessmen, the writer continues, are not slow to appreciate the time and money which this means, "and the rapidly increasing use of Esperanto for business is the result." If enthusiasts will spend *seven months* in order to get in touch with a handful of fellow-enthusiasts, the rapidity with which Basic might conquer the world of commerce will be obvious to all who have followed us so far.

Basic has the initial advantage of being able to avoid all appeal to authority.

It is already so simple that it can be mastered theoretically in a day, practically in a week, orientally (with a suitable intensive course) in a month.

It has both the wind and tide of simplification in its favor. Every conscious effort at simplification, every advance in

[36] *International Language,* April 1930, p. 81.

phonetics, every fresh achievement of radio, of gramophone, and of talkie make its progress more assured; and the whole of the analytic tendency of the newer English-speaking communities will work to render its idiomatic irregularities less numerous, its word-order more elastic, and its resources more extensive.

When the founder of Esperanto looked into the future, he could only say in the preface of the *Fundamento:* "If any authoritative central institution finds this or the other word or rule in our language is too inconvenient, it must not remove or change the said form, but may propose a new form which it will recommend to be used parallel with the old form (until usage decides)." But for the advocate of Basic the formula might run as follows: "As soon as analogical contamination shall have rendered any irregularity unnecessary (for purposes of idiomatic communication), that form or phrase can be abandoned; and as soon as any term or symbol becomes internationalized in any of the rapidly developing international sciences, that term is then automatically added to the vocabulary of Basic *qua* scientific medium."

Nor must it be forgotten that when once Basic is established as a universal linguistic foundation, its technique of expansion is chiefly the acquisition of further invariable names; and since such names can be added at an average rate of one every two minutes, a few hundred addenda could at any time be acquired over the week-end. In other words, the time may not be far distant when governments will initiate special Language Weeks to focus attention on the benefits accruing to a community through any extension of its power of communicating with other communities; when the public prints will feature the year's most plausible guess at the next most useful word; and when philanthropists will solace their retiring years by watching Basic Institutes rise around them for the diffusion of defter definitions and dumpier dictionaries.

PART TWO

A Short Guide to Basic English

1. What Is Basic English?

Basic English is an attempt to give to everyone a second, or international, language which will take as little of the learner's time as possible.

It is a system in which everything may be said for all the purposes of everyday existence: the common interests of men and women, general talk, news, trade, and science.

To the eye and ear it will not seem in any way different from normal English, which is now the natural language, or the language of the governments, of more than 600,000,000 persons.[37]

There are only 850 words in the complete list, which may be clearly printed on one side of a bit of notepaper. But simple rules are given for making other words with the help of those in the list; such as *designer, designing,* and *designed* from *design,* or *coal-mine* from *coal* and *mine.*

The word-order is fixed by other short rules, which make clear from an example such as

"I will put the record on the machine here"

what is the right and natural place for every sort of word.

Whatever is doing the act comes first; then the time word such as *will;* then the act or operation (*put, take,* or *get*); then the thing to which something is done, and so on.

[37] Estimates today put the number of English-speaking people in the world at about 700 million. ED.

It is an English in which 850 words do all the work of 20,000, and has been formed by taking out everything which is not necessary to the sense. *Disembark*, for example, is broken up into *get off a ship; I am able* takes the place of *I can; shape* is covered by the more general word *form;* and *difficult* by the use of *hard.*

By putting together the names of simple operations—such as *get, give, come, go, put, take*—with the words for directions like *in, over, through,* and the rest, two or three thousand complex ideas, like *insert* which becomes *put in,* are made part of the learner's store.

Most of these are clear to everyone. But in no other language is there an equal chance of making use of this process. That is why Basic is designed to be the international language of the future.

In addition to the Basic words themselves, the learner has, at the start, fifty words which are now so common in all languages that they may be freely used for any purpose. Examples are *radio, hotel, telephone, bar, club.*

For the needs of any science, a short special list gets the expert to a stage where international words are ready to hand.

Those who have no knowledge of English will be able to make out the sense of a radio talk, or a business letter, after a week with the word-list and the records; [38] but it may be a month or two before they are talking and writing freely.

In fact, it is the business of all internationally minded persons to make Basic English part of the system of education in every country, so that there may be less chance of war, and less learning of languages—which after all, for most of us, is a very unnecessary waste of time.

[38] See the Book List at the end of the book. ED.

2. Basic as an International Language

Even the experts who give all their time to words are unable
to get a working knowledge of more than 20 or 30 of the 1,500
chief languages still in use; and those who have a knowledge
of Chinese or Japanese in addition to one of the languages of
India or Africa may be numbered on the fingers of the hand.

Today the great languages of Europe are important from
an international point of view, not only or chiefly as the mother
tongues of this or that group but because of their use in other
parts of the earth. Spanish and Portuguese, for example, have a
future in South America, though English is increasing as the
second language of all South American countries. It has taken
500 years for English to become the second language of the
East, in addition to its development in the United States, Canada,
and Australasia; and of the 30 languages now at the head of
the list, English has the first place among the eight which are
used by more than 50,000,000 persons. It is the natural language,
or the language of government or trade, of some 650 millions.[39]
The seven others are:

Chinese	450
Russian	166
French	112
Japanese	100
German	95
Spanish	85
Bengali	60 [40]

Though 'Chinese' is generally given as the mother tongue of
400 millions, it is not certain how far these are clear to one
another in talking and writing. Some authorities put the num-

[39] See footnote, p. 47. ED.
[40] These figures are of course long out of date. ED.

ber at 200 millions, others at 300, but the words have quite different senses at different voice levels, and the time needed for the learning and writing of Chinese picture-words gives such a language very little chance of becoming more widely used.

Before the Great War, it was clear to most persons with a knowledge of history and an interest in international organization that one of the chief needs of Europe was fifty more dead languages. Every year the Earth is getting smaller, through the discoveries of science; but there are still more than 1,500 languages in use in the different countries which the radio, the telephone, and advertisement in all its forms have suddenly put in touch with one another. In fact, the experience of the past ten years makes it possible to say with some hope of agreement, at any rate from men of science, that the chief need of our time is 1,480 more dead languages.

Even today, it is hard to get a working knowledge of more than three or four, so 20 would be quite enough (in schools) to keep teachers at work; and men of letters would be quite happy with almost 2,000 (in libraries).

In a year or two it may be possible for voices in China or Peru to come through quite clearly to any English workingman with an apparatus about the size of a hat and at a lower price than the present small gramophone. Twenty or thirty years back it was possible to put together a language based on European roots in the belief that it might one day become international; but now that the East is fully awake, and in the very front of our political picture, such an idea is foolish.

English has been made part of the school system of countries with interests as widely different as Japan, the Argentine, and Estonia; it is the language of the talking pictures and of over 500 radio stations; and experts in all countries have for a long time been of the opinion that if only it was simpler it would quickly become international for trade and for all other purposes.

Basic English is this desired simpler form. The complete

word-list goes on the back of one bit of business notepaper, and takes only 15 minutes on a small folding record. In theory, anyone with no knowledge of English might get it into his head in less than 24 hours; but it is wiser to take two hours a day for a month, giving one hour to the words and the other to word-order and to the 250 special uses ('idioms') which are needed to get the natural effect of everyday talk.

In science, this effect is equally possible, as may be seen from any of the Basic science books. But it is less important, because in science the chief need is to get the sense clear without troubling about the details in which men of letters are interested; and this is what Basic is designed to do. With the addition of 50 special words for any branch of science, and 100 words for general science, the field of knowledge may be completely covered for international purposes. At a higher level, different in every branch, international words are ready to hand; and Basic is the quickest way of getting to that level.

The value of making the discoveries of science international is not seriously questioned; but it might be 1,000 years before the necessary language was produced by the process of natural selection. A strong attack on the forces of reaction is the only hope; and with the right organization, on the lines of the International Bureau of Weights and Measures, the work might be complete while some of us are still living.

In this connection, it may be noted that those who have not given much thought to language are frequently in error as to the number of words used for the purposes of normal education. Even before they go to school, young learners are generally making use of between 2,000 and 3,000 separate word-forms, and there is an American list of the 20,000 most frequently needed by teachers. Most readers of these pages will have a working knowledge of 20–25,000 words ready for all purposes, and there are more than 7,000 so common that they might any day be seen in advertisements or headlines designed for the general public. So statements in the papers, saying that we may

get on happily with 500, are based on the chance ideas of some
office boy. All this makes the value of a word-list limited to 850
units very clear.

For the expansion of trade, for the organization of peace, and
for the development of science, an international language is
at least as important as the gold question; and if it is true that
men of science are in touch with less than 10 percent of their
public, it is very much more important for the future.

3. How the 850 Words Do Their Work

The best way to get agreement about the value of a new invention is to let it be seen in operation, and this is no less true
of a new system of language like Basic English than of a machine
or a process in industry. Basic may now be seen at work in
more than 1,000,000 printed words by more than 50 different
writers.

But when the public has seen the invention at work it becomes interested in the question *how* that work is done. Basic
is not a sort of schoolroom trick, or a simple form of English
put together from the commonest words for school books, which
may be taken at their face value; and the teacher will be in a
better position to make its purpose clear if he has some knowledge of the structure and working of the machine he is using.

How is Basic able to get so far with only 850 words? The
reason may be given in simplest language.

The greater part of the words used in science and for everyday talk are what may be named *shorthand* for other words;
that is to say, they are taking the place of other words which
are clearly, in some sense, nearer to the facts.

The greater part of the things we generally seem to be talking
about are what may be named *fictions:* and for these again there
are other words in common use which get nearer to fact.

The greater part of the statements we make about things and persons are unnecessarily colored by some form of *feeling:* they do, no doubt, say something about things and persons, but most common words are colored by our feelings—or the feeling by which the thought of our hearers is to be consciously or unconsciously guided; and it is frequently possible to keep thought and feeling separate.

The most important group of 'shorthand' words in European languages is made up of what are named 'verbs'—words like 'accelerate' and 'ascertain'; 'liberty' and 'blindness' are examples of fictions; 'credulous' and 'courteous' say something about our feelings in addition to their straightforward sense.

At the back of such forms of language there is something simpler for which we may or may not have the right words. In English it is generally possible to get to the lower level without much trouble. To 'accelerate' is to go more quickly, when we have 'liberty' we are free, and a 'credulous' person is one who (in our opinion) is over-ready with belief; and this lower level is one stage nearer that solid base in pointing and acting from which the structures of language go up into the clouds.

There is no need to go further down till we come to science, and for the purposes of an international language it is not wise to go higher than this common-sense level—which is where the 850 Basic words have their place.

The first step to a simpler word-list, then, is to take out all the more complex sorts of 'verbs,' in which, in addition to the *operation* of one body on another, the *direction* of the act is more or less clearly named. Sometimes the thing talked about, in addition to the operation, is covered by one word, as when we 'rise,' 'shave,' 'feed,' and 'grumble'—where bodies and beds, hair and faces, food and mouths, feelings and the weather may be part of the word-picture; but these 'shorthand' forms are chiefly names of acts and directions only—as when we 'enter' (go into) a room, 'break' (go against) the law, 'contract' (go down with) a disease, 'precede' (go in front of), and so on.

In this way we see that it is possible to have a working language in which about 4,000 common 'verbs' have been dropped out. At the same time a first attack on the other groups gets the list down by another 1,500; so that, in place of at least 7,500 at the start, we are now only troubled by about 2,000.

These numbers are not far wrong, but in fact not more than 1,500 words are needed for the list from which the expert will make his selection and to which all the most serious thought has to be given.

We have to get well under the 1,000 level if the outcome is to be of use for international purposes or as an instrument in education, and the first stage in the development of Basic was the invention of an apparatus with the help of which it might be possible to get a clearer idea of the behavior of words and a more certain test of their value.

By putting the word to be tested in the middle of a circle with lines going out from it like the arms or rays of a starfish, so that on every line we get a relation or connection with some other possible word, questions may be framed in the form—
"What word takes the place of the word in the middle in this connection?"
These other words will then be placed at the end of the lines, all round the circle. For example, if the key word *dog* is in the middle: What is another name for a dog in connection with time? Answer: *Puppy.* Clearly the word *puppy* will not be needed if we have *dog* and the connection with time is covered by *young.* The same will be true of *bitch,* in relation to (sex) behavior, if we have *female* in our Basic list. And when our range of questions is complete, we have a complete picture of the word in relation to all the other words in a language which have a connection with it.

If, for everyday needs, the word in the middle, used with the words on the joining line, will take the place of the new word at the end of the line, that word may go. It is not necessary in this connection. So if we have *young* and *dog, puppy* will not be kept in the Basic list. The question "What is a puppy?" is answered fully and readily by 'a young dog' on the line marking the time-relation.

In making a map for all sorts of words there are thirty lines for thirty sorts of possible questions; though for a word like *dog*, some questions will not be answered. Dogs do not come into all the relations talked about in connection with men, mountains, machines, or music; so there is, for example, no special word (such as *litigant, plaintiff, client*) for a dog in relation to law.

This, then, is the apparatus used in 'Panoptic Definition'[41]; and when the answers are all put in on any one map, with special uses underlined, or colored, we get a picture with an important and interesting story for the Basic expert; and with its help he is in a much better position to make up his mind about the value of words for which an argument might be put forward. With his working selection of key words, he will be ready to go through the *Pocket Oxford* to make certain that every one of its 25,000 commonest words has a place somewhere on one of the maps.

Naturally, those who made decisions about the Basic 850 had before them all the work done in America by Thorndike, Horn, Dewey, and the rest, on the most frequent words. Not that it is of any great interest at this stage, because anyone who has been working for years with such word maps is in no doubt about which English words are very common, or common enough for the Basic list. What a word will do for us has little relation to the number of times it is used in newspapers and business letters; and to say that one word is more common than another over the 1,500 level, when the statement is based on observations of less than 50,000,000, has very little sense. Such statements are clearly dependent on the size and purpose of the selection, and the amount of detail noted about expansions of sense, which no one has so far taken, or would ever be able to take, into account, in listing even 10,000,000 uses.

[41] For details, see *Psyche*, Vol. X, No. 3, January 1930, pp. 9–17.

In this way, in 1928 a selection of between 800 and 900 words was ready for the last stage of testing; and in January 1929 the 850 words were printed, though no decision had been made about some 50 words which were still under discussion as possibly 'international.' In 1930 *Basic English* was put out in book form with less than 15 percent of the list in doubt; and after another year's experience, getting the views of representatives of all countries, 50 international words were fixed, and the Basic list was printed in its present form.

For the purposes of science, Basic is a system by which special word-lists, most of them international, may be put into operation. There are about 20 words in the 850 at a level high enough to make the connection; and in addition there are 100 words for general science and 50 for any special branch.[42] These lists are only needed by the expert who is writing or talking about some one part of science, and are not for the general reader; but in the same way as Basic puts such groups of words into operation it takes the number system and weights and measures, which are different in different countries, as an addition for everyday purposes. The numbers themselves are international for writing, and the learning of their English names takes less than half an hour.[43]

Of the 850 Basic words, it will be seen that 600 are names of things, and 150 are names of qualities. That makes 750, and the last 100 are the words which put the others into operation and make them do their work in statements. After the names of acts and directions which, as we have seen, are pointers, come the other Basic words which make the language complete. All of these (62) are clearly taking the place of other words which would say the same thing in a more roundabout way, or are of use in oiling the wheels of our talk so that it may not seem strange to persons who are used to normal English.

The chief form-changes in Basic are those which make the

[42] See *Basic for Science, Basic for Geology, Basic for Economics.*
[43] See *Basic Step by Step,* pp. 50–51.

behavior of the 'verbs' and 'pronouns' the same as in normal English; together with 'plurals,' -*ly* for 'adverbs,' the degrees of comparison, and the -*er*, -*ing*, -*ed* endings to 300 of the names of things. In this way the learner is not troubled by a great number of forms and endings which are not regular, and the outcome is a simple, natural English in which there is room for addition but no need for change at a later stage.

Every word is first given in its root sense, and any other senses which may be used in Basic writing are made clear in relation to this root sense, which, whenever possible, is based on pointing or on a picture. In the Word List, as a guide to teachers, only 200 of the names of things are listed as 'pictured' (that is, best made clear in pictures). These are words representative of physical things which may be pictured so clearly and simply and separately that there will never be any doubt as to what the picture is representative of. (For example, an apple is seen to be an apple whatever sort it is, and may be pictured quite by itself, unlike, let us say, a road.) But though physical things outside this limited list may not be as clearly pinned down, in fact a great number of them may quite well be pictured, and frequently are pictured, as a help in teaching.

The same process of going forward from what is clear and simple to what is more complex or less regular takes the learner from root uses to special uses or 'idioms.' There are 250 such special uses numbered and listed with great care in *The ABC of Basic English*, and when he is clear about most of the normal senses of the 850 words, these are given to the learner to make the system complete. In reading, he may come across some of the 250 other special uses which it would be hard for an Englishman to put out of his mind; but these are unnecessary tricks, to be noted when they come in but not troubled about for everyday use.

In addition to pictures, there are a number of ways of profiting by the structure of Basic in teaching and learning how the words do their work. Among the 150 names of qualities, for example, are fifty which are best taken together with their opposites (*good-bad, right-left,* and so on); at the same time we have *front-back, profit-loss,* and a great number of others among the names of things; and the chief operation-words go two and two together—*come-go, put take, give-get, keep-let, be-seem,* like the directions *before-after, over-under,* and so on.

All these helps for the organization of the material give an idea of the existence of scales and ranges among the thoughts, things, and feelings which are talked about. But the chief reason why it is possible to do so much with the limited word-list is because Basic has been able so completely to do without 'verbs.' That English had two equally good ways of saying most things had long been common knowledge, because Latin and French roots are mixed with those from an earlier system; but it was a surprise to make the discovery that so much which has been valued by men of letters, and supported by teachers as necessary, was, in fact, a sort of shorthand growth on top of a very much more straightforward growth. For hundreds of years these two tendencies have been in existence side by side, and Basic has taken from the more complex forms what is needed to give the effect of natural English. The same degree of organization would not be possible in any other language, and in some ways the structure of Basic is not far from that which science itself has so long been looking for as an instrument of thought.

4. Basic as an Instrument of Thought

For the last thirty or forty years, teachers in English and American schools have been putting up a great fight against the old forms of 'Grammar'—against the learning of rules based on the structure of dead languages. By protesting against a book-knowledge with little or no relation to the needs and interests of present-day society, they have certainly taken a step in the right direction.

There was, however, an idea at the back of the old rules: the idea that because our thought is based on language, and because it is important for our thought to be clear, a great respect for form might be a help in the development of our minds. A good language is a machine for thought, and the delicate adjustment of words to changes of thought and shades of feeling is certainly dependent in some measure on attention to the parts and structure of the machine. But, by degrees, the machine became the manager of the man, and the cry went up for the right to be free from the dead weight of machine-made rules.

So far, so good; and more power to the supporters of brighter school books talking the language of the market place. But there is a great danger of turning out a mass of automatic talking-machines in a desire to get the 'right' reactions to the sort of questions now common in school tests. The selection and learning by heart of words and word-complexes, for no other reason than that they are the most frequent, is a new form of the old idea of basing language-teaching on the structure of the machine. If the learner is made conscious of his instrument, not only will his power of thought be increased, but much memory-work will become unnecessary.

Education, for Basic, is the expansion of experience by experts. Even in the earliest stages of reading an important part may be taken by the Basic framework. The natural development of the material is from simple pointing, at the level of a sign-language, to the more complex needs of normal talk; and for this purpose stories about the doings of some improbable Landru from the Never-Never-Land are clearly out of place.[44] In addition, the use of Basic is an insurance that the words most necessary to the structure will be worked in frequently enough for the learner to get them completely under control.[45] Most simple word-lists for early reading and writing are not truly limited, but

[44, 45] Footnotes here had to do with reading books for use at different stages which are now out of print and have been superseded by others. An up-to-date list of books is given at the end of this volume. ED.

are increased, without system, at the pleasure of whoever is responsible for the teaching-material.

For those to whom it is only a first step, the expansion of Basic into normal English may be viewed as a natural growth, so that the learner goes from level to level as he would up this or that branch of a tree—and not from words to more words for no better reason than that some of the later words are less frequently used by writers of school books.

'Expansions' are made clear from root uses, and 'idioms' from the more regular and straightforward forms of the language. In the same way the senses of new words outside the Basic range will be put before the learner with the help of the 850, so that even the most complex ideas of science may come before the mind as parts of a shorthand system and not as fictions to be given substance in some structure of air.

The small word-list of Basic has a special value at all stages of word-learning. The list is representative of every sort of word, and gives us all the material necessary for a more detailed knowledge of the behavior of languages of unlimited range. It is a sort of instrument for testing the use of words in newspapers and the effects desired in verse. When we put a language such as Spanish or Russian into English there is a danger of going only from words to words, with the least possible adjustment. In Basic it is necessary to keep in mind all the time what is being said, so that we are never exchanging one fixed form for another at the same level.

This process is frequently a great help to those whose word-reactions are slow, and who may have a clear idea of the simple sense without the power of quickly pushing the right buttons in the delicate language-machine. And at the same time Basic will make teachers less surprised that those who seem when young to have the best minds so frequently do not come up to their hopes under conditions where words have to take second place.

To put the argument shortly, Basic at last gives us a chance of getting free from the strange power which words have had over us from the earliest times; a chance of getting clear about the processes by which our ideas become fixed forms of behavior before we ourselves are conscious of what history and society are making us say.

The words which give us this chance may themselves become a help to thought, and through Basic even the very young may be trained to a sense of true values; in fact, those with no education are frequently quicker in their reactions than persons who have been through the school-machine. In England and America, that machine is badly in need of attention today, and through Basic the teacher may give, and be given, a truer view of the relation between thought and feelings on the one hand and words and things on the other. It is wise to let experience be the only judge of the value of such suggestions; but if the attempt is not made, there will be no experience on which decisions may be based. In most countries the decision is being taken for international reasons; and everywhere science and common sense are working together for the development of an island language from which journeys may be taken with profit into that mist of words of whose dangers education is at last becoming conscious.

5. The Learning of Basic

To become expert in some forms of knowledge and behavior no teaching is needed; in others a teacher may be a help for the early stages; in others, again, the learner is dependent on the teacher till his education is almost complete.

Language-learning comes under all three heads; but because the business of living and making a living takes up so much time in later years, it is very frequently limited to the school—where the sort of knowledge and behavior which seems most necessary to the organization of society, such as the reading and writing of one or more languages, is forced on the young. In schools we are up against special conditions, among which the mind and the training of the teacher are not less important than the stage of development of the learner, the size of the group in which he is a unit, and the tests by which knowledge is judged. The tendency is for schools to go at whatever rate may be necessary to let the slowest keep up with the rest; but where the learner is in control, and is clear about his purpose from the start, the process may be much quicker.

Learners of Basic, old and young, will have no need for schools and teachers of any sort if they have the necessary books. This is true even of those languages in which there is still no special guide to Basic.

At the end of 1939 there were such guides, and one or more of the Basic books, in Chinese, Japanese, Russian, Czech, Polish, Danish, Swedish, Latvian, and a number of other languages. In *The Basic Words* are the French and German words for all the senses of the 850, and the *ABC* and *Basic Step by Step* have now been printed in French, German, Dutch, Italian, and Spanish.[46]

It is a good idea to get the senses of the 850 words for reading purposes before going on to talking or writing. With this general knowledge of the system, the private learner will be able to give special attention later to those parts of it which are of most interest to him—for example, business, news, science, or a journey to England or America. It is a waste of time for those who are chiefly interested in writing business letters, or in reading and writing science, to give the same amount of thought to the sounds as if they were starting on a journey, where talking would be a pleasure.

For reading Basic, it is possible to take 30 words an hour after

---

[46] Basic being only a selection from normal English, the learner who has no other guide will be able to put the words into his natural language with the help of any word-book. He will then have no trouble in reading *Basic Step by Step,* where they are grouped for learning purposes in the simplest possible way.

the first two or three steps. Some learners go much quicker than this (between 50 and 100), even without the use of the story form as a help to the sense. In *Basic Step by Step* and *The Basic Way to English*, the words in the earlier steps come in over and over again, where the sense of new words is being made clear, and in reading (though not in writing) the form-changes almost take care of themselves. After working, then, for between 24 [47] and 30 hours, or say, four hours a day over a week, the back of the system will have been broken.

Anyone who is learning a strange language seriously is ready to give it two hours a day for a month, and of the 60 hours 30 will be free for a serious start in writing and talking. Experience makes it quite certain that this is no theory, but a statement supported by solid fact. So even those who are working all day for a living, and have to go to bed before eleven to be up by seven, may get control of this international language of the future, without a teacher, by taking out their books from 8.30 to 10.30 P.M. every night for one month.

For talking, it is best to get by heart a number of statements, and a story or two, as early as possible, and to say them quickly enough to keep in the right rhythm those 12 words which are only weighted for some special reason.[48]

The directions generally given for getting a natural English rhythm are so complex that it might take years to get the secret; and much time may be wasted in the attempt. Here again, however, Basic has something new to say, though this is not the place to say it in detail. It will be enough to give those who are interested some idea of the lines on which an answer to the question "What is English rhythm?" may be framed—and of the

---

[47] That is why it has been said that in theory (for example, on the condition that his head would be cut off if he was unable to get the sense of any straightforward Basic statement after 24 hours' hard work) any European language expert might be reading Basic after a 'day.'

[48] *A, the, and, of, for, from, to, than, is, some, have, that.* For other details see *Basic Step by Step,* pp. 52–55 [and "Word Stress and Sentence Stress." ED.].

reasons which make Basic the best guide to the more complex developments of the English language in its complete form.

In an English of 10,000 words—or even 2,000—rules for what little is regular are not much help; and when the teaching of English has no special relation to its structure, or to the sense and purpose of every unit in that structure, the learning of unnecessary tricks gives the memory more than enough to do even without the addition of the current theories of rhythm. In Basic, the number of words is so small, and their behavior so straightforward, that rules are possible which would have little value, as such, for any other selection from the English language.

To get a natural effect, force or weight has to be put on the right words for the sense, and on the right division of the word for the sound. Every English word with more than one sound-division (*let-ter, di-vi-sion*) is weighted on one or other of these— by force of breath or muscle. So first we have to give a rule for this.

Only 337 of the 850 have more than one division, and the Rule is: *The weight is on the part before the last.*

No less than 254 of the 337 are covered by this rule; and here are examples from every group (of two, three, and four divisions):

réason, símple: exámple, impórtant, educátion, automátic.

All but 22 of the rest come under three simple heads; and the 22 which might give trouble take less than half a minute on a record.

The first business of the learner is clearly to get the sounds of the words right. If the weight is not on the right part, the effect may be quite as unnatural as an error in the sound itself. But in addition to this there are two rules for weighting words when they are put together in statements. It is not enough to say the words one after another like a word-list, because (*a*) any word may be given *special* force to make the sense clearer, and (*b*) some very frequent little words are generally given much less force than is normal. So the Rules for weighting words in statements, to get nearer to the English way of talking, are:

I. Put force on at least one word in every 10—the word which the sense makes most important.

II. Let the 12 words which are only weighted for some special reason be joined in sound to the word which comes after them. For example:

"I will give a good rule to the *boy* slowly." That is to say, I will give it to the *boy* and not to (as against) the girl.

Almost every statement of 10 words may be said in at least 10 different ways; and the effect of the addition of force is chiefly to make the weighted word louder. Naturally, more than one word in a statement may be marked out in this way, but one will be enough to give quite an 'English rhythm' to any statement. Certain ups and downs of the voice will probably be part of the effect, but we may let these changes take care of themselves as long as they are not the outcome of a sort of song-rhythm based on the special behavior of some other language. Such song-rhythms have to be watched and taken out if they are seen to be very strong; but there are no rules for English 'song' which are important enough to be forced on the learner's attention—at any rate at the early stages.

Learners who have no English or American friends will get the natural rate from the shortwave radio; and when Basic is regularly used for news by shortwave stations in forward-looking countries, and for international talking pictures, there will be a new chance of learning the language of the future without a teacher.

The selection of international words which have so far been listed for use with the Basic system is at present small, but a further expansion of its range, with the authority of an International Radio Committee, may be looked for in the near future. The 50 about which experts have come to a decision are printed in *The Basic Words.*

Though some of these will come to the attention of the reader when he makes a start on the Basic books, there is no reason for making them a part of the learning system in the earlier stages.

They have no place, for example, in *The Basic Way,* Books I–IV. Even less will his memory be troubled by the further 50 starred in *The Basic Words* which may be used with care in different sorts of material for testing reactions.

For writing, make a start by putting down the events of the day in a book, noting at the same time any uses which are markedly different from those in your natural language. Turning pages of your language into Basic is not so good for a start, because you will be giving attention to *words,* which may have no parallel form in Basic, and not to the things, thoughts, and feelings about which you are writing. These things, thoughts, and feelings *are* covered in Basic, and if your mind is on *them* you will be certain of what you are saying and will see better how to say it simply and clearly.

The tendency to let our thoughts be controlled by words is very deeply rooted, and a month with Basic is much the best way of training the mind to put up a fight against it. When we have to do without a word, we frequently become conscious for the first time of what we were saying with it. And sometimes we see that we were saying nothing—or nothing for which a special word was needed. So here is the great value of Basic for those who come to it with a knowledge of normal English.

It might seem at first as if they were being requested to put 10,000 or 20,000 words out of their minds for no better reason than that part of their language had become an international instrument. That, it is true, would be a good reason for making use of a smaller number of words when talking internationally, in the hope that most of them would be Basic; and on this view, much may be done for the more general exchange of ideas. The addition of words to a telegram does not necessarily make it clearer, and in the same way the Basic part of what is said with the help of words outside the 850 might be clear enough for the exchange desired. Why, then, take the trouble to get the Basic right, or nearer to the rules? The answer is that, as we have seen, the training is of great value in itself, and is very little trouble if started in the right way. There is no question for the Englishman or American of learning the list by heart. He will be comforted to see that most of the words on which his normal talk is based are there. Let these be marked; and at the same time it will be seen that all the rest are very common—even those, from the last 50, which make the connection with science and are not needed by anyone under 14. He will quickly become conscious that the 100 words which are representative of 'prepositions,' 'pronouns,' 'conjunctions,' 'adverbs,' and so on, give him all the framework which is necessary.

But there are certain very common words which are not in the Basic list, and he will make a note of these and of the reasons why they are not there. Some, he will see, are covered by the names of acts and directions, which he will take through their tricks (every operation-word in turn with every direction) till he has listed one or two hundred of the 'verbs' whose place is taken by them.[49] To get a clear picture of the system at this stage he will be wise to go all through the *ABC* with care, taking at least two or three hours on the details and answering for himself the harder test questions at the end of every part.

A further step is to put ten lines from a newspaper roughly into Basic, noting which words were in Basic at the start, and underlining any word which will not go straight across into the simpler form of writing. By then turning to these underlined words in *The Basic Dictionary* for suggestions, he will be able to make the necessary changes. After that, things will go more quickly, and one by one his doubts and questions will be answered. The system is working, but it is a good idea to see it working smoothly in some book which has the full English on one page and the Basic opposite line by line.

A good example of this is *International Talks*, by Mr. Wickham Steed. Mr. Steed was for a long time in control of *The Times*, and his English is clear and straightforward. Reading the Basic first is not much help, but take Mr. Steed line by line with the

---

[49] See *The ABC of Basic English* [Section Two of this book, pp. 140–46. ED.].

opposite page covered over, turning to it only when a decision has to be made or there is a doubt as to how the Basic might go. Three or four pages will be enough to give a feeling of the Basic way of saying things.[50]

At this point we may say to the learner: You now have a working knowledge of the structure and the units of the system— enough to make a test of where you are still going wrong. So now take anything you are reading, 1,000 words from the morning paper, for example, and put a line under every word which seems to you to be Basic. Then go through them with the Basic list, writing down every word about which you were wrong. Do the same the day after with the words which are not Basic, again making a detailed comparison with the list. If you make any error twice at this stage, put the word in a special list. This list— possibly of not more than ten or twelve—is a guide to your special tendencies (others would make different errors); and after a little more work with these words they will give you no further trouble. You will be stopping from time to time over a new word, but after a week you will be writing freely, and only looking at the printed list itself when you get in a hole.

When you go down the street or in trains, you will have a chance of putting advertisements and other signs into Basic; and experience in talking may be got from an attempt to keep up with the radio news as if you had a Basic friend from China or the Hebrides in the room, and you were giving an account in clearer language of what had been said. And have a look at *Brighter Basic*, pages 28–44, to see if any of the words which do not come readily to your mind are fixed in the sayings made up of words starting with the same letter, as a help to the memory. Take note of the way the *-er*, *-ing*, and *-ed* endings are used,[51] of the possible

---

[50] Unhappily, this book is now out of print, and there is no other of quite the same sort at present available. Another parallel translation was Shakespeare's *Julius Caesar*, done by A. P. Rossiter. ED.

[51] That is, as 'nouns' and 'adjectives,' so that we may say "The book is printed," as we say "The book is small" or "The boy is tired"; but not "I printed the book," which would come under the quite different rules

use of *un-* before the 50 names of qualities which take it,[52] and of the higher and lower limits for the special uses which have to be made clear to those whose natural language is not English.

The uses of more than 95 percent of the words are those which common sense would give them on first seeing them in the list. The only question is how far to go with possible expansions if you are to be clear to a Basic learner, and the rules on this point are based on the test of long experience. Every expansion in Basic has some connection with the root sense, but about 50 words have second senses in normal English needing special attention. A number of these *are* kept in Basic to make the system complete, though for some of them different words would be necessary in most languages; the other half are not used because they give so much trouble to learners and the second sense is covered by other Basic words. A *stick*, for example, being a bit of wood, clearly has no connection with getting stamps fixed on letter-covers; *lead,* as a substance, does not give us the 'leader' of a group, and 'backing' horses is clearly one step farther from the *back* of anything than is necessary in a language which naturally "puts money on" these animals. On the other hand, you would be safe in using *arms* as 'weapons,' a *blow* for a 'set-back,' *carriage* for 'transport charges,' *change* for 'money change,' *common* for 'vulgar,' *company* for 'companionship,' *crying* for 'weeping,' *dear* for 'beloved,' *ice* for 'ice-cream,' *taste* for 'good taste,' and *waiter* for the 'garçon' who is waiting on you in a restaurant.

Here, however, are 20 words which writers with a knowledge of English frequently take in wrong senses. *Still* is not used for 'quiet,' *even* for 'level,' *that* for 'who' and 'which,' or *will* for anything but future time. Among the names of things, a *ball* is not

of 'verb' behavior as such. The reasons for this and for not using the word *print* itself as a 'verb' ("I print books") are given on p. 25, and further details are in the *ABC* [Section Two of this book, pp. 176–77, and 182].

[52] See Section Two, p. 131. The learner who is uncertain which names of qualities regularly take *un-* will keep to *not* for forming their opposites, till his Basic is smooth enough to make use of the *un-* with profit.

a dance, a *balance* is not scales, or a *board* a committee; a *box* has no connection with a fight, or a *fly* with airplanes; *hard* does not give us 'hardly,' *light* is not to be used of weight, or *measure* of laws, or *net* of prices; a *ring* has nothing to do with a bell, or a *scale* with a fish, a *start* is not a jump, a *match* is not a competition, and *base* is not bad. Of the names of qualities, *present* is no help in giving.

And here are 20 which do more than they might be given credit for, so that there is a true stretch for any learner whose language makes use of a different word for the second sense, though the connection is clear enough. They are all so common that even the addition of a different word would not make them unnecessary. *Chest* has an expansion to chest for clothing, *fall* to the fall of the year, *fire* to gun-fire, *interest* to interest on money, *join* to joiner (in wood-working), *key* to music key, *meal* to meal from grain, *nail* to finger-nail, *note* to note of music, *plane* to the wing of an airplane, *rest* to the rest (what is over), *right* to the opposite of wrong, *shade* to shades of the dead, *sign* to signing letters, *spring* to the spring months and water springs, *stage* to the theater stage, and *stamp* to post stamp. And when the endings -er, -ing, -ed are used with *train, unit,* and *watch,* the senses of *training, uniting,* and *watching* almost put them in a group by themselves.[53]

With these examples, covering 99 percent of what is not regular, and noting the suggestions in this book, you may go straight forward with the word-list and the short rules given on the bit of notepaper. Thousands have done so, and have sent us their work.[54]

[53] For more details of this sort, see Section Two, pp. 183–91. ED.
[54] There followed an invitation to anyone desiring help with his Basic to send in a sample to the Orthological Institute. This service is not available at present. ED.

6. The Teaching of Basic

The learning of Basic in schools is only one part, though a very important one, of the process by which a knowledge of its value may become general in all countries. Radio and the talking pictures will do much, but the schools have a better chance because they have more time.

It is not uncommon for five or ten years to be given to a language, and at the end, reading, writing, and talking may all be equally impossible.

This has been true of Latin and French in English and American schools for more than a hundred years. After five years' work the reading of French newspapers is still only possible with a word-book, and such talking as is attempted is certain to be a cause of amusement in Paris. In the same way, the English talked by our friends from other countries is not a good advertisement for any but their best schools; but the level of English in schools under English control overseas is even lower.

What is responsible for the present position of language teaching? Chiefly, no doubt, a bad teaching system, in which attention is given to fixed forms of words—'idioms,' 'collocations,' and the like—before the structure and the root senses have been made clear; but in addition, certainly, the dead weight of a mass of unnecessary words, chiefly 'verbs' whose behavior is not regular. The memory is over-taxed when English is given to the learner as if it was no more regular, and only a little simpler, than French, which is truly a language of complex forms and fixed uses at every turn.

English is the simplest of all languages in form and structure, but if a start is made with a limited word-list in which more than 100 'strong verbs' are given a place, it will never seem so. With this 100 go their 200 strange 'past definites' and 'past participles' —and much more.

Take the word *bear* (*bore*, *borne*), used freely of parcels (carry), news (bring), fruit (produce), babies (give birth to), pain (tolerate), and so on. Even if these are kept separate in the word-list we have still to get away with

"I cannot bear him."
"He bears himself nobly."
"Bear this in mind."
"He bore down on us."
"He lost his bearings."

His 'proud bearing' is as different from the 'lost bearings' as the 'bear ring' with fighting animals is from a 'bare ring' with no ornaments, or a 'bare baby' from a baby 'born' but 'unbearable.' Every word of this sort has its train of tricks, and the learner is certain to get it mixed up with other words of the same sound and much the same form.

The makers of 'simple' school books go happily through the range of senses, frequently without noting any change; and after the first 1,000 comes another 1,000 equally without reason or system. All this is done in the interests of a natural English which will never be natural as talked in China or Japan, India or Africa, even after ten years of school work. Such a process is only a way of humoring bad teachers, on whom the learner is made dependent—and the teacher is dependent on a book which gives no reasons for anything, but is full of tests by which the learner may be marked for memory-work and even more memory-work.

This may be seen by a comparison of Basic with any of the word-lists produced in competition with Basic. There have been a number of other attempts at limited word-lists for learners, a great number of them clearly copying, if not profiting by, the example of Basic. But these selections, when they have not been made without any system at all, have at best been based on simply noting the most frequently used words in newspapers, etc., which is a long way from noting those which are of most use.[55]

There is a tendency for those who have not given much attention to Basic to take the view that the learner might be happier to have two or three hundred more words than to get control of what in most language books are named 'prepositional phrases.' The answer to this is that all the uses of the names of operations and directions given in the early stages are needed for any purpose; that those which come in later are at least as necessary for reading and talking any sort of English as the new words would be, and are of value in building up a knowledge of the root uses; that every new word, however simple it may seem, is a new sound which may not be common in the learner's natural language, and may be a cause of trouble with other Basic words; that all common words have their tricks and special uses (like *bear*), of which teachers are generally quite unconscious; and that any such additions, outside a small number of 'strong verbs' which are the hardest of all, would be little help in covering the field till after the 850 themselves had done their work.

Basic is as much a protest against this new school which, with the 850 words before it, is attempting to make the first steps to English simpler without system, as against the old, which has no war-cries such as 'Correct English' but is at least wasting the learner's time with some belief of the value of hard work. Simple English as an instrument of education is something more than a short way to reading *Tit-Bits*, and Basic will only be of use to education authorities when they are conscious of the damage which is being done by viewing the schools as a forcing-house for hotel-porters. The porters may be able to say the right thing

---

[55] Ogden here referred specifically, though without naming any names, to three or four rival systems which in their day had a certain notoriety. Today, this old history is long forgotten and the references would be not merely of no interest but quite mysterious to most readers. The general statement made in the last two sentences has therefore been substituted. ED.

in three languages, but so are the birds at the Zoo who have been
learning by the 'Direct Method' from sailors.

It is the business of the school to do something more than this;
and a start may be made with *The Basic Way to English*, in
which the 850 words are covered in four Language Books. All
four have pictures on every page, with questions for testing the
learner's knowledge at the end of every division. In addition,
there are four Teaching Books for those who have no time for a
complete training with the *ABC*. Simple reading-material goes
with these.[56]

Before making a start it is important to give the learner a
clear idea of the range and purpose of Basic. Even the very
young do better when they have a bird's-eye view of the country
through which they will be journeying by slow stages. They see
that the end of the journey is not so far away, that there are good
reasons for the rules, that there are no unnecessary details, and
that if they are going on to an English of 10,000 or 20,000 words
the 850 are an instrument by which new words may be controlled
as they come in.

The list itself will be kept before the learner till the sounds
and senses are clear and every word has been marked off in
connection with the group in which it was first given. For learning and general use 'the bit of notepaper' is the right size for the
pocket, and it is a common experience that even those who have
never before done work out of school hours will come back with
more in their heads than before.

Older learners who may have got a certain distance with some
sort of English before attacking Basic will naturally be surprised
if they are given something which seems to them to be designed
for the first year's work only. The attraction of words is like that
of money; more words seem to be a sign of power, and even if

[56] *The Basic Way to English*, Books I–IV (Teaching Books separate) from
Evans Brothers, "Our Changing Times" from The Basic English Publishing
Co., and "The Basic Reading Books" from Sir Isaac Pitman and Sons. [The
last two are now out of print. ED.]

when we 'disembark' we only get off a ship, 'disembarkation' gives the simple-minded the same sort of feeling as the colored *acqua pura* which is so much used by medical men for other diseases of the mind. The teacher who is ready to keep away from complex and shorthand forms of language till the building of the framework is complete will be able to make the position clear. The learner has to be made to see that he will not be limited in any way after two or three months, that walking comes before running, and that he is certain to be making foolish errors all the time if he is unable to get control of the 850 words which are the key to the rest before airing his chance knowledge of additions from newspapers, verse, and the market-place.

The thought to keep in mind is that 850 words come before 851, and that the 851st word may be any one of those which, like other additions outside its list, Basic is able to put into operation. And if, as is clear, the 850 themselves make it possible to do all the work, even in business or science, for example, a discussion of the place of Basic in these important fields may be a further help to the teacher in getting his learners to see why they are taking the right first step.

7. Basic for Science

Little more than a hundred years back, one man might have been able to make himself an expert in almost every branch of science. There are some now living whose fathers were friends of the man who made the discovery of O_2 (Oxygen), and who were themselves at school when Darwin was writing *The Origin of Species*. While they were young, the first books on science were making their way to the East, and only yesterday were the new developments which have been changing the face of the earth taken seriously by the millions of China and Japan.

Today Biology has to take into account the work of Sir Jagadio

Bose, but if equally important observations were now being recorded in Chinese or Japanese it might be a long time before
they got attention. In certain fields new ideas are more or less
readily exchanged through international 'Abstracts,' but these
short accounts are frequently not very clear, and for material
printed in any but the chief European languages, even Russian,
the range covered is not very wide.

There is still no English-Japanese or English-Chinese Dictionary which is of any value for the purposes of science, though
hundreds of good brains from China and Japan are being trained
in English and American universities. Before long these hundreds
will become thousands, working with a curtain of strange signs
between them and their friends in other countries. The loss on
this side may still be small, but let us keep in mind the other
side of the picture.

Readers in the East, in tens of thousands, are interesting themselves in medical questions and the sciences of biology, chemistry,
engineering, and so on—whose development, at least in theory,
is going forward in Europe at an unparalleled rate. Is the Siamese
medical man to get his training in the language of his country or
in the languages of science? If he gives five years to English and
then comes to France or Germany, his time will be wasted on
another unnecessary list of 20,000 units.

It is frequently said that the East will quickly get tired of its
new plaything, but there are no signs of such a change. The same
arguments were used in Europe two hundred years back; and it
is not surprising that education authorities are turning at this
point to Basic, not only for the training of the expert but for giving the general public an account of complex ideas in the simplest
possible form.

At a time when public opinion may have increasingly important
effects on the future of education, the current view that any newspaper story is good enough for the public may do great damage
to the cause of science. With the help of Basic, such accounts
may be made simple without becoming bad science. Mr. S. L.

Salzedo's *A Basic Astronomy* is an interesting example of what is being done in this connection; and of the papers in *The Outlook of Science* and *Science and Well-Being*, Professor J. B. S. Haldane was even ready to say that in some places his argument was the better for being put into Basic.

In fields such as economics, where everyday questions are frequently under discussion, Basic may be a help to anyone who is troubled by statements such as this (by Sir Josiah Stamp):

"Narrow dispersions, skewed negatively, signify deliberate human restriction of output. Skewed positively, after the introduction of selection of employees by test or examination, a narrow dispersion indicates a successful system of selection."

This goes into Basic quite simply at the level of the general reader, and, it would seem, without serious loss, as:

"The tendency to a common level of output being more frequent, is a sign that output is being consciously kept inside a certain limit. When the lowest outputs are most frequent and the output of workers not widely different and generally high, after selection of workers by test has come into use, the tendency may be taken as a sign of the efficiency of the system of selection." [57]

Here only one word from the list of 50 special economics words has been made use of. On the other hand, for material in which no one but the expert is interested, words which are international in all the seven chief languages of science will be used frequently. Then we get accounts of this sort:

"The explanation of the fact that the range of radio waves is shorter by day than by night is based on the absorption of the electro-magnetic waves in the ionosphere. By day the ionization of the air is very strong. The highest degree of ionization in Picture 3 will be in a much lower position, and the deeper layers have a great power of electric conduction. For this reason the radio waves (those ranging between 200 and 600 metres in wave-length) undergo reflection at lower levels, and would come back to earth if there did

[57] *Basic for Economics*, p. 25.

not take place in the layers of reflection a great absorption caused
by the frequent violent meetings of ions and electrons at such levels.
Further, it is clear from the latest investigations of the 'fine structure'
of the ionosphere that there are present in the lower air other layers
of electrons and ions by which absorption is effected, and the range
of the rays limited. (The level of ionization may be as low as 50 km.)
At night the ionization becomes less; there is no chance of refraction
or reflection till very high levels (where the mean free paths are
very great), and at these levels the numbers of meetings in a second
is very much smaller, so there is much less absorption. This makes
possible a much greater range, and that is the explanation of the
increased range of radio waves at night." [58]

To those working in this field, international words such as
ionosphere and *ionization* are necessarily clear. For others there
will be the Dictionary of 10,000 science words whose senses are
given in Basic; [59] and whatever is designed for the wider public
will make no use of any words outside the Basic 850 other than
the simplest internationals. Notes may give the sense of a new
word here and there to make the reading smoother, but no
special knowledge is needed to get this sense fully. The level of
such writing may be judged from Professor Haldane's discussion,
in Basic, of the future behavior of the moon.

"In the last four or five million years the moon quickly came nearer
to the earth. When it was clear that the end would not be long in
coming we got news that the use of sea-power had in a great degree
been given up, and wind and other forms of power were used in
place of it. But the earthmen were not certain that the smashing up
of the moon would necessarily be their destruction, and the turning-
motion of the earth-moon system was still used for getting some
power. In the year 36,000,000 the moon was only a fifth of the

[58] From an 800-word outline in Basic of a ten-page paper on "The Investigation of the Ionosphere through Electro-Magnetic Waves," by Professor
Hans Zickendraht of Basle, printed in the *Annales Guébhard-Séverine*,
No. 11, 1935.
[59] See pages 389 and 395–97. ED.

distance it had been from the earth at the start of history. It seemed twenty-five times the size of the sun, and made the sea-level 200 metres higher about four times a year. The effects of the force of the earth's attraction on it might now be seen. Great landslips were seen in the mountains of the moon, and cracks were sometimes formed on its face. Earth-shocks became more frequent on the earth.

At last there were signs that the moon was getting broken up. It was so near to the earth that about ⅒th of the sky was covered when the first bits of stone came off its face. The part nearest to the earth, which was very much cracked before, now came away bit by bit in the form of great stones up to a kilometre across, which went round the earth separately. For about a thousand years this process slowly went on, and at last no further interest was taken in it on the earth. The end came quite suddenly. It was watched from Venus, but details about the earlier stages were sent from the earth in addition. The hollow part in the side of the moon facing the earth was suddenly cracked open and there came out of it a current of liquid stone at white heat. When the moon went round the earth, the heat in the middle band of the earth was increased to such a degree that all the rivers and stretches of water became dry and no plants were able to go on living." [60]

The great need now is for Committees to be formed by those responsible for the organization of science in different countries, so that workers in every branch may be in no doubt as to which words are international. Signs of all sorts are becoming more and more necessary and are getting a wider distribution every year; so a new form of picture language is taking the place of words for a great number of purposes.[61] Science has its international signs in chemistry, where the structure of a substance is pictured by letters and numbers without any words. Basic puts such systems of words, letters, numbers, or signs into operation, and the more of them there are the quicker the Babel of the experts will come to an end and the mind be free to get

[60] J. B. S. Haldane, *The Outlook of Science*, pp. 130–31.
[61] *International Picture Language*, by Otto Neurath (in Basic), 1936.

on with the work mapped out for it by Bacon and Bentham, Euclid and Einstein, Napier and Newton, Orpheus and—Orthology.

In *Basic for Science* there is a full account of the language question in science, and the history of attempts so far made to get agreement about the next step. Examples for the general reader and from a number of special fields (physics-chemistry, mathematics-mechanics, geology, biology) are taken from ten of the Basic Science Books, and the senses of the 100 General Science Words are made clear. A first list of science internationals is printed on pages 307–14.[62]

[Ogden's account of the language question in science and of Basic as the answer to it is as true today as when it was penned. Time has only made the need for an international language for science greater and clearer. By now, there is almost no country where science is not a part of higher education, and where its most surprising uses are not facts of everyday experience. First-rate brains are ready and able everywhere to make their additions to the store of knowledge. But the exchange of ideas, which is so necessary to the development of science, has not become any simpler. It is still necessary for those taking up science to have a knowledge of at least one of the chief European languages, and for such as do not have it as their birthright this is frequently a serious tax on their time and powers. In England, at any rate, it is not very uncommon for learners from the Afro-Asian countries to come for training to our universities and colleges and be unable to get any profit from it because their knowledge of English is not good enough, so that they go back to their countries with broken hopes after a most unhappy experience.

A further word is needed in connection with Ogden's second example. *Les Annales Guébhard-Séverine*, from which this was

[62] For an account of the general and special lists for science, and examples of their use, see Section Three, Part Two. ED.

taken, was a science paper produced in Neuchâtel in which the writings might be in any one of the four European languages, French, German, Italian, and English. It was, that is to say, an attempt at an 'international' paper, answering the need for a free exchange of ideas among science workers of different nations. But clearly, a paper limited to those languages would go only a small part of the way, and was, in addition, still dependent on a knowledge of more than one language by its readers. In 1935 Dr. Emil Mühlestein, the producer of *Les Annales*, had the idea of printing at the end of every paper a short outline of it in Basic English. In this way, anyone with a knowledge of Basic would be able to get a general idea of everything between the covers of the paper, even if he had no knowledge of any of the languages used. Dr. Mühlestein got in touch with the Orthological Institute, which undertook to put such outlines into Basic from any of the languages in question, and the system was put to the test. Supported by the warm approval of readers and writers, it went on regularly up to 1939, when the war made it impossible for Dr. Mühlestein and the Institute to keep in touch. It would be hard to get a better example of the feeling of need for a common language on the part of men of science, on the one hand, and of the value of Basic for the purpose on the other.

After 1944, Basic went on producing science books till in 1953 it had in print sixteen at all levels (see the Book List at the end of this book for some of them), of which two had done so well as to have been put out in paper covers by Penguin Books. In September, 1962, at the Meeting of the British Association at Manchester, two papers were given on (and in) Basic, one on "Basic English as an International Language for Science," the other on "Basic English for the Social Sciences."

Last, in 1965, after more than twenty years, *The Science Dictionary in Basic English* came out. In the end, the number of words and word-groups covered by it came nearer to 25,000

than to the 10,000 looked forward to by Ogden in 1944. A year
later (1966) it was put out in the United States under the
name *The Basic Dictionary of Science.* ED.]

8. Basic for Business

Mountains and rivers are chiefly responsible for the early division of men into small warring groups whose expansion, as
nations, is effected by crushing other nations. The tendency of
every group to make noises in a different way has given the
different forms of language by which their thought is limited
and their troubles are increased. Language, which might be
a uniting force, keeps men separate so that their common interests are still seen through a mist darkly.

What, then, are the uniting forces working for the future and
against these unnatural divisions which are natural only in books
on geography? Rivers may be controlled by one or another of
the groups living near them, but the sea is still a highway for
international *trade.* Mountains may be the property of nations,
but the air is still free—at any rate for international *radio.*
Radio, like the airplane and the talking picture, is the outcome
of *science;* and science, though its produce is still being used
for destruction, is a help to that international development which
will only be possible through a common international language.

English is one of the international languages for trade, which
is dependent on peace and common sense for its increase, so
Basic as a complete second language for all purposes has a special value for businessmen. But a wide field is covered by the
word 'business.' We get no clear picture of a businessman. He
might be anything from a bookkeeper to an insurance expert.
Makers of goods, bankers, storekeepers, and those responsible
for operations on the Exchange are all equally businessmen,
though they have little in common but an interest in making

money. Most of them, however, are more certain of making money in peacetime than when everything is being turned upside down by the military; and all of them get more comfort from the thought of themselves on a seat in an office or a club, getting bits of paper signed by the softer part of the public, than on a bed in a hospital having bits of metal taken from the softer parts of their bodies.

To the peace-loving sort of businessman common sense says: "Sweet are the uses of advertisement. Send letters (with the 850 Basic words on the other side) to business houses in other countries. When new orders are coming in by every post it will be possible to get from you support for inventions which might have had no other chance but self-help. And a new invention is a safer mother for new business than a flag or a gun."

Any branch of business may have 50 special words, in addition to the 850, for its special purposes. There are certain words, such as *liability, purchase,* and *guarantee,* which are common to all the branches, but the number of these is very limited. Clearly then, it will be necessary to have separate lists for bankers, insurance men, and so on, in the same way as we have separate lists for zoology, chemistry, and psychology, though they are all sciences.

On the other hand, there is one branch of business which is, in a very great measure, the key to all the rest. The backbone of business is trade. Industry is nothing but an organization for producing goods for the trader; the chief purpose of insurance is to make the transport of goods a safe undertaking; and trading operations may have important effects on banks and the money-market.

For these reasons the decision was made that a Business List of the widest and most general use possible would be formed by putting together 50 words from among such necessary words as are common to all the branches of business and the special words which are needed for trading purposes. There is no doubt that this is the field which teachers of 'Business English' have chiefly in mind when writing their books. In *Basic for Business* sixty Basic examples are given of the sorts of letters which are sent through the post by someone every day.

There is more profit to be got from learning examples by heart in connection with business letters than in most other special fields, because in business a small number of conditions and decisions have to be faced again and again, and the forms used have a tendency to become fixed. For this reason it is possible to get a very long way with a rubber-stamp knowledge. That is why the shorthand experts have been able to make a working system based on the use of unit signs for long groups of words, a system which would not be possible if there were a great number of such word-groups in frequent use. It may be pointed out that Basic gives the experts a chance of taking this system even farther than they have been able to do at present, because in Basic the number of different ways in which one statement may be made is much more limited than in normal English, and for this reason the forms of letters will necessarily become more regular.

A reader who has any knowledge of business will see for himself which parts of the examples it will be wisest for him to get into his head. He will do well to give special attention to the words with which the letters are started and ended. Openings such as "In answer to your letter of the . . . about . . . we have pleasure in saying . . . ," "To our regret we have to say that . . . ," "We are surprised that we are so far without any answer to our letter of the . . ." might be listed for learning purposes.

A list of endings would have an equal value. Examples which will be of very general use are "Hoping that you will be pleased with this suggestion, and will send an early answer . . . ," "Waiting for the receipt of my order . . . ," "Looking forward to your orders in the future . . . ," "With regrets for the trouble you have been caused. . . ." It is important to get these details right because the purpose and outlook of the sender are frequently judged by the words with which the letter is started or ended. The parting words, "It is our hope that there will be no more trouble about this," make it quite clear that the writer is not pleased, while keeping well inside the limits of good taste; and an ending such as "Hoping that you will not be greatly troubled by my request . . ." has probably more chance of getting attention for a letter than one worded with less care. It will be noted that 'Yours truly' is the form used at the end of all Basic business letters as a sign that there is no more to be said. Anyone who gets tired of putting this may make small changes such as 'Yours very truly' or 'I am yours truly,' but it is our belief that nobody will be very much troubled by the fact that 'respectfully,' 'faithfully,' and 'I have the honor to be' have been put on one side.

The fact that certain ornaments and additions normally exchanged in letters between businessmen are overlooked by Basic gives equally little cause for regret. Any attempt to put what we have to say more simply and straightforwardly is a step in the right direction. Much good ink and time are wasted in writing about 'an esteemed firm' or being 'favored by an inquiry.' There is no need for creditors to be 'reluctantly compelled' to make their requests for payment; even less is it necessary for someone desiring simple details from another business house to say, before putting his question, "May I trespass on your indulgence in the following matter." Forms such as these are only like the silver paper round the chocolate, and when the chocolate is a bitter one, the silver paper does not make it any sweeter. Basic has quite enough smooth-sounding words to be able to do everything necessary in the way of giving a soft answer or making a delicate request. Here are some suggestions: "We have pleasure in saying . . . ," "Will you be kind enough to . . . ," "To my regret I am unable . . . ," "Kindly let me have. . . ." A long list of this sort might be made; but the degree to which such forms are necessary is all a question of what one is used to. A Frenchman has more taste for polish than an Englishman; while in the Far East the ornaments of language seem quite overpowering to most Europeans. If everyone equally is forced by Basic to get to the point as quickly as possible, we may safely say that nobody's feelings will be wounded.

From one point of view, then, Basic English will be hard even for the English themselves. The businessman seems to have a strange love for using long words where simple words would do as well and better. In this way there has come into existence a special business language which is not based on business needs or interests, and whose only purpose is to make whatever is under discussion seem more important than it is. A businessman will 'furnish' details where a normal person would 'give' them; he 'renders' an account when he might equally well 'send it in'; letters are talked of as 'favors' and payments as 'remittances.' To give a clearer idea of how unnecessarily complex business letters are made in normal English here are some examples of the self-important forms which are frequently used, together with Basic parallels:

We are compelled to have recourse to your services.	We are forced to make our request to you.
It afforded us great pleasure.	It gave us great pleasure.
Furnish particulars.	Give details.
I shall esteem it a great favor if you will send.	Will you kindly send.
You may rest assured that.	You may be certain that.
We venture to suggest.	We make the suggestion.

It may be doubted if anyone would seriously say that there is any loss of sense in putting such statements into Basic, and it is to be hoped that the number of those to whom the simple Basic words are more pleasing and more natural to the ear is increasing.

Traders undertake the exchange and transport of all sorts

of goods, but naturally the names of a great number of these are not among the general 850 words. The trading operations of most business houses, however, are limited to certain groups of goods—fruit, cloth, writing materials, and so on—and wherever this is so it would be very simple to make short lists of the names which are needed in connection with any special group of goods. The question of the general trader is a harder one, and for him some use of word-books will probably be necessary. But if the form and purpose of a letter are clear, the fact that two or three words in it have to be looked up will give no trouble to anyone.

9. Sixteen Years, 1927–1943

Though English might have automatically become the international language, it would not necessarily be the best answer to the question—What sort of language does its work with the least waste? It would certainly be a waste of time to make a language international if it was nothing more than the chance outcome of competition for trade and other sidelines of history, or a form of Esperanto based on word-roots with a wide distribution in a number of European languages.

The theory of language is a very complex business. It is dependent on new sciences which have only come into existence in the last hundred years. Thoughts, words, and things are hard enough to keep separate; and all of them have a tendency to get mixed up with feelings. Five years may be a short time in which to come to a decision about what is what in such a field, but in 1923, when *The Meaning of Meaning* [63] was complete, it was possible to go back to the special field of grammar with some new light on the ways in which words do their work, and from that time to 1927 Basic was in the making. Early in 1928

[63] International Library of Psychology, 6th printing, 1944.

it became clear that 850 English words, put into operation by the Basic system, would give us something which was supported by science while offering to teachers and businessmen what they had been looking for.

The system was first made public by limited distribution, so that the reaction of the best brains might be tested for two or three years, with a view to forming a group of workers in certain key countries. But interest was everywhere so great that letters and requests for further details kept coming in hundreds, and a wider organization became necessary. With the help of English friends and the Payne Fund of New York, the necessary material was got ready in a number of languages, and in 1933 a serious start was made in the Far East with a program supported by the Rockefeller Foundation.

Less than seven years after that, Basic had its representatives in more than twenty countries, and interest was everywhere increasing. By the end of 1939 more than 150 books in and about Basic were in print, and the year 1944 will be marked by the addition of more reading material for schools and the printing of the complete *Basic Bible* by the Cambridge University Press.[64]

Special attention has been given to the needs of the education authorities in China, where the Orthological Institute (Peking), under the direction of Professor R. D. Jameson of Tsing Hua University and Dr. I. A. Richards of Magdalene College, Cambridge, was working (till 1938) on the organization of material for the Middle Schools. They had the help of a Chinese Committee, and were profiting by the new developments in radio, which is now coming to the front in all countries of the East. The parallel program in Japan would have been complete in 1942, when the *Japanese-Basic Dictionary*, on which Mr. F. J. Daniels had been at work for five years, was almost ready to be printed for the use of teachers. The place of Professor Okakura, our representative from 1932 till his death in 1936, was taken

[64] In fact, *The Bible in Basic English* came out in 1949. ED.

by Mr. T. Takata, who was responsible for the Japanese form of *The ABC of Basic English,* and *A New Guide to Basic English* for Middle Schools.

In countries such as Japan, where the value of English for international purposes is very great, not only in trading with America, Australia, India, and Europe, but for science, invention, and general thought, language teaching has generally been started on the wrong lines. In addition, Japan had been guided in the past twenty years chiefly by English teachers of the old school who had no knowledge of psychology. Even when Basic came to their attention through the work of Mr. Rossiter in Etajima (1929–1932), their attempts at copying it were limited to making word-lists designed for story-writing. Lists of this sort, based on the old ideas of memory-work, get the learner nowhere, and it will not be surprising if a form of English needing so much time and giving so little power of saying anything clearly is taken out of the schools in the near future.

This might give Basic its chance, and certainly more would be done in one year by a private learner than has so far been possible in three or even five years in the present schools. By 1941 between 2,500,000 and 3,000,000 Japanese had enough knowledge of English to make a new start with Basic as a guide, and it would be sad for teachers who have been working so hard to be put out of business for no better reason than that errors have been made by others. But if, when the present troubles are over, Basic is given a test in the last year before the Middle School, the Japanese will quickly be profiting by short-wave Radio News (page 93).

A first need in all countries where English has been started on the old lines is the training of a body of teachers who will be able to get the best out of the new system. That is what Dr. Purcell was doing for two years in Singapore. Even without such training, "The Basic Way" in language learning may be used with profit, but when the reasons for a change are made clear, the process of adjustment goes more smoothly—and a month or two will be quite enough for anyone who makes the comparison with an open mind.

An important chance of training teachers came in 1938–1940 when a start was made in Hyderabad and other parts of India. The organization was put into the hands of Mr. Adolph Myers, who, working with *The Times of India* in Bombay, has been building up a great future for Basic for the 300,000,000 living south of the Himalayas. Among others who are supporting Basic in India is Mr. Jawaharlal Nehru, President of the All-India Congress.

For some learners in the East the sounds of a European language are hard. In India, Burma, and the Near East a natural rhythm comes readily if attention is given to the Basic rules. This is equally true of Russian, and our first representative in Moscow, Mrs. Litvinoff, whose Basic school books were in use for more than three years, was surprised by the record time in which learners got control of the system in the U.S.S.R.

The first Basic group in Moscow was that in the Institute of Legal Psychiatry in 1933. A short time after, others were formed in the Radio Committee, in one of the Military Academies, the Stalin Industrial Academy, the Stanko-Instrument Institute, and the Cinema Institute. In 1935, after a meeting in the Leningrad House of Science, teachers' circles were started, and the Arctic Institute became interested. At the same time, helpers were trained in the Foreign Language Combinat, from which the Red Army gets most of its teachers. From 1937 to 1940, Mrs. Litvinoff was in the Urals, teaching in Sverdlovsk, before she went to America; so the work is no longer limited to the West.

In Australia, the Modern Language Association of New South Wales now has a Basic English division. The first meeting took place in February 1936, with a talk by Senator the Hon. Macartney Abbott on "The Need for an International Thought Exchange." In 1935–1936 there were discussions of Basic in the Federal Parliament. Senator Arkins has kept the question before the public and Professor Sir C. Stanton Hicks of Adelaide University has been interesting himself in the use of Basic for the purposes of science. At the same time, Mr. H. Walpole of Queen's University, Ontario, was able to put Basic on the map in Canada before going to Bogotá to make a start with some of the chief schools in Colombia.

In 1932–1933 Basic was headlined in the news in America, and came to the front again in 1939 through the use made of it in Boston, Massachusetts, for the teaching of those whose knowledge of English is still less than normal. Miss Mary Guyton, an expert on Adult Education in Boston, Massachusetts, came over to London in 1935 to make detailed notes on the step-by-step material then being printed. In 1936–1939 talks in Basic were given on the Boston short-wave radio (WIXAL); and in 1943 Dr. Richards and his Committee at Harvard were able to make good use of what Churchill had said about their work on September 6.

In Europe, the organization of Basic is going forward quickly wherever war, or the fear of war has not put education in the hands of the military. Events in Spain have made Buenos Aires and Montevideo seem more important than Madrid or Barcelona, where the schools so well started by Mr. Calvert and Mr. Teague were needed for machine guns. When Geneva came under a cloud, Dr. Vočadlo made himself responsible for a Danubian Center in Prague; Dr. Otto Neurath undertook the designing of pictures for Basic school books at the Mundaneum Institute in The Hague; and new support was given to the system from 1938 to 1940 in Athens, where between 4,000 and 5,000 were learning English through Basic at the Institute of English Studies.

The first European country to make Basic a part of its education system was Denmark, where a Copenhagen night school went on the air from the Kalundborg station in 1932 after only 50 hours' work. A start was made in the day schools in 1934, and in the first stage there were more than 40 of these with about 2,000 Basic learners. With the help of Mr. August Lerche, through whose *Hvad er Basic Engelsk?* the system came to the attention of the authorities, our representative, Mrs. Kamma Taylor, was quickly getting together the material necessary to give the teachers a good chance; and in 1938–1939 no less than 85 out of 105 taking English in Copenhagen were making use of her books.

In a number of other countries governments are moving slowly, even where teachers of the old school seem at present to be completely in control; and though it may take another ten years for the new ideas to get on the top of the wave, the wind is blowing in the right direction.

So much for the sixteen years which have gone to make Basic a living force in education and a new hope in international relations. They have been years of spadework, and those who have taken part in the planting and watering now may get comfort from watching the growth of new seed in fertile fields.

10. The Future

There were good reasons for the belief that the Great War was in fact only a little one—a sort of one-act play before the curtain was lifted on more serious military operations. But long before we get back to normal, something will have to be done for the development of international feeling. What is chiefly needed at the present time is some new idea, by which the mind of man may be lifted out of its narrow prison house, where food, sex, and money, or the political troubles of the nation are its only interests outside sport.

What makes a nation is a common language. What will make men international will be a common language. That is one part of the great idea.

Basic is the only chance. The earth is getting smaller through the discoveries of science, and radio is now putting Babel into the houses of those who have no knowledge even of the names of the languages they are hearing. One great step forward would be news every hour of the day and night, in a common language, from one or other of 24 stations working with a common purpose through Basic.

Five minutes would be enough—five minutes every hour, on the hour—to give everyone the feeling that this little earth was pulling itself together. And with that feeling would come a new hope for all the forces moving for peace. It is 4 P.M. and we are turning on Copenhagen; 5 P.M., New York; 6 P.M., Geneva; 7 P.M., possibly Peking. We have been hearing for five minutes a Basic account of those events which, in the opinion of the experts responsible for the news given out by the country or station in question, were of international interest. Not much organization would be needed, and there are a number of businessmen who are in a position to get the idea started in less than six months.

Any school in any country would then have the chance of hearing Basic, the second language of all (no longer looked on as the language of England or America), and that language would quickly become as much a part of its everyday experience as the knowledge of the names of the countries from which the voices were talking. That would make it possible for books to be produced in any country for every country, and the second step would be a Basic Library of General Knowledge covering the sciences in 1,000 divisions—all so cheap that no workingman would be without them.

A third step on the same scale would be a Basic Parallel Library of 1,000 books giving the Basic form of the works of great writers of the present and past and on the opposite page the words of the writer himself, so that everyone would at least have a chance of learning any language in which he might be interested. The private learner has generally gone forward more quickly because he has been given, or has been able to get, the answers *with* the questions. The schoolboy who was a jump in front of the others, because he had seen the Key in secret, went in fear of punishment; but in his heart he said to himself: "The quickest way of learning languages is clearly to have the answers on the opposite page; so when I get away from school, I will have no more of their tricks." And if, later on, he was interested in a new language, as a private learner, he got as much as possible from a comparison of stories in two forms, with the words in his natural language as a guide. Sometimes he went wrong, by getting the sense without the structure; but this was because his comparisons were made without any system, and the stories were not put before him in parallel form, step by step, with the necessary notes.

The Basic Parallel Library will be designed for three purposes:

1. To give the sense as quickly as possible, so that after getting a bird's-eye view of the 850 words at work the learner may go back over the details.

2. To give the reader a clear idea of the rules on all points in which two languages are different in use or structure, in special notes.

3. To make the teacher a guide and a helper where the going is rough, so that the full value may be got out of the printed word, and no time may be wasted on unnecessary tests to which only the teacher has the key.

At first, only the better teachers will be ready to make use of such material; the others will go on with the old tests without seeing that the makers of such tests were laughing at them, and saying that the only safe way with the foolish is to keep them to fixed forms of question and answer. "Let the teacher keep to the book and he will make no errors; let him be given new forms and new uses *as new words*, because he has not enough knowledge to make the connections clear." Basic is on the side of the learner all the time, and it is better for the foolish teacher to make a small number of errors than to give orders from his book to an army of badly trained little monkeys—who will make the right answers only as long as they are kept to the forms of question locked up in the expert's secret Key.

Books of 100,000 words are now printed for sixpence, ten cents, or 50 sen: so books of 20,000 words at one penny, two cents, or ten sen would be quite possible—even without the help of a moving picture star to get things started.

At any rate, it is safe to say that international talking pictures in Basic will come automatically, but the quicker the better now that the stars are getting tired of learning new languages. In March 1937, Mary Pickford said as much, but had no suggestion to make about the language which would take her through every country.

Long before 1939 Henry Ford gave the answer to this and other questions of the same sort when, in agreement with President Masaryk and H. G. Wells, he made English for Everyman his new peace-cry to take the place of war-cries of the past; but the different language groups got at one another's throats again, before the idea had time to take root. Now with the growth of that Everyman's English which is named Basic, the old arguments become ten times stronger. So, though the lights have gone out in country after country in Europe, there are hundreds of millions looking out from the dark into a future which is still bright with hope.

A. Basic English—Its Present Position and Plans

A paper read to the Commonwealth Section of
The Royal Society of Arts on April 26, 1966, and following a paper
by Dr. E. C. Graham on Basic English.

by J. A. LAUWERYS, D.Sc., D.Lit., F.R.I.C.
*Professor of Comparative Education, Institute of Education,
University of London, and Chairman of the Trustees,
Basic English Foundation*

There is no need to describe Basic English; that has already been done. Its nature, functions, and purposes were summarized by C. K. Ogden in his 1943 Memorandum to the War Cabinet: 'Basic English is a selection of 850 English words, used in simple structural patterns, which is both an international auxiliary language and a self-contained first stage for the teaching of any form of wider or Standard English.' And, as Sir Winston Churchill said in his 1943 Harvard speech: 'Here you have a plan. There are others, but here you have a very carefully wrought plan for an international language capable of very wide transactions of practical business and of interchange of ideas . . .'

If the qualities and virtues of Basic are indeed what they are claimed to be, questions immediately arise. Why then has its progress been slow and rather halting during the last twenty years? What use could and should be made of Basic? What could it contribute to the spreading of scientific knowledge in the countries of the Commonwealth and, indeed, of the world? What program of activities ought now to be planned?

Before attempting to give tentative answers, it seems fitting that I should explain the reasons for my own interest. In the 1930's, I was responsible for the training of teachers of science and mathematics in the London Institute of Education. Among these were many from Commonwealth countries in Asia and Africa. Many had language difficulties caused by inadequate and poor quality teaching of English. But, equally important, on their return home they would have to convey to their pupils scientific knowledge using as a medium of communication vernacular languages heavily tainted by animistic and super-stitious beliefs. Standard English, too, has many words with such overtones—as etymology makes clear. But the overtones have been weakened, worn away, by hundreds of years of use in an industrializing society, permeated by scientific thinking. For this reason—there are, of course, many others—it is somewhat harder to teach science in Africa or Asia than in Northwestern Europe or the United States. In addition, it is obvious that *all* science teaching, like all teaching, is an affair of communication between teacher and pupil largely through the medium of spoken language: the problems presented are in part semantic. There was also another, distinct point: working in an institution which, like the University of London, attracts students from many countries, is bound to create interest in the possibilities of international auxiliary languages.

The outcome of these influences was renewed and intensified interest in the theory of language and, in particular, in *The Meaning of Meaning* and Bentham's *Theory of Fictions.* I well remember my delight on first learning about Ogden's work on Basic English. Here, it seemed, was an approach completely consonant with that of the sciences. Here was something re-freshingly different from the pseudo even anti-scientific word-counting and frequency evaluations, with their bogus sampling techniques. It appeared to me then, as it does now, that to decide that certain words should be taught because they are among the 2,000 or 5,000 words most frequently used in conversation or writing by some Englishmen at some date or other was about as wise as to decide to teach pupils all about test-tube holders or glass beakers just because they are frequently used in laboratories.

Basic English also seemed a better answer to the problem of devising an Auxiliary than, say, Esperanto. This, partly because the artificial languages were in reality little more than European hash, but chiefly because, in Ogden's words, Basic harnessed 'the impetus behind the spread of the English language to the development of an international means of communication.'

My deepening interest in all this led to a long and close friendship with C. K. Ogden, and I am happy to have this opportunity of expressing both my gratitude and my great indebtedness to him.

I became Chairman of the Basic English Foundation at a time when it was known that the government grants were to be withdrawn and when financially its affairs were at a very low ebb. If I may be allowed to say so, however, I have never thought that the material success or prosperity of a policy or of an organization was *the* criterion that should decide whether it should be supported. Furthermore, the history of science and technology provides many instances of the fact that it usually takes at least fifty years for a good idea or invention to be accepted and acted upon. H. G. Wells expresses the same view in *The Shape of Things to Come* . . . 'Basic English was a by-product [of attempts to improve the language mechanism]. The new science was practically unendowed, it attracted few workers, and it was lost sight of during the decades of disaster. It was revived only in the early twenty-first century . . . It became the common language for use between nations . . . By 2020 almost everyone was able to make use of Basic for talking and writing.'

Let me turn away from these personal details and take up the story where Dr. Graham left off. There are points to be added and a record to put straight. First, the Cabinet committee appointed by the Prime Minister was neither quick nor efficient.

A month after his Harvard speech, in October 1943, we find
Sir Winston writing to the Secretary of State for India, Mr.
L. S. Amery: 'I was shocked to find on my return to this country that the Cabinet committee appointed on July 12th had
never once met. You volunteered for it . . . If you feel the
pressure of your other duties is too heavy on you I will myself
take on the duty of presiding. . . .' How sad that he did not!
The final recommendations, while in favor of Basic as an international auxiliary language, were weak, half-hearted com-
promises.[1]

The financial negotiations—after all nothing could be done to
spread Basic without cash and Ogden was absolutely opposed
to commercializing it to his own advantage—were dragged out
to tremendous length. The failure of the authorities to provide
the necessary paper for printing made it impossible to take advantage of the publicity caused by Churchill's support. In 1945,
a stock of more than 100,000 volumes valued at £18,000 was
destroyed by damp in Cursitor Street, Chancery Lane, while
the Inter-Departmental Committee which had been set up de-
layed the decisions which would have provided the necessary ac-
commodation and removal facilities. At no time was any help
given—those were difficult days—to renew the contacts abroad
which had existed before the war. Since no paper was made
available, even to print textbooks for export, piracy flourished;
while American texts, clearly making much use of the theory of
Basic, exploited even the European market.

It is not going too far to say that this first stage of the negotiations (that is, from 1944 to 1946) was a complete justification
of President Roosevelt's opinion. In June 1944 he wrote to his
Secretary of State, Cordell Hull: 'If in regard to Basic English
we get the views of "competent Government specialists" we shall
certainly sound the death knell of Basic English or anything like
it. I never knew of any group of such people to agree to any-

[1] See the Prime Minister's Statement with original and Basic versions,
pp. 376–80.

thing really different from the existing system or for that matter anything new. Basic English has tremendous merit in it.'

A claim for damages and liabilities amounting to £56,000, which included the 100,000 books, had been submitted in March 1946. An offer of £23,000 was accepted by Ogden in settlement, and the payment of this amount was agreed by the Inland Revenue in the following year to have been made entirely for that purpose. It is important to insist upon this point because a widespread impression exists, based upon inaccurate and misleading answers in Parliament, that the £23,000 was a payment for copyright in Basic English. It was *not:* it was compensation for damages. The papers in the files of the Basic English Foundation leave no doubt whatever about this point. No payment was ever made by the Government for the copyright—only for material loss caused by delay and incompetence. It is not without interest to note that the amount paid, the £23,000, is recorded in the Civil Appropriation Accounts as set off against the vote to the British Council, of which in that year £1,000,000 was shown as unexpended. The Chairman of the Council at that time, Sir Malcolm Robertson, had never concealed his hostility to Basic. Later in 1946, on the intervention of Mr. Ernest Bevin, then Foreign Secretary, negotiations were resumed and finally brought to a conclusion in May. As Dr. Graham has said, the Basic English Foundation was established as a result, in 1947. In the following year, at the request of the Foreign Office, the copyright in the Basic word-list and system, an option on which had been retained by H.M. Government, was assigned by Ogden to the Foundation. The copyright in the United States and in India was expressly excluded from this assignment. The Orthological Institute was to receive, through the Foundation, an annual grant from the Ministry of Education, to be used for those of its projects which the Foundation approved. Altogether a total sum of about £100,000 was allotted to the Foundation over a period of six years. This sum may appear large, but in fact the size of the sums given by American

foundations or by the Nuffield Foundation for the improvement
of science teaching explains why some think of it as peanuts.
Still, I suppose it would be worth more then than now.

Moreover, there was an insistence upon wasteful appointments
as a precaution against the misuse of funds, although the
Foundation was subject to Government Audit and any profit
from publications accrued to the Trustees under Ogden's deed
of assignment and declaration of Trust. So, much of the grant
was frittered away. In any case, *none* of the money could be
spent abroad, for instance, to start experiments on the teaching
of English or to pay the expenses of representatives—evidently a
crippling restriction making almost impossible the diffusion of
the Basic system abroad.

The protracted negotiations which followed the Harvard
speech had yet another unfortunate outcome. Because of what
was said in the White Paper it was generally assumed that the
Orthological Institute would be receiving official support, and
most of its sources of income in consequence stopped. In 1946
the Payne Fund, its last main benefactor, ceased its grants.

At this time, I think for the same reasons, came another set-
back. At the end of 1943, George Bernard Shaw wrote to Ogden
to say that he was contemplating leaving a great deal of his
estate to the Orthological Institute. 'Basic,' he wrote, 'can hardly
become a universal spoken language without a phonetic script:
its pronunciation would soon be all over the shop in a dozen
dialects.' Then in March 1944, in a long letter, he explained
that he had previously named the Orthological Institute in his
will as the agent for devising and launching the British 42-
letter alphabet but that he would now look for some other fad-
executor. Ogden replied that he regretted the decision to dis-
inherit the Orthological Institute since in fact there was still
no certain financial support. I should add that he made it clear
he had deep doubts about the 42-letter alphabet. In a letter to
The Times, a few days later, Shaw said that 'Basic English is
a natural growth which has been investigated and civilized by

the Orthological Institute on the initiative of Mr. C. K. Ogden, whose years of tedious toil deserve a peerage and a princely pension.' He added that, once Basic had been mastered 'any foreigner who can live in England can [then] pick up as much of the rest as he needs, from Chaucer to Chesterton, just as we all pick it up, by reading and conversation.' But he made the will we all know about, and when I consider the continuing success of his plays, *My Fair Lady* and all, I view with regret the enormously useful work that could have been done for Basic English with all that wealth.

The story I have sketched in outline is evidently one which illustrates the way in which administrative incompetence, procrastination, and timidity can defeat the best intentions of men of vision. Even statesmen of the stature of Churchill and Roosevelt at the height of their power were unable to overcome the inertia of the gigantic machines of which they were in nominal control. Or, if you like, to avert the bedevilment which at that point befell Basic English—'bedevilled by officials,' as Ogden entered in *Who's Who* for those years. There is really no need to suppose that there was active malevolence anywhere —in the Treasury, the Foreign Office, the Ministry of Information, or the British Council, which *inter alia* were represented on the Inter-Departmental Committees. That too many cooks spoiled the broth may perhaps be the explanation. Of course interested parties, such as some publishers and authors of widely used textbooks, did what they could, by innuendo, misrepresentation, and obstruction to defend their vested advantages. But this is another matter. Many of these people, in fact most of those who have an interest in some particular theory of English teaching, are concerned chiefly with paddling their own canoe. Occasionally they lead some visitor or other down the garden path for a trip into some backwater. Content with their own profitable little splashings, they do not want to hear anything about engines or motors.

Personally, I have little doubt that the chief reason for the

slow and halting progress of Basic since the war is the absence
of the solid official support needed to implement the policy decisions of the Harvard speech. I attribute very little importance
to the criticisms that have been made of the system, largely because I have not come across any that are sound and relevant.
Consider, for example, the argument that Basic is under-
privileged English unacceptable to people in developing countries—a point I at least have never heard raised outside England.
Prime Minister Nehru wrote to Ogden in 1947: 'My partiality
for Basic English continues and I think it can help us in India.'

Or think of the argument that English must be taught through
the medium of literature. Possibly true—in England with
English-speaking students or abroad at University level. But
with children or adolescents in India, Japan, or Africa? As Ogden
put it: 'The Basic System, in spite of the fact that the Bible has
been translated into it with some success, does not lay claim
to literary merits, which no simplified vocabulary can possess.
At the same time, every one of the 850 words is as necessary for
literature as it is for conversation or science, while the peculiar
analytic power of Basic English can be used with great effect,
as Dr. I. A. Richards and Mr. A. P. Rossiter have shown, for the
development of a new approach to intelligent reading and
literary appreciation.'

Since then, in Northern Ireland, Mr. Wynburne proposes to
use it to train his pupils in literary appreciation and critical
ability, while in Japan Mr. Masaru Muro uses Basic translations
of Shakespeare's sonnets. As he puts it (in Basic): 'It is not my
desire to say that my Basic form of the "sonnet" has any value
as a work of art, but it is my belief that it does have value in
making clear where the true value of this "poem" is to be looked
for. It seems to me that the "sonnet" is still beautiful even in my
Basic form. That makes it clear that what is beautiful in this
sonnet is for the most part the thought which Shakespeare has
put in it, and not chiefly in the use of words whose business is
to have an effect on the reader's feelings or in some trick of
putting words together, or in the sound of the words.'

With regard to criticisms of a theoretical and specific kind, a word of warning is essential. Anyone who wishes to evaluate them must, really *must,* check up every statement made and refer to the book called *The Basic Words.* Consider fairly recent examples. In a book first published in 1950, now distributed over here in paperback edition, an American professor of linguistics, Robert A. Hall, tells his readers that, as Basic English 'uses the separate words *fancy, dress,* and *ball* (in all the different meanings which Standard English attaches to these words), it is permissible to use also the combination *fancy dress ball.*' But neither *fancy* nor *ball,* except in the sense of spherical object, is a Basic word. In a book published in 1963 Lancelot Hogben, Honorary Senior Fellow in Linguistics at Birmingham, whose achievements in science and education we admire and acclaim, and for whom as a person many of us feel deep respect and affection, put forward a scheme which is intended to be an improvement on Basic. He says that Ogden adopted 'highly multivalent entries for his list, e.g., *fair* (= 1. Equitable, 2. Pale, 3. Pleasing to the eye)' and also that the Basic *formula* for *ask* includes *give an invitation.* Apart from the fact that the mention of formulas in the sense of fixed phrases in Basic English which could always be substituted for words not included in the system shows a misapprehension of the nature of Basic, neither *fair* nor *invitation* is a Basic word. An anonymous writer in the *Times Educational Supplement* last year used the publication of the Basic English *Science Dictionary* as an excuse for a patronizing and misleading description of Basic. He wrote from the point of view of one of those schools of linguistics which have grown up during the past thirty years, so removed from psychology and so narrowly conceived that obviously their practitioners no longer have any business to speak about language learning or teaching. They have been engaged chiefly, as the scholastics were, in spinning 'cobwebs of learning admirable for fineness of thread,' but of no 'substance or profit.' This reviewer asked how a foreigner who knew the meaning of *go* and a number of prepositions could be expected to form the compounds *go by* (meaning *judge by*) or *go for* (meaning *aim at*). The implication that foreigners are expected to produce English idioms without being taught them is plainly contrary to every exposition of the system; and *The Basic Words* shows that neither *go by* nor *go for* with the meanings stated are among the six idioms with *go* which may be included in a beginners' course. It is really saddening to see the degree to which prejudice and premisconception can cause writers to fall so far below normal standards of scholarly accuracy.

But I should not like to give the impression that all students of linguistics are hostile or ignorant. On the contrary: many write very fairly and are to some degree supporters. For instance, Professor Stephen Ullmann of the University of Leeds in his *Principles of Semantics.*

It is also most cheering suddenly to come across, quite unexpectedly, real understanding and support. On a bookstall the other day I picked up Dr. P. H. Nidditch's *Development of Mathematical Logic* and, to my surprise, found it to be written in Basic. Nidditch explains his purpose: 'The writing of all this discussion of Mathematical Logic is in Ogden's Basic English. One is forced when keeping to the apparatus of this form of the English language to take more care than one commonly does to make the dark and complex thoughts that are at the back of one's mind as clear and simple as possible. We will be attempting in what is to come to get across to the reader the substance of the story of Mathematical Logic. In this attempt Basic English will certainly be of some help to some, possibly even to almost all, readers, and will certainly not make things harder for any.'

PLANS AND PROSPECTS

In spite of all difficulties and obstacles, a good deal of solid work is being done, and the record of the last fifteen years is by no means negligible. There is the Basic *Science Dictionary*, published in this country last year, which has been described in an overseas broadcast as a godsend for students of science. It will shortly be published in the United States for the use of American students. There is the work being done in Japan. Professor Daniels's Japanese-into-Basic dictionary is in process of printing, there are books like Nidditch's or Wynburne's *Vertical Translation*. Among applications of the Basic techniques there is the work of I. A. Richards at Harvard in connection with the illiteracy problem in the United States, which has had the support of the Ford and other foundations. Practical experiments in teaching, too, are going on. I remember a few years ago, at the Rhodesian Selection Trust's vast installations near Ndola, watching the highly successful teaching of Basic to hundreds of new recruits drawn from scores of different tribes. Basic was to them both a *lingua franca* and a gateway to the modern world of machine technology.

What sort of program could the Basic English Foundation now support, if the material and financial resources were available? Let me try to list a few—not in order of priority—just as examples.

1. A revision of the initial courses in Basic (*The Basic Way to English*) for beginners as well as of *The Basic Teacher* in order to improve them and to bring them into line with recent publishing standards.

2. A revision of the textbooks which have recently gone out of print and on which Dr. Graham is already working on behalf of the Orthological Institute. We know these can be improved.

3. Preparation of entirely new vernacular courses in Basic. There is something for French, German, Dutch, Italian, and Spanish—though the books could be improved—but not, for instance, for Swahili, Hindi, Tamil, etc.

4. Planning of courses of training for teachers using Basic.

5. The preparation and publication of Basic Mathematics—already partly ready—and Basic Social Science Dictionaries, parallel to the Science Dictionary.

6. The establishment of offices and training centers, in the various countries of the Commonwealth.

Now, turning more specifically to science:

1. C. K. Ogden envisaged as the first and chief contribution of Basic the publication of a Science Library covering in Basic all the main departments of science and technology. A provisional start was made on this in his lifetime with the publication of sixteen books dealing at various levels with various branches of science. A comparatively modest target would be about 100 books, which number would meet the most urgent needs.

2. Drawing up Basic Science Lists in respect of sciences for which these do not already exist.

3. Publication of a Journal of Abstracts in Basic.

4. Translation Bureaus, providing Basic versions of scientific papers to be sent out on request.

CONCLUSION

Let me stress, in conclusion, that my faith in Basic English and its possibilities is now stronger than it has ever been. The claims of rivals, such as the artificial auxiliaries, are fading away. The demand for English is stronger than ever in all newly emerging countries and in the U.S.S.R. and China as well. It is evident that Standard English, with its immensely rich vocabulary and its subtle and intricate forms, cannot become a world language in any future I can foresee. At the same time it is not possible to run the business of a World, speaking and writing hundreds of languages, without a common medium. What is needed is a very simple, easily learned *auxiliary* to facilitate verbal face-to-face communication as well as the spreading of scientific and technical knowledge and know-how. The use of Basic would strengthen links between countries already associated, as in the Commonwealth, and would facilitate the flow of ideas between them, enriching them materially and spiritually.

Other factors, too, go to swell the tide. One instance must suffice. How are the memory banks of computers to be furnished? With the entire vocabulary of the *Oxford Dictionary* and the whole apparatus of Standard English? Impossible. Computers must be taught to respond to a limited vocabulary and to a simplified grammar and syntax. Is it altogether fanciful to imagine that the routine business of the world of A.D. 2100 will be run by a population of computers chattering to one another in Basic? What else should they speak? In the *Guardian* (20th April 1966) there was an article on 'Making Computers Compatible.' I quote: 'The Imperial College [research] program, [calls for] a general purpose compiler processer. . . . Most computer programs . . . are written in a high-level language and before they can be used on the machine for which they are written they have to pass through a device known as a compiler. This translates them into terms which the machine understands. . . . The purpose of the new research will be to find ways of describing in computer terms both computer languages and computer systems. . . .' Another task for the Foundation.

But leave aside computer and industrial routines. Finally the real business of the world is concerned with human happiness and dignity, with spiritual and aesthetic values, with peace and freedom. Churchill put it well at Harvard. Those concerned with the use of Basic were, he said, 'the headstream of what might well be a mighty fertilizing and health-giving river; for it would certainly be a grand convenience for us all to be able to find everywhere a medium, albeit primitive, of intercourse and understanding. Might it not also be an advantage to many races and an aid to the building up of our new structure for preserving peace? . . . Let us go forward as with other matters and other measures similar in aim and effect . . . Such plans offer far better prizes than taking away other people's provinces or land or grinding them down in exploitation. The empires of the future are the empires of the mind.'

I am convinced that the empires of the mind have nothing to do with empires of political or military power. Nothing to do with either Washington or London, nor with Moscow or Peking. The empires of the mind rest upon reason and knowledge, animated by brotherhood and love. I think of Basic as an instrument of communication, not of dominion; of cooperation, not of power.

I wonder and speculate. I think of the world political scene, its storms and stresses. I think of the needs of the emerging and low-income countries of the Commonwealth. I ponder over the relations of science to society.

Is there any chance whatever that the Government might be induced to take a fresh look at Basic English? Churchill at Harvard spoke of a second Boston Tea Party, all together, to see what could be done. But the tea pot was cold and the water lukewarm. In the end the tea party turned out to be a Mad Hatter's Party. Is there any chance now—it is not too late—to warm up the kettles afresh?

B. Churchill and Roosevelt on Basic English

1. From Sir Winston Churchill
The Second World War

Prime Minister to Sir Edward Bridges (Secretary of the War Cabinet) [July 11, 1943]

1. I am very much interested in the question of Basic English. The widespread use of this would be a gain to us far more durable and fruitful than the annexation of great provinces. It would also fit in with my ideas of closer union with the United States by making it even more worth while to belong to the English-speaking club.

2. I propose to raise this tomorrow at the Cabinet with a view to setting up a committee of Ministers to examine the matter, and, if the result is favorable, to advise how best to proceed. The Minister of Information, the Colonial Secretary, the President of the Board of Education, and perhaps Mr. Law, representing the Foreign Office, would all seem suitable.

3. I contemplate that the B.B.C. should teach Basic English every day as part of their propaganda, and generally make a big push to propagate this method of interchange of thought.

4. Let me know your ideas about the committee, and put the matter on the agenda for tomorrow.

2. Extract from the Prime Minister's Speech at Harvard University [1]

September 6, 1943

Some months ago I persuaded the British Cabinet to set up a committee of Ministers to study and report upon Basic English. Here you have a plan. There are others, but here you have a very carefully wrought plan for an international language capable of very wide transactions of practical business and of interchange of ideas. The whole of it is comprised in about 650 nouns and 200 verbs or other parts of speech—no more indeed than can be written on one side of a single sheet of paper.

What was my delight when, the other evening, quite unexpectedly I heard the President of the United States suddenly speak of the merits of Basic English, and is it not a coincidence, that, with all this in mind, I should arrive in Harvard, in fulfillment of a long-dated engagement, to receive this degree, with which President Conant has honored me? Because Harvard has done more than any other American University to promote the extension of Basic English. The first work on Basic English was written by two Englishmen, Ivor Richards, now of Harvard, and Ogden, of Cambridge University, England, working in association.[2]

The Harvard Commission on English Language Studies is distinguished both for its research and practical work, particularly in introducing the use of Basic English in

[1] From the London *Times*, September 8, 1943.
[2] The Prime Minister was misinformed on this point. Dr. Ivor A. Richards had collaborated with Ogden in writing *The Meaning of Meaning* (published 1923), a theoretical work on language, but Ogden was the sole originator of Basic English. ED.

Latin America; and this commission is now, I am told, working with the secondary schools in Boston on the use of Basic English in teaching the main language to American children and in teaching it to foreigners preparing for citizenship.

Gentlemen, I make you my compliment. I do not wish to exaggerate, but you are the headstream of what might well be a mighty fertilizing and health-giving river; for it would certainly be a grand convenience for us all to be able to move freely about the world—as we shall be able to do more easily than ever known before as the science of the world develops—to be able to move freely about the world, and to be able to find everywhere a medium, albeit primitive, of intercourse and understanding. Might it not also be an advantage to many races and an aid to the building up of our new structure for preserving peace? All these are great possibilities, and I say: "Let us go into this together. Let us have another Boston Tea Party about it."

Let us go forward as with other matters and other measures similar in aim and effect—let us go forward with malice to none and good will to all. Such plans offer far better prizes than taking away other people's provinces or land or grinding them down in exploitation. The empires of the future are the empires of the mind.

3. From Sir Winston Churchill
The Second World War

Prime Minister to Secretary of State for India (Rt. Hon. L. S. Amery, M.P.) [October 3, 1943]

I was shocked to find on my return to this country that the Cabinet committee appointed on July 12, 1943, had

never once met. You volunteered to undertake this task,
and I certainly thought you would be admirably qualified
for it. Pray let me have a report of your program up to
date. I have received a letter from Mr. Ogden suggesting
that a special investigator should be sent to spend a week
with him to learn all about Basic English, and I think it
would be very wise to accept this invitation so that your
committee can be advised on details at an early date. The
matter has become of great importance, as Premier Stalin
is also interested. If you feel the pressure of your other
duties is too heavy on you I will myself take on the duty
of presiding over the committee, but I hope you will be
able to relieve me of this.

4. From *Onwards to Victory: War Speeches by the Rt. Hon. W. S. Churchill 1943*

Answering questions regarding Basic English, the Prime
Minister said he hoped to receive the recommendations of the
Committee of Ministers on the subject before very long. He
continued:

> Basic English is not intended for use among English-
> speaking people, but to enable a much larger body of
> people who do not have the good fortune to know the
> English language to participate more easily in our society.
> People are quite purblind who discuss this matter as if
> Basic English were a substitute for the English language.

5. From *F.D.R.: His Personal Letters*

The White House
June 5, 1944

Memorandum for the Secretary of State:

If in regard to Basic English we get the views of "Competent Government specialists," we shall certainly sound the death knell of Basic English, or anything like it. I never knew of any group of such people to agree to anything really different from the existing system—or, for that matter, anything new.

Honestly, I do not want either to kill the idea or pour icy water on it. The reason is that Basic English has tremendous merit in it. The reason is that for practical purposes it is relatively easy for non-English speaking peoples to pick up sufficient vocabulary to carry on a conversation.

For instance, if you and Molotov and Eden had had Basic English and if Stalin, Chiang Kai-shek and I had had Basic English, our conferences would have been infinitely easier and far less tiring than having everything go through interpreters.

Secondly, Basic English is extremely easy for English-speaking peoples and would soon take the place of French as the so-called "language of diplomacy." You or I could learn it in our spare moments.

I wish you would pursue the check-up with the Congressional people first of all. It might be possible for a sympathetic Congressional committee (emphasis on the "sympathetic") to take the matter up with an English committee and see if we can arrive at a complete meeting of the minds that would cover the whole English-speaking world.

If this could be done, I really believe that the other nations would go along with us.

F.D.R.

Churchill had discussed the possibilities of Basic English with Roosevelt at Quebec in 1943, and in April 1944 had sent him a British Cabinet Committee report on means of promoting its wider use. The President prepared a reply, which he never sent off, but which concluded: "Incidentally, I wonder what the course of history would have been if in May 1940 you had been able to offer the British people only 'blood, work, eye-water and face-water,' which I understand is the best that Basic can do with five famous words."

[No doubt there were people who took this jocular rendering seriously, but it is hard to believe that a man as acute as Roosevelt could be for a moment unaware of the fallacy on which it was based, namely, the naïve idea that translation is simply a matter of word-for-word substitution. It is much easier to think of him chuckling over the joke—as who did not?—and enjoying pulling Churchill's leg about it. The actual Basic version of Churchill's words, achieved by entering into the spirit and intention of them, would have been more like: "All I am offering you is death and pain, bitter trouble and hard, unending work." ED.]

The System
in Detail

comprising

The ABC of Basic English
(in Basic)

and

The Basic Words
(a detailed account of their uses)

PART ONE

The ABC of Basic English

*

On Learning the Basic Words

This account is designed as a simple guide in three stages (A, B, and C), covering all the chief points in Basic English.

In some ways it is different from other accounts of language, because the learner has, at the start, on one page, almost all the material which will ever be needed. The complete word-list takes about a quarter of an hour on the records (see the Book List at the end of this book) which makes it possible to get a rough idea of the sense of anything said or printed in Basic English after only one week's work; and a little time given to the examples in Section Three of this book, or taken from the Book List at the end, will do the rest.

Even if you have a good knowledge of normal English, or have made a start with some other system, it is a good thing to put yourself first of all in the position of someone who is taking his very first step. But if what is said seems far more simple than is necessary, keep in mind the fact that what comes later will sometimes be dependent on statements made in these early pages.

The chief business of the learner, then, is to get a good knowledge of the words and their senses, with the help of the records (and of signs and pictures), and the nearest words in his natural tongue. At the same time, by putting every word into some simple statement at an early stage, he will get an idea of its natural uses for talking and writing. With most languages two or three years may be necessary to get a knowledge of 5,000 words; and every new word up to 10,000 may still have its special tricks, which will only be overcome by slow and bitter experience. In Basic English, the end of the work is in view all the time.

The learning of the system may best be done in three stages:

1. The 850 words and their order.

2. Expansions of the words in form and sense.

3. Special uses of the words, and their use for special purposes.

The number of words in the Basic list is so small that it is possible to go through them *all* in fifteen minutes every day before any other work is done, till their sounds are quite clear and their simple senses are fixed in the memory.

A *very* quick learner, with special training, might get 100 words in an hour.

A *good* learner, with a knowledge of more than one language, may get 50 in an hour.

A *normal* learner whose natural language is not unlike English will get 30—at least after the earlier stages.

A learner who takes an hour to get only 20 words will probably have a bad memory for words, or will be one whose natural language is very different in structure from Basic English.

A normal learner, who is able to take two hours every day for the work, will be wise to give one of these hours to the sounds and simple senses of the words. He will then get the complete list in a month (or if he makes it two hours, he will probably get through this part of the work in two weeks). The second hour every day would then be free for putting the words together, and learning everything which is important about Word-order.

But after a very short time, it is a good idea to make a small selection of words, so as to have enough for some simple statements; and by the time you come to the end of A, you will be able to make five different sorts of simple statements:

1. A *word is a sign* (page 132).
2. *Words give* (*do not give*) *clear signs* (page 138).
3. *Words will give signs to men* (page 137).
4. *Words will give signs to men clearly* (page 140).
5. *Stop! Please give new rules to the quick boys now* (pages 150–51).

This *ABC* and *The Basic Words* give the teacher with some knowledge of English everything needed for building up further material; but guides in a number of other languages, and in forms designed by experts in different systems, are now in print. In *The Basic Dictionary* the 7,500 commonest words of normal English are put into Basic—which makes it possible to do the same for any other language in the near future; and in *Basic by Examples* there are 120 pages of simple examples.

A list of the other books to be used in connection with the *ABC* is given on the last pages [see Book List, at the end]; and naturally it is a good idea to make a start with some sort of story or general reading-material as early as possible.

This book is all in Basic English, but in the forms of it designed for use in other countries it has been put into the learner's language and only those words (here generally in italics) to which he has to give attention at the different stages, and the statements needed as examples, are kept in Basic. But when the learner gets to the end (that is to say, after giving about a week to A, a week to B, and an hour to C) he will be in a position to go through the complete story by himself in its Basic English form—as an example of the way in which the words may be put together.

So that the First Step may be of value to the very young in addition to its more general interest, the words in the examples in this part are chiefly such as are commonly used before six years old; from these the teacher will be able to make a simple selection.

The First Step

In learning any language it is necessary first of all to have some idea of the different sorts of words in that language. There are more than 1,500 separate languages still in use, and they are as different as the clothing of those who make use of them; so that no sort of word or form of dress has so wide a distribution as to seem natural in all parts of the earth.

In one country it may be the right thing to put a gold ring or a silver chain round the neck; in another, the space between the chest and the chin may be covered by jewels and ornaments, or by a colored cloth, for comfort; or a soft collar may be common—changed to a stiff one at night. So it would be foolish to go everywhere with the question, "What sort of collar do they have here?" It is better to say: "What, if anything, do they put on their necks?" Or, again, "How are the legs covered?" Then we are at least taking a general point of view, and there is less danger of getting a wrong answer—or no answer at all.

It is the same with words. There may not be 'nouns,' 'adjectives,' 'verbs,' or 'pronouns' in every language; but everywhere there are things. So the first and most natural question about a language is, "What names has it for *things?*"

So we will make a start with the names of things; but first of all it is necessary to get a sort of map of the system in its complete form.

1. THINGS

Of the 850 Basic Words, no less than 600 are names of *things.* It is important to have a good number of names for things, because if we went about with a knowledge only of the names of things, we would be able to make ourselves clear for a very great part of the time.

Even without the names of things, we might, no doubt, get a long way by pointing, and by other acts and signs. The trouble is that sometimes it is not clear what we are pointing at; one thing gets in the way of another, and we may not be near enough to make ourselves clear. But if we have a knowledge of the *names of things,* it is much more probable that our hearers will be in a position to see from the signs on our faces, or from our behavior, what we would have said if we had made use of other sorts of words.

The names of things take the place of pointing; the other words, to which we are coming later, take the place of the other signs which we make.

a. Names of Things Which May Be Pictured. At a meal, for example, if we say "apple" when the fruit comes in, we may be almost as clear as if we say—"Please give me an apple."

The simplest words of all, then, are the names of the separate things which it is possible to get by pointing; the things round the room, the things which are moved or marketed everywhere, one by one.[1]

In Basic there are 200 of these, and when the things of which they are the signs are not themselves present to be pointed at by the learner, a picture will do equally well.[2]

QUESTIONS AND EXAMPLES

If you are good at making pictures or copying them from books, see which of your pictures are rightly named by your friends; and

[1] If you are ready to make complete statements from the very start, you may say *This is* . . . every time you do any pointing at things in the room or at pictures. But most learners will be wiser to go quickly through the First Step before making any decision about the best form of simple statement.
[2] Among the 200 there are four words which are a little different from the rest. These are *angle, circle, line, square.* They are not material things; but they may be pictured, and the pictures make them quite clear.

why they go wrong when they give a wrong answer. Might your pictures have been more clear?

Is it a help to your memory to get some of the names two by two; like *boy* and *girl, sun* and *moon, hammer* and *nail, horse* and *cart, needle* and *thread?* If so, make a list of those which go naturally together.

Put together all the words in the 200 which are names of different parts of clothing (*boot, coat, collar, dress, glove, hat, pocket, shirt, shoe, skirt, sock, stocking, trousers*). You have, in addition, *button, hook,* and *band,* which may go with them.

Now do the same with the parts of the *body* (such as *arm, chin, hair, leg, knee, muscle, nerve, stomach, throat, toe,* and *tongue*).

Then take the things in connection with the building of a *house* (*arch, board, brick, floor, pipe, roof, screw, wall, window,* and the rest); and from those go on to such as may be seen in a *room* (*bath, book, box, curtain, cushion, drawer, lock, oven,* and the like). In this way you will quickly get an idea of the different groups of words in the Basic system.

What is this group representative of: *cup, egg, fork, plate, potato, spoon, tray?* (*Meal*)

Make a list of 10 names among the 200 about whose sound, form, and sense you have no doubt whatever. Let them be names of things which are generally near—to be touched or seen. These will be of use later as a sort of frame in which new words may be fixed for purposes of learning. A different list will probably be necessary for every country; but if the sounds are simple enough, here are 12 from which you may be able to make a selection: *arm, hand, head, book, box, door, paint, paper, pen, side, table, tree.*

b. General Names. Sometimes, though there may be no doubt that a word is used for a material thing, it is hard to give a clear picture of the thing itself; a *building,* for example, or a *mine.* This is because there are different sorts of buildings which themselves have pictures (such as *church, house, hospital, library*); and because a *mine* is not a separate thing. All such words are grouped among the 400 'General names.'

Then there are solid *substances; metals,* for example, such as *copper.* These are certainly very material. In fact they are what things are made of; but only a little of them is in any one place, and even then it generally has the form of some other thing with a common name. So it is hard to make good pictures of substances. But it is possible to take a bit of any one of them and make a change in its form or, with the help of a business-man, get money for it. With these come the *liquids,* like *blood* and *milk.*

Air, mist, smoke, and *steam* may be put in the same division because they are made up of material parts and their behavior is like that of substances; and *foods,* like *bread, butter,* and *cheese.*

There are 50 words of this sort, and because they are names of substances they are almost as simple to get fixed in the memory as the words which go with pictures. Here is the list:

air, blood, brass, bread, butter, canvas, chalk, cheese, cloth, coal, copper, cork, cotton, dust, earth, glass, gold, ice, ink, iron, lead, leather, linen, meat, milk, mist, oil, paint, paper, paste, powder, rice, salt, sand, silk, silver, smoke, snow, soap, soup, steam, steel, stone, sugar, tin, water, wax, wine, wood, wool.

Another important group of the general names, of which it is frequently possible to give the sense by pointing (and some-times by pictures), is that of the *parts* or *divisions* of material things. Such are *back, base, body, cover, edge, end, front, mid-dle, page, side, top.*

Then there are *persons,* named sometimes in relation to *sex* or *family* (*man, woman, father, mother, son, daughter, brother, sister*), and sometimes because of what they do (*cook, judge, manager, porter, servant*); common *acts* (a *shake,* a *bite,* a *grip,* a *kick,* a *kiss,* a *laugh,* a *smile,* a *cough,* a *sneeze*—or *driving, reading, teaching,* and *writing*); the divisions of *time* (*minute, hour, day, night, week, month, year*); *birth* and *death, summer* and *winter, peace* and *war, question* and *answer, cause* and *effect, work* and *play, profit* and *loss, art* and *science, color* and *form, law, crime,* and *punishment, prose* and *verse;* words for the *feelings* (like *pleasure* and *pain, hope* and *fear, love* and *hate, belief* and *doubt*); words for the *senses* (like *touch, taste,* and *smell*).

At this point you will have got some idea of more than half the names of things and almost half the complete Basic word-list. So this is the right place for a little note about the other general names which are not names of material things, or parts of material things, like the great mass of the words which we have taken first. As separate words, they are happily all quite as simple in form as the names of material things; but their behavior when put with other words is sometimes not so regular. A little more attention has to be given to them, till any tricks they may have are clear from examples. With so small a number of words this is not hard; and most of the necessary knowledge will come automatically from the examples themselves, from hearing others, and from reading.

QUESTIONS AND EXAMPLES

Make a list of general names used for a number of things which themselves have pictures (*animal, apparatus, building, insect, instrument, machine, plant, structure, vessel*). Make a list of those which are not separate from the other material things round them (*harbor, mine, mountain, river, road, wave*).

Put the 50 names of material things into four groups so that you may say 'a *bit* of' (*chalk, bread,* and so on), 'a *mass* of' (*coal, stone,* and so on), 'a *drop* of' (*blood, water,* and so on), 'a *grain* of' (*powder, rice, sand*). Which will come into more than one group?

Because it is possible for all of them to be measured, you may say 'an *amount* of' (any of them). What other things (in addition to material substances) are frequently said to be measured, in the sense that 'more or less of' them is talked about for purposes of comparison, though we are not able to put them in the scales? (*agreement, approval, change, competition, expansion, growth, increase, organization, pleasure, shame,* and so on).

Here is a list of 100 of the simplest names of things which the learner will be wise to get into his head at a very early stage:

apple, baby, back, ball, bed, bell, bird, boat, book, box, boy, bridge, brother, cat, coat, color, country, cow, day, dog, door, dress, drink, egg, fall, father, fire, fish, floor, flower, fly, front, garden, girl, grass, hair, hand, hat, head, help, hole, horse, house, light, look, man, milk, money, mother, name, night, nose, paint, paper, picture, pig, place, plant, play, pull, rain, ring, room, run, sand, school, shoe, side, sister, sky, sleep, snow, song, start, stick, stop, story, street, summer, sun, table, tail, thing, thought, top, town, train, tree, turn, wall, walk, wash, water, way, wind, window, winter, wood, work, year.

c. Forms for Number. RULE. When a word is used for two or more things of the same sort, an 's' is put at the end of the word.

There are four which make a change of form—*foot* (*feet*), *tooth* (*teeth*), *man* (*men*), *woman* (*women*). *Trousers* and *scissors* are themselves 'plural' (that is, more than one) as is clear from the form, but we may say "one *leg* of his trousers," or "one *blade* of the scissors." There is no change for *sheep.* For talking, only these have to be specially kept in mind; [3] and if you do go wrong it is not very important.

QUESTIONS AND EXAMPLES

Make a list of all the words with the endings *s* and *x*, and put the 'plural' forms in writing, so that you may see how simple and natural the business of 'plurals' is in Basic English. Would 'glasss' or 'taxs' seem natural to you if you were free to give all 'plurals' their most simple form in writing?

The wool of *sheep* is cut with scissors to make *trousers* for *men* (and sometimes *women*). That gives you 5 of the changes of form.

---

[3] In addition to the four changes of *form,* there may be some change in the last three letters (though the sound is much the same as if only 's' had been put at the end) of words ending in *f, fe, y, s, x, sh, ch,* or *o,* for writing. Here is the complete list—but you will probably be wise to make no attempt to get it into your head at this point:

1. *Leaf, leaves, self, selves, shelf, shelves, knife, knives.*
2. All ending in *y* with a stopped sound before it (that is, all but *boy, day, key, monkey, play, ray, tray,* and *way*) have the *y* changed into *ies;* as *army, armies,* and *berry, berries.*
3. All ending in *s, x, sh, ch* (but for *stomach*), or *o* have *es* at the end and not simply *s;* as *arch, arches,* and *match, matches.*

Make a statement giving the other 2 changes of form—*feet* and *teeth*.

Put a mark against any of these words which have been given the wrong 'plural' form: *leafs, boxes, seas, arches, crys, potatos, traies, horses, sleep, sheep, smashs.*

There is one word which is not ever used in the 'plural.' Have you any idea which it is? (*News*)

Give some examples of words which, even without the addition of 's,' give the idea of number (*group, committee, family*).

What is the use of the *s* on all these words? We say: "I have two *sheep.*" Why not say: "I have two *brother*"? The answer is that in this example it is clear enough, but "Come with your *sheep*" is not clear if more than one sheep is to come with you. So Basic, like other languages, is happy to make the change, even if a small number of the 850 words are not quite regular.

Two words, *house* and *mouth,* undergo a small change of sound with the addition of 's': in *houses* the middle 's' is sounded as in *was,* and in *mouths* the 'th' is sounded as in *the.*

d. A (AN [4]) *and* THE. Sometimes a thing is talked about as any one of a group which has the same name; sometimes as a special example about which something has been said before.

> *A man* = "any one man."
> *The man* = "that man of whom you have knowledge."

If anyone says, "Please give me *a camera,*" you are then free to make the selection from all the possible cameras in the stores. But if he says *the* camera, you are limited to the special camera which he has in mind (one which, in his opinion, is equally clear in your mind).[5]

We do not normally put '*a(n)*' before the names of substances, such as, '*gold*' or '*snow,*' because gold, for example, is not one of the things which are all in front of us to be talked about or pointed at; only part of it is ever there. Some other 'things' which are not substances, such as qualities or processes, are looked on in

---

[4] '*A*' before an open sound becomes '*an*': *an apple.*
[5] So *the* is a sort of pointing 'adjective'—not quite as strong as *this* or *that,* to which we are coming later (p. 149).

the same way. For example, we do not say 'a behavior' or 'a damage.' But there is one special purpose for which $a(n)$ is used before names of substances and other such words, and that is to give the sense 'a sort of.' So we say 'a gold unlike any other.'

If we are on an island and we have only one knife, would you say: Give me *a* knife, or *the* knife?

If your house has 4 doors—one at the front, one at the back, and two at the sides—would you say: Let us go in at *a* front door, or *the* front door? Would it be possible to go in at *the* side door?

On a bright night we generally take a look at *the moon*, not *a moon*. Why? Are there any other things which would generally be talked about with *the*, because there is only one of them? (Yes, *the sun, the sky*.)

Why do we generally give *a push* and *a kick*, not *the push* and *the kick*?

Make a selection of words like *behavior*, with which, because of their sense, $a(n)$ will probably be least used (*attention, control, cotton, silver, thunder*, and so on).

What would be the sense of *a cotton, a silver, a paint*?

What words are there which do not ever take *a* before them? (For example, *damage, learning, news, transport, waiting, weather*.)

2. QUALITIES

There are 150 names of *qualities* ('adjectives').[6] They are used before the names of things to give some special idea about the thing—*a red book, the hard seat, cold air*.

See what groups of names of qualities it would be possible to make; in relation, for example, to color, form, size, and feeling.

Put together all the words like *red*, which are names of simple

[6] *A, the, any, all, every, no, other, some*, and *such* are generally said to be 'adjectives,' because they are put before the names of things; but we may let them come in separately as and when they are needed. See pp. 128, 138, 150, 158, and 172.

qualities, starting with the colors (*blue, green, yellow, brown, black, gray, white*); words like *sharp, hard* and *soft, sweet* and *bitter, warm* and *cold* which are the nearest to the senses; then the names of simple feelings like *happy, sad, tired.*

Make a list of the 'adjectives' which are least like names of simple sense-qualities (*cheap* and *dear, hanging, political,* and so on).

A third selection will have in it all the words which do not seem to come naturally into the first group or the second. You will probably put *quick* into this third group; if so, it will be because *quick* is used of motion, and motion is not a material thing, or a sense, or a feeling, but a change of place. There may be more than one opinion about the sorts of qualities, so that the size of the groups given in different answers will be very different. But your answer will be of use in getting a general idea of the sorts of 'adjectives' in the Basic language.

These 25 names of qualities will probably be the simplest to get by heart first: *black, blue, clean, cold, dirty, first, good, great, green, hard, high, kind, last, like, long, new, old, open, ready, red, right, round, same, straight, white.*

Give five names of qualities which might be used of a dog.

a. Opposites. Words like *good* and *bad* have opposite senses, and it is a good idea to get such words into your head together; 50 of the names of qualities have opposites, and 40 of these are themselves names of qualities:

good–bad, straight–bent, sweet–bitter, warm–cold, kind–cruel, bright–dark, living–dead, cheap–dear, same–different, clean–dirty, wet–dry, true–false, strong–feeble, male–female, wise–foolish, past–future, red–green, first–last, early–late, right–left, tight–loose, quiet–loud, high–low, separate–mixed, wide–narrow, young–old, private–public, smooth–rough, happy–sad, long–

short, open–shut, complex–simple, quick–slow, great–small, hard–soft, hollow–solid, general–special, normal–strange, thick–thin, black–white.

50 opposites are formed by putting *un-* before the name of the quality, though till the learner becomes expert in the art of writing it will be best to make use of *not*.[7]

Make a list of the 10 words among the 50 opposites which are not in the list of twos (*awake, blue, certain, complete, delicate, ill, opposite, safe, secret, wrong*). Of these, *opposite* is another opposite of *same* (page 130); *blue* is the opposite of the color of an *orange* (page 188); *wrong*, of an expansion of the sense of *right*; *secret*, of an expansion of the sense of *open*. The opposite of *delicate* is frequently *strong* or *rough*; of *ill*, *healthy* or *well* (page 147); of *old*, *new*. What General Names give opposites of *awake, certain, complete,* and *safe*?

Make a list of 'adjectives,' like *electric* and *political*, which have no opposites of any sort in the Basic list.

What are the opposites of: *tight, smooth, separate, sweet, private*?

Is *present* or *past* the opposite of *future*?

Do you see any quality which might be the opposite of *fat*?

Here are most of the opposites in verse:

> *Sweet–bitter, wide–narrow, quick–slow,*
> *Thick–thin, living–dead, any–no,*
>> *Shut–open, first–last,*
>> *Short–tall, future–past,*
> *Cheap–dear, late–early, high–low.*
>
> *Hard–soft, simple–complex, black–white,*
> *Red–green, public–private, wrong–right,*
>> *Left–right, feeble–strong,*

[7] *able, automatic, beautiful, bent, broken, certain, chemical, clean, clear, common, complete, complex, conscious, cut, elastic, equal, expert, fertile, fixed, free, frequent, happy, healthy, important, kind, like, married, medical, military, mixed, natural, necessary, normal, open, parallel, physical, political, probable, quiet, ready, regular, responsible, safe, smooth, solid, straight, sweet, tired, true, wise.*

Un- may be used in addition with a number of the *-ing* and *-ed* forms (see p. 176).

> Rough–smooth, short and long,
> Solid–hollow, male–female, loose–tight.
>
> Wise–foolish, bent–straight, old and new,
> Young–old, cruel–kind, false and true,
>   Bright–dark, happy–sad,
>   Clean–dirty, good–bad,
> Loud–quiet, wet–dry, orange–blue.

For which of these are two opposites given here? (*Old*, *short*, and *right*.)

b. IS *and* ARE. *Is* and *are* are two forms of the word *be* (about which more is said on page 191).

To make simple statements, the word *is* (*are*, when there is more than one thing) is put between the name of the thing and a quality, or between two names of things.

Was (*were*, when there is more than one thing) takes the place of *is* for the past.

A ball is round. A bee is an insect. Words are signs. The cows are married. The last example was foolish.

Round, married, and *foolish* are said to be qualities or properties of the things named.[8] But some qualities and names, when put together, do not make sense, like example 4, and you will have a better knowledge of any language if you are able to give reasons why any two words will not go together.

c. AND *and* OR. *And* is used for joining words together:
The man and the woman are married.
Or is used for the idea of one of two:
The man or the woman is married.
For other uses of the 'conjunctions' *and* and *or*, see page 159.

---

[8] Most languages have this group of quality words, and strange errors of thought may be produced by them. But in general talk or business letters it is not hard to put the words together so that they will make some sort of sense.

Take the name of anything in the list, such as *payment*, and put different 'adjectives' with it in turn (*an able payment, an acid payment, a violent payment, a sticky payment*, and so on). See which of them make sense in your opinion. Then take those which make good sense, such as *a quick payment*, and put the word *is* (or *are*) before one of the other 'adjectives' which go naturally with payment (*A quick payment is strange; slow payments are natural; a second payment is necessary*, and so on); till you are quite certain how a payment may be talked about. Then do the same with *burst, flag, flame, pig*, and *verse*. Now for the first time you are making complete statements, such as are used in normal discussion.

Put all the natural statements you are able to make about *the sad story* and *sad stories* (*The sad story is ready; sad stories are frequent*) into past time. What makes you so certain that some of the possible statements would be foolish? If it is the sense of the words, take care to get all the possible senses of the statement quite clear; if it is our experience of things, keep in mind the fact that our experience may get wider.

Certain names of qualities are in need of special attention because they are less freely used than the others. Some, such as *chief, future*, may only be used before the name they go with. *Awake* is not put before the name of a thing or person, but generally comes after some form of *be*. *Same* is never used without *the* (or *this* or *that*) before it. In most languages the senses of certain words make the same sort of adjustments necessary; but ten minutes with a selection of examples, when all the rest of the work is done, will put anyone right with any that give trouble in Basic.

The baby is awake.

A

I. Simple Statements

1. OPERATIONS

We now come to the words representative of the acts or *operations* of our bodies and of bodies generally.

What is it possible to do to things with our arms and legs, with our hands and feet?

We *make* them, *get* them, *have* them, and *keep* them. We *give* them a *push* or a *pull* (or a *bite*, or a *blow*, or a *kick*); and they are moved in different directions.

We *do* all these acts; or, if we do nothing, we *let* things be where they are (or be moved by others).

We put our bodies in motion in different directions; we *come here* and *go there*.

But, chiefly, we *put* and *take* other bodies, other things—in different directions; so that it is important to be clear not only about the names of acts but about the names of the directions in which things are moved.

a. The Names of Simple Acts. Among the names of the things themselves there are some which are in fact names of simple acts. Such are, a *push*, a *pull*, a *bite*, a *blow*, and a *kick*, which came into the account of what we 'give.' Others are: a *crush*, a *fall*, a *jump*, a *run*, a *step*, a *rub*, a *turn*, a *twist*, a *walk*; but these are all the names of forms of behavior, which are only acts pinned down, as one might say, for observation (like an insect on a card), and viewed as something which may be talked about.

When it is necessary to get the motion itself into a statement and to have separate signs for what is going on or being done,

134

language makes use of a special sort of word which is generally named a 'verb.' These words are frequently very hard for the learner, because they have a long history of changes of form and are full of tricks, whatever attempts are made to get regular rules for them; and most languages have about 4,000 of them in common use.

Basic English has only 15 such words, in addition to *be* and *have* (pages 137, 169, 171–73, 191, 195).[9]

The 10 which come first are:

come–go, put–take, give–get

(which may be taken in twos, because in their chief senses they are opposites),

make, keep, let, and *do.*

There is not very much to say about these little words at the present stage, because it is best to keep before you the acts and motions for which they are the signs, and to go through the acts themselves with your body.

At a motion picture house, for example, there are generally two doors. By the one we *come;* by the other we *go;* and so on.

We *put* the food for birds; the birds *take* it.

We *give* food; the birds *get* it.

We *make* money; the banks *keep* it; we *let* them; they *do* the work.

Seem may be grouped with *be,* as the word for what is not certainly a fact, but is only a question of opinion, or has the air of being something.

The walls are wet.

The walls seem wet (but may be dry).

[For a complete picture of the root senses of the first 12 operation-words, see Section One of this book, page 27.]

Then there are three words of the same sort at a higher level. These are *say, see,* and *send.*

---

[9] In its simplest sense *be* is the word for existence; but, as we have seen, its forms (*is* and *are*) are used for making simple statements (p. 132).

They are said to be at a higher level, because, if necessary, other simpler Basic words might be used in their place. *Say* is a form of talking, or use of words; *see* is a form of looking, or use of the eyes; *send* is a form of putting in motion, or use of transport. But they are so very frequently needed, and the other possible words are so roundabout, that it is best to have them in the list.

Last, there are the two 'auxiliaries' (*may* and *will*), which give us help in saying things about the time at which an act is done, or the degree in which it is possible.

In addition to these, *be* and *have* have important uses as 'auxiliaries.'

QUESTIONS AND EXAMPLES

Do the acts named by the words, *put, make,* and *take;* or make pictures of someone doing them.

Give suggestions for pictures to make clear the senses of *keep* and *let.* (*It is hard to keep a ball balanced on the end of a walking stick. There was a kind girl who let a poor rat go free.*)

It may seem harder to get a good picture for *seem.* But take a look in the looking-glass, and *you* will seem to be there.

Why is it a complete statement to say *the girls take plates,* though it is not a complete statement to say *the girls put plates?*

Motion is a name for change of position in space, as, for example, when things are pushed or pulled by other things or by us. When we do the moving, we make use chiefly of our hands, so which are the 2 simplest acts of the 10 which come first?

We not only *put* and *take* things with our hands, moving them from place to place; it is with our hands that we generally *give* and *get* them (at the simple physical level). What other act is done chiefly with the hands?

Though we *put, take, give, get,* and *make* with our hands, the other 5 acts are done by other parts of the body or by the complete body. We do not come and go on our *hands* but on our ——. (Why not our 'foots'? Because that would be as bad as biting with our 'tooths'.)

b. BE, HAVE, WILL, MAY. The four words which give the help talked of on page 136 are *be, have, will,* and *may.* Of these, *be* and *have,* in addition to the help they give in making statements with the operation-words, may be used by themselves.

We *have* things (*are* their owners); and we ourselves *are.* But the other uses of *be* and *have* may all be grouped with those of *will* and *may,* which are not ever used by themselves. All these 'auxiliary' uses are made clear in connection with the other forms which are given in the complete account of the language of acts on pages 171–73. For the present, it is only necessary to have in mind these simple examples of the way in which they come into statements:

The pencils have come (and so they are now here).

The birds will get the food (when we give it to them).

The rat may go (if the hole is open).

Have come is different from the use of *have* in *the pencils have points.* When the pencils *have points* they are *sharp,* and when they *have come* they *are here.* So it is clear that this use of *have* is quite a simple expansion of the first sense.

Will get is the future form of *get.* It says that the getting of the food by the birds is going to be done at some later time.

May has two uses which are not hard to get clear.

It is important to be clear when two uses of a word have no connection, and when they are simply two forms of a wider use. There are white men, black men, yellow men, and brown men; but we do not say that the word *man* has four different uses, with no general sense running through them all. The general sense of *may* is 'It is possible . . .'; and it may be possible in two ways:

In the first, the person talking makes it possible—by giving the power, the authority, or the chance—(to go), as in: *You may go now* (= I let you go now).

In the second, general conditions make it possible, by putting nothing in the way of a desire—(to go), as in: *If the dog is not chained he may go* (= it is possible that he will).

The two uses of 'may' will be made clearer by this very touching story:

One day last *May* there was a rat in a hole. It was a good rat which took care of its little ones and kept them out of the way of men, dogs, and poison. About sundown a farmer who was walking that way put his foot into the hole and had a bad fall. "Oh," was his thought, when he got on his legs again, "a rat for my dog, Caesar!" Naturally the rat had the same idea and kept very quiet. After an hour or two, Caesar got tired of waiting, and the farmer put his spade over the top of the hole, so that the rat was shut up till the morning when there might be some sport. But the farmer's daughter, May, had seen him from her window. "What a shame," said May. "Poor rat! There is no sport in letting cruel dogs loose on good mothers! I will take the spade away. There—*the rat may go.*" Then she took the spade to her father: "See! your spade was out there in the field, and I went to get it for you. Here it is." "You foolish girl," was his answer, "I put that spade over a rat-hole till the morning, and now—*the rat may go.*"

The girl was saying: "It is now possible for the rat to go," with the thought—"For my part, I let her go." The farmer was saying: "It is now possible for the rat to go," though his thought was— "For my part, I would not have let her go." So *may* is used in two different connections—but that is not a cause of trouble; any more than the further fact that the name of the girl was *May* and the name of the month was *May* (see page 236).

c. DO NOT. When a statement using any of the operation-words but *be* and *have* is made with *not,* the word *not* is placed before the operation-word, and the needed form of do is put before the *not:*

> *Simple rules do not give trouble.*[10]
> *The woman does not seem to be happy.*

[10] We might equally well say: *Simple rules give no trouble.*

The 'auxiliary' *do* is not used with *be* (or with *will* and *may*), and only in a special sense, which it is not necessary to go into at this stage, with *have*. When *not* is used with these words it comes after them. *Dead men are not conscious.*[11]

Like *have*, *do* has a special use by itself, in addition to the help which it gives in statements made with the word *not:*

Good men do kind acts (see page 192).

(see page 192)

QUESTIONS AND EXAMPLES

Here are some examples of the future formed with *will:*

> *The cook will make the cake.*
> *A porter will take the boxes.*
> *The meal will be late.*

The use of *may* is equally simple:

> *Kind friends may come.*
> *The place may be unhealthy.*
> *Animals may have thoughts.*
> *The woman may get the meat.*

Put *not* (with *do*) into the statements: *The birds take the berries. The banks keep the money. Quick payments seem strange.*

Not comes after *will* or *may*, and before the name of the act. Put *will* (or *will not*) and *may* (or *may not*) into the statements: *Birds take money. Banks keep food. Slow payments seem necessary.*

We say: *An umbrella will be necessary*, when rain is certain, and *An umbrella may be necessary*, when rain is possible. When would you say: *A warm coat may not be necessary?*

[11] In talking, it is very common to say little words like *not* so quickly that the *o* is not sounded. *Do not*, in writing the words, then becomes *don't* (with a change of sound to *doant* as in *road*). But at first there is no need to give any attention to such details. *Do not, have not, is not,* and *may not*, for example, are quite natural English, though in everyday talk *don't, haven't, isn't,* and *mayn't* are commoner.

Another trick with *not* is the change of *not ever* to *never,* but here again it is wiser to keep the learning of these special forms to the very last. When you are expert enough to say what you have to say clearly and simply it will be time to make your talk more natural and more polished.

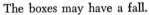

The boxes may have a fall.   The man may be ill.

2. DIRECTIONS

We now come to the *directions* in which things go when they are moved.

It would not have been surprising if there had been hundreds of these; but happily there are only twenty.

Whenever anything is moved it goes *to* one thing and *from* another which is then said to be in the opposite direction. Letters are sent *from* America *to* England; a wheel may be turned *from* the left *to* the right; water goes *from* the bath *to* the drain; a man goes *from* his office *to* his club. When he gets there he is *at* the club and *among* his friends. The water, however, will not be *at* the drain but *in* it, and before that it will have gone *through* a pipe (that is to say, it will have gone *into* [12] the pipe at one end and *out* [13] of it at the other). But the drain is at a lower level than the bath, so we might equally say that the water goes *down* the pipe. A monkey going *up* a tree to get fruit at the top is a good example of motion in the opposite direction. He goes *about* the tree looking for a good place, and when he gets *on* a branch and takes fruit *off* it he gives us a picture of two other opposites. Part One of this book comes

---

[12] *Into* is formed by putting together *to* and *in* (for the process of getting inside anything). (See p. 141.)

[13] For an account of *out* in relation to *in*, see pp. 207–08.

before Part Two; this page comes *after* page 53, and *between* them is page 54; when the book is shut and on the table, this page comes somewhere *between* the front cover which is *over* it and the back cover which is *under* it.

To go *across* is to go from one side to another. We go *across* a river, a street, a bridge, and so on. When we are waiting and looking at the water before getting into it, we are *by* or near the river, and the river is going *by* us. If we took a swim in one direction the current would be pushing *against* us, but if we went the other way the current would be *with* us; that is to say, it would be going in the same direction, like a dog or a friend going *with* us for a walk.

Here, as a help in keeping some of these things in mind, is the story of the young man whose death was caused by the noise which got on his nerves after an operation in hospital, though a dog, a rat, and a fly all did their parts in putting him in hospital in the first place.

> The dog went *after* the rat, *by* the drain, *across* the street, *over* the wall, *with* the fly, *through* the door, *against* the rules, *to* the meat.
>
> The fly got *in* the meat, *into* the mouth, *down* the throat, *among* the muscles.
>
> The poison got *off* the fly, *at* the digestion, *about* the system.
>
> The noise came *from* an instrument, *under* the window, *up* the steps, *through* the hospital, and got *on* the nerves, *after* the operation, *before* death.

Take note in this account of the word *into*, which is formed by putting *to* and *in* together to give the sense 'to a position *in*' (something). This is your first example of a 'complex word' (see pages 156–58). You will see in addition that the uses of *against, after,* and *before* in this story are a little different from their root uses (pages 201, 202–03). They are examples of simple and natural 'expansions' (see page 183).

Some of the words we have been talking about are not names of directions but names of positions in which things come to rest after moving in the different directions. For purposes of learning, however, they may be put in the same group.

When the fly goes *to* the meat, it may come, at the end of its journey, to be *on* it. So we may equally well say that it goes *on* the meat. It may be resting *in* the meat, or *between* two bits of meat, or *among* the bones in the meat, or *at* the edge of the meat.

All this will be much clearer when the full account is given of the ways in which the senses of words are stretched. [For a clear picture of the root senses of all twenty of the words naming physical directions, see Section One of this book, page 30.]

Two of these little words may seem at first to be quite different from the others. They are *of* and *for*.

But if we *take a bit off the top*, it is clear that this is very like taking a bit *of the top*. In fact, *of* is frequently used after words like *part*, as in *a part of the animal*, and, as a further development, with words like *number* and *amount, a number of friends*. From the use with *part* one may readily see how *of* has come to be used as a sign of the relation between property and its owner: *the leg of the boy, the shoe of the boy*.[14]

For has gone a greater distance from its early use as the name of a position (in front of, before), till it now only takes the place of other groups of words, to make statements about *exchange* and *purpose* go more smoothly.

The porter will go for money (= in exchange for money).

The porter will go for the box (= with the purpose of getting the box).

The father will get the reward for the family (= in the place of, in the interests of).

It is not important to give much time at the start to these special uses. Take note of them as you come across them in examples, and more will be said about them on pages 204 and 206.

[14] Sometimes in place of using 'of' to give the idea of property, *'s* is put after the name of the owner as in *the animal's tail* (for *the tail of the animal*).

These little words are like drops of oil put into a machine when necessary. When is it necessary? Experience with the machine is better than a long list of possible reasons.

a. The Names of Directions. Because the names of directions generally come before the names of the things to which we go (or from which we take other things, and so on), they have been named 'prepositions,' that is to say, words 'placed before' others. But it is no harder to get the idea of a direction than to make the discovery later that names of directions frequently do not come before anything.

For example, we may say, we *will go up* (simply in the direction *up*), without the name of any special thing being given. It may be up the mountain, or up the steps (or up the list of names, by an expansion which will be made clear on page 210). When *in, up, over,* and the rest are used by themselves in this way, they are said to be used as 'adverbs,' to which we are coming on page 146.[15]

QUESTIONS AND EXAMPLES

In the group of words we have been talking about, the idea of direction is more important than the idea of position, because in our account of acts it is made clear that an act is done in a certain direction to some thing: *bees take sugar from the flowers; the men give food to the horses; the guides go up the mountains; monkeys come down the trees.*

It then seems natural to go one stage farther and say: *bees put the sugar in wax; the food is by the horses; the horses take the food off the floor; the guides are on the mountain; the monkey is at the foot of the tree.*

Put the words *after, by, across, over, with, through, against,* and *to* in different places in the first part of the story of the causes of the young man's death (The dog went *to* the rat, *against* the drain, *through* the street, *with* the wall, and so on). See how far the story

[15] Two other words used as 'adverbs' of direction may here be noted: *back* (opposite of *forward*) and *round.*

still makes sense; and give the reasons when the act is not a possible one.

Which of the names of directions will go together two by two; like *up* and *down, to* and *from?*

When the time comes to give attention to such details, it is a safe general rule to make use of *of* when talking about things and fictions as if they were owners, and the *'s* form when talking about persons and animals in this connection. For example, say: *the stem of the flower, the end of hope;* but: *the cow's horn, the men's trousers, the horses' food.*[16]

b. How to Make Verbs. There are some languages, of which English is one, in which statements are frequently made with 'verbs,' but by making a sort of X-ray picture in our minds of those complex forms, we see that they are made up of operation and direction words. For example, 'enter' (a room), 'disappear' (into the garden), 'retire' (to bed), 'traverse' (a bridge), 'pursue' (a man) are all forms of 'going,' in one direction or another. It is equally simple to see that 'mount' (a horse), 'extract' (a tooth), 'approach' (a town), 'ascend' (a mountain) are unnecessary when we are able to say 'get on,' 'take out,' 'come to,' and 'get up.'

Let us take again the story of the young man in hospital as it might have been given using 'verbs':

> The dog 'pursued' the rat, 'passed' the drain, 'crossed' the street, and 'climbed' the wall, 'bearing' the fly; it 'entered' the door, 'broke' the rules, and 'approached' the meat.
>
> The fly 'invaded' the meat, 'penetrated' the mouth, 'descended' the throat, and 'infested' the muscles.
>
> The poison 'left' the fly, 'attacked' the digestion, and 'permeated' the system.

[16] After a form for more than one ending in *s,* we put simply '.

You will see that there are no names for directions here; but sometimes they are used in addition to the 'verbs':

> The noise 'emanated' from an instrument 'located' under the window, 'proceeded' up the steps, and 'diffused' itself through the hospital; it 'worked' on the young man's nerves, 'following' after his operation.

Some acts have a natural tendency to go in one special direction. *Give* generally goes with *to*. Is this clear from the sense of *give?* If not, make the motion of giving something, and see if *under* or *down* would come naturally into your mind for the direction taken by your hand. In the same way you will probably get a feeling that *take* has a natural connection with *from*, because taking is the opposite of putting and giving.

You may be able to make a suggestion for *come* and *send*. But even an expert in making signs will be in doubt as to the special friends of *get* among the directions.

The uses of *seem* are not quite parallel with those of the others in this group. But if you see your face in the looking-glass, it will certainly seem *to* you to be at the back of the glass.

Things may *seem strange,* or *seem to*[17] *be strange* in the same way as they may *be* ready; and *get*, like *seem*, will go with most 'adjectives,' because it is the name of the process of change or development. For example:

An old dog will not get young again.

Every time you put together the name of one of the 10 simple acts (six of which are free to go in almost any direction) with the name of one of the 20 directions or positions in space, you are making a 'verb'; that is to say, in some languages a new word would be necessary for the complete act. In France, for example, they do not *get down* a tree, or *get down into* a hole, but there is a special word ('descendre') for *get down,* and another spe-

---

[17] This use of *to* is one about which more will be said later when we come to the 'infinitive' (p. 209).

cial word for *get up* ('monter'), another for *get across* ('traverser'), another for *get ready* ('préparer'), and so on.

Normal English has a great number of 'verbs' of the same sort, like 'ascend,' 'descend,' 'climb,' 'traverse,' and 'prepare,' and every one of them is itself a new sound for the learner and has a number of special forms in addition. Months, or even years, of training are needed to get 4,000 of these sounds and forms fixed in the memory, so that the value of a good working knowledge of the 30 little words for acts and their directions in Basic English will be clear to all who are interested in cutting down the time which it now takes to get a knowledge of English.

QUESTIONS AND EXAMPLES

Give a Basic substitute for the 'verbs' in these examples:

The men 'extract' the root with a spade.
The boys 'deposit' nuts in the basket.
The girls 'manufacture' stems for pipes.
The women 'can obtain' fowls at the market.
The nation will 'prepare' for war.
Some goats 'leave' the garden.

Get is the most general of all the names of acts. In fact it will take the place of almost all the others and so may frequently be used when in doubt. For example: *the men get the root out with a spade, the boys get nuts into the basket,* and so on.

3. HOW, WHEN, AND WHERE

The way in which an expansion of our knowledge of things takes place is, first, by the addition of the names of their qualities, so that we get *a man, a good man;* and, second, by the addition of the names of acts, so that we get *the good man, the good man comes.*

The act may be done in any one of the different *directions,* all of which have their names, as we have seen; or it may be done in some special *way.* There are only twenty names of directions, but there is no limit to the number of ways, and a separate sort of word (an 'adverb') is frequently used for the way in which we do things.

RULE. 'Adverbs' are formed by the addition of *-ly* to an 'adjective.' [18]

There are some very common 'adverbs' which are not made from 'adjectives.' They are chiefly words for place, time, or amount:

again, ever, far, forward, here, near, now, out, still, then, there, together, well, little, much.

Of these, *far–near, now–then, here–there* will go two by two as opposites; and *well* (which has another use as an 'adjective' opposite *ill,* see page 131) is the special form taken by the 'adverb' of *good.*

Most of these are generally put after the operation-word:

He will go again (far, forward, near, now, out, then, there, and so on).[19]

Then there is another group made up of the 'adverbs' of degree: *almost, enough, even, only, quite, so,* and *very.* These are used chiefly with 'adjectives' and other 'adverbs.'

---

[18] Because of the sense or the sound, it is not possible to make this addition to every one of the 150 'adjectives,' but over 100 have this regular ending. We do not say *cut-ly* (because of the sense), or *parallel-ly* (because of the strange sound).

Tallly, smallly, and *longly* are not formed; and there are no adverbs for *like* and *same.*

In writing the adverb forms from adjectives ending in *y,* the *y* is changed into *i;* for example, *angrily, healthily.* In addition there are the not quite straightforward forms: *truly* (from *true*), *fully* (from *full*); *automatically, elastically,* and *electrically; ably, feebly, possibly, probably, responsibly,* and *simply.*

[19] *There* is frequently used for making everyday statements like: *There is a kettle on the fire,* or *There are no cracks in the glass* (p. 220). Such statements are not unlike those starting with *it* (see pp. 172, 173), where *it* is not used for the name of something talked about earlier.

The special places of other adverbs, like *ever* and *still,* will be made clear when we come to word-order (p. 165).

Make a list of all the 'adjectives' which would probably not be given the ending *ly*, because of their sense (*cut, hanging, yellow, male, married, past, tall*, and so on). The names of the colors all seem to come naturally in such a list; it would only be possible to do things 'in a blue way' by a strange stretch of the sense.

Do the same with those where the sound might be against the addition (*complex, early, parallel*, and so on).

For every one of these examples make a list of 6 'adverbs' which make sense in the spaces.

"You are a foolish boy," he said ——.

He went to the house ——.

The airplane came down ——.

The statement was —— true.

'Adjectives' of position in space or time may be used as 'adverbs' without a change of form; for example, *high, deep, flat, early, last.* Make a list of these.

Is the picture representative of any of these 'adverbs':
near, badly, happily, secretly, cruelly, strongly?

A special note is needed about *hard*, which has no *-ly* form in Basic, but may itself be used as an 'adverb' in the sense 'with much force,' as in: *It is raining hard.*

4. I, HE, YOU; THIS, THAT

You now have a language in which things may be talked about by giving their qualities ('adjectives'), and by saying what they do ('verbs'), the directions in which they go ('prepositions'), and the ways in which the acts are done ('adverbs').

The most necessary words are those which take the place of the simplest sign—pointing; then come those which do the work of the other signs we make when pointing is not enough. And there are some words like 'adverbs' which take the place, not of pointing, or of simple signs, but of other words, so that as little time as possible may be wasted in making our ideas clear to others.

Sometimes we are pointing at ourselves, which is the same as saying *the person here;* or at others (*the person there*). But at a very early stage some languages get special words for this purpose. We say:

I will come, He will come, and *You will come.*

And in place of *the thing here* and *the thing there* we say: *this* and *that,* or *this thing* and *that thing.*

If we are talking about more than one thing or person, *this* and *that* become *these* and *those.*

Who (with *which* and *what*) is in this group, but it is not needed till we come to put words in their right order in longer statements.

When I am talking about myself together with others, or when a word is needed for 'you and I together,' the 'plural' form *we* is used, as in

We will come tomorrow.

When it is two or more of your friends who are coming, you say:

They will come.

But if you are talking to your friends, you say:

You will come,

using the same form for a number of friends as you would for one.[20]

[20] For other such forms (*she, it*) see p. 170.

QUESTIONS AND EXAMPLES

If you make a picture of a house, you may say about this house, *This is a house, I will make this house,* and so on; or if there are two or more houses, you say about these houses, *These are houses, I will make these houses,* and so on. Do the same with *that* and *those,* and make use of the names of all the buildings (*library, house, church,* and so on) and all the vessels (*boat, bottle, bucket, basin, pot,* and so on) in the list.

When you have given money for a house, you are its owner, and *you have the house.* When two or more of your friends have a house, they say *We have a house;* and you say *They have a house.* If you are going to give a house to two friends, you say *I will give a house to you.* What would they then say to their friends, if they made use of the word *get?*

Such is a less straightforward pointing word than *this* and *that,* having the sense 'of this (that) sort,' or even 'of this (that) sort of size (degree)': *such ideas are foolish, the gloves are not such a dark color.* Take note of the word-order—*such* before *a* (it is never used with *the*).

5. CRIES AND ORDERS

The use of one word by itself with the mark '!' after it is the sign of a strong feeling about the thing or the act named by the word— *Fire!, Danger!* Sometimes the feeling is a desire—*Water!* Very commonly such a cry is an order: *Come! Stop!*

The sense is dependent on the place or the conditions in which such words are used. If a man is ill in bed, and he says *Water!*— we may be certain that he would be pleased to have a drink. But if some boys are looking about for a place where their boats may go sailing, and one of them suddenly sees water, and says *Water!* —the others do not give him a drink.

Three Basic words which are specially used by themselves are *Yes!, No!,* and *Please!* Their use in this way is so common that the '!' sign is not necessary.

A 'cry' may sometimes be made up of more than one word:

> *Go back!*
> *Oh, what a shame!*

Orders are given by using the root-form of an operation-word without a name or 'pronoun.' In this way they are like cries but in other ways they may be like full statements, keeping the same word-order as in a normal statement:

Come to the theater tomorrow.
Put the gun down.

The 'l' sign is not generally used after orders or requests formed of more than one or two words, but may be if they are cried out:

Keep away from the edge!

When 'not' is needed in an order, the 'auxiliary' *do* has to be used:

Do not go in there.

There are a number of noises which, though not internationally used, are probably clear to everyone when the conditions in which they are used are given.[21] *Oh!*, *Ah!* are 'interjections' of this sort, which might have been listed with the group of international words (page 235), if they had been important enough.

Not all the 'interjections' are made with the purpose of saying something to another person. Sometimes they are only an outlet for one's feelings, as when we say 'Ow!' on coming up against a door suddenly, or 'Phew!' when the heat is very great. It is clearly not necessary for this private language of the feelings to be

QUESTIONS AND EXAMPLES

One special use of these cries is for military purposes. *Fire!* is the order for a gun to be made to go off with a loud noise and smoke. given an international form.

---

[21] Basic makes no general use of words which might seem to be international because they are formed from sounds ('onomatopoeia'). But a small number of names of noises, such as 'the *buzz* of a bee,' 'the *pop* of a cork,' or the '*tick* of a clock,' will have a limited value as simple sounds. Naturally, other languages may have other names for such noises; but a *cuckoo*, a *hiccup*, and a *miaou* will probably give little trouble. Other suggestions made in *Basic English* (p. 37) are *cluck, crash, croak, flap, splash,* and *wheeze;* but, naturally, they are only to be used in connection with the things or acts by which they are caused, and chiefly for ornament or amusement.

Attention! is the order to take a stiff position and get ready for another order: *Eyes front! Left turn!*—and so on. Make a selection of words which might be of use for giving orders in a school (*Attention! Quick! Come here! Books shut! Quiet, please!*).

When you are surprised, or overcome by strong feelings, do you make noises which would be clear to everyone in any country? Do you say: *Oh! Ah! Pooh! Bah! Shssh!?*

Make these examples into short cries:

I have a desire for a porter for the bags. (Porter!)

That was a cruel act. (Shame!)

That is a very good thing. (Good!)

Make this order into its opposite by the use of *not:*

Get the meal ready before I come back.

At this point, most learners will probably have a good working knowledge of the 850 words and their senses. On pages 126–27 there was a list of the first 100 names of things for general use. Here is a suggestion for the last 100:

addition, adjustment, agreement, amusement, apparatus, approval, argument, art, attraction, authority, base, brass, cause, committee, comparison, condition, connection, control, credit, crime, current, debt, decision, degree, development, digestion, discovery, discussion, disease, disgust, distance, distribution, education, effect, error, event, existence, expansion, experience, expert, fact, fiction, flight, government, harmony, history, humor, impulse, increase, industry, instrument, insurance, invention, level, limit, manager, mass, metal, nation, observation, offer, opinion, organization, position, power, process, produce, profit, property, prose, protest, purpose, range, rate, reaction, regret, representative, respect, rhythm, science, selection, sex, shame, shock, society, structure, substance, suggestion, support, system, tax, tendency, test, theory, transport, unit, value, vessel, weight, wine.

A

II. Word-Order

Generally, it is a good thing to put every word into some form of statement when you have its sound and its sense clear. It is much less hard to get a story into the memory than a list of words; and in a story such as the one about May and the rat, or in any of the examples in Section Three of this book you will have all the words in the right places, even if at first you are not quite certain about some of the details. This is very important because even though you may be quite clear about the sense of the words and how they are used, if you do not put them together in the right order, your statements may be taken in the wrong way by all your friends. For example, if you say *"have I an idea"* in place of *"I have an idea,"* it will seem as if you are uncertain about the condition of your mind, when in fact your purpose was to say that something of value was going on inside it.

1. STATEMENTS

Take a simple statement, such as you might have made when you got to page 137,

> *I will give simple rules to the boys now.*

So long as you make no change in the *order* of the words you may put any of the 600 names of things in the place of *rules* (which will make 600 different statements), and any of the 150 'adjectives' in the place of *simple*. This gives you 90,000 possible statements; though, naturally, not all of them will make equally good sense.

153

Other simple changes in this one example (by taking words from the Basic list which you are now quite certain might go into the places of *I, will, give, to, the, boys,* and *now*) will quickly give you more different statements than it would be possible to make by going through them for 1,000,000 years without a stop.[22]

This would not be very interesting, but there is certainly enough in that one example to give anyone something to do for an hour or two on a wet day. But till we have some more rules, so that there is a chance of making use of other forms of words than those given in the First Step, we are limited to a small number of fixed statements; and we have no way of putting these statements together into longer ones, with connections between them such as are necessary for discussion and argument.

So let us take a look at the sort of complex statement which it will be possible to make when we get to the end of the division on Word-order, and have a little more knowledge about word-forms and the expansions of the simple senses of the words themselves.

This process is not unlike the behavior of readers who go to the last page of a story to see if it has a happy end. But in learning a language there are no surprises to be kept secret, and the only reason for not starting at the end is that it is not so simple. In fact, there are some teachers who do put boys into deep water before their first swim; but if they are not very good teachers, it is unnecessarily cruel, and a feeling of disgust may be produced by the shock. This book is designed to get the best out of their system by having a quick look at the middle, after a good start has been made on a solid base. So it is more like going to the top of a mountain for a wide view of the land before us; and then we see in the distance:

[22] This 1,000,000 is not a printer's error. Get the numbers yourself. It takes one second, at least, to make the statement; and $60 \times 60 \times 24 \times 365 \times 1{,}000{,}000$ is much less than $1205 \times 2 \times 16 \times 200 \times 600 \times 20 \times 204 \times 600 \times 119$.

The camera-man who made an attempt to take a moving-picture of the society women before they got their hats off did not get off the ship till he was questioned by the police.

There are eight separate points here about which we have so far had no rules.

1. 'Camera-man,' 'society women' (the use of two names of things together, page 156).
2. 'Who' (page 162).
3. 'Before,' 'till' (as connections for two statements, page 161).
4. 'Off' (placed before and after a thing, pages 206–07).
5. 'Moving,' 'questioned' (the addition of 'ing' and 'ed,' page 176).
6. 'Made,' 'got,' 'did' (= *make, get, do,* in past time, page 169).
7. 'Their' (= of them, page 170).
8. 'Police' (international word, page 235).

The first four of these come into the account of Word-order; the others are later details.

QUESTIONS AND EXAMPLES

Make changes in the statement, *I will give good rules to you now,* by the addition of other words (*No, I will not give . . .*).

Now make changes by changing some of the words.

(*I will give bad rules . . .*)

When one of the statements formed by changing a word like *good* to *electric* does not make sense, it is interesting to put the question: Would this ever be possible? Care is needed in coming to a decision. For example, in the year 1734, it would not have made sense to say, *I will give an electric bell to the servant now.* If you had been living then you might have said that it would not ever be possible.

Make some simple statements like the example you have been given. Here are some suggestions:

I take a sweet cake from the shelf quietly.

I give soup to the family regularly.

The man will put a new roof on the house tomorrow.

Put these words in the right order:

Tired dogs after rats do go not.

Of Basic English a good opinion have I.

Slowly do we will the work.

It would be a good test of the learner's knowledge of the system at this point to make certain how the numbers given in the footnote on page 154 were worked out. For example, 1205 = 400 general names + 200 picturables + 596 'plurals' (there is no change of form for *news, trousers, scissors, sheep*) + *I, he, you, we, they, this, that, these, those;* 2 = *will* and *may*. The numbers 200 and 119 do not take in all the words which might be put in these places. (For example, the '200' takes into account only the 150 names of qualities, with their 50 *un-* forms, though there are clearly some words among the 'Operations' which might be used.) What additions are you able to make for these positions?

Like is an 'adjective' pointing from one thing to another, so it is quite natural to put the name of the thing with which the comparison is made after it: *an instrument like a plow.* Two like things may be said to be *like one another.*

2. COMPLEX WORDS

We have seen how an 'adjective' comes before the name of a thing and says what sort of a thing it is. In the same way, you may put the name of one thing before the name of another, and so get a new name for a new thing.

The word coming first says something about the word which comes after it. *House-coal* is coal for use in the house, but a *coal-house* is a place where coal is kept. It will be quite simple to get the sense of other complex words with this example as a guide.

RULE. Complex words are formed by putting together two names of things. *Word-order* and *word-form* are two which are being used in this book.

An *account-book* is a book in which money accounts are kept, and the sense of *music-book* and *story-book* will be equally clear.

So we get a *milkman,* who comes with the milk; a *postman,* who comes with the post (international word, page 235); a *dust-man,* who takes the dust away in his cart; or a *camera-man,* who makes his living by taking pictures.

In writing complex words, the parts may simply be put together as one word or they may be joined by '-'. Very common complex words, which give no trouble to the eye or tongue, are formed without the joining-sign (*bedroom, newspaper, raincoat, sundown*), but much the greater number of complex words are formed with it (*baby-carriage, cow-house, machine-gun, ticket-box*), and it is safer to make use of it when in doubt.

Sometimes the words are simply put side by side. Any number of words may be put together to make one complex name in this way, but '-' is not generally used for joining more than two: *motion-picture house*.

You may go on to say *motion-picture house fire*, or put an 'adjective' in front of the complete new word, as in *sudden motion-picture house fire*, or *good, cheap, motion-picture house fire-apparatus*.

This is an uncommonly fertile field for new ideas in language-making; the only limit being what the public is ready for.

In addition to these simple examples, there are certain words which are made up of two Basic parts—not necessarily names of things—but have now got fixed senses or special uses (like *into*, on page 141). Though the sense is different from what would be the normal suggestion of the parts, the sounds are generally not changed; so they have not been listed as new words among the 850.

Here are some which are used very frequently, and which might give trouble:

away (= at or to some distance). *Go away.*

become (= come to be). *Boys become men.*

cupboard (= *boards* or shelves for *cups* and other things, with a door). *The glasses and spoons are in the cupboard.*

income (= amount of money *coming in* regularly every year, and so on). *Incomes go down after a war.*

inside (= the *side* or part which is *in*). *The inside of the house.*

into (= to a position *in*). *Go into the house.*

outcome (= what *comes out* as the end of a process, and so on). *These events had a sad outcome.*

outlet (= way by which anything, for example a force or a liquid, is *let out*). *Music is an outlet for the feelings.*

outside (= the *side* or part which is *out*). *The outside of the house.*

today (= this *day*; formed like *tomorrow*). *They will go today.*

undertake (= *take* on work, and so on). *They will undertake the building.*

upright (= straight *up*). *An upright stick.*

without (= not *with*, not having). *He is without a raincoat.*

When we have to make it quite clear that an act was done by (or to) one person or group and no other, *my, your, its,* and *our* (the owner-forms of *I, you, it,* and *we,* see page 170) are put with *self* or *selves: I will do it myself, you yourself say, we saw him ourselves.* There is only one 's' in *itself,* and about *he* and *they* we say *himself* (female form *herself*) and *themselves.*

There is an important group formed by joining *one, body* (in the special sense of 'person'), *thing,* and *where* on to *any, every,* and *some,* and all but the first on to *no.* (*Anyone, anybody, everyone, everybody, someone, somebody, nobody,* but *no one.*) In addition, we have *anyhow* and *somehow.*

QUESTIONS AND EXAMPLES

In late years a *he-man* and a *yes-man* have come into use in some circles. Is the sense of these clear to you?

Fire-apparatus is used to put out a fire by *firemen.* See what other words come naturally before or after *fire* (*fire dust, coal fire,* and so on).

Do the same with *face* (*face-cloth, face-powder,* and so on).

There are two or more possible senses for some common complex words. Which of the two senses of *snowman* would seem most natural to boys playing in the snow?

Why are *glass flowers* different from *flower glasses?* (Because you see with an *eye-glass,* but not with a *glass eye.*)

What words would you put together to give the sense of: 'doctor,' 'pavement,' 'perambulator,' 'calligraphy,' 'sailor,' 'journal'? (*medical man, side-walk, baby-carriage, handwriting, seaman, newspaper.*)

What in your opinion would be the sense of these: *anybody, footnote, good-looking, however, outlook, overcome, undergo, upkeep, downfall, mother-in-law, outline?*

Put two words together to give this picture a name.

3. JOINING WORDS

All the statements we have made so far are simple, separate statements, with no expansions or ornaments.

When simple statements come one after the other the effect is like that of a number of jumps. It is much the same as putting the names of things together and letting the other person make the connection between your ideas:

Fly—meat—poison—danger.

The connection is clear when you are in a meat store; and someone may put a cover on the meat. At a meal, the effect might be to send someone running for medical help. In a Science building, where there may be flies of great value, someone might give help to the fly.

If you say, *A fly is on the meat. Poison is on the fly. Take care of that dog!*—you are doing the same thing with statements; and a number of different sorts of joining words ('conjunctions') are necessary to overcome the jumping effect.

And and *or* are used to make the same sort of connections between statements as between words:

I will come and you will go. I may get the money, or it may go to the Government.

But gives a different sort of connection, with a sense like 'on the other side' or 'on the other hand.'

He is happy, but you are sad.

Everyone is happy, but you are sad.

But is used between words as it is between statements.

Everyone is happy but me.

In statements such as:

They say that the dog is dead,

the two parts, *The dog is dead* and *They say that,* are clear enough.

That, in addition to its other uses (page 149), is the joining word for all sorts of statements about sayings, opinions, and so on, where there is a connection between the first part and what comes after. The connection is generally clear. We say:

The opinion of the owner is—the dog is dead.

The dog is dead—that is the opinion of the owner.

The opinion of the owner is that—'the dog is dead.'

The opinion of the owner is that the dog is dead.

The only trouble is with past time, where the *is* becomes *was:*

The opinion of the owner was that the dog was dead.

But till it is quite clear from examples how the change is made, you may keep the statement in the form, *The opinion of the owner was, 'the dog is dead,'* by giving the words of the person talking.

There are four other words which are specially used for joining statements:

Because, if, though, while.

Because = for this cause or reason. *I will go because he is there.*

If = on this condition, chance, or theory (which is in doubt).[23]

---

[23] *If* has come to be used in a general way where there is a doubt or question about something: *They are not certain if he is there, but they will see if there is an answer.*

He may be there; and if he is there, I will go.
He may not be there; but if he is there, I will go.
I will go if he is there.

Though = even if it is true (that). *The road is wet, though there was no rain.*

While = in the same stretch of time. *I will go while he is there.*

Before, after, and *till* are used in the same sort of way for the purpose of joining two statements; the dependent statement then takes the place of the name of a thing or person.

I will go before the boys.
I will go before the boys get ready.
I will go before you.
I will go before you are ready.
I will go before you come.
He is sad after they go.
He is happy till they go.

Because *so* has the sense 'in that way' it frequently does the work of a 'conjunction':

I will come; so you may go.

Another group of joining words is made up of *when, where, why,* and *how,* which are used in addition for putting questions (see page 166).

I will go when he is there.
I see where the ship is.
He will say why he is angry.
It is not clear how the box got broken.

QUESTIONS AND EXAMPLES

We were able to make the use of *that* as a 'conjunction' clearer by putting the four stages of its development side by side. The same may be done for the two uses of *if*:

1. *I will go, if the parcel is there* (on that condition—but I am not certain that the parcel will be there).

2. *I will see the parcel, if it is there* (on that theory—but it may not be there).

3. *I will see if it is there* (because I am in doubt).

4. *He is not certain if it is there* (it may or may not be there).

Do you see the connection between the first two and the last two? And are you clear that they are different? (No sort of stop is necessary before the *if* in the last two. Why? Because there is no stop in the sense.) In (2), what I will see is the parcel; in (3), what I will see is 'if the parcel is there.' And when it is there I see *that* (it is there).

Put *He was certain that* in front of *They are in the room if it is true that the door is still shut;* and make the necessary changes for past time.

Put joining words between the parts of:

"*Men may come—men may go—I go on for ever.*"

"*He will have heart-trouble—he is at work all day,—a medical man has said, 'Stop!'*"

"*—there is no doubt—it is foolish to put a lock on the cupboard—the loss of the spoons—you have no more silver, the lock-maker will not say—it is a waste of time—the lock is safely fixed.* (The words needed are *when, after, though, till, that*—but not in that order; one of them is needed twice.)

4. WHO AND WHICH

We have now seen how an expansion of the names of things is possible by the addition of other names of things, and how statements about things may be made longer by the addition of other statements side by side with them or dependent on them. The use of an 'adjective' was the first way of saying something more about a thing; and some 'adjectives,' such as *automatic*, say more than others.

An 'automatic *writing-machine*' would be a writing-machine doing its work without the help of men. But a 'writing-machine' is itself a machine for putting signs on paper; and there is clearly a limit to the number of complex ideas which it is possible to put in this 'adjective' form. If, for example, the machine is 'quick,' we get a 'quick, automatic writing-machine,' and then it would be hard to put in a word like 'electric.' So *who* and *which* may take off some of the weight.

Who is used for persons; *which* is used for things and animals.

"I have a tall father" may become: *I have a father, who is tall.*

"I have a small, gray hat" may become: *I have a small hat, which is gray.*

In the same way, *who* and *which* may take the place of *and he* or *and it.*

In complex statements formed with *who* and *which* it is sometimes necessary, if the sense is to be clear, to make a change in the position of the 'adverbs.' For example, in the statement, *I will go with the man who is here now*, *now* seems to say something about 'the man.' To give the sense, 'I will go now,' the 'adverb' would have to be placed after *go*, to make clear that its connection is with the first part of the statement.

What is used for 'the thing which,' as in *I see what is wrong.*

QUESTIONS AND EXAMPLES

In the statement, "I will give *good, clear, short rules* to you," take out one or more of the 'adjectives' with the help of *which.*

Two *whiches* may be joined by *and.* Put *which* in two places into *They have an old monkey, and it is able to get a lock open with a key.*

Do you see an 'adjective' which would make it possible to say *Here is some water which is at 100° C.* in 5 words?

Make the necessary changes in the statement, *This is the cat who was the property of the man which is dead.*

Put *who* or *which* into the spaces in this story:

There was a story in the newspaper yesterday about a woman . . . . is secretary of a hospital for babies . . . . is on an island. She was at a meeting . . . . was very important, when there was a sudden burst of wind, ... was the cause of the trouble. The records are still in the sea because the only rods . . . . were in the hospital were not long enough to get the papers back.

5. HOW, WHEN, WHERE, AND WHY

We have seen from our simple example of word-order (page 147) that the safe rule for normal 'adverbs' is to put them at the end of a statement or of a part of a statement complete in itself (page 163). But there are some special 'adverbs' whose sense makes it necessary for them to be placed differently. These are of 5 sorts:

1. 'Adverbs' of degree, which come before the word or group of words with which they are used—*it is almost six; I was quite ready; we are very happy*. But—*I am old enough*.

2. *Not* (see page 139), which comes after *be* or the auxiliary—*I was not happy; he will not come; it was not cold*.

3. Joining 'adverbs,' which, like *who* among the 'pronouns,' are used in making complex statements. These naturally come between the two parts of the statement to which they give the necessary connection—*this is* HOW *the apparatus is put together; there is a reason* WHY *he is sad; take this coat* WHEN *you go; this is* WHERE *the fire was*. For the use of these words in forming questions, see page 166.

4. 'Adverbs' of place which are the names of certain positions *in relation to some point*, and so are not complete in themselves. If the point in mind is quite clear from the rest of the statement, then there is no need for it to be named, and the 'adverb' is used by itself, as in *Do not go far* (the sense of *far* being naturally taken as "far from where you are"). But if it is necessary for the point to be named, then the name of a direction has to be put after the 'adverb'—*from* after *far* (*London is far from Tokyo*), *to* after *near* (*We are near to a tea-room*), and *of* after *out* (*They go out of the house*).[24]

---

[24] Naturally such 'adverbs,' like other 'adverbs,' may have their sense limited by names of directions and so on giving further details of the place or time in question. For example, the boys go *out into the street*, or *far up the mountain*, in the same way as events take place *early in the morning* or *late at night*. But such additions are clearly different from those noted here as necessary to the sense of the 'adverb.'

5. The two 'adverbs' of time, *still* and *ever*. *Still*, like other such words, may be put at the end of the statement, but when used with *be*, *will*, and *may*, it generally comes after these words, and with the simple past and present of every other 'operation-word' it frequently comes before it: *she is still here: I still have this: he will still have that*. *Ever* is generally used with *not* or in questions. When used with *not*, it comes after the *not* wherever this may be. In questions it is placed after the person or thing doing the act—*I do not ever go: have you ever been?*

QUESTIONS AND EXAMPLES

How would you put these two statements together with the help of an 'adverb':

I have an interest in fiction; there is a reason.

It is time; I will have a meal.

Put *almost* and *near* in their right places in the statement: *It will be dark when we get to the house.* Do the same with *quite* and *enough* in: *We are happy if we are warm.*

Put *still* and *ever* where they make the best sense in the statement: *If I have money I will be a friend to the boy.*

Put *ever* and *not* into the statement:

You take sugar.

Make it into a statement with *still*.

Quite may be used in two senses. *You are quite right* = *You are completely right.* *The book is quite good* = *The book is good but not very good.*

What is the sense of: *This is quite the wrong answer?* Take note of the word order.

Though *near* and *far* are opposites in sense, they are not quite parallel in form, because *near* has a use as a 'preposition,' which *far* has not. In place of *near to* we may make use of *near* by itself: *the table is near (to) the wall, the ships go near (to) the land*, but we have to say *the house is far from the town, the boys will go far up the mountain*.

6. QUESTIONS

A simple statement using any form of *be, will, may,* or *have,* may be made into a question by changing the order in this way: *Is sugar sweet? May I have the sugar?* [25]

With all other names of operations, questions are formed by putting *do* (or *did* for past time) before a statement.

Do you take sugar?

Do you come here frequently?

Did they give you a full account of the play?

How, when, where, and *why* may be put in front of any such question, to get an answer about the way, the place, the time, or the reason of any fact, act, or event.

Why is sugar sweet?

Where is the station?

When will he get the news?

How do you get there?

How frequently do you go?

Who is used for questions about persons.

Who is that?

Who will you give that to? [26]

What (or *which,* when the things are limited to some special group) is used for questions about things.

What is that strange thing?

What will you put in the box?

Which apple will you take?

Which of these is your book?

QUESTIONS AND EXAMPLES

Put in the form of questions:

The ink is dry.

[25] The rule is equally true for *be* and *have* used as 'auxiliaries' (see pp. 171–73): *Have the boxes come? Were they sent today?*

[26] Here we might have put *whom* (see p. 170), but it is a form which is going out of use.

You give money very freely.
They will go tomorrow.

If you have two cats and one of them has been poisoned, would it be right to say:

What is dead? Which is dead? or *Who is dead?*

Here is a story:

On the way to the office in an automobile in the morning, it was necessary to [27] *put on the brake suddenly because a man was in the road.*

To what questions, then, might these be the answers:

1. Because a man was in the road.
2. On the way to the office.
3. In an automobile.
4. Suddenly.
5. In the morning.
6. The brake.
7. A man.

---

[27] For this use of *to,* see pp. 208–10.

B

I. Other Word-Forms

With the 850 words, and a knowledge only of the forms which
have so far been used, a surprising number of statements are now
possible, and a still greater number would be quite clear to every
reader. This is because the other forms are chiefly designed to
make things go more smoothly. A rough idea of the sense may
be got without their help; and most of the expansions of the
senses of the words are quite natural developments when taken
in connection with the rest of a statement.

Let us go back to the example on page 155 and put the nearest
form about which we are certain in the place of any word which
we have not come across so far:

"The camera-man who *make* an attempt to take a *move* picture
of the society women before they *get they* hats off, *do* not get off the
ship, till he was *question* . . ."

There is no doubt that the story is all in past time, so the sense
is clear even here. It is only necessary to get the right time-forms
of *make, get,* and *do,* the pronoun-form *their,* and the rule for
making 'adjectives' when needed, from names like *move* and
question. When you are clear about the behavior of the very small
list of 'operation-words' and 'pronoun'-forms on pages 169 and
170, and the working of the rule on page 176 about the addition of
the endings *-er, -ing,* and *-ed* when needed, you have the complete system.

This is interesting for two reasons:

1. In other languages (and in normal English) there are

FORMS OF 'OPERATION-WORDS'

Present			Past	-ing Form	Special Past Form
	ONE	MORE THAN ONE			
1, 2	COME	COME	CAME	COMING	COME
1, 2	GET	GET	GOT	GETTING	GOT
1, 2	GIVE	GIVE	GAVE	GIVING	GIVEN
1, 2	GO	GO	WENT	GOING	GONE
1, 2	KEEP	KEEP	KEPT	KEEPING	KEPT
1, 2	LET	LET	LET	LETTING	LET
1, 2	MAKE	MAKE	MADE	MAKING	MADE
1, 2	PUT	PUT	PUT	PUTTING	PUT
1, 2	SEEM	SEEM	SEEMED	SEEMING	SEEMED
1, 2	TAKE	TAKE	TOOK	TAKING	TAKEN
1	AM * †		WERE		
2	ARE	ARE	I ⎫ WAS	BEING	BEEN
3	IS		HE ⎭		
1, 2	DO *	DO	DID	DOING	DONE
1, 2	HAVE *	HAVE	HAD	HAVING	HAD
1, 2	SAY	SAY	SAID	SAYING	SAID
1, 2	SEE	SEE	SAW	SEEING	SEEN
1, 2	SEND	SEND	SENT	SENDING	SENT

* Has a use as a helping word.
† The forms of *be*.

The present form used with *he, she,* or *it* is made by the simple addition of 's.' Only *be, do* (*does*), *go* (*goes*), and *have* (*has*) are not regular.

Number	Sex	Form for Doer of Act	Form for Thing to Which Act Is Done	Form for Owner
One More than one	M. F. N.	THIS THESE	THIS THESE	
One More than one	M. F. N.	THAT THOSE	THAT THOSE	
One More than one	M. F. N.	WHO WHICH	WHOM WHICH	WHOSE
One More than one	N.	WHAT	WHAT	
One More than one	M. F.	I WE	ME US	MY OUR
One	M. F. N.	HE SHE IT	HIM HER IT	HIS HER ITS
More than one	M. F. N.	THEY	THEM	THEIR
One More than one	M. F.	YOU	YOU	YOUR

M = Male.   F = Female.   N = No sex.

One, in addition to being part of the number system (page 236) has two uses as a 'pronoun.' The first has the sense "a person or thing" (of those, or of the sort, being talked about): *I have no pencil. Please give me one.* The other has the sense "*any* person" (and from this is formed *oneself*): *If one has money, one generally has friends. When one is old, one has to take care of oneself.*

For "this is *my* book" and so on, we may say "this (book) is *mine*" (*yours, his, hers, ours, theirs*). That is, these new owner-forms may take the place of *my* (*your* and so on) *and the name of a thing* whenever it is clear from what is being said what the thing is: *those are their seats and these are ours.* The owner-forms of names are used in the same way: *John is not my brother, he is Mary's.*

generally pages and pages of 'special' time-forms (which take years to get fixed in the memory for ready use).

2. Even the most strongly supported of the different attempts to make an international language with new words has at least 50 different endings which may be put onto its root-words; and you have to be an expert with most of these endings (and with about 3,000 separate roots) before you are able to make any but the simplest sort of statements, such as those which have been possible in the earlier pages of this 'A B C.'

1. 'VERB'-FORMS (WITH 'PRONOUNS')

The different forms of the operation-words and 'pronouns' may be given in examples which make it clear when and how they are to be used.

Here is *be,* used with the different 'pronouns' in the present.

1. I *am* where he (she, it) *is;* so we (you, they) *are* all in the same place.

Then we have *be* in the past, and with it the special form which is only used with *have* or *be.*

2. This (that) *was* where these (those) *were seen* (*made, kept, put, given, sent, taken*) yesterday.

Example 3 (and 5) gives us the form of the operation-word with the sense 'in the process of,' which is used with all the different past, present, and future forms of *be.*

3. I *am* (*was, will be*) *going* (*coming*) where he *is* (*was, will be*) *getting* (*making, putting*) what we *are* (*were, will be*) *having* (*giving, keeping*) for our meal.

Example 4 gives the present form of *have.*

4. I (we) *have* some things which he (she, it) *has.*

Example 5 gives two complex ways of making the past by using the 'auxiliary' *have* or the complex auxiliary *have been* with the special forms seen in 2.

5. I (you) *have had* (*got, seen, taken,* and so on) what he *has been having* (*saying, seeing, sending, taking*).

Examples 6 and 7 give the simple present of all the operation-words other than *be* and *have*, with examples of the complex present formed with *be*.

6. Whenever he *lets* us, we *take* (*do, get, keep, make, say, see, send*) what he *makes* (*does, puts, says, sees, sends, gives*); but now he *is being* (*seeming*) kind, and *is letting* me see how he *is doing* it.

7. Whose are these (those) dogs which *come* (*go*) where my (his, her) dog *comes* (*goes*), and *gets* (*keeps, puts, takes*) its food?

Examples 8 and 9 (10 and 11) give some simple past forms of the operation-words.

8. Our (your, their) dogs *came* (*went*) and *got* what the other dog *kept* (*put, took*) there.

9. Before he *went* (came), I *saw* how he (they) *did* (*had, kept, said, made, sent*) it.

Example 10 gives us another complex way of forming the past by using the past of *have* with the special past forms which came into example 2.

10. Others, who *had done* (*had, said*) it before, *gave* me (him, her, us, you, them) no help.

Now comes an example of *do* when used to make a Past statement with *not*. In addition, you are given the Past of *may* and *will*.

11. It *seemed* that if I (we) *let* (*did not let*) the boy whom I *saw* have it, he *might take* what he *did* (*would*) *not take* before.

Last of all, we get two more ways of putting words together to make complex pasts, for which *may, might,* and *would* are used.

12. He *says* that we *may have been* wrong, because we *might* (*would*) *not have seemed* so foolish if we *had not let* them take it.

For those who have no knowledge of English, or are only in the early stages, the learning of these different forms and their uses will probably be the hardest part of their work. Putting together examples of all sorts is the best way; and the learner will do well to make lists of such forms which he comes across in reading.

QUESTIONS AND EXAMPLES

Here is a bit of prose:

"Caesar *take* most of the men *what* had been with Pompey into *her* army, and *makes* peace with the important persons among *they*. Brutus, *which* later *putting* Caesar to death, *is* one of these, and they *says* that Caesar *be* full of regret when, after the fight, no one had *saw* him, and that *she* was very happy when he *gives* himself up."

Put the words in italics into their right form, using the past form for the names of acts. Then put them into the present and future form. If Caesar and Brutus were women what changes would have to be made?

We may now give some examples of the special use of *it* for starting statements (see page 147). In *it seems to me* . . . , *it is true that* . . . , *it is wise to* . . . , the *it* is pointing to what is going to be said. In *it is raining* (see page 178) the sense of *it* is open to argument, but seems to have some suggestion of a strange power which is responsible for events.

The use of *have* with *had* in example 5 is very like the use of *have* with the name of a quality. *I have the food ready* = *I have the food got* = *I have got the food*. Here are some other statements in the same form:

I have done the work.
A rat has taken the cheese.
The experts have made a test.
The workmen have made a hole.

2. COMPARISON

In the same way in which there are different degrees of heat, it is possible to have different degrees of any quality, and different amounts of a thing or substance. How are these degrees made clear in Basic English? For this purpose, there are the 'adverbs' *almost, enough, little, much, only, quite, so, very;* but sometimes we have to make statements about one thing in comparison with another, and these comparisons are made possible by *more* and *most,* which are formed from *much.* An example will make the use of these two words clear: If I had *much* money yesterday, and my friends had the same amount; and if I get *more* money today though my friends do not, I will then have *most* money. This gives us a sort of rough scale which is used in the same way with qualities. An event may be *frequent, more frequent,* or *most frequent;* a person may be *tired, more tired,* or *most tired;* an act may be done *quickly, more quickly,* or *most quickly.*

RULE. Statements of comparison are made by putting *more* and *most* in front of an 'adjective' or 'adverb.'

Though *more* and *most* may be used with any quality word, a certain number of these words take the endings *-er, -est,* which have a more natural sound to English ears. These are generally the shorter words like *fat, long, red, true.*[28] The learner will best get these into his head by reading and talking; the sense is the same whichever form is used. But it is necessary to give special attention to two words which are not regular: *bad,* which makes comparisons with the forms *worse* and *worst,* and *good,* forming *better* and *best.*

The 'adverb' *little,* like *much,* has special forms for comparison.[29] These are *less* and *least,* and when used with names

---

[28] Take note of the forms: *fatter, flatter, redder, sadder, thinner, wetter;* and of the fact that in words ending in *y,* the *y* is changed to *i* before the addition of *-er, -est: dry, drier, driest.*

[29] There are only three other 'adverbs' which have such forms: *far, farther*

of qualities, they make the opposite end of the scale to that which is formed by *more* and *most*.

The only quality words about which statements of comparison are not made are those whose sense gives no suggestion of degree. Examples of these are *first, last, male, female, same.*

To make a statement of comparison complete the joining word *than* is used when the comparison is between unequals, as in: *the country is more beautiful than the town; women are less strong than men;* and equal comparisons are put into the form *as . . . as,* so that we say *she is as good as her sister; butter is not as cheap as it was.*

In addition, this *as* form is used for making comparisons with the help of some of the 'adverbs' of degree. We say *he is almost as old as the manager, the leaves are quite as green as the grass, the coat is only as new as the hat.*

Another form of comparison is possible with *as* and *such;* for example, *such comforts as these,* or *comforts such as these.*

QUESTIONS AND EXAMPLES

When one is talking to businessmen it is a good thing to make one's statements as short as possible. How would you say this in 9 words: *There is not as great a number of snakes in England as there is in Africa?* (*There are less snakes in England than in Africa.*)

Does it seem strange to you that there are some quality words which do not ever come into statements of comparison? If two things are the *same* is it possible for them to be more or less like one another than they are? Have you ever been earlier than the *first* person at a meeting? If so, you may be of the opinion that it is possible for an *only* son to have brothers.

Put the right words into the spaces in the statement:

When you go ——— from the north you get ——— to the south. Would this be equally true if we put *west* and *east* in place of *north* and *south?*

Are there any words of which you are able to say certainly from

(*further*), *farthest; near, nearer, nearest; well, better, best.* In addition, *inner* and *outer* are formed from *in* and *out.*

the sound that they do not take the endings *-er, -est?* What about *dependent, necessary, foolish?* Would you put *flat* and *thick* in the same group?

What are the errors here:

The baddest boy did wellest in the test?

Pointing at one or other of these pictures, make statements like *These birds are wiser than these birds, these birds are less wise than these birds,* with *happy, angry, foolish, quiet, kind,* and *violent.*

3. ENDINGS IN -ER, -ING, -ED

RULE. 300 of the 600 names of things may take the endings, *-er, -ing, -ed* [30] to make new words having a straightforward connection of sense with them.

Of these names, 200 are general and 100 are the names of pictured things.

The name of a thing is formed by the addition of *-er* (person who, thing which, does a certain act), and *-ing* (the doing of the act); the name of a quality by *-ing* (in the process of doing the act) and *-ed* (having undergone the act). Though all these endings may be used with any of the 300 names, there are some with which *-er* and *-ed* will probably not ever be needed because of the sense. 'Rainers' and 'snowers' have no place in our experience, and it is a little hard to see what sort of thing would be 'smiled.'

The names of acts are the most straightforward. Here the *-er*

---

[30] There are other words in the Basic List which take some but not all of these endings. For example, *run, runner, running* (but not 'runned'). It is not necessary to have a knowledge of them, but anyone with enough experience may make use of them.

form becomes the name of the person or thing which does the act in question; -*ing* makes the 'adjective' used about the doer and the name of the act when in process of being done; and the -*ed* form gives the 'adjective' of the person or thing to which the act is done.

Act,[31] *attack, exchange, kiss, roll, smash, turn* are among the words in this group.

Another simple group is made up of the names of conditions of feeling or being. With a number of these the change of sense is parallel to that which takes place with the names of acts, -*er* forming the name of the person or thing having the condition, -*ing* the 'adjective' used about such a person, and so on. Examples are *desire, fear, love, regret.* With the other words in this group, -*er* makes the name of the thing causing the condition: *comfort, heat, surprise; -ing* then naturally gives the 'adjective' used of this cause, and -*ed* that of the thing in which the condition is caused. It may be noted that *'resting'* and *'balancing'* are used in two ways—of persons or things in a condition of rest or balance and of those causing such a condition. The only condition word which is not like one of the two sorts of examples given is *motion.* This is because it is only a special use of the word, for a sign made with the arm or hand, which takes the endings.

There is a very important group of words in which the -*ing* form is used for the doing of some act for which the thing named is used, or in which it takes the chief part. With substance words the act is frequently that of putting the substance onto something. *'Oiling'* is putting *oil* on, an *'oiler'* is a person or apparatus which does this, and an *'oiled* machine' is a machine into which oil has been put. *Butter, chalk, coal, ink, polish, sugar, water,* and a number of other words are of the same sort. (*'Dusting,'* on the other hand, has the sense of taking *dust* off.) Some words which are not names of substances, such as *cover, feather, letter,*

---

[31] A person acting on the stage is an *actor,* a seaman is a *sailor,* and a person to whom the payment of a debt has to be made is a *creditor.* But the sounds are the same as if the endings were in -*er.*

stamp, have the same behavior. Another list might be made of names of things whose -*ing* ending gives the sense of putting. '*Bottling*' is putting into a *bottle,* '*pocketing*' is putting in one's *pocket,* and '*potting*' is putting into a *pot.* With most of the other words in this group the -*ing* act is clear enough from the purpose for which the thing in question was made. *Brush, cart, comb, drain, hammer, plow* will give no trouble to anyone. But possibly it may not be quite so clear that '*detailing*' is giving all the *details* of something, that '*wheeling*' is pushing a thing on *wheels,* or even that '*handing*' is offering in the *hand.*

A fourth group is made up of words to which the addition of -*ing* gives the name of the act by which those things are made. Some of these words are fictions; for example, *answer, damage, effect, request, stop.* But others are the names of things which are formed by a quite straightforward physical process. We may see a bit of wood '*cracking,*' or a house '*burning,*' and we ourselves do the '*folding*' which makes a *fold,* and the '*roofing*' which gives us a *roof.* It may seem a little strange to some that '*raining*' is the process of making *rain,* because it is the rain itself which comes down. But because the rain does not become rain till it comes down in the form of rain, there is a good reason for placing it in this group. With *flower* it is the process of producing flowers which is named by *flowering,* so it frequently, as an 'adjective,' means simply 'in flower,' 'having flowers out.' *Branch, curve,* and *arch* are a little different from the others, because the '*branching,*' '*curving,*' and '*arching*' generally go on all the time, that is, they are representative more of conditions than of acts. One sense of '*forking*' (as used, for example, of a road branching into two) comes into this group.

In addition to the four chief groups which have been given attention so far, there are some words which make up only very small groups, or even do not go into any group at all. One such group is that formed by *cook, guide, judge,* in which the -*ing* form gives the name of the work which it is normal for a *cook, guide,* or *judge* to do. The -*er* form is here unnecessary, though '*cooker*' is used for a cooking-apparatus. From *farm, garden, market,* and *mine* are formed by the *-ing* ending the names for the work which is done in those places. But '*harboring*' is acting like a *harbor* to, '*landing*' is coming to *land,* '*placing*' is putting in a *place,* and '*schooling*' is a form of training which is not necessarily given in *school.* '*Causing*' (being a *cause* of), '*milking*' (getting *milk* from a cow and so on), '*pricing*' (putting a *price* on) are examples of words with which the endings may be worked quite simply from a knowledge of the root sense. '*Viewing*' (looking at something as if it was a *view*), '*facing*' (turning one's *face* in the direction of), and '*skirting*' (going round the edge of) seem a little less natural. And the learner will probably not see how '*training*' becomes teaching or education, or '*watching*' has the sense of keeping an eye on, without a word of help from the teacher, pointing out the connection between a *train* of carriages and the *train* of events which makes up the process of learning, and between the *watch* which a man's eye keeps on the clock and the *watch* which keeps an automatic finger on the time.

Where the act named by a word with the *-ing* ending may be done in a certain direction or to some thing, it is natural to say *looking at the sky, painting a picture.*

Another sense given by *-ed* is 'with, having, whatever is named by the root word.' Some *-ed* forms have only this sense, others have it as a second sense: *flowered* (of material)—'with (a design of) flowers on it'; *hooked*—'fixed on (by) a hook' or 'with (the form of) a hook.' Some words take *-ed* in this sense only for forming *complex* 'adjectives,' as *bright-eyed.*

Certain words which do not take the other endings may have *-ed* in this sense, as *winged, dark-haired, glassed* (a *glassed*-in summer house), *leaded* (*leaded* windows). These are not listed for the learner, but will be come across in his reading.

In addition to the 300 names which take 3 endings, all those ending in *-ing* have a use as 'adjectives' and all but *meeting* may take *-er* in place of the *-ing.* A '*builder*' may be '*building*' a building, a '*learner*' may be '*learning*' (*learning*) and so on. With them are grouped the *-ing* 'adjectives'—*boiling, hanging, living,* and *waiting.*

There are twelve names of qualities with *-er* and *-ing* endings: *clean, clear, complete, cut, dirty, dry, free, open, separate, smooth, shut,* and *wet.* Of these, all but *cut* and *shut* may take *-ed* as well. The rules for changing certain letters before the endings are the same as with names of things, so we get *dried, dirtied, wetted, wetting, wetter,* and so on. 'Cleaning' is making clean, and a man who does this is a *'cleaner.' Please,* like the names of qualities, takes two of the endings, *-ing* and *-ed.*

Here is a list of the 300:

200 General Names

act, air, answer, attack, attempt, back, balance, base, breath, burn, butter, cause, chalk, chance, change, cloth, coal, color, comfort, condition, control, cook, copper, copy, cork, cough, cover, crack, credit, crush, cry, curve, damage, design, desire, detail, disgust, doubt, dust, edge, effect, end, exchange, experience, fear, fire, flower, fold, force, form, front, grip, group, guide, harbor, hate, heat, help, hope, humor, ice, increase, ink, interest, iron, join, journey, judge, jump, kick, kiss, land, laugh, letter, level, lift, light, limit, list, look, love, machine, mark, market, mass, measure, milk, mine, motion, move, name, need, note, number, offer, oil, order, ornament, page, pain, paint, paper, part, paste, place, plant, play, point, poison, polish, powder, price, print, process, produce, profit, protest, pull, purpose, push, question, rain, range, rate, ray, reason, record, regret, request, respect, rest, reward, roll, rub, rule, salt, scale, seat, sense, shade, shame, shock, side, sign, silver, slip, slope, smash, smell, smile, smoke, sneeze, snow, soap, sort, sound, space, stage, start, steam, steel, step, stitch, stone, stop, stretch, sugar, support, surprise, talk, taste, tax, test, thunder, time, tin, top, touch, trade, transport, trick, trouble, turn, twist, unit, use, value, view, voice, walk, wash, waste, water, wave, wax, weather, weight, word, work, wound.

100 Picturable Things

arch, arm, band, bath, bed, board, bone, book, bottle, box, brain, branch, brick, bridge, brush, button, cake, cart, chain, circle, cloud, coat, comb, cord, curtain, cushion, drain, dress, drop, eye, face, farm, feather, finger, fish, floor, fork, frame, garden, glove, hammer, hand, hat, head, hook, house, jewel, knife, knot, line, lock, map, mouth, nail, nerve, net, parcel, pen, pencil, picture, pin, pipe, plane, plate, plow, pocket, pot, prison, pump, rail, receipt, ring, roof, root, sail, school, screw, seed, ship, shoe, skin, skirt, sponge, square, stamp, star, station, store, sun, thread, thumb, ticket, train, wall, watch, wheel, whip, whistle, wire, worm.

QUESTIONS AND EXAMPLES

Here is a list of words. Every one gets the same sort of sense from the addition of the endings as some other word in the list. See which of them go together: *pump, polish, fold, roll, ornament, mass, crush, brush, group, damage.* You may be at a loss to see which word to put with *group. Mass* is the answer, because *grouping* is forming into groups in the same way as *massing* is forming into *masses.* Which 2 words would you put these with: *sponge, whip, wire, cord?*

Put the 4 words *dress, range, cloud, map* [32] in their places in these examples:

1. *We have jewels —ing in quality from the poorest to the best.*
2. *The mother is —ing the baby.*
3. *Take the digestion into account when   ing out a meal for persons in hospital.*
4. *The glass was —ed with steam.*

---

[32] Most words ending, like *map,* in one letter representative of a stopped sound (but not *r, w, x,* or *y*), with one letter representative of an open sound before it, put in the last letter again before *-er, -ing,* and *-ed: control(ler), net(ting), regret(ted).* With all words ending in 'e,' the 'e' is dropped before *-er* and *-ed,* and with all but two (*shoeing, eyeing*), before *-ing: hated, lover, hoping. Uniting* and *united* are said with a long first 'i' as in *night.*

Make sense of this statement by completing the *-ing* form with all the words possible from the list on pages 180–81:

She is —ing the machine.

Put these letters in the right order to make words with one of the three endings: GITWINTS, DONIDONICET, CURDODEP, ARESUDEM, RESRUPTOP.

Might one say *raining the field* or *smiling the man?* (No, because only rain is 'rained' and only smiles are 'smiled.' But we might say *raining on the field, smiling at the man.*)

A rough guide to the use of the *-ed* form is: Do not make use of it where it would be wrong to put another sort of 'adjective.' For example, we do not say *I have blue the wall,* so we may not say, in Basic, *I have painted the wall.* But *The wall is blue* is quite right, and so is *The wall is painted.*

B

II. Expansions and Special Senses

1. NAMES OF THINGS AND QUALITIES

In addition to changes in its form, which give us new words, there are two chief ways in which a word may be made to do overtime—by a stretch of the sense to something a little different, or by limiting the sense to some special sort of thing covered by the name.

The greatest number of expansions are formed by using the name of one thing for the name of another which seems in some way to be like it. Starting with that which is nearest to us—ourselves—we readily see parallels between the parts of the body and certain common things. For example, *head* is used for the round top of anything; *foot* becomes the general name for a base; any branch or rod roughly in the position of an arm is said to be an *arm*, while the important use of the arm in the early days for fighting made it seem natural for instruments of war to be looked upon as longer and stronger *arms;* the connection between the leg of an animal and the *leg* of a seat or bed is even clearer, and the fact that the chest is the box where our breathing-apparatus is kept, gives us the more general use of *chest* for 'box' and 'chest of drawers.' Other important expansions in this field are *mouth* (an opening), *heart* (for the seat of the feelings), *neck* (the narrow part of a bottle, a violin, and so on), *tooth* (for anything pointed like a tooth), and *face* (the side which is in front, or before one's eyes).

Things may be like one another in a number of different ways. The simplest comparisons to make are those dependent on sense

183

STAMP

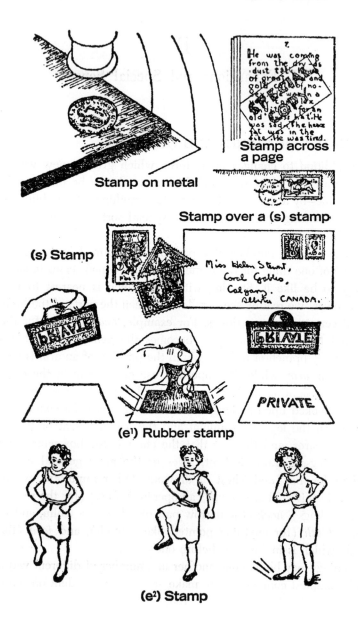

Stamp on metal

Stamp across a page

Stamp over a (s) stamp

(s) Stamp

(e¹) Rubber stamp

(e²) Stamp

ARM

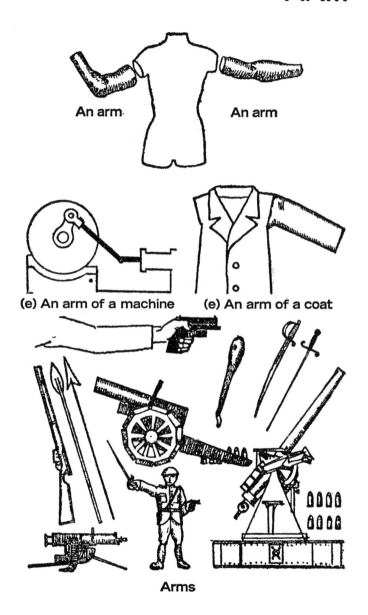

An arm. An arm

(e) An arm of a machine (e) An arm of a coat

Arms

qualities—size, form, sound, and so on. Great things are frequently said to be *mountains,* small things, *babies;* a number
of persons become an *army. Plates* of steel and glass are so
named because they are flat and smooth; thinner substances,
such as paper, are *leaves.* A hollow is a *basin,* a long, thin bit of
anything, a *stick;* we have *cakes* of soap, and even family *trees.*
In much the same way the sound of guns comes to our ears like
thunder, and some are more moved by the *music* of the river
than by the music of the band.

The comparisons based on purpose or behavior are more complex, and these make up the widest group. The bodies in space
which are named *suns* and *moons,* are in form and behavior
very like our *sun* and *moon.* A *breath* of wind is quite like the
breath we give out, and the *carriage* of a train is used for the
same purpose (the transport of persons) as a *carriage* pulled by
horses. But the chain of connection is longer between the *bed*
of a river or a *flower-bed* and the bed in which we take our
rest, between the crimes for which a man is sent to prison and
the *crimes* of the government, or of society, between an automatic machine in the station and a man who is said to be a
machine because he does the same sort of thing all the time,
or between the kick of an animal and the *kick* of an engine.

Going a step farther, 'fictions' are formed by these 'as if'
comparisons; that is to say, things which have no true existence
are talked of as though they were like what we see round us. It
would not be possible to take a walk in a *field* of interest, though
there is something in common between the range of our thoughts
and a limited space; strong though the *attraction* may be which
cakes have for a small boy, he is not physically pulled to them
as the needle is to the north; and the work of the church puts
no weight on the money *support* it is given, though the roof
of the church is certainly resting on its supports of wood or
stone.

Certain names of qualities give us another group of 'expansions' which have an even more complex connection with the qualities whose names they take, the connection here being dependent on our reactions to the things of which they are used. What is there in common between a bitter taste and a *bitter* experience, *stiff* material and *stiff* behavior, a smooth floor and *smooth* words, a bright color and a *bright* face? Most of us have as little desire for a second bitter experience as we have to take a second bitter fruit; a person who is *stiff* in behavior generally has the look of being made of stiff material; *smooth* words are as kind to our feelings as a smooth floor is to our feet; we are made as happy by a *bright* face as we are by a bright color. Only psychology is able to give a complete answer as to why these expansions come naturally in such a number of languages, but the comparisons may be of some help in pointing out the connections we have been talking about.

We now come to a group in which the connection is based on a tendency for things which have one quality to have a second. Cheap things are frequently in bad taste, so things which are in bad taste are said to be *cheap*, even though a high price may have been given for them. The less complex an act is the less hard it is to do, and so acts which give us little trouble are said to be *simple*.

Not all expansions of sense are based on the relation of like to like. For example, the name of a feeling or thing may be used for its cause, as with *amusement, comfort, pleasure, surprise*. Or the name of a thing may be used for the process by which it is produced, as in *addition, advertisement, building, discovery*. A third group of a like sort is made up by the expansion of the name of a thing to its use, such as *brush, sail, whistle*.

Sometimes a thing which is part of a greater thing gives its name to it. A number of *letters* when put down on paper, in the form of words and statements, make *a letter* which we send to someone; those who come from towns like Tokyo or New York have as much right to say that Japan or the United States is the *country* of their birth as farmers living in the country of fields and woods; and when a number of men get together to do something they become one *body* in the eyes of the law.

Then we have the use of the name of a substance for something which is commonly made of it, a *glass* for a drinking-vessel, an *iron* for a dress iron, a *tin* for a tin box or pot; or the use of the name of a thing for the substance forming it, as *horn* for the material of horns, *card* for that of which cards are made.

Last of all, there are a number of expansions based on true connections, which do not, however, go into any group. Most of these are, happily, quite simple. Examples are *gold* and *orange,* which give their name to their color, *relation* for a person in a family relation, *force* for something which has force, *library* for the books which go in a library. Not quite so simple are *Spring* and *Fall* for the times of year before and after Summer, a *note* in music for a sound in a scale, (*the*) *rest* for what is in addition. It takes a little more thought, or knowledge of the history of words, to see the connection between the point of a pin and the *point* of a story, between the plane which makes wood smooth and the *plane* of an airplane, between the frame of a picture and the *frame* of a structure, or between being certain (of something) and being of a *certain* (but unnamed) sort. If they have no parallel in his natural language, the learner will probably be wisest to get these last expansions by heart and keep his questions till a later stage.

A special sense is different from an expansion because it gives a word a narrower, not a wider, sense. Special uses are formed when a bit of a substance used for a purpose is covered by the name of the substance. In this way we get a *chalk*, a *cloth*, a *paper*. When a thing becomes important in our experience it is generally given a separate name from its group. We have, for example, *shoes* and *boots, watches* and *clocks*. But sometimes the special need is only responsible for the development of a special use. A ball, if no other details are given, is a *ball* for sport, a *business* man is one whose business is trade, a *judge* is a representative of the law, a *stamp* is a post office stamp, and *the pictures* are the motion-pictures. With some words, however, their special sense is not their most important one. The *curtain* in front of the stage in a theater is not as important as the curtains in our houses, though it is *The* Curtain; and most of us have less to do with the *gloves* of the fighter than we have with the gloves which keep our hands warm.

So far, we have given attention only to the expansions and special senses of words in their root form. But the addition of the -*er*, -*ing*, and -*ed* endings frequently makes new expansions and special senses possible. A certain number of these give us words which are necessary in the Basic system. A list may be of use. First, among the expansions, we have *clothing, crying, facing, gripping, moving, noted, painting, parting, playing, rubber, shocked, stretcher, training, united, working.* Some of the most important special uses are: *actor, duster, feeler, maker, producer, sailor, stopper, used.*

Quite a number of words have no special sense and no expansion. Some have only a special sense or only an expansion; and though no word may have more than one special sense, because if there were more we might get mixed between them, it may have any number of expansions. For example, starting with the idea of a *law* as a man-made rule, the word is then used for a general statement of fact, the system of laws in society, and the men responsible for putting these laws into effect. Again, a *line*, from being a long mark, comes to be used for the way between two points, for things placed in the form of a line (side by side like houses in a street and so on), for the rails of a train, and for a cord (for certain purposes). With a little experience, this sort of word will not give trouble; the sense is made clear by what is being talked about.

Among the names of qualities some have a different sort of expansion in their use as names of things. The simplest example of this is the use of the name of a quality with *the* before it in the sense "that which is . . ." or "those who (which) are . . ." (for example, *the beautiful, the old, the dead, the first, the last*). But a number of these names of qualities are used as names of things with somewhat more special senses. These are:

acid, chemical, chief, cold, complex, cut, dark, elastic, equal, fat, female, flat, future, good(s), hollow, living, male, material, opposite, parallel, past, present, public, quiet, right, safe, second, secret, solid, sweet, waiting, wet, wrong, young, and the color words.

QUESTIONS AND EXAMPLES

What are the special senses of *current, engine, rail, ring?* (electric current, railway engine, engine rail, finger ring). You might make a list of any other Basic words which have a special sense in your experience.

Give the sense of the expansions of the words in italics from their use in these examples:

The door has a new *coat* of paint.

Fear of change was responsible for a government of *reaction*.

Some men are not happy in the *society* of women.

The girl puts polish on her *nails*.

They have put a new *wing* onto the school-building.

Do you see how the words get a different sense? These ideas may be a help. A door is covered by paint as a man is by a coat; a government of reaction is not unlike the small boy whose reaction to being put into deep water is to have a reaction against anything new; society is made up of a number of persons together, so 'society' has a connection with the idea of being with others, or 'company'; uncut finger-nails get long and pointed like the nails used by the joiner; the side parts of a building sometimes give the idea of the outstretched wings of a bird.

If you have got the different groups of expansions into your head, you will be able to say into which group these words go: *invention, iron, stage, solid, deep, paper, net, star, bone.* Where would you put *humor* and *wash?*

In what branch of work is *industry* most valued? (Among those who make things. That is why we say *Trade and Industry*.)

What is the connection between a *serious person* and a *serious event?*

2. WORDS FOR OPERATIONS

BE

Be has no special uses which are not clear from its normal behavior as a connection between whatever is talked about and what is said about it (*he is a cook, he is good, he is across the street, he is here*). *There is* in statements like *there is enough* is listed under *there*. In this last example the idea of existence is more marked.

In addition, see *let*.

COME

Come is the opposite of *go* from the point of view of anyone at a fixed place, but it is not quite so widely used for motion generally. Things may *come* in all the directions, but whenever *come* is not clearly needed, there is a tendency to make use of *go*.

From our point of view, then, thoughts *come into the mind* in the same way in which smells *come into the house*. A statement may *come out of a book*, a new star may *come into existence*, flowers may *come from* bulbs, or a meeting may *come to an end*. Two uses frequently needed, because hearing and hoping are very common, are *it came to his ears* (that), and *this did not come up to my hopes*, which is like the water not coming up to our necks in a bath, or the sea not coming up to some fixed mark.

When the thing to which anything comes is not named, it is because everyone will be able to make the necessary addition in his mind. So the *sea comes in* (to the land), *money comes in* (to a business), the *sun comes up, flowers come up, prices come down, buttons come off,* and so on.

There are 5 special uses of *come.*

DO

Do is most frequently used with the name of some act, or of what is produced by some act. We *do a kind act, do the right thing,* or *do the cleaning;* or we may *do a picture,* and when learning music, we *do music. Do* by itself, in the sense of *do what is necessary, be enough,* is used in *I will make this do,* or *this will do (the work,* what is necessary). In addition, it may be put in the place of some other operation-word which has come earlier in the statement: *He put his hands up and the others did the same.*

There are 2 special uses of *do.*

In addition, see *good.*

GET

When anything is our property, it may have been given to us, or we may have taken it, or it may have come to us in some other way. *Get* is the most general word for all these processes, in relation to everything which may be talked about.

We *get money for a living,* and we *get a living* by making money. So we *get control, experience, help, support;* or we *get an answer, a light, a shock.*

When things have to be moved, we *get them up, down,* and so on—in all the directions of space. We *get a tree up* (by the roots), or *down* (by cutting), or *down a mountain;* we *get a bridge across* a river, or *food into* the house, or *an idea into* a person's head, or *liquid out of* a bottle, or *a secret out of* a person.

Among the commonest things which get moved about in this way are our bodies. In fact, moving our bodies is so common that we generally say nothing about it, and simply *get up* (from a seat, or from bed in the morning). So *get* may be used in the same way as *go* and *come,* as in *get to the office early.* But it is more frequently used when the way in which the act is done is not a simple form of motion like walking, or a normal one like taking a train. He *went out of* the house (by walking out), or he *went into* the country (by the morning train). But he *got out of* the house (through the window, by a trick, secretly), or he *got into* the country (by running, after some trouble, in the end).

So we *get off* a ship, or *away from* danger, or *over* a wall, or *down* a tree, or *through* a test; and by a natural expansion we may *get through work* or *get over a disease*.

In the same way *get* is used with an 'adjective' for all changes of condition caused by any act. We *get the food ready*, or *get our fingers sticky*, or *get the work started*. And we ourselves *get married, get old, get near the end,* and *get ready for the future.*

There are 5 special uses of *get*.

In addition, see *nerve* and *good*.

GIVE

As we have seen, the natural direction of the act of giving is *to,* so that the milk is *given to the cat;* and in the same way we *give an answer, a reward, a name, a look, a touch, a push,* or *a kick* to whoever gets them.[33]

We *give time* or *attention to* our work; *experience gives value to* our opinions; attention to details *gives a sense of knowledge;* knowledge of facts *gives support to* our statements. At a meeting we *give a talk;* the papers *give news* of what is said; false news *gives trouble.*

There are other ways in which it is possible for things to be given, in addition to the natural direction *to.* We may *give out* stores, *give away* money or a secret, or *give back* a book; the waiters may *give* food *round* (to everyone at table); the water

[33] Sometimes the name of what is given is put after that of the getter and the *to* dropped. This is the normal form when what is given is not material (*I gave the ball a kick*), and is common when the getter is named by a 'pronoun' (*I gave him food*). But if the thing given is itself named by a 'pronoun,' that has to come first (*Give it (to) me*).

may *give off* steam or gas, the sun *gives out* light. All these are probably clear to anyone who will *give a little thought to* the sense of the words.[34]

There are 5 special uses of *give,* of which the two last are in need of special notes.

Give up has first the sense of giving to someone *over us* in power or authority ('up'), so we *give up our tickets,* and in war the side which is overcome *gives up its arms.* From this, frequently colored by the suggestion of putting up one's hands as a sign that one is not going on with the fight, comes the use of *give up* by itself as 'let oneself be overcome,' or simply 'not keep on.' So, by a short further step, we *give up hope, smoking,* or *our rights.*

Given to has the sense of 'with a tendency to'—*given to saying foolish things, given to sport, pleasure, drink*—generally with the suggestion that the tendency is not a good one.

GO

Whenever anything is in motion, or is put in motion, or puts itself in motion, it *goes.* Machines *go smoothly,* the moon *goes round the Earth,* men *go to* and *from places.* But in the root sense *go* is the natural opposite of *come.*

As we have seen (page 134), we generally *come here* and *go there; here* being the place where we now are, and *there* being some other place to which we are going.[35] So, the natural direction of go is *away.* But because it is the most general word for all sorts of motion, it may be used freely in every sort of direction and expansion.

[34] Though *put* is the opposite of *take,* and *get* of *give, put* and *get, give* and *take* are opposite in the sense of being the opposite acts which make a complete operation. For example, we would generally say:

> *The servants put water on the plants.*
> *The plants get water.*
> *Plants give fruit (to men).*
> *Men take the fruit.*

[35] When we are going to see a friend we take *his* point of view in such a statement as "I will *come* to see you in the morning."

If, for example, you are able to *take* a dog *to a house*, or *for a swim*, or *about*, or *back*, you may say that it goes *to a house*, for *a swim*, or *about*, or *back*. If it is a well-trained dog, it *goes after* a rat—and gets it.

When a number of possible directions seem possible for an operation, all of them may be right. So we may *go into* the accounts, *over* the accounts, or *through* the accounts. We may go *against authority, against the government, against good taste, against the rules*, or *against public opinion*. In the same way, it is possible to go *to* any thing or place *to business, to work*, or even *to one's death*.

Sometimes a little common sense may be necessary to take into account the conditions in which something is said. When will the food not *go round?*—When there is not enough to go round the table. When do two things *go together?*—When they are parts of one thing, such as a machine, or have some connection in fact or thought. When do we *go on?*—When *on* is used in the sense of *forward*. And so on.

In addition, go is used with 'adjectives' like *wrong, bad, solid*, as in *everything went wrong today, the food went bad, the jelly went solid*.

There are 5 special uses of *go*.

In addition, see *without*.

HAVE

The things which we *have* in the most natural sense are the things of which we are the owners—our *houses*, our *money*, and our *land*. These things are our *property*. But there is a wider sense in which *have* is very generally used.

The things which are most like our property, and which we *have* in the wider sense, are our bodies. We *have arms* and *legs, a head, a throat, muscles, a brain, a mind*. In the same way we *have a pain, a thought, a desire, a feeling, a disease*, or *a religion*.

A man may *have a good voice, a poor digestion, a sense of humor*, or *respect for others*. We may say of a machine that it has *had no oil,* or *no attention,* or *a smash;* and of an opinion that it *has no arguments* against it; or, after getting the arguments ready, that we *have them ready.*

Very different things may in some way, or at some time, be talked about as being in this special relation to us; and it is clear that whenever we get or are given anything we then *have* it.

There are 5 special uses of *have.*

In addition, see *face, mind, name.*

KEEP

When we have anything for some time, or go on having it, we *keep* it for a certain time; and when it is our property, we simply *keep* it. We say:

"I *will keep the book for a week,*" and "May I *keep the book* which you gave me?"

We *keep things* in some position or condition which they would not be in if we let them go. If I put a ball on the end of my nose, it is hard to *keep it there,* or to *keep it balanced there.* It is sometimes equally hard to *keep a secret,* or to *keep a person from* doing wrong.

As with *get,* it may be ourselves or our bodies which we *keep* in this way, so we *keep off the grass, to the right side of the road,* or simply *on,* in the sense of keep going forward (see *on*). So we see signs in public places such as

"*Keep off* the grass."
"*Keep to* the right."

In the same way we may *keep (ourselves) ready,* or *keep young,* or *keep doing* (something), or *keep where we are,* or *keep our money safe.*

We *keep the fire burning in the fire-place,* and *we keep the glasses in the cupboard;* and everything which may be put away (sad thoughts), or together (threads, ideas), may be *kept away* or *kept together.*

There are 5 special uses of *keep.*

In addition see *eye* and *word.*

LET

The opposite of keeping something is *letting it go*. But in addition to *letting things come* and *go*, and *letting our friends put* and *take*, *make* and *have*, *seem* and *be* whatever is desired, we may *let anything in* or *out* (or in any other direction), or *let a gun (go) off*. When we *let the dog loose*, it will probably be clear that we let it be loose, free, unchained, and so on.

Let has in addition a use as an 'auxiliary' with '*us*,' to make a request or suggestion for some other person or persons to do something with the person talking:

Let us go to see her.

It is a sort of order, given to the person talking himself, as well as to others.

There are 5 special uses of *let*.

MAKE

The simplest act of *making* takes place when some new physical thing is caused to come into existence, by the *maker*. Sheep have wool on their backs; men *make cloth* with the wool.

In a more general sense, most things of which we are the cause may be said to be made by us, such as *a law, a decision, a statement*, or *a religion*. Important events are said to *make history*.

We go into business so as to *make money*. It is true that the money is not new money, but the process of making it seems to the businessman quite as much an art as that of the man who makes cloth or pictures; he puts it in the bank with a feeling of having *made an addition* to the income of his family or his country. Clearly he does not *get* it from his father, or *take* it by force from those in competition with him. And if he *makes use of* his money in the right way, it will not be hard for him to *make a great number of friends*.

If the condition of things or persons is changed by our acts, we *make them different*. We may *make a statement clear, make a talk interesting*, or *make a friend happy*. Hope seems to *make all things possible*, and a bad cold *makes one meal as uninterest-*

ing as another. Make goes in the same way with all the opera-tion-words; so that we may *make a person do* any act, or *make him come, go, put, take,* and so on.

There are 5 special uses of *make.*

In addition, see *certain, face, love, much,* and *of.*

PUT

Put is the natural word for the operation by which a bottle is caused to get into a box. But the same sort of act which *puts* the bottle into a box *puts it on the table,* or *puts it down,* or *puts it away.*

So, by an expansion, we may *put our troubles* or *doubts away,* or *out of our minds;* or we may *put a person down,* in the sense that we get ourselves into a position where we may be said to be on top and he will give us no more trouble. Or we may *put an idea before* a person, in much the same way as we *put food be-fore* him. We may *put a question* to a friend, and he may *put his answer into words.*

If things are on record, it is because someone has *put them on record;* and we may be *put in the wrong,* or *put out of doubt,* in the same way in which we are put, physically, *in (a) prison* or *out of a room;* but because the more important things are generally put before others on a list, one thing is said to be *put before another* when it is given greater value. There is no limit to the number of things which may be talked of as if they were places or spaces, and for all such purposes *putting* is the natural operation.

There are 5 special uses of *put.*

In addition, see *mind, off, stop,* and *up.*

SAY

When we put an idea into words, we *say the words;* but even if our words are not clear we *say something.* We *say things,* much as we (are *said to*) *do* them or *make* them, and when we make any statement we may *say it* in a number of different ways (*to ourselves, through the nose,* and so on). We may (make it

clear or) *say that we have a cold* in the same way as we may *say*
(*do* and so on) *what is needed.* These different uses are a
natural outcome of the account of *to* (pages 208–09), *what* (page
163), and *that* (page 160).

SEE

Whenever we make use of our eyes we *see* things: but by an
expansion common in most languages we *see the point* of a statement when we get its sense.

We *see through glass* or through a keyhole, and when anyone
makes a false statement or comes to us with some trick, we may
say that we *see through him,* or *see through the trick.* But it is
our hope and belief that it will give no trouble even to the
oldest reader.

SEEM

Seem is generally used with *to be* or one of the other operation-words: *He seems to have* (*do, say, see,* and so on) *nothing.*
He seems to be angry. To be, however, may sometimes be
dropped and *seem* used by itself in the sense of 'seem to be'; *He
seems angry.* But this is never possible with the name of a
quality ending in *-ing: He seems to be waiting* (*living, hanging*).
When there is any doubt, it is never wrong to put in *to be.*
For *it seems to me,* see page 173.

SEND

Things may be *sent* or made to go in all directions in which
they *go.* So we *send a parcel by post,* and at the other end of its
journey someone may *send it forward.* In sport, a ball is *sent
through the air,* or *across the field,* and so on.

TAKE

The word *take* will give us a good idea of the step from the
natural use to the expansions of sense which are possible for the
operation-words.

We *take* what is *put* for us (generally with our hands), and
when we have *taken* it we ourselves may *have* it, *put* it, or *give*

it. When, for example, there are different drinks which have been put out, the question is *What will you take?* A great number of things which are put for us are given; so *take* will go with most of the things which are said to be given to us, such as *food, a name, an order, a chance, a cold, a position, a suggestion.* The chief thing which almost everyone is ready to take, if it is given freely or in payment, is *money.* In the same way (when it is offered to us, or is not in use) we may *take a seat,* by seating ourselves.

In exchange for money we get a number of things of which we become the owners, and of which, for this reason, we *have* or *take control.* So we *take a house,* or *a box* at the theater, or *a ticket.*

Whenever we *take something* into our body we simply *take* it; so we *take a drink,* or *a breath,* or even *a smell. We make an attempt, a decision, a sign, a statement,* or *a protest,* because by such acts something new seems to come into existence; but we *take a look* (*at*), *take an interest* or *pleasure* (*in*), because these things are looked on as waiting for us to take them. Another use of the same sort is *taking a part* (in a play). If we *make trouble,* it is frequently because we do not *take trouble* or *take care;* and the trouble we *make* is there for others to see and put right.

When we *go for a walk* we are sometimes said to *take a walk* (*a run, a journey*); and as in walking we *take a step* (forward) to get somewhere, so we *take steps to* get something, or to get it done.

When we come to the directions in which things may be taken there is little chance of serious error. If you have got over any doubts about the division between *take* and *put* by making the motions yourself, it will be clear to you that you *take hope from a person.* You do not *put hope from him,* because you do not *put coal from a box.* In the same way in which a cart *takes away dust,* sleep may *take away pain.* We *take off our clothing, take forward designs,* and *take back statements* when facts make it clear that they are false. Amusements *take our minds off work.*

In the same way as we *take in food* (into the mouth), we may be said to *take in details*. As we *take work* which is offered to us in the sense of making it our business to do it, so by a little stretch we *take care of* something when we make the care of it our business; and as we *take down a book* (from the shelf), so, by a not unnatural expansion, we *take down words* (from the mouth, on a writing-machine). We *take a part* of anything (*away*) *from it*, and we *take* a small number *from a greater one*, as when we *take* 3 *from* 5.

There are 5 special uses of *take*.

In addition, see *hand, note, part, place, root,* and *side*.

3. NAMES OF DIRECTIONS

ABOUT

When we are among things, the things are *about us;* but *round* now generally takes the place of *about* in statements like *he had a number of friends round him*. We still say *there was no one about when the crime took place;* but *about* is more commonly used in expansions such as *a book* (*talk, discussion*) *about religion; he is clear* (*right*) *about the facts; he has no doubts about it*, or he is *making trouble about it*.

There is 1 special use of *about*.

In addition, see *come*.

ACROSS

As we may *go across the road,* so one line may *be across* another.

See *come* and *put*.

AFTER

Though *after* still sometimes has the sense *at the back of*, in the same way as *before* may be used for *in front of*, it is generally used as the opposite of *before* in statements about time. So something may be a *long time after an event*, or *after my coming* or *after I came*.

There are 2 special uses of *after*.

AGAINST

From the simple use of *against* in talking of a spade *against a wall* we get *sailing against wind* and *working against change.*

AMONG

A thing which is in a group with others is said to be *among them;* so I am *among my friends,* or a fork is *among the knives.* In the same way, a man may be *among his books;* and *among other things* he may do *work among the poor* and make a *distribution of food among his boys.* If the distribution is unequal, there may be a *fight among them.*

AT

At is used for marking position in space or time. We may make a start or a stop *at any point* on a line, or *at the end.* In the same way we may be *at Tokyo,* on our journey, or get to the hotel *at four* on a certain day. If the door is the point at *which* we come in, we may be said to come in *at the door* (though generally we come in *through* doors and windows).

A man may be *at the top of* a tree, or *at the head of* the government, or *at a meeting.* The water may be *at a high level,* goods may be *at a low price,* or *at any price* (levels and prices being taken as measured on a scale). We may take our meals *at any time,* or *at regular hours.* Points of time are marked by an event; so we may go away *at the request of* a friend, and a gun may go off *at a touch.*

There are 10 special uses of *at.*

In addition, see *all, angle, hand, loss, present, rate, school.*

BEFORE

Though *before* is generally used of time, it still has its earlier sense of 'in front of' when we *come before* a judge, or *put the facts before* him. On the line of time, we come across some things *before others;* one event is *before another event,* or *I will see him before coming.* And from this it is a natural step to the use of *before* as a joining word between statements—I will see him *before I come* (page 161). We generally do first the things which are most pleasing to us; and so the sense is clear if I say, "I will go to prison *before* I will let my friend down."

BETWEEN

Whenever only two things are in question, *between* is used in the place of *among*. They have *a space* or *a distance* or *a material between* them; *time* comes *between events*, and there is music *between the acts* of a play. There is a *connection between*, or a *relation between*, any two things *between which* we make a *comparison*. When one or other of two parcels is offered to us, we have to make a *selection between them*; when two boys are given one cake, they have to make a *division of it between them*, and the end will probably be a *fight between them*.

BY

When a tree is near a river it is *by it*. In the same way, I may take a walk *by the river*, and if I go *by* something on my way somewhere, I generally go past it, so the two senses are united in *the train went by* (me). From *I go to Leeds by London*, it is a simple expansion to say that *I go to town by a different way* [36] or *do a thing by daylight*. One further step gives us *it was done by a trick* or *he did it by a new process*, which makes *by* a pointer to the 'way' in which any effect is produced, and so to the cause, doer, or maker of anything. So we may have *a picture by Rubens* which is *covered by our insurance*, or be *troubled by ants, ruled by the authorities*, or given *punishment by death*.

There are 10 special uses of *by*.

In addition, see *side, surprise,* and *word*.

DOWN

Even those who are clear that the sun *comes up* in the morning and *goes down* at night, and that they *go up* to the top of a mountain or *go down* to a lower level, are sometimes troubled by the fact that they *go down a street*. Why *down?*

[36] But we say that we *go by steamer* (*train, automobile*), and *by land* (*sea*).

If the end of the street is at a lower level the answer is simple, and if the numbers of the houses go up from 1 to 100, that is another reason for going up or down. But if the street is flat, and the houses are not numbered, it is only a question of feeling, so this gives us one of the 2 special uses.

In addition, see *let*.

FOR

When we have come to an end of all the names of directions in which we do things with our arms and legs, and all the expansions for the directions of time and of thought, we are still at a loss for ways of talking freely about purpose.

Our purpose is the direction in which our desires and thoughts go. When a friend is late we may be kept *waiting for him*. When food is in our minds, we have a *desire for food,* we have a *need for food,* we go *for food* (= to get food).

So there are *places for food, rooms for dancing* or *used for dancing.* We send in our names *for a position,* put up our goods *for offers,* go into business *for profit;* we are given food *for thought,* when we do not get enough *for our needs* from what we do *for a living;* and we have *time for it* when there is no *work for us to do.* When we give support to a person or a suggestion we are *for them.*

It is a very short step from the idea of purpose to the idea of exchange, as is clear from the fact that what we do *for a living* or *for money* is done *in exchange for a living* or *for money.* We do not get money *for nothing;* we make *payment for goods.* If we are acting *for another* (for his purposes), we get *credit for our care and trouble,* or *punishment for being foolish.* We give *a check for a certain amount,* because that amount will be given *in exchange for it.*

Some statements about purpose are made by using the word *to* with an operation-word (pages 208–09); *for* gives us another way of getting round most of these:

I am ready *for food* (= *to have* food).

This is timed *for tomorrow* (= *to take place* tomorrow).

There is no need *for noise* (= *to make a* noise).

There are 10 special uses of *for*.

In addition, see *as, bad, exchange, eye, name, take.*

FROM

The natural opposite of *to* is *from*. We go *from* a place, in the same way as we go *to* it, and the use of *away*, as in *he was going away from the meeting*, makes the sense of direction stronger. So we *put food* (*away*) *from us*. If we *get away from the point*, we make an attempt to get back to it; and if we have *got away from danger*, we are *free* or *safe from it*.

When we take anything out of a box we equally *take it from the box;* so we are said to get *profit from a business*, or *goods from a store*. In much the same way, it is clear *from the history of language* that one word frequently *comes from* another.

The chief expansion of *from* is as a general word for 'starting from,' and so (frequently) 'caused by.' We may say that *from this time forward* (or *on*) the weather was bad, or that a mark on our skin was *from a blow*.

There are 2 special uses of *from*.

IN

One of the words with the greatest number of uses is *in*. From the physical use (*in the pot, in the water, in the room, in the road, in the field, in space*) there is a ready expansion to whatever is talked about as if it was a space (*in the year, in flames*), or a solid or liquid thing (*in the light, in trouble*), or a vessel (*in the mind*). So we get: Be *in business, in comfort, in danger, in doubt, in error, in fear, in need;* or (of spaces of time), *in the week, in* (*the*) *summer, in* (*the*) *winter*, or again (of the mind), *in thought*.

So a person may be *in a hat* (that is to say, his head is in a hat), or *in shoes*, or *in chains*, or *all in black*. He may be foolish *in company*, experienced *in* crime, or *in the dark* about what the government is doing.

Sometimes an 'adjective' is necessary to give the right sense:
in bad condition, in some degree, in my opinion, in my hearing,
or *in such a form (that)*—which is not far from *in the hope
(that).*

A little harder are *in so far (as), in relation (to), in comparison (with), in connection (with)*; but no language, old or new,
has any better way of getting these complex ideas across, so that
in takes a very high place among words, because of the great
amount of work which it is able to do for us.[37]

There are 10 special uses of *in.*

In addition, see *addition, belief, bit, common, detail, end,
fertile, front, hand, interest, knot, memory, mind, order, part,
question, request, step, store, support, take, taste, time, touch,
turn, view, voice, way.*

OF

The expansion of *of* from *a bit of the cake,* through *a day of
the month,* to *a sort of box,* is so very natural that no account
of it is necessary. Let us put down some other simple uses *of this
sort: a group of friends, a store of apples, a bucket of great size;*
or again, *the property of the owner, a copy of an old picture,
the invention of radio; a representative of the government* and
memories of the past. It would probably be *a waste of time* to
give any more *examples of* such natural *developments of 'of.'*
Everyone has the *power of making* more with *any of* the words
in the list.

There are 10 special uses of *of.*

In addition, see *front, get, good, make, memory, mind, note,
support, tired, touch, view, way, word.*

OFF

There is very little to say about *off* which would not be clear
to anyone who has *taken the skin off an apple.* There is no doubt,
for example, about the sense of *he put me off doing it* or *what*

[37] There is a small number of fixed uses with common things—*in bed, in
church, in prison, in town.*

you say is off the point. A bit of wood *off a table* may be *cut off* or *broken off*, the light may be *turned off*, and one part of a room may be *curtained off*.

There are 2 special uses of *off*.

In addition, see *go, let, put*.

ON

Most of the uses of *on* are very near to the physical sense. *On the top, on one side, on the same side, on the right side,* are all quite natural. We may be *on our feet, on land,* or *on the water;* a coat may be *on a hook,* a name *on a list.* Not far from these are the words *on one's lips,* the trouble *on one's mind,* the song *on one's brain,* rules and knowledge *based on facts,* or the goods *on the market.*

Music may be *on the piano* or all *on one note* and our hair may be *on end.* An event may take place at 5 *on a certain day,* in a certain week, month, or year.[38] *Living on one's income* is specially hard when there is a *tax on goods.*

There are 10 special uses of *on,* the last of which is the use with *go* and *keep* with different operation-words or *with,* as in *go on doing, keep on going, go on with* the work, and so on.

In addition, see *act, approval, attack, condition credit, de-pendent, design, effect, eye, foot, get, hand, hard, impulse, keep, look, nerve, put, record, side, so, watch, work.*

OUT

Though *out* as a simple direction is the opposite of *in,* it is not possible to say: "I am *in* the room and you are 'out it.'" The opposite of *being in* (or *coming into*) a place is *being* (or *going*) *out of* it. So we get *out of* as the opposite of all those uses of *in* with physical things or places, among which we may put, for this purpose, *mind;* and with these are to be grouped *out of control, out of danger, out of hearing, out of touch, out of work.*

---

[38] See pp. 202 and 205. The key to the right direction-word in connection with time is "*at* a point, *on* a line, *in* a circle." (But take note of the special use *at night,* see p. 216.)

(See *of,* page 217.) A small number of fixed uses like *he went
out* (of the house or room), or *the light (fire) went out* (of existence) will be clear enough in the statements in which we
come across them.

There are 2 special uses of *out.*

In addition, see *get, go, let, make.*

OVER

As the natural opposite of *under, over* is equally simple and
limited in all its chief uses. Some things which are *over* others
may be much farther away from them than the cover which is
over the meat, or the fat which is *over* (or *on*) *the bone.* A
window may be *over a door,* or an airplane may be *over a house,*
so that *over* becomes a more general way of saying 'on top of'
or 'higher than'; and by a simple further development we go
over a wall and *over the side* of a ship, or a road goes *over a
mountain.*

A very common expansion gives us *authority* or *power over
a person;* and a number on any scale which is more than another may be said to be *over it,* so that a person 22 years old is
over 21.

There are 3 special uses of *over.*

THROUGH

When we go *through the air,* or take breath *through the nose,*
our going and our breathing are made possible by the air and
our noses—much as the hole *through which* the rat goes is the
cause of its getting away. So *through* comes to have the expansion, *as an effect of:* he got his position *through* you, or he made
a friend *through being ill.*

TO

The chief expansions of the simple use of *to* give very little
trouble,[39] and are common in most languages. There are great

---

[39] There is a small number of fixed uses of *to* with common things—we go
to bed (*church, prison, school, sea, work*).

numbers of words which give us a feeling that *to* is needed after them. *Attention to details* is as natural as *an addition to the family,* an *answer to a question,* or a *right to property.*

Another very frequent use of *to* is for the idea of *in relation to* (see page 206). For example, we generally say *this line is parallel to that line* (though *with* would be equally possible here), or this amount is *equal to* that amount. We say this is *joined to* that, *near to* that, *special to* that, or *a danger to* that; again, a man may be *in debt to,* or *married to,* a woman.

The *behavior of a girl to her lover* may be *a blow to his self-respect,* and if she was *kind to* him at the start *a wound to his feelings* will be very much harder for him to put up with.

The connection between *to* and *for* in *a desire for food* has been made clear under *for.*

There are 10 special uses of *to,* the last of which—*able to (do)* —is in need of a separate note. It will probably become clear if we say first that *to* is used before an operation-word whenever there is a desire or purpose to do or have something:

He is ready to go.

He is making an attempt to get away.

He has a desire to go up the mountain.

I sent (took, got) him to have some food.[40]

Generally, whenever 'for the purpose of' might be used, *to* may be put before the operation-word:

He has enough trouble to make him angry.

He has authority to get the baby back.

This is a place to be in for a long time.

It is time to go.

In the same way we say *he is able enough to do this;* or more frequently and simply, *he is able to do this.* And from such uses it is not hard to get the expansion *he is said* (an 'adjective') *to be doing this,* or *he is said to be able to do this.* For *he has to do this,* see *have* (page 214).

---

[40] But *I let (made, saw) him go,* as is made clear in the account of *let.*

To is the only name of a direction which has this sort of special use with the simple form of the 'verb,' which is named the 'infinitive' in books on language.

In addition, see *about, addition, angle, as, bit, come, credit, face, from, get, give, go, have, in, let, make, mind, of, put, scale, seed, so, stop, that, way, word.*

UNDER

The idea of being *under* something is very simple and limited. In all languages its possible expansions are almost all quite straightforward. The position of authority or control is clearly the same as that of the dog which is on top in a fight; and so we are *under a ruler,* or *under his power,* or *authority.* In the same way we are *under the control* or *direction* of a manager, or *do our work under him.*

The sense of *going under,* or *being under a cloud,* or *under a person's thumb* is not hard to make out, even when seen for the first time; but we might equally well make use of some other comparison such as *being overcome by hard conditions,* or *with public opinion against one,* or *under a person's power.*

There are 2 special uses of *under.*

UP

Most of the uses of *up* do not get far away from the physical direction which is given by going from some point or place to another at a higher level. Water has to come down a slope of some sort to get to the sea, so we go *up a river* as we go *up a mountain.* And in the same way we go *up and down a scale* or *a list.*

If we take a bit of paper or cloth, or the collar of a coat, and give the edge a turn, it will be *turned up* or *down.* By going one step farther materials or bedding may be *rolled up.*

Up is very freely used where it is not truly necessary, in examples like *building up a business.* So it frequently has the sense of '*up to* the top,' or '*up to* some complete form,' or '*up to* some natural limit.'

There are 10 special uses of *up*.

In addition, see *get, give, keep, make, put, take*.

WITH

From the use of *with* = 'together with,' it is a very natural step in most languages to the sense of 'having' or 'making use of.' What we have is *with* us. So we say a *man with a hat,* or *with wide interests;* sand may get *mixed with* salt; a *story with a purpose* may be about *a person with authority*.

In all forms of agreement, comparison, connection, and competition, the fact that the two sides are said to be *in* agreement (comparison, connection, or competition), and so, in a sense, are together in that agreement, makes *with* the right joining word—even when they are having a *fight (an argument, a discussion, angry words) with* one another. So we may be *in business with* anyone; or when we make use of books we may be *rough with* them, because the idea of having them (in the hands) and doing something with them is stronger than the sense of *to* which would make good sense (as in *kind to*); but in *quick with his fingers* (= in the use of his fingers) there is no feeling of *to,* so *with* is the most natural connection.

In the same way we give a person a *blow with the hand,* or *with a stick,* because hands and sticks are what we have *with* us and make use of. But frequently *by* is equally possible, as in *a table covered by (with) a cloth*.

There are 2 special uses of *with*.

In addition, see *get, go, have, keep, step, touch, up, young*.

B

III. Special Uses

1. THE 250 FIXED WORD-GROUPS

We now come to certain uses of the Basic words which are not expansions of the sense but changes of sense (sometimes not clear from the senses of the separate words) which come about when certain words are used together, as a group. They are named 'idioms' in the language books, and have three chief causes:

1. Attraction to the uses of other words—when we *come to a stop* (like *a place*).

2. Loss of some of the words normally used—as when fear of change *keeps a government in* (the same place, that is, keeps it in power).

3. Some special picture formed in the past, but no longer clear to everyone—as in the example of *put up with.*

There is no need to take much trouble about these special uses if your interest in Basic is limited to business letters, or to hearing radio talks; or if you will be talking chiefly to persons without a knowledge of normal English. But it is a good thing to have them all together, so that the learner may see the complete story in front of him.

The best way is to get used to them by experience—by reading books in Basic and making a note of uses which do not seem natural to you from a knowledge of the words by themselves.

Then you may go quickly on to the list of Fixed Uses which

are necessary; there you are given a selection of 'idioms' which it would not be possible to go far without.[41]

The only words for which more than a very short note is needed are in two groups:

1. *Come* and *go*, *put* and *take*, *give* and *get*, together with *let* and *keep*, *have* and *make*. (All with 5 examples.)

2. *At*, *by*, *in*, *on*, *to*, and *up*, together with *for* and *of*. (All with 10 examples.)

This gives us 130 examples, and there are 20 other special uses with words in this group. In addition, there are 100 special uses with the rest of the Basic list—making 250 in all. In fact, a quick writer would make a copy of the complete list (giving *every* use in Basic English which is not quite regular) in less time than it takes to get through a normal meal.

These fixed uses are unnecessary for anyone who is going through the Basic system for the first time; but they are listed here, so that at the end there is nothing more to come. The learner may then go back to them when the working of the rest of the system is clear. Most of them are important chiefly for purposes of ornament or smooth writing, but there are some by which very common needs are covered without going a long way round. These are specially listed on pages 231–32, where the learner is given a Basic Selection. It may be noted that for memory purposes all the 250 special uses are given in the form of stories, and the reader may be interested in working out the connections.

Acts (10 groups of 5)

COME

    1. The governments will *come to an agreement* about the taxes.

    2. The train will *come to a stop* at the station.

[41] In *The Basic Words* are listed another 250 special uses (marked, **) which are of great help in writing high-level Basic, but are not necessary for the learner.

    3. Strange facts will *come to light.*

    4. A newspaper man *came across* some private papers under
       the seat.

    5. How did this *come about?*

GET

    1. He had no money because he *got a book out* last year.

    2. His friends said they would *get a play up* for him.

    3. But he did not *get on* (*well*) *with* the chief actor.

    4. He *got* (himself) *into bad ways* through drink.

    5. He *got* (himself) *out of doing* any more work.

GIVE

    1. Mothers *give birth to* babies.

    2. She *gave her word* to the family that she would take care
      of the little boy.

    3. The wall *gave back* the sound (light).

    4. They did not *give up* hope till the news was certain.

    5. Newspapers are *given to* printing false statements.

GO

    1. The color of the walls did not *go with* my dress.

    2. An old man in the front had *gone to sleep.*

    3. Something (the gun) *went off* with a loud noise.

    4. The light *went out* in the middle of my talk.

    5. I am *going to make* a protest to the gas company.

HAVE

    1. I *had a talk with* him this morning.

    2. His arguments *had* no *effect on* me.

    3. Our thoughts *have* no *existence* outside our heads.

    4. They *have to go* into such questions because of their in-
      terest in history.

    5. I will *have* nothing *to do with* foolish discussions.

KEEP

    1. She *keeps house* for her father.

    2. He has only her to *keep him company.*

    3. We *kept* the manager *on* till everyone was out of work.

4. He *kept* his interest *up* all through the winter.

5. I will *keep up with* the changes in public opinion, and take his place.

LET

1. The teacher *let* the boy *off* (punishment) when she saw how unhappy he was.

2. She will not *let* us *into* her *secret*.

3. She had been *letting out* the skirt because it was getting tight.

4. A good man would not *let* his friends *down*.

5. Please *let* me (the machine) *be*.

MAKE

1. He *made up* a story which was not quite true.

2. It was not hard to *make out the sense* of his words.

3. He had *made* the material *into* trousers in error.

4. She *made much* (*little*) *of* it.

5. It is unkind to *make sport of* persons dressed in a strange way.

PUT

1. A common way of *putting* an idea (suggestion) *across* is by advertisement.

2. He *put up* an argument (fight) when the trainer said the horse had been poisoned.

3. Someone had made an attempt to *put* it *to death*.

4. They *put* the discussion (talk, meeting) *off* till the morning.

5. The chances are generally against you if you *put* money *on* a horse (event).

TAKE

1. He *took up* the question (painting) with great interest.

2. He did not *take into account* all the details.

3. He said he would *take a picture*, but he had no camera.

4. We *took* him *for* an expert.

5. The news *took* us *by surprise*.

Directions (8 groups of 10)

AT

1. The men are *at war* (*peace, work, play, rest*).
2. They were happy *at first* (*last*).
3. They were *at* a great *distance* from their country.
4. They did not go to bed *at night.*
5. *At times* they were covered with small insects.
6. There was some *surprise at* their desire to get back.
7. There were *at least* (*most*) 1,000 persons at the station.
8. They had the interests of their country *at heart.*
9. They were *bad at* (*good at, quick at, slow at, expert at, working at*) languages.
10. They are *looking at* (*pointing at, laughing at, firing at*) the camera-men.

BY

1. Robinson Crusoe was on an island *by himself.*
2. He had to make everything for himself *by hand.*
3. I was working there *by night* (*day*).
4. I had come across some coal on the island *by chance.*
5. *By the way,* have you ever been down a coal mine?
6. No smoking, *by order.*
7. A young miner got the Basic words *by heart* in less than a week.
8. He got the word order into his head *by* slow *degrees.*
9. *Little by little* (*bit by bit, day by day*), he made himself expert at the special uses.
10. He is coming here at 4, *by this clock.*

FOR

1. He has no *regret for* his acts.
2. *For example,* he was cruel to his sister.
3. He was *responsible for* her death.
4. He went away *for* this *reason.*
5. He kept away *for fear of* the law.
6. He will go to prison *for the first* (*second, last*) *time.*

7. He will be there *for* a long time.
8. There is no *cause for* protest.
9. Every judge would say the same thing, *word for word*.
10. Men are like animals, *but for* their brains.

IN

1. The Judge said that the prisoner was *in the right* (*wrong*).
2. He took a tin tray *in exchange for* his picture.
3. The picture itself was done *in metal* (*wood*).
4. The head is turned *in a strange way* (*direction*).
5. Strange things are done *in the name of* art.
6. He is *in love with* a woman who is not in love with him.
7. The machine was *in motion* when he got out.
8. It will be *in operation* (*use*) again today.
9. He gave the facts *in answer to* a question.
10. Basic is a very good system *in fact* (and *in theory*).

OF

1. Do not go *out of* the room so quickly.
2. You were *talking of* writing a book of general knowledge.
3. I am *full of* good ideas.
4. These facts may be *of use* (*value, help, interest*) *to* you.
5. Clothing *made of* wool is best in a cold country.
6. The Englishman's *love* (*care, control*) *of* animals (the boy's *grip of* the facts) is surprising.
7. A man *of 50* (*years*) is not old.
8. In the future, we may be *conscious of* events at a distance.
9. Basic is the best system *because of* its simple rules.
10. That was very *kind of* you; and your last point is a good example of advertisement.

ON

1. The *light* (*water, gas, play*) is now *on*.
2. The pictures are *on view*.
3. I came *on purpose* to see them.
4. This design is *on a great* (*small*) *scale*.
5. I have a friend *on the committee*.

6. He is an *expert on* old prints.
7. He has gone *on a journey* to the East to get some more.
8. The *profit* (*loss, interest*) *on* his business is chiefly through insurance.
9. Look! The house is *on fire!*
10. Let us *go* (*keep*) *on putting* water on it. We will *go on with* the fight till the firemen come.

TO
1. That music is not *to my taste*.
2. They are *dancing to* bad *music*.
3. The question is not *open to argument*.
4. The machines are *face to face* (*back to back*).
5. Your answer is not *to the point*.
6. *To my surprise* and *regret*, it is still going on.
7. Bad music is *dear to* the public.
8. The chances are 10 *to* 1 that it will be better in the future.
9. Most of us are slow to get *used to* new forms of art.
10. I was *able to* make this last use clear earlier.

UP
1. At school, *dressing up* was one of my greatest pleasures.
2. Now, it is hard even to get my overcoat *buttoned up*.
3. In a cold country, all one's force is *used up* in the attempt to keep warm.
4. Bread has to be *cut* (*broken*) *up* for the birds.
5. Even if your house is *shut* (*locked*) *up*, the rain may get in.
6. Yesterday there was ice in the bath and the drains got *stopped up*.
7. Get the pipes *fixed up* again before the spring!
8. The wet places on the walls will have to be *touched up*.
9. There is no need to get *worked up* about it.
10. In England, they have to *put up with* small troubles of this sort.

In addition to the special uses so far listed, there are 10 more names of operations and directions with separate special uses, making another 20. These are:

1. The bricks will DO *damage* to the window.
2. They *did well* (*badly*) because they had the support of the authorities.
3. The glass is ABOUT *to* be broken.
4. It was a foolish act, but AFTER *all* they were young.
5. A girl was *looking after* the store.
6. He took a walk DOWN (*up*) *the street* (*road*).
7. If you are good at fighting, that is no reason for *looking down on* lovers of peace.
8. His ideas took form FROM *day to day* (*year to year* and so on).
9. It was clear from their strange behavior that they were almost OFF *their heads.*
10. His experience in the war did not put him *off his balance.*
11. He said *straight* OUT what he had in mind.
12. All the details of the Basic system have been *worked out.*
13. The teacher is reading the list *out loud.*
14. When the page is *turned* OVER, you will see another list.
15. You will get the words into your head if you *say them over* frequently.
16. Being UNDER *fire* makes learning harder.
17. The idea was *under discussion* for a long time.
18. A simple system has *weight* WITH the education experts.
19. There is no need to be *angry* (*pleased*) *with* slow learners.
20. I *went without* sweets for a month to get the money for this book.

We are now at the end of the 150 special uses of names of acts and directions. Here are 100 more with some of the other words in the Basic list, making the 250 complete.

First come those with the other words in the group headed 'Operations':

1. To some it seems AS *if* there is very little hope of change in language teaching.
2. *As to* (*for*) that view, it is natural but probably false.

3. Such questions are not *at* ALL interesting to the normal man.

4, 5. He and his friends are happy *all day* (*night*) talking to *one* ANOTHER about business.

6, 7. THAT *is to say,* they are better at making money than at forming theories; though HERE *and there* a man with money may have respect for someone who has ideas about language.

8, 9. But, talking generally, it is *as true as* (*truer than*) EVER that THERE *is* little in common between them.

10, 11. So *as to* get language taken seriously by governments, schools, *and so on,* some new system is necessary.

12, 13. So *that* Basic may be the VERY thing for that purpose *as* WELL (*as* for those we have been talking about).

With General Names

14. The hole was produced by an acid ACTING *on* the material.

15, 16. *In* ADDITION *to this,* the color was taken out, which was sad because the coat had been sent *on* APPROVAL.

17, 18. The story is that a young woman made *an* ATTACK *on her lover* with acid *in the* BELIEF *that* he had been false to her.

19, 20, 21. The police had no belief *in his story* till they saw that his coat was *in* BITS (had come *to bits*).

22. The woman was *out of* BREATH when they came up to her.

23. She was let go *on* CONDITION *that* she got married to the man.

24. He got a new coat *on* CREDIT.

25, 26. But it was *to his credit* that he had no DESIGNS *on her money.*

27, 28, 29, 30, 31. This story is given *in* DETAIL because it is an example of how, *in the* END, even *in* FRONT *of* one's lover, *acting on* IMPULSE is sometimes not *in one's* INTERESTS.

32. If you are *at a* LOSS for something to do, why not go to Chicago?

33. In a short time you will probably be *making* LOVE *to* the daughter of a gunman.

34, 35.   Then I will be able to put up a stone *in* MEMORY *of* you, with a beautiful design I *have in* MIND.

36.   This *puts me in mind of* another friend who came to a bad end.

37.   I *have a (good) mind to* make a book about him.

38.   He *had a* NAME *for* keeping on the right side of the law.

39, 40.   Some businessmen *took* NOTE *of* this fact when their accounts were not quite *in* ORDER.

41, 42.   *In* PART because he was their friend, and *in part* because he saw a chance of profit, he said he would *take part in* the organization of their company.

43, 44, 45.   A meeting *took* PLACE at which the public took a different POINT *of* view from the controlling body about the accounts *in* QUESTION.

46, 47.   What story the other men gave is not *on* RECORD, but *at any* RATE they went free and my friend was sent to prison.

48.   While in prison he made little ships which were much *in* REQUEST.

49, 50, 51.   One day he was walking *in* STEP *with* the other prisoners, SIDE *by side* with one of his new friends, when one of the prison watchmen *took him on one side.*

52, 53, 54.   "I am going to *put a* STOP *to* this talking," he said, and *in* SUPPORT *of* this statement he gave him a blow across the face, which was not *in (very) good* TASTE.

55, 56, 57.   *In* TIME, the wound became serious, and he was *out of (not in)* TOUCH *with* a good medical man, so it was not long before he, *in his* TURN, was taken dead from the prison.

58, 59, 60, 61.   *In* VIEW *of* these sad experiences, if you have *a* VOICE in the business of your friends, don't let them *give* WAY to bad impulses, or they may get *in the way of* the law.

62, 63, 64.   I had this story *by* WORD *of* mouth from my friend at his death, and *to keep my word* to him, I am now WORKING *on* a book about crime and punishment.

With Pictured Names

65, 66.   They put their boxes in the train *at right* ANGLES *to* one another, and sent them 'CARRIAGE *forward.*'

67.   The man on the train said he would *keep an* EYE *on* them.

68, 69, 70.   The camera-man *had an eye for* form, but he *hadn't the* FACE *to* say that she was *making a face.*

71, 72, 73,   He went to the mountains *on* FOOT, *on the one* HAND;
74.   she, *on the other hand,* went by train, though her knowledge of the country was *at first (second) hand.*

75, 76.   When they got there, she *took in hand* the cooking operations, and he went to get some fish, but his fishing-line was *in* KNOTS.

77.   After a time this *got on his* NERVES.

78, 79.   Resting in the shade of a tree which had *taken* ROOT near the river, he let his memory go back to his days *at* SCHOOL.

80, 81, 82.   These flowers will have *gone to* SEED before I get up from here, he said to himself, unconscious of what might be *in* STORE *for* him from the woman *on* WATCH by the fire.

With Names of Qualities—general

83, 84.   *Make* CERTAIN before you get married that you have something *in* COMMON.

85, 86.   Everything is DEPENDENT *on* his comfort, so be FERTILE *in* bright ideas.

87, 88.   *Do your* BEST *to get the better of* bad humor.

89.   Do not let your GOOD-*mornings (days, nights)* become automatic.

90, 91.   It is HARD *on* a man if he *no* LONGER has any peace because he is married.

92, 93, 94.   The days may *go* PAST quickly enough *at* PRESENT, and everything may seem *all* RIGHT.

95, 96.   Though two persons do not get TIRED *of* one another STRAIGHT *away*, they may later.

97, 98.   But it is clear from watching the happy faces of animals *with* YOUNG that my worst fears may not *come* TRUE.

With Names of Qualities—opposites

99, 100.   Is this a record? I am 100 *years* OLD and have not ever been *the* WORSE *for* drink.

C

A Key Selection

1. SOME COMMON NEEDS

a. Simple Acts To be expert in Basic it is necessary to have a knowledge of the best ways of covering names of common acts and things which do not have a place among the 850. A number of ready-made answers to the questions with which the Basic writer is most frequently faced have been produced after long experience with the system, and much time will be wasted if you do not make use of them.

Naturally it is with words representative of acts that we have most trouble, because we have to get round the 'verb' form. Let us first take some of the simple physical acts and see what Basic is able to do with them. When you 'speak' to a person, you *say something* to him; but if you are 'speaking' at a meeting, you *give a talk*, or you may *make a statement on*, for example, a political question. If you are able to 'speak' a language, it would be said in Basic that you *have a knowledge* of it. 'Telling' a story is *giving* it. In the same way, we may *give an account*, or *the news*. But to 'tell' a person how to do something is to *give directions*, and for 'as I was telling you' we say *as I was saying*. When the voice is used in 'singing,' we *give a song*. The music *comes to the ears* of those who 'hear' (*are hearing*) it, and if they are 'listening' they *give it their attention*. If, however, someone only 'heard' of it later, he would *have news of* it. The newspaper man who 'wrote' about it *put* his account *into writing* or *down on paper*, and those who 'read' of it, *saw* it in the paper, or *were reading* it, or possibly *went through* it with care, and they may *send a letter to* the paper, giving a different opinion.

223

The mouth has an even more important use than talking, and that is 'eating,' which is *taking food,* or *having a meal.* When we are given more to 'eat' than we have room for, we are unable to *get through* it. Sometimes (when the meat is old) you may have to 'bite' it very hard, or *get* your *teeth into* it much as the dog gets his teeth into your leg; but generally it is enough to *give it* the necessary number of *bites.* When you 'bite' off a bit, you *have a bite of* it or *at* it. And if what you 'bite' has a bad taste you may quickly 'spit' it out, which is to say *put it out of your mouth.*

In most operations of the body it is necessary to 'touch' something. In Basic we *put a hand,* or *finger,* or some other part of the body *on* it, or *give it a touch.* When we 'touch' or 'bump into' things by chance we *come up against* them. When we 'touch' a thing very hard, as when we are angry, we 'hit' it or *give it a blow.* If we 'touch' new paint with something pointed, like our nails, we will 'scratch' it—that is to say, we will *make a mark on* it. When we are 'scratching' an insect bite, we *give it a rub;* and when a cruel little boy 'scratches' his sister's arm till the blood comes, he *gets his nails into* it. If a sharp blade had been used in place of the nails, he would have 'cut' her or *given her a cut,* but if he had been cutting through something like thread or a cake, he would have *got it cut.* It is quite possible to 'break' a number of things which we 'cut.' The thread would then *be broken,* or we would *get it broken.* If we 'broke' a plate it might equally well *be smashed,* but if it 'broke' itself it would probably *come to bits.* 'Cutting' and 'breaking' are two of the most important operations in connection with changes of form.

We now come to acts by which the places of things are changed. The quickest way to get a thing from one place to another is to 'throw' it. In Basic we *send* the ball *to* a baby, or *over* the wall, or *across* the river. A sudden noise may 'throw' or *put* us off our balance, and a blow, given hard enough, will *send* us violently *against* the table. Whoever 'catches' the ball *gets* it (in his hand), and if he is able to *get a grip of* it (as when he 'catches' someone's arm) he 'holds' it, that is to say he *keeps* it or *has* it *in* his hand. When we are simply given something to 'hold' we *take* it, and when we have 'hold' of it, we *have a grip of* it. Most of us are not very good at 'catching,' so it is wiser to 'bring,' *get* or *take* things to our friends and not to 'throw' them. In other words, it is safer to *come with* them.

Another group of 'verbs' is made up of those for the different positions of the body. A person or thing which is 'lying' on something may be said simply to *be on it*, or to *be resting on* it. When a person who is 'lying' down gets into an upright position, he 'stands' or *gets up*. But he is still 'standing' when he is *on his feet*. Things which 'stand' in a certain position *are* (*placed*) there. If you are tired of 'standing' or 'lying' you will probably 'sit,' that is, *take a seat* or *be seated*. If not, you will make a move in some direction. If time is short you will 'run' or *go quickly;* if you are doing this to keep healthy, you will be *taking a run*, but if there is some danger which you are getting away from you will *go* (*off*) *at a run*. A little ice on the road would then make you 'slip' so that you *had a slip* or *fall*. It is not a long step from *slipping* in this sense to its use to give the idea of doing some simple act quickly and smoothly—and generally quietly—as in: *slipping your arm out of your coat*, or *slipping the money into your pocket*, or *slipping out of the house.*

b. Complex Acts Turning now to acts which are more complex than those of which we have been talking in the simple, physical group, we come first to the processes of the mind. To 'think about' is to *give thought to* and simply to 'be thinking' is to *be in thought*. But to 'think' that a thing is so is to *be of the opinion* or *take the view that;* and to 'know' that it is so is to *be certain of* it, or posibly only *conscious of* it. Other facts which we 'know,' we may *have knowledge* or *experience of*. If we are talking of 'knowing' a person we say we *are a friend of* that person or have *come across him*. This last is used, more widely, of books, pictures, and any other things which we *have seen*. To 'understand' what we 'know' we have to *be clear about* it or *have a grip of it,* though when we 'understand' horses, all we are saying is that we *have a good knowledge of* them. But we do not 'understand' a friend till we *see his point of view,* which is not unlike *seeing the point* of a person's statement, or, in other words, what he 'means.' This may be what he *is talking of,* but is sometimes only what he *has in mind.* When our words 'mean' something, they *have the sense of* it. Two words which clearly have a connection with 'knowing' are 'remember' and 'forget.' We only 'know' things so long as we *have a memory of* them or *keep them in mind.* When we 'forget' them, we *put them out of our mind,* or they *go out of our mind,* or we *have no memory of* them, and so they are no longer a part of our knowledge.

When we 'feel,' we *have a feeling of* pain or pleasure, or *a feeling* (in the sense of an idea) *that* a thing is so, or we may *be feeling* angry or *be conscious of* a touch. If we 'feel' the wall to see if it is dry, it is possible to say that we *put our hand on* it. We *are pleased with* things, or *friends of* persons when we 'like' them; or we may *get on well with* them. Of good food and pictures we sometimes say we *have a taste for* them. More generally, anything which we 'like' *has our approval,* and we *give our approval to* it. It is natural for us to 'want' such things, and then we *have a desire for* them. If they are very necessary for our well-being, we will *be in need of* them. And when we 'want' things of which we have not got enough, we *are in need of more.*

One way in which we 'learn' things is to *get facts into our heads.* We *get knowledge of* them somehow (in the process of which we *are learning*), generally by being 'taught.' We will probably go to someone who *is a teacher of* the branch of knowledge in which we are interested, and he will *give us training* or *teaching.* If he is a teacher of history he will 'show' us the effect of the past on the present and so *make it clear* to us; and he may 'show' us pictures by *letting us see* them—or *putting them on view*—and examples of old buildings by *taking us round.* We, on our side, will 'show' the interest we take by *giving signs of it.* If buildings have no attraction for us, we may even have to 'try,' or *make an attempt,* to give signs of an interest which is not there.

The organization of society is dependent on the two operations of 'buying' and 'selling.' When we 'buy' things we *get them* (in exchange *for money* or *at a price*) or we *give money for* them. If we have no money we may 'promise' to give it later by *giving our word* to do so. The person who 'sells' *gets money for* what he gives us. If he 'sells' things regularly he probably *keeps them in his store,* and if he 'sells' what he makes he *puts it on the market.* One way of getting things without payment is to 'find' them. We may *come across* money in the street, or *see* that free meals are being given to the poor, and if we *make a discovery* of some new land there will no doubt be money in it. Unhappily most of us 'lose' things more frequently than we 'find' them. We may only be *unable to put our hands on* a thing when it is needed, or *have no idea where it is,* but if *it has been taken from* us it will probably have gone for ever. Certainly we will not see it again if it has been 'destroyed' because then it will *have been burned* or *smashed* or *broken.* When a number of things are 'destroyed' at the same time *great destruction is done.* We 'destroy' animals by *putting an end to* them. Some attempts at 'destroying' them do no more than 'hurt' them, *giving them pain,* and possibly *wounds* which may *do serious damage* to them.

A great part of existence is taken up with 'growing' and 'sleeping.' Boys and girls *get taller,* trees *get higher,* old men generally *get fatter,* while one's powers, up to a certain point, *get greater.* When things *are increasing* in these ways they *are in the process of growth* or *development.* We 'fall asleep' very simply by *going to sleep,* and then we *are having a sleep.* At the end of all we 'die.' We are said to *go to our death, come to our end,* or, as writers put it, *take our last breath.* In our experience everything which 'begins' will later 'finish.' We *made*

a start with the physical acts, and you *got started* at the same
point. We have now *come to the end* of the names of acts which
may give you trouble, and though you have not quite *got to
the end* of the Basic story, you will *get it done* in a very short
time.

c. Other Suggestions   Our third and last group is made up of
words of all sorts which may be a cause of trouble.

There are three words which are used in a special way with
operation-words, 'can,' 'ought,' and 'shall.' What I 'can' do I
am able to do or *it is possible for me to* do. Things I 'ought' to
do, *it is right (wise) for me to* do or my *business to* do; in the
statement, "the train 'ought' to be here in half-an-hour," the
sense is that *it is probable* from the facts that it will be so. 'Shall'
is covered by *will* in statements which are not questions; but
"Shall I do it?" becomes *"Am I going to do it or not?"* or *"Am I
wise to do it?"*

Here are some words of number and amount with which care
is necessary. When 'each' person in a group gets something, the
distribution is made to *everyone (separately)*. If there were six
of them 'altogether,' they would *make six;* but if this number
was 'altogether' wrong it would be *quite* or *completely* so. The
'whole' group is simply *all the* group, and the 'whole' story about
them is the *complete* story. A 'few' men are very frequently
two or three, but it is safer, if you are uncertain, to say that they
are a *small number*—the opposite of 'many,' which is *a great
number* or *quite a number.* 'Too many' is *more than enough,* or
over-much; 'too' tired is *over-tired,* but a person who is 'too'
tired to go is *so tired that* he is unable to go. If he is ill 'too,' he
is ill *in addition.* Things which are done *once* are done *one time*
only, but things which were true 'once' were true *at one time*
or *in the past.*

Some suggestions in connection with time-words may make
things go more smoothly. A long time 'ago' is a long time *back,*
or *in the old days,* and an event which has taken place 'already'
has taken place *in the past* or *before.* An account of such events

is an account of what has taken place *so far* or *up to now*. A person who is 'already' there is there *now;* but if he is not there 'yet,' he is *still* not there, or *so far* he has not come. "And 'yet,'" as a joining statement, has the sense of *but even though this is so.* Friends we have not seen 'since' last year we have not seen *for a year.* Events which have taken place 'since' then have taken place *after* then. But in the statement, "'Since' it is late let us go to bed," 'since' has the sense of *because.* What we will do 'next' is what we will do *after this,* but when we 'next' do it is when we do it *again;* and the house 'next' to this is the house *nearest* to it. 'Always' is generally *at all times,* which used loosely may sometimes be *frequently.* When we have the future specially in view, as in "I will 'always' be your friend," *for ever* is a better way of putting it. *Without change* and *without end* are the right words in other connections.

'Unless' is a very common word which is quite simply got round with *if* and *not*. For example, "It will not be done 'unless' I do it" becomes "It will not be done *if I do not do it.*"

Here are two examples of the sort of quality words, much used in everyday talk, which do not go in quite a straight-forward way into Basic. A 'busy' person may simply be one *with much business,* but it is generally better to say he *is working hard* or *has much to do.* A 'deaf' person is one whose *hearing is bad.*

Last of all, if you are given the tricks with a representative selection of general names you may get the idea of how others are covered. The 'world' is the *earth* when we are talking of space, but when 'all the world' is shocked it is *everyone.* In again another sense, the 'world' may be *things* or *conditions,* as in "The 'world' is changing." That which has 'life,' has *existence;* but 'life' when used for the things which have 'life' is *living things,* or *all living things. Living* by itself is sometimes used for 'life,' as in "Living is interesting." A 'hill' is a bit of land *at a higher level* than the country round. Our short ways of saying this are *a slope,* or *small mountain* (when the size makes this possible), or, of country which is full of 'hills,' *highlands.* Though everyone who has a 'home' has not necessarily a *house*, he has at least a *place where he is living* (though one night in a hotel does not make it a 'home'), and when he is happily at 'home' it may be because he is *with his family*. *Where one is living* will, in addition, be one's 'address' for private purposes, but the 'address' of one's business letter will be at one's *place of business*.

2. WORDS FORMED BY ENDINGS

Most of the forms made by the addition of endings are needed only at the second level—that is to say, when we give as much attention to *how* things are said as to *what* is said; but a certain number of them are necessary even in the early stages. From among the -*er* words a list may be made of names given to persons doing different things, all of which are important. Some of these are *actor, builder, carter, designer, driver, farmer, fisher(man), gardener, jeweler, joiner, learner, miner, painter, potter, printer, producer, reader, ruler, sailor, teacher, trader, trainer,*[42] *waiter, worker, writer*. From among the names of operations we get *keeper* and *maker*. Then there is a small group of things which have some special purpose: *burner, cooker, duster, folder, hanger, pointer, roller, rubber, steamer, stopper, stretcher*.

Some forms are needed as part of a special fixed use with the name of a direction. With *up* we have *buttoning, dressing, locking, stopping, touching,* and *working. Firing, laughing, looking,* and *pointing* go with *at*. Others are *acting* (*on*), *dancing* (*to*), *talking* (*of*), *turning* (*over*), and *working* (*out* or *on*). In all these the -*ed* form may equally well be used. In addition, there are *pleased with* and *used to*. To be *used to* anything is to have had experience of it, so that it is no longer new or strange.

Then there are some words to which the endings give an important new sense. A *prisoner* is a person kept in *prison* and so on, and a *reader* may be a school book for learning *reading* (as well as a person reading). *Clothing*[43] is a name for the

[42] See p. 179.
[43] Said with a long 'o' as in 'roll' and a 'th' as in 'though.' In 'breathing'

covers we put on our bodies, to keep ourselves warm and so on. *Crying* is needed for the behavior of those who are unhappy. A *marked* man is one who is marked out for punishment or destruction, and a *noted* man is one who is in the public eye. *Pained* is troubled in mind or feeling. A *painting* is a picture done with paint. A *parting* is a line of division in the hair as well as a separating. *Training* is teaching or education (see page 179).

The -*ing* and -*ed* forms of certain words, though not much changed in sense, are important because so common. These are *base* (*basing, based*), *burn* (*burning, burned*), *cook* (*cooking, cooked*), *drop* (*dropping, dropped*), *heat* (*heating, heated*), *play* (*playing, played*), *rain* (*raining*), *shock* (*shocking, shocked*), *snow* (*snowing*), *trouble* (*troubling, troubled*), *waste* (*wasting, wasted*).

3. THE MOST NECESSARY FIXED WORD-GROUPS

Here is our list of 50 (of the 250) fixed word-groups which are hardest to do without:

at war (peace, work, play, rest)	worked *out*
bad (good, quick, working) *at*	go (be turned) *over*
at last (first)	be able *to*
by himself	put *up* with
for example	angry (pleased) *with*
but *for*	*come* to a stop
responsible *for*	*get* (a book) out
in motion (flight)	*got* out of doing
in use (operation)	*give* up
out *of* the room	*go* to sleep
control, grip *of*	(guns) *go* off
full *of*	(lights) *go* out
off his head	*have* an effect on
go (*keep*) *on* (*doing* and so on)	*make* up a story

(in which the 'ea' is sounded as in 'increase') and 'mouthing,' there is a like change in the sound of 'th'; and in 'housing' the 's' is sounded as in 'was.'

put off (a meeting)

as if

one *another*

there is

in *addition* to

in the *belief* (that)

in *bits*

in *memory* of

take *part* in

take *place*

and *so* on

put a *stop* to

give *way* to

in (out of) the *way*

at right *angles*

dependent on

good morning (day, night)

at *present*

tired of

straight away

10 years *old*

as *well* (as)

The Last Step

1. POINTS TO KEEP IN MIND

The general account of the Basic system is now complete but you will not have the necessary working knowledge till you have gone through all the words in the Basic list in turn to get a clear idea of their behavior and special uses.

The Basic Words is the guide for this purpose. In this book, every word of the 850 is given its parallels in French and German; so anyone with some knowledge of these languages will have a key to the sense of the words. It is not possible, however, to do more than give rough parallels, because words which seem to be used for the same thing in two languages are in fact frequently used in very different ways, and a word in German, one of whose senses is the same as one of the senses of an English word, may have other senses which the English word has not.

In addition to the French and German parallels examples are given and there is some account in Basic of every expansion and special sense. Naturally, it is not possible to get round the senses of the 850 words very happily inside the limits of the system, because the selection of these words has been based on our most important needs. So the only point of putting Basic into Basic is to make the sense clearer. It is not an attempt to give 'ways round' which may be seriously used.

In *The Basic Words* it will be seen which words take endings, and which may be used as other sorts of words. All the words now used as International are listed. With them may be grouped the necessary material for measuring and numbering (see page 236). In addition, all the Special Uses (first-level and second-level) are listed, and examples are given of all the special tricks of separate words. For example, it will be seen that *fruit* is generally used as if it was the name of a substance, and that *fish* may be looked on in the same way. Such details do not all get attention in the *ABC*.

In Basic, full use is made of the fact that words of a narrow range may be covered by words of a wider range, if account is taken of the way in which the sense of a word is pinned down by the connection in which it is used. We do not, for example, have the word 'husband' among our 850, and the Basic parallel given in *The Basic Dictionary* is *married man*. This is all right in a general way, but when it comes to statements other words may be happier. If we are talking of "her first husband," we may say "the man she was first married to," but if the question is put, "How is your husband today?" it would be better to say "How is Mr. X today?"

In *The Basic Dictionary*, the Basic parallels are given in detail, but in any special connection it is generally possible to say something very much shorter; and though some suggestion is made as to which words will most probably be of use, experience and common sense are the best guides. For example, a 'claim' is given as "a request based on a right," but a "claim for insurance" is a "request for payment of the insurance."

Again, when there is an expansion of the sense, care may be needed to get the right effect in Basic. 'Severe' is 'hard' or 'cruel'; but if used about a cold in the head these words would be quite foolish. Clearly, in this connection, 'bad' is the right thing to say. In other words, when two or three suggestions are put before you, give some thought to the point of what you are saying before making a selection.

2. INTERNATIONAL WORDS

An international language has to be as simple as possible for the learner, and for this reason all words which are truly international are naturally looked on as part of the Basic system. To give a new word in place of one which is common to every language would clearly be foolish. But what is an international word? Or, and this is more to the point, who makes the decision as to what words are international? In the end it is you, the men and women of Japan, of China, of Russia, of Scandinavia, of Africa, who will be the judges. But though the last word will be yours, the first decisions have been made by a smaller body, a representative committee of experts, who have gone through the material with care to get a small group of words which, in their opinion, will not be questioned by most. In addition, there is a waiting-list of 300 suggestions which will not be taken as international till the general reaction to them has been tested more fully by a special committee of radio authorities.

The words about which the experts have come to a decision are printed in *The Basic Words*. There are 51 of these, the 'adjective' *international* itself, and the names of things:

alcohol, aluminum, automobile, bank, bar, beef, beer, calendar, chemist, check, chocolate, chorus, cigarette, club, coffee, colony, dance, engineer, gas, hotel, influenza, lava, madam, nickel, opera, orchestra, paraffin, park, passport, patent, phonograph, piano, police, post, program, propaganda, radio, restaurant, sir, sport, taxi, tea, telegram (*telegraph*), *telephone, terrace, theater, tobacco, university, whisky, zinc;* together with 12 names of sciences:

Algebra, Arithmetic, Biology, Chemistry, Geography, Geology, Geometry, Mathematics, Physics, Physiology, Psychology, Zoölogy.

With these, 15 words may be noted which come into special names used internationally:

College, Dominion, Embassy, Empire, Imperial, King, Miss, Mr., Mrs., Museum, President, Prince, Princess, Queen, Royal.
These words are not necessarily international.

In addition to the 50 words which have been fixed as international and are of value for Basic, a further 50 may be listed

about which there is at present more doubt. These will be used
with care for a year or two for the purpose of testing reactions.
Here is the list:

*ammonia, asbestos, autobus, ballet, café, catarrh, champagne,
chauffeur, circus, citron, cocktail, cognac, dynamite, encyclopaedia, glycerine, hyena, hygiene, hysteria, inferno, jazz, liqueur,
macaroni, malaria, mania, nicotine, olive, omelette, opium,
paradise, penguin, platinum, potash, pyjamas, pyramid, quinine,
radium, referendum, rheumatism, rum, salad, sardine, tapioca,
toast, torpedo, vanilla, violin, visa, vodka, volt, zebra.*

As little change as possible is made in place-names, but when
a form would seem very strange to an Englishman or an American it is given as in normal English. Examples are *Germany* and
Rome. Happily there is a tendency to take such names over into
the English language untouched.

In addition to what has been listed, measuring words, number
words, and words in the money systems of the different countries are said to be international, and given in their English
form.

The days and months of the year are worked in the same way.

Here are the days of the week:

*Monday, Tuesday, Wednesday, Thursday, Friday, Saturday,
Sunday.*

Here are the months of the year:

*January, February, March, April, May, June, July, August,
September, October, November, December.*

Here are the necessary words for numbers:

*one, two, three, four, five, six, seven, eight, nine, ten, eleven,
twelve, thirteen, fourteen, fifteen, sixteen . . . , twenty, twenty-
one . . . , thirty, forty, fifty, hundred, thousand, million, once,
twice, half, quarter, third, fourth, fifth.*

3. SCIENCE

The learner who has got so far in the system and is able to
make use of it for general purposes may at this point put the

question "Of what use is Basic to me in my special field?" The answer is that by getting 150 more words into his head, making the number up to 1,000, he will have everything necessary for talking about a branch of science, or any other special field. 100 of these words are general science words (there may be other such general lists for other fields), of value in the discussion of any branch of knowledge which comes under the heading 'Science.' The other 50 are made up from the narrower field in which special interest is taken. An account of these lists is given on pages 391–93 of Section Three. Happily, much more is international for science than for general purposes, and it is hoped that, in the future, all true science words may become international by agreement, making Basic necessary only as the framework of discussion.

PART TWO

The Basic Words

Editor's Note

This book is designed as a handbook for use by learners of English in connection with one of the Basic teaching books (for example, *Basic Step by Step* or *The Basic Teacher*), and by teachers with a knowledge of English in connection with *Basic English* and *The ABC of Basic English*. It is, in addition, quite necessary for anyone, even if his mother tongue is English, who is attempting to make use of Basic in writing.

What *The Basic Words* does is to make clear the senses covered by every word in the Basic list and the ways in which these words may be used. *The General Basic English Dictionary* gives in Basic the senses of 20,000 common English words, and there the 850 themselves are in their places, with all the senses possible to them in full English. Here, on the other hand, the 850 Basic words are given with only those senses to which they are limited in Basic. With them are listed such international words and names as are made part of the system in *Basic English* and *The ABC* together with a certain number of complex words (formed by putting Basic words together) and 'onomatopoeic' words (words based on sound-effects)—of which straightforward additions Basic is free to make use.

It is pointed out which words take the *-er* (n.), *-ing* (n., a.), and *-ed* (a.) endings, and which have forms for more than one, or for comparison, which are not regular. In addition, those words in the Basic list which may take *un-* [1] before them or *-ly* after them are noted. But not every possible use of *un-* or *-ly* is covered because a great number of words formed with the *-ing* and *-ed* endings may have these additions as well.

Un- and the endings sometimes go only, or chiefly, with the root sense, sometimes with an expansion or special sense, and sometimes with all senses. These details are not noted, but attention to the examples will make them clear. Examples are not given for all possible forms, but they are given for every one about which there might be any doubt.

GUIDE TO THE USE OF THE BOOK

1. The nearest French and German words are given for the root sense, special sense—marked by (s)—and expansions—marked by (e)—of every Basic word. Where the French and German words are the same for all the given senses they are printed only for the root. Naturally not every special use is covered by the French or German words, because these languages frequently have ways of saying the same thing without making use of any parallel word.

2. A key to the special senses and expansions is given in Basic; and the sometimes strange effect is a sign of the important part played in the language by the words whose sense is made clear in this way.

   The sign : is put between the different expansions.

3. The same short forms for naming the different sorts of words (n., a., prep., v., and so on) are used as in *The General Basic English Dictionary*. The one printed first is that under which the word is listed for Basic purposes. If a word is noted as coming into more than one group, the French and German parallels for the other possible ways of using the word are

---

[1] Where the *un-* is changed to *in-, im-,* or *ir-* in full English, these forms are given. Though it is not necessary for them to be forced on the learner's attention, they are used freely in Basic writing.

given only when, in those languages, the connection with the root is not clear.

4. For making clear the sounds of the words as they are said on the records by Mr. J. C. Catford,[2] the 'phonetic' system of *An English Pronouncing Dictionary*, by Professor Daniel Jones, has been used.

5. The first examples are representative of normal uses, special attention being given to ways of getting round 'verb' forms. Full stops are put between root-use examples and those of special senses or expansions. The same division is made between examples of different expansions. Examples of a word used as another sort of word (for example, an 'a.' used as an 'n.') come last.

6. After these examples of straightforward uses, come the special word-groups of which the word makes part.

    * is put before the 250 special uses listed for learners in *The ABC of Basic English*. Those inside ( ) are based on another word in the group, and come under it without ( ). Those which are numbered are taken from the 130 printed in *The ABC*, in lists of 5 and 10, under names of acts and directions.

    * is used, in addition, for marking the 50 least important international words.

7. ** is put before special word-groups which are listed in *The ABC* among the second 250 (not for learners).

8. In the French and German parallels, words or parts of words which are given only to make the sense clearer are put between [ ]. ( ) are used where there are two possible parallels, one with and one without the part between ( ).

---

[2] There are four records playing for 22 minutes.

The Basic Words

a (an), a. ei; *un, une; ein, eine.*

A man; give the ball a kick; the selection of a paint; a bit of; quite a good book; he has £100 a year; an apple; an hour.

ABC, n. *Basic words.* The letters; the first steps.

able (un, -ly), a. 'eibl; *capable, intelligent; fähig.*

An a. teacher; an a. book; the work was ably done.

*(*A. to* make).

about, prep., adv. ə'baut; *environ, autour de; um, herum.*

(e) Roughly: on the question of; *à peu près: au sujet de; fast, ungefähr: über.*

Trees a. the house; walking a. the streets. There are a. enough; at a. 4. A book a. history; be right a. the facts. The servants are a.; looking a. for a place.

*The glass is *a. to be* broken. (How did this *come a.*?)

**(*Hanging a.*).

account, n. ə'kaunt, *récit, compte rendu, explication; Bericht.*

(s) Money account; *compte; Rechnung, Konto.*

Give an a. of. Have an a. with; keep aa.; put it on the a.

*(*Take into a.*).

***On no a.; on a. of;* goods *on a.*

acid (-ly), a., n. 'æsid; *acíde; sauer.*

(e) Sharp in feeling.

The fruit has an a. taste. She gave him an a. look; "Don't be foolish," he said acidly. It was burned by an a.

across, prep. ə'krɔs; *en travers de, sur; (quer) über.*

A bridge a. the river; go a. the road; put one stick a. another.

*(He *came a.* some papers; *put* an idea *a.* by advertisement).

act (-or, -ing, -ed), n. ækt; *action; Tat, Handlung.*

(e) Division of a play; *acte; Akt.*

-or, (s) Person acting in a theater; *acteur; Schauspieler.*

Do a kind a.; he was in the a. of taking the money; acting as a brake. A good third a. He is an actor.

*Acid *acting on* material.

addition, n. ə'diʃən; *addition, surcroît; Zusatz.*

(e) Act of addition; *action d'ajouter ou d'additioner; Addition, Ergänzung.*

Make an a. to a building; a good a. The a. of water to milk; do a.; bad at a.

In a. to this.

adjustment, n. ə'dʒʌstmənt; *réglage, mise au point, adaptation, réglement; Richtigstellung, Anpassung.*

Make an a.; an a. of the amount; by the a. of a screw.

advertisement, n. əd'vəːtismənt; *annonce, affiche, réclame; Anzeige, Reklame.*

(e) Public attention: act of advertisement; *publicité: réclame; Reklame: Ankündigung, Reklame.*

Put an a. for a secretary in the paper; the store has an a. for soap in the window. Do it for a.; get good a. Undertake the a. of goods.

after, prep., conj. 'aːftə*; *après: après que; nach: nachdem.*

Some time a. an event; go a. a rat. I took it a. he came.

*A. *all,* they were young; *looking a.* a store.

**A picture *a.* Rembrandt.

aftereffect, n. *Basic words.* An effect coming about after a time.

aftertaste, n. *Basic words.* Taste experienced in mouth after taking food or drink.

afterthought, n. *Basic words.* A later thought.

again, adv. ə'gein; *de nouveau, encore; wieder.*

He did the work a.; then, a., he is old; say it a. and a.

against, prep. ə'geinst; *contre; gegen.*

(e) On opposite side to (in war, feeling, and so on).

Resting a. the wall; come up a. a stone. Fighting a. an army; be a. change; have something a. a person.

agreement, n. ə'griːmənt; *pacte, contrat; Vereinbarung, Vertrag.*

(e) Condition of agreement; *accord; Undereinstimmung.*

Make an a. with; keep (to) an a. Be in a. with; there is not much a. between them.

*(Come to an a.).

air (-er, -ing, -ed), n. ɛə*; *air; Luft.*

(e) Behavior, look; *Miene.*

Out in the a.; take in a.; birds in the a.; airing the room; go out for an airing; put on an a. of interest; foolish aa.

aircushion, n. *Basic words.* Cushion full of air.

airman, n. *Basic words.* Driver of airplane.

airplane, n. *Basic words.* Winged machine for flight.

air-tight, a. *Basic words.* Not letting air in.

alcohol, 'ælkəhɔl. *International word.*

algebra, 'æ1dʒibrə. *International name of science.*

all, a., adv., pron. ɔ:l; *tout; all* (*-er, -e, -es*), ganz.

A. men are the same; a. the day; at a. times. A. in black; a. covered with dust. A. were happy; a. is quiet.

*°He is *not at a.* interesting; *a. day* (*night*). (*A. right; after a.*).

**(For a. that; a. the year round; a. the same*).

almost, adv. 'ɔːlmoust; *presque; fast, beinahe.*

A. ready; a. there; the boy is a. a man.

aluminum, ælju'minjəm. *International word.*

am (*are*). See *be.*

ammonia°, ə'mounjə. *International word.*

among, prep. ə'mʌŋ; *parmi, entre, unter, zwischen.*

Be a. one's friends; a. one's books; working a. the poor; a. other things; make a division a.; we have 5s. a. us.

amount, n. ə'maunt; *quantité, montant* (*d'une somme*); *Menge, Betrag.*

Have a small a. of food; gold in great aa.; he made payment of the full a.

amusement, n. ə'mjuːzment; *amusement; Belustigung, Spasz.*

(e) Pleased interest; thing causing a.; act of causing a.; *Unterhaltung.*

Such humor gives me no a.; a look of a. Get a. out of watching trains. Sailing is a good a. Plays for the a. of the public.

and, conj. ænd; *et; und.*

He a. I; I came a. he went; it was round a. fat; a. then he said; I went a. saw him.

*° (*A. so on*).

angle, n. 'æŋgl; *angle; Winkel, Ecke.*

(e) A. of a room: point of view; *coin: angle, côté; Winkel, Ecke: Winkel.*

An a. formed by two lines meeting. Put the table in the far a. of the room. Looking at the picture from a different a.; seeing the question from a different a.

*The boxes were *at right aa.* (*to* one another).

angry (-ly), a. 'æŋgri; *en colère, fâche; zornig, böse.*

Be feeling a.; an a. face; an a. man; a. words; an a. red; make oneself a. about; they were talking angrily.

* (*Be a. with* a learner).

animal, n. 'ænimǝl; *animal; Tier.*

(s) All animals but man.

Man is an a. Be kind to aa.

another, a., pron. *Basic words.* A different or further (one).

* (They saw *one a.*).

answer (-er, -ing, -ed), n. 'ɑːnsǝ*; *réponse; Antwort.*

Give an a. to a question; answering a letter (bell); answering for a friend.

* (*In a. to* a question).

** *Answering to an account.*

ant, n. ænt; *fourmi; Ameise.*

There is an a. in the food.

any, a., pron., adv. 'eni; *aucun (-e), n'importe lequel; irgendein (-e), irgendwelche (-r, -s).*

I haven't a. friends; have you a. wool?; come at a. time. I haven't a. of that; take a. of them. He is not a. wiser.

* (*At a. rate*).

anybody, pron. *Basic words.* Any person.

anyhow, adv. *Basic words.* 1. Whatever takes place. 2. In any way.

anyone, pron. *Basic words.* Any person.

anything, pron. *Basic words.* Any thing.

anywhere, adv. *Basic words.* In (at, to) any place.

apparatus (apparatuses), n. æpǝ'reitǝs; *appareil; Apparat.*

Put up an a.; different apparatuses; an a. of tax-control.

apple, n. 'æpl; *pomme; Apfel.*

The aa. are still green.

approval, n. ǝ'pruːvǝl; *approbation; Billigung, Beifall.*

Give a. to; say with a.; have a feeling of a.

*Get goods *on a.*

arch (arches, -er, -ing, -ed), n. ɑːtʃ; *arc, arche; Bogen.*

(e) Archlike form.

-er, (e) One using as an instrument of war a curved bit of wood or other elastic material with a cord stretched between the ends; *archer; Bogenschütze.*

The a. of a bridge; the church has pointed arches. A foot with a good a.; the cat is arching its back. The bird was wounded by an archer.

argument, n. ˈɑːgjumənt; *argumentation; Auseinandersetzung, Wortwechsel.*

(e) Line of reasoning; *argument, raisonnement; Argument.*

Have an a. with somebody. A good a. for putting an end to war; his a. was.

arithmetic, əˈriθmətik. *International name of science.*

arm (-er, -ing, -ed), n. ɑːm; *bras; Arm.*

(e) Long structure like an a.

aa. = Instruments of war; *armes; Waffen.*

Working-men get strong aa.; with open aa. The a. of a machine; the a. of a coat. The nation has no aa.; arming for war.

***A baby in aa.;* nations *in aa.* (They went *a. in a.;* the men *took up arms*).

army (armies), n. ɑːmi; *armée; Heer.*

(e) A number of persons; *multitude.*

The boy is going into the a.; the a. has a new chief; armies were smaller then. An a. of boys went to the house.

art, n. ɑːt; *art; Kunst.*

(e) Way of doing.

A work of a.; he puts his a. first; a museum of bad a. A. came before Science. The a. of cooking; I am learning the a. of seeming interested.

as, adv., conj., pron. æz; *aussi* (. . . *que), comme;* (*so* . . .) *wie, als.*

A. hard as iron; he came a. slowly as before. As far a. I see; look on a. wrong; a. an example; please be so good a. to come; a. we go higher the air gets colder. Such things a. drink.

*It seems *a. if; a. to* (*for*) that. (*So a. to* get it right; he has horses *a. well a.* cows).

***A. a* man; *a.* you are here.

asbestos*, æzˈbestɔs. *International word.*

at, prep, æt; *à, chez; an, um, bei, in, zu.*

A. a point; a. Tokyo; a. the top; a. 4; a. his request; a. what price.

*1. The men are *at war* (*peace, work, play, rest*).

2. They were happy *at first* (*last*).

3. They were *at a great distance* from their country.

4. They did not go to bed *at night*.

5. *At times* they were covered with small insects.

6. There was some *surprise at* their desire to get back.

7. There were *at least* (*most*) 1,000 persons at the station.

8. They had the interests of their country *at heart*.

9. There were *bad at* (*good at, quick at, slow at, expert at, working at*) languages.

10. They are *looking at* (*pointing at, laughing at, firing at,* and so on) the camera-men.

(*Not a. all* interesting; be *a. a loss;* knowledge *a. first* (*second*) hand; days *a. school; a. present; a. any rate; a. right angles to*).

**A. *a run; a. a profit* (*loss*). (*Have a go a.; a. all events;* three *a. a time; get a.* details; *a. table; a. sea; a. pleasure; make eyes a.*).

attack (-er, -ing, -ed), n. ə'tæk; *attaque; Angriff, Anfall.*

An a. against his views; the army made a sudden a.; a new line of a.; attacked by a disease; attacking a question.

*An *a. on* a man.

attempt (-er, -ing, -ed), n. ə'tempt; *essai, tentative; Versuch.*

Make an a. to get the news; wounded in the a.; attempting to do.

attention, n. ə'tenʃən; *attention; Aufmerksamkeit, Achtung.*

(e) Care, looking after; *soin(s); Pflege, Behandlung.*

Give a. to; keep one's a. on; great powers of a. The baby gets no a.

attraction, n. ə'trækʃən; *attraction; Anziehung[skraft].*

(e) Pleasing quality (thing): condition of (undergoing) attraction; *attraction, attrait: attraction; Reiz, Attraktion: Anziehung.*

The a. of the earth for bodies. She has no a. off the stage; have an a. for; the a. of the idea; coming aa. The a. of the sea by the moon; their a. to one another.

authority, n. ɔː'θɔriti; *autorité, autorisation; Autorität, Vollmacht, Ansehen.*

(e) Person or body in authority: person with special knowledge; *autorité: autorité; Behörde: Autorität.*

Have a. over the army; what a. have you?; be in a.; be under the

a. of the chief. Go to a higher a.; come before the aa. An a. on the Great War.

°°(*On good a.*).

autobus°, 'ɔːtoubʌs. *International word.*

automatic (un-, -ally), a. ɔːtə'mætik; *automatique; automatisch.*

Get chocolate from an a. machine; his behavior was a.; an a. reaction; he got up automatically.

automobile, 'ɔːtomobiːl. *International word.*

awake, a. ə'weik; *éveillé; wach.*

The baby is a. very early; I came a. suddenly.

°°(*Wide a.*).

away, adv. *Basic words.* At (to) some distance; out of view.

baby (babies), n. 'beibi; *bébé; Baby.*

He was ill when he was a b.; the woman had two babies with her; the b. cat; my b. brother.

°°(*A b. in arms*).

baby-carriage, n. *Basic words.* Push-carriage for a baby.

back (-er, -ing, -ed), n., adv. a. bæk, *derrière, arrière; Rückseite: zurück: hinter.*

(s) Back of man's body or like part of other things; *dos; Rücken.*

(e) Top of animal's body.

The b. of the house; the b. of the book; at the b. of the station; a picture backed with linen; backing an automobile. A pain in the b. The monkey was on the dog's b. Come b.; get money b.; a year b. The b. door.

°(*Give b. a sound*).

backbone, n. *Basic words.* Bone down the back of man or animal.

back-cloth, n. *Basic words.* Painted cloth at back of stage.

backside, n. *Basic words.* Back end of person's body.

backwater, n. *Basic words.* Quiet water near a river.

backwoods, n. *Basic words.* Out-of-the-way place.

bad (worse, worst, -ly), a. bæd; *mauvais; schlecht; schlimm.*

(s) Bad in behavior; *méchant; böse.*

(e) No longer good for food; *gâté; verdorben.*

A b. day; b. weather; have a b. time; a b. idea; a b. bit of wood; a b. book; a b. friend; be badly wounded. A b. boy. The milk will be b. tomorrow.

°*The worse for drink.* (*B. at* languages; he *did badly*).

bag, n. bæg; *sac; Beutel, Tasche, Sack.*

A b. full of wool; a paper b.; a porter took my bb.

bagpipes, s. *Basic words.* Music pipe with bag for wind.

balance (-er, -ing, -ed), n. 'bæləns; *équilibre; Gleichgewicht.*

Keep one's b.; a b. of forces; balancing on a wire; have a well-balanced mind.

* (Be *off one's b.*).

ball, n. bɔːl; *boule; Kugel.*

(s) Playing-ball; *balle; Ball.*

A silver b.; make butter into bb. The little girl has a b.

ballet*, 'bælei. *International word.*

band (-er, -ing, -ed), n. bænd; *bande; Band.*

(e) Group: music-playing group; *bande: orchestre; Schar, Rotte:* [*Musik-*] *Kapelle.*

Put a rubber b. round; fixed by a b. of iron; a b. of red; banded with red. A b. of young men; banding together against the police. Playing in the b.

bang, n. *Onomatopoeic.* Noise made by burst.

bank, bæŋk. *International word.*

** (A check *on the b.*).

bar, bɑː***. *International word.*

base (-er, -ing, -ed), n. beis; *base, fondement; Grund (lage).*

(e) Base of military operations; *base; Basis.*

The b. of a building; basing opinions on facts. The wounded are sent back to the hospital at the b.

baseball, n. *Basic words.* An American sport in which a ball is used; ball used in baseball.

basin, n. 'beisn; *bol, cuvette; Schüssel.*

(e) Wide hollow; *bassin; Becken.*

Food in a b. A river b.

basket, n. 'bɑːskit; *panier; Korb.*

Eggs in a b.; a b. of flowers.

basket-work, n. *Basic words.* Material made like a basket.

bath (-er, -ing, -ed), n. bɑːθ; *baignoire, bain; Bad.*

(e) Wash in a bath; *acte de (se) baigner, bain.*

Put water in a b. Have a b.; give the baby a b.; bathing the baby.

bathroom, n. *Basic words.* Special room with (gen. fixed) bath.

be (am, are, is, was, were, being, been), v., aux. v. biː; *être; sein.*

(e) Have existence, take place.

been (e) Gone (or come) to and away from a place.

-ing, (e) Living thing; *étre; Wesen.*

She is a cook; he is good; it is wise to do nothing; they are talking; I will be there. I am; such things have been and will b. again; there is no answer to that question. Have you ever been to Paris? A strange being.

(*That is to say; let (a person, thing) be).

beautiful (un-, -ly), a. 'bjuːtəful; *beau; schön.*

A b. woman; a b. day; a b. picture; the theory is beautifully clear.

because, conj. bi'kɔz; *parce que; weil.*

He was angry b. she was late.

*(Best b. of its rules).

become, v. Basic words. Come to be.

**What has b. of it?

bed (-der, -ding, -ded), n. bed; *lit; Bett.*

(e) Stretch of material, specially under, forming base of, something: flower-b.; *lit, couche: plate-bande;* [Fluss-]Bett, Unterbau, Lager: Beet.

-ding, (e) B.-covers: *literie; Bettzeug.*

Put the covers on the b.; go to b.; be in b. The b. of the river is deep; the discovery of a new coal b. Put flowers in the bb.; bedding out plants. Soft bedding.

bedroom, n. Basic words. Special room with bed(s) for sleeping in.

bee, n. biː; *abeille; Biene.*

There is a b. on the flower.

beef, biːf. International word.

beer, biə*. International word.*

beeswax, n. Basic words. The wax made by bees.

before, prep., conj., adv. bi'fɔː*; *avant, devant; vor: bevor, ehe: vorher.*

Come b. tea; the word b. "have" is not clear; go b. a judge; the work b. us; work comes b. play; death b. prison! Have a meal b. you go. He did it once b.

**(Before long).

behavior, n. bi'heivjə*; *conduite, comportement; Benehmen, Verhalten.*

His b. is good; rough in b.; the b. of a chemical; the b. of nations.

belief, n. bi'li:f; *croyance; Glaube.*

    (s) Belief in religion; *foi; Glaube.*

    (e) What one has b. in: feeling that a thing is probable; *croyance: opinion; Uberzeugung.*

    B. is an event in the mind. To be a Christian it is necessary to have b. They had a number of strange bb. It is my b. that we will have snow.

    °In the b. that; have *b. in* a story.

bell, n. bel; *cloche, sonnette; Glocke, Klingel.*

    The church b. is sounding; that is the front-door b.

bell-boy, n. *Basic words.* Boy servant in a hotel.

bent (un-) n. bent; *plié, courbé; gebogen, gebeugt.*

    Using a b. stick; a b. old man; his arm was b.

berry (berries), n. 'beri; *baie; Beere.*

    The fruit of this plant is a b.; birds take the berries.

better (best). See *good* and *well.*

between, prep. bi'twi:n; *entre; zwischen.*

    A river b. two mountains; time b. events; there is no connection b. these events; make a comparison (selection) b. foods; make a division of the sweets b. the two boys.

biology, bai'ɔlədʒi. *International name of science.*

bird, n. bə:d; *oiseau; Vogel.*

    A b. in the air; going after bb. with a gun.

bird's-eye view, n. *Basic words.* View from the air.

birth, n. bə:θ; *naissance; Geburt.*

    (e) Position in society by b.; start; *naissance: origine source.*

    Bentham's b. took place in 1748. All are given an equal chance, whatever their b. The b. of a new idea.

    ° (Mothers give b. to babies).

birthday, n. *Basic words.* The day of the year on which a person's birth took place.

birth-mark, n. *Basic words.* Mark on the skin from birth.

birth-place, n. *Basic words.* Place of person's birth.

birth-rate, n. *Basic words.* Number of births for every 1,000 persons in a given time.

birthright, n. *Basic words.* Right given by fact of birth.

bit, n. bit; *morceau, pièce; Stück(chen), Bischen.*

    (e) Unit of metal money.

Have a b. of bread; bb. of news; put the bb. together. A two-shilling b.

*The dress is *in bb.;* the plate has *come to bb.* (*B. by b.*).

**He was *a b.* sad; I *did my b.* in the organization.

bite, n. bait; *coup de dent, pique; Biss.*

(e) What is taken at one bite: wound from a bite; *bouchée: morsure; Bissen: Biss.*

The dog gave him a b.; have a b. at an apple. I took a b. of it. A bad b. in the leg.

bitter, a. 'bitə*; *amer; bitter.*

(e) Bitter in feeling; *acharné; verbittert.*

A b. taste; a b. drink. A b. thought; her troubles have made her b.

black, a., blæk; *noir; schwarz.*

A b. night; a b. man from Africa; make one's hand b. as coal. Dressed in b.

blackberry, n. *Basic words.* Dark berry of the fields and roadsides in England used as food.

blackbird, n. *Basic words.* Bird of Europe noted for song.

blackboard, n. *Basic words.* Black board for writing on used in school.

blacklead, n. *Basic words.* Black polishing substance (for iron fireplaces and so on).

blackout, n. *Basic words.* Keeping of town(s) dark in war-time.

blade, n. bleid; *lame; Klinge.*

(s) Blade of war; *épée.*

(e) Flat, narrow, b.-like leaf or part of any thing.

The b. is not sharp; a knife with two bb. Waving his b. in the air. A b. of grass.

blood, n. blʌd; *sung; Blut.*

(e) Family.

There was b. on the coat. There is Irish b. in him; they are of the same b.; a b. relation.

bloodvessel, n. *Basic words.* Blood pipe in the body.

blow, n. blou; *coup; Schlag.*

(e) Motion of air-current: shock; *coup de vent, souffle: coup; Blasen, Schnauben: Schlag.*

Give a person a b. A strong b. of wind; giving one's nose a b. The news was a great b. to him.

blowpipe, n. *Basic words.* 1. Pipe for increasing heat of flame by blowing air into it. 2. Pipe for blowing sharp-pointed, frequently poisoned, sticks through, used in war and so on by certain Indians of
America and the West Indies.

blue, a., n. bluː; *bleu; blau.*
    The sea is b. on a bright day. A dark shade of b.

bluebell, n. *Basic words.* Blue, spring, woodland flower.

board (-er, -ing, -ed), n. bɔːd; *planche; Brett, Diele.*
    (s) Advertisement board; *enseigne, écriteau; Tafel, Brett.*
    The floor-bb. are cracked; boarding up a window. Put up a b.;
I saw it on the b. outside.

boat, n. bout; *bateau; Boot, Schiff.*
    Take a b. on the river; go by b.

body (bodies), n. ˈbɔdi; *corps; Körper.*
    (s) Dead body; *cadavre; Leiche.*
    (e) Body without legs, head, or arms: material thing: group
(organization) of things or persons; *torse: corps: corps; Rumpf:
Körper: Gruppe, Körperschaft.*
    Have a healthy b. They were on watch by the b. He had a short
b. and long legs. The attraction of bodies to the earth. The decision
of the ruling b.; a b. of law.

boiling (boiler), a., n. ˈbɔiliŋ; *bouillant; siedend, kochend.*
    -er (s) Steam-making apparatus; *chaudière;* [*Dampf-*]*Kessel.*
    Put an egg in b. water; the water is b.; he is b. the coffee. Cook-
ing the fish by b. it. A ship's boiler.

bone (-er, -ing, -ed), n. boun; *os; Bein, Knochen, Gräte.*
    (e) Bone material; *Bein.*
    No bb. are broken; boning fish. A spoon made of b.; a b. button.

book (-er, -ing, -ed), n. buk; *livre, cahier; Buch, Heft.*
    -ing, (e) Taking tickets for; *acte de retenir* (*une place*); *Belegen.*
    Writing a b.; see it in a b.; a b. of pictures; noting it in a b.;
have no more copies of a b. Booking seats for a play.

book-keeper, n. *Basic words.* Person who keeps accounts.

bookrest, n. *Basic words.* Support for books when reading.

boot, n. buːt; *botte, chaussure; Stiefel.*
    Put on one's bb.

bottle (-er, -ing, -ed), n. ˈbɔtl; *bouteille, flacon; Flasche.*
    Put wine in a b.; bottled beer.

box (boxes, -er, -ing, -ed), n. bɔks; *boîte, malle, caisse; Kiste, Schachtel, Koffer.*

(e) Theater-box; *loge; Loge.*

Keep gloves in a b.; send the boxes to the station; this part is boxed off. Seated in a stage-b.

boy, n. bɔi; *garçon; Junge, Knabe.*

The b. is making a noise.

brain (-er, -ing, -ed), n. brein; *cerveau; (Ge-)Hirn.*

(e) Good quality of brain (freq. **bb.**); *intelligence; Verstand.*

Something wrong with his b.; cooking sheep's bb.; he was brained by a blow. The man has bb.; he has no b.

brake, n. breik; *frein; Bremse.*

The bb. are loose; put the b. on.

branch (branches, -er, -ing, -ed), n. brɑːntʃ; *branche; Zweig.*

(e) B.-like part; b. of business (organization): division; *embranchement: succursale: section; Abzweigung: Filiale: Zweig.*

A broken b.; a tree with low branches. A b. of the railway; branching to the left. The bank has a b. in Hull. A b. of science.

brass, n. brɑːs; *laiton; Messing.*

A bit of b.; a b. pot; a b. plate on the door.

bread, n. bred; *pain; Brot.*

Cutting b.; b. and butter.

breath (-er, -ing, -ed), n. breθ; *haleine, respiration; Atem(zug).*

(e) Soft blow of wind; *souffle; Hauch.*

The dog's b. was warm; take a deep b.; not breathing well. Moved by every b. of wind; a day without a b. of air.

*Be out of b.

breath-taking, a. *Basic words.* So surprising, beautiful, and so on as to take one's breath away.

brick (-er, -ing, -ed), n. brik; *brique; Backstein, Ziegel.*

Putting bb. on the wall; a red-b. house; bricking up a hole.

brickwork, n. *Basic words.* Bricks joined together forming material of wall and so on.

bridge (-er, -ing, -ed), n. bridʒ; *pont; Brücke.*

Make a b. across the railway; bridging the river.

bright, a. brait; *brillant; hell, glänzend.*

(e) With a quick brain: happy; *intelligent: joyeux; hell, aufgeweckt: heiter.*

A b. fire. A b. girl; have a b. idea. A b. and smiling face.

broken (un-), a. ′broukən; *brisé, rompu, fracturé;* [*zer-, unter-, ge*]
brochen.

(e) Crushed (by loss); *abattu; gebrochen.*

The plate is b.; a very b. sleep; the house was b. into by the
police; a bit b. off; the box was b. open; an unbroken line of trees.
He is a b. man.

* (The bread is *b. up*).

brother, n. ′brʌðə*; *frère; Bruder.*

She has a b. in the army; the two boys are bb.

brother-in-law, n. *Basic words.* Brother of man (woman) one is married to.

brown, a., n. braun; *brun; braun.*

Dark b. hair. There is not much b. in the picture.

brush (brushes, -er, -ing, -ed), n. brʌʃ; *brosse, pinceau; Bürste, Pinsel.*

(e) Brushing; *coup de brosse;* (*Ab-*)*Bürsten.*

Using a b. to get the floor clean; a paint b.; the painter is cleaning his brushes. Give the dog a b.; brushing one's hair.

brushwood, n. *Basic words.* 1. Small, low trees. 2. Thin sticks from b.

bucket, n. ′bʌkit; *seau, baquet; Eimer.*

Milking into a b.; a coal b.

building (builder), n., a. bildiŋ; *bâtiment; Gebäude.*

(e) Act of building; *construction; Bauen.*

The highest b. in London; there was no other person in the b.;
that is work for a builder. B. is his trade. They are b. ships (walls);
b. up a business.

bulb, n. bʌlb; *bulbe; Knolle, Zweibel.*

(e) Thing having the form of a bulb; *poire, ampoule;* [*elek-
trische*] *Birne, Gummiball.*

These flowers come from bb. A rubber b.; this electric b. gives a
good light.

burn (-er, -ing, -ed), n. bəːn; *brûlure; Brandschaden.*

-er, (s) Gas burner; *bec, brûleur; Brenner.*

Put oil on a b.; the acid is burning me; the fire is burning
brightly; burning with shame; burning a hole; a smell of burning;
a burning pain. You will get a better light if you have a new burner.

burst, n., a. bəːst; *éclatement, rupture, explosion: crevé; Bersten,
Bruch, Platzen: geplatzt.*

(e) Outburst; *éclat(ement), explosion; Ausbruch.*

There has been a b. in the pipe. A loud b. of sound; a b. of angry feeling. A b. pipe.

business (businesses), n. 'biznis; *occupation; Geschäft, Beruf.*

(s) Trading business: *affaires, commerce: Geschäft.*

(e) Business house: what has to do with one; *maison de commerce: affaire; Geschäft: Angelegenheit.*

His b. is farming. My father is in b.; a good b. man; do b. with. An insurance b.; an old family b.; the two businesses have no connection. It is not your b.

**You *have no b. to* say it; he came *on b.;* they are *going out of b.*

but, conj., prep. bʌt; *mais: sauf; aber, sondern: ausser.*

He is old b. she is young; I went to the house, b. he was not there; I had no desire to go, b. he made me; not only rain b. snow. All b. the foolish have ideas.

* (Men are like animals, *b. for* their brains).

butter (-er, -ing, -ed), n. 'bʌtə*; *beurre; Butter.*

Put the b. on thickly; buttering bread.

buttercup, n. *Basic words.* Yellow, cup-like field-flower.

buttermilk, n. *Basic words.* Liquid from butter-making.

button (-er, -ing, -ed), n. 'bʌtn; *bouton; Knopf.*

(e) small round structure.

The b. has come off my coat; buttoning his shoes. Touching the b. of the bell.

* (My overcoat is *buttoned up*).

buttonhole, n. *Basic words.* Hole for putting button through.

button-hook, n. *Basic words.* Hook for buttoning shoes, gloves.

buzz, n. *Onomatopoeic.* Sound like that of a fly.

by, prep., adv. bai; *près de; neben, bei: vorbei.*

(e) Cause or instrument; *par, au moyen de; bei, von, durch, mit.*

A house b. the river; he went b. me on the road. Picture b. Rubens; go b. train; troubled b. ants; covered b. insurance; punishment b. death. Time goes b. quickly.

*1. Robinson Crusoe was on an island *by himself.*

2. He had to make everything *by hand.*

3. I was working there *by night (day).*

4. I had come across some coal on the island *by chance.*

5. *By the way,* have you ever been down a coal mine?

6. No smoking, *by order.*

7. A young miner *got* the Basic words *by heart* in less than a week.

8. He got the word order into his head *by slow degrees.*

9. *Little by little* (*bit by bit, day by day*), he got expert at the special uses.

10. He is coming here at 4, *by this clock*

(*Take b. surprise;* a story *b. word of mouth; side b. side*).

**Come *b.* to-morrow. (Playing *b. ear; b. request*).

bygone, a. *Basic words.* Long past, no longer in existence.

*café**, 'kæfei. *International word.*

calendar, 'kælində*. *International word.*

cake (-er, -ing, -ed), n. keik; *gâteau; Kuchen.*

(e) Cake of substance; *pain, morceau; Stück.*

Make a c.; have chocolate c. for tea. A c. of soap; the wheel is caked with earth.

camera, n. 'kæmərə; *appareil photographique; photographischer Apparat.*

Taking pictures with a c.

canvas, n. 'kænvəs; *toile, canevas;* [*Maler-*]*Leinwand, Zeltbahn, Segeltuch.*

Painting on c.; sleeping under c. A c. cover on the boat.

card, n. kɑːd; *carte; Karte.*

(s) Playing-card; *carte à jouer; Karte.*

(e) Material of which cards are made; *carton; Karton.*

cc. (e) Play with cc.; *cartes;* (*ein*) *Spielkarten.*

Send a c. to. Put down a higher c. Pictures done on c.

The men were playing cc.

cardboard, n. *Basic words.* Stiff card.

care, n. kɛə*; *soin; Sorgfalt, Obhut, Vorsicht.*

(e) Feeling of trouble; *souci; Sorge.*

Put on the dress with c.; the jewels are in my c.; take care. The cc. of his position.

((Take) c. of).

carefree, a. *Basic words.* Without any feeling of care.

caretaker, n. *Basic words.* Person looking after house and so on.

carriage, n. ′kærid₃; *voiture; Wagen.*

(e) Division of train: transporting: payment for transport; *wagon: transport; port; [Eisenbahn-]Wagen: Transport: Fracht.*

Driving in a c. with two horses. A train with six cc. Undertake the c. of goods. How much is the c.?

*Send the box c. *forward.*

cart (-er, -ing, -ed), n. kɑːt; *charrette; Karren, [Fracht-] Wagen.*

A c. came round with coal; carting the earth away.

cat, n. kæt; *chat; Katze.*

The c. is on the roof.

catarrh, kə′tɑː*. *International word.*

cause (-er, -ing, -ed), n. kɔːz; *cause; Ursache.*

(e) Purpose: question up for decision by law; *cause: procés, cause; Sache, Zweck: Rechtsfall.*

Get angry without c.; it has an interesting c.; the c. of the trouble. Give money for a good c. The hearing of a c.

* (There is no c. *for* protest).

certain (-ly, un-), a. səːtn; *sûr; sicher.*

(e) Special but unnamed; *certain; gewiss, bestimmt.*

Be c. one is right; seem uncertain; they are certainly not here now. He has a c. disease.

*Make c. *before you do it.*

chain (-er, -ing, -ed), n. tʃein; *chaîne; Kette.*

(e) Things looked on as a c.: range of mountains.

The dog is on a c.; chaining the prisoners together; chained to the railing. A c. of events. A c. of mountains.

chalk (-er, -ing, -ed), n. tʃɔːk; *craie; Kreide.*

(s) Stick of chalk for writing with.

The earth here is full of c. My c. is broken; chalking numbers on a board.

champagne, ʃæm′pein. *International word.*

chance (-er, -ing, -ed), n. tʃɑːns; *hasard, chance; Zufall.*

(e) Possible hope, time when chance is on one's side; *occasion, chance de réussir, Möglichkeit, Gelegenheit.*

A question of c.; c. is against us; take one's c. of getting a seat; a c. meeting. Here is your c.; he hasn't a c. of getting away; the cc. are against him.

    * (I came there *by c.*).

    **Come *on the c.* that one's friend is there.

change (-er, -ing, -ed), n. tʃeindʒ; *changement; Wechsel, (Ver-) Änderung.*

    (e) Small money: money handed back after taking payment out of money offered; *petite monnaie: différence; Kleingeld; Überschusz.*

    Make cc. in the book; see a c. in him; men are changing; she is changing her dress. Get c. at the station. Give the right c.

    ** (*Small c.*).

chauffeur,* ʃou'fəː*. *International word.*

cheap (-ly), a. tʃiːp; *bon marché; billig.*

    (e) Poor in quality, common; *inférieur; gering.*

    A c. meal. C. fiction; a c. trick; be cheaply dressed.

cheese, n. tʃiːz; *fromage; Käse.*

    A great round c.; cc. made from goat's milk; a bit of c.

chemical (-ly, un-), a., n. kemikəl; *chimique; chemisch.*

    A c. process; chemically, it is unchanged. A strong c.

chemist, 'kemist. *International word.*

chemistry, 'kemistri. *International name of science.*

check, tʃek. *International word.*

    **A c. on the bank.

chest, n. tʃest; *poitrine; Brust(-Kasten).*

    (e) Box for storing things in; *coffre; Lade.*

    A pain in my c. Locked in a c.; a c. of drawers.

chief, a., n. tʃiːf; *principal; chef; haupt(sächlich): Haupt, Häuptling, Führer.*

    Fishing is his c. interest. The c. is wounded.

chin, n. tʃin; *menton; Kinn.*

    She has a small c.

chocolate, 'tʃɔkəlit. *International word.*

chorus, 'kɔːrəs. *International word.*

church (churches), n. tʃəːtʃ; *église; Kirche.*

    (e) Organization of which a c. is representative, gen. C.

    The c. is full; the town has 4 churches; be in c.; go to c. every Sunday. The opinion of the C.; the C. of England.

cigarette, sigə'ret. *International word.*

circle (-er, -ing, -ed), n. 'səːkl; *cercle; Kreis.*

    (e) Group of persons.

A c. on the paper; the little girls were in a c. round the teacher; circling round the tree. An interesting c. of friends.

circus*, 'sə:kəs. *International word.*

citron*, 'sitrən. *International word.*

clean (-er, -ing, -ed, un-, -ly), a. kli:n; *propre; sauber.*

(e) Without dirty suggestion; *pur; rein.*

A c. room; send a dress to the cleaner; my coat has been cleaned.
A c. story; unclean thoughts.

**Cleaning up after work.

clear (-er, -ing, -ed, un-, -ly), a. kliə*; *clair; klar.*

(e) Clear to the mind: sharply outlined to eye or ear: free; *évident: net, clair: libre; deutlich; bestimmt, hell: frei.*

A c. day; c. water; the sky is clearing. Make a point c.; get c. about something; see his purpose clearly; the sense is unclear. His writing is very c.; the c. sound of a bell. The road is c.

**Get (keep) c. of.

clock, n. klɔk; *horloge, (une) pendule; Uhr.*

This c. is right.

*(4 *by the c.*).

clockwork, n. *Basic words.* Machine like that of a clock.

cloth (-er, -ing, -ed), n. klɔθ; *étoffe, drap, toile; Tuch, Stoff.*

(s) A bit of cloth; *torchon, nappe.*

-ing, (e) Dress; *vêtement; Kleid(ung).*

A roll of c. Here is a c. for drying the plates. Put on clothing; clothing oneself.

cloud (-er, -ing, -ed), n. klaud; *nuage; Wolke.*

(e) Thick mass: cloud of trouble; *nuage: ombre.*

Cc. in the sky; the sky is clouding over. A c. of smoke. A c. on her face; be under a c.; clouding their pleasure.

club, klʌb. *International word.*

coal (-er, -ing, -ed), n. koul; *charbon; Kohle.*

Burning c.; a c. fire; coaling the ship.

coat (-er, -ing, -ed), n. kout; *veston, manteau; Rock, Jacke, Mantel.*

(e) A cover; *couche [de peinture etc.]; Anstrich.*

A winter c.; put on a c.; a c. and skirt. A new c. of paint; coating the house with whitewash.

cocktail*, 'kɔkteil. *International word.*

coffee, 'kɔfi. *International word.*

cognac*, 'kounjæk. *International word.*

cold (-ly), a., n. kould; *froid: rhume; kalt: Kälte; Erkältung.*

(e) Cold in behavior (feeling): ill condition marked by coughing and sneezing; *froid: rhume; kalt: Erkältung.*

A c. day; the soup got c. She was c. to her friends; be looking at him coldly. Feeling the c. Have a c.

collar, n. 'kɔleᵉ; *col, collet, collier; Kragen, Halsband.*

A shirt c.; put on a clean c.; a dog-c.

college, 'kɔlidᴣ. *International name.*

colony, 'kɔləni. *International word.*

color (-er, -ing, -ed), n. 'kʌləᵉ; *couleur; Farbe.*

A bright c.; coloring the wall.

comb (-er, -ing, -ed), n. koum; *peigne; Kamm.*

(e) Combing; *action de (se) peigner; Kämmen.*

A brush and c. Give one's hair a c.; combing the dog.

come (comes, came, coming), v. kʌm; *venir, arriver; kommen.*

C. into the house; thoughts c. into the mind; nations c. into existence; one page comes after another; his name comes at the end; prices will c. down; the sea comes in; he came first in the list; in the coming year; boats c. and go; buttons c. off; these words c. out of a book; the story came to my ears; all these examples c. under one rule; flowers c. up; the sun comes up; it comes up to my hopes.

*1. The governments will *come to an agreement* (*a decision*) about the taxes.

2. The train *came to a stop* at the station.

3. Strange facts *have come to light.*

4. A newspaper man *came across* some private papers under the seat.

5. How did this *come about?*

*(Your fears may not c. *true*).

**C. *to blows; c. to grips; c. to one's senses;* it *comes to this; c. up for* discussion. (*C. into line; c. into play; c. round;* men *c. out*).

comfort (-er, -ing, -ed), n. kʌmfət; *confort; Bequemlichkeit.*

(s) Comfort to the feelings; *reconfort, consolation; Trost.*

(e) Thing giving comfort; *reconfort; Trost, Annehmlichkeit.*

Resting in c.; a comforting drink. Take c. from the fact; comforting a friend. My son is a c. to me.

committee, n. kə'miti; *comité, commission; Komitee, Ausschuss.*
Put it before the c.; forming a c.
* (He is *on the c.*).

common (un-, -ly), a. 'kɔmən; *ordinaire; gewöhnlich.*

(e) Of low birth, behavior, in bad taste, unpolished: taking place frequently: with more than one owner; *vulgair: commun: commun; gemein: alltäglich: gemein (sam).*

That is the c. view. A c. person of rough behavior. Quite a c. event; an uncommon disease; it is commonly said. Talking a c. language.

*Things *in c.*

commonsense, n. *Basic words.* General good sense.

company (companies), n. kʌmpəni; *société; Gesellschaft.*

(e) Group, sp. an organization for some purpose, as a business c.; *compagnie; (Handels-) Gesellschaft.*

She went to meetings for c.; be happy in a person's c. The business was made into a c.; two companies of actors.

* (*Keep* a person *c.*)

comparison, n. kəm'pærisn; *comparaison; Vergleich.*

Make a c. between things; this is small in c. with that.

competition, n. kɔmpi'tiʃən; *concurrence; Konkurrenz; Wettbewerb.*

(s) Competition with rules; *concours; Wettbewerb.*

The groups are in c. with one another; c. is strong between them. The paper is having a c. for cooks.

**C. *in.*

complete (-er, -ing, -ed, in-, -ly), a. kəm'pliːt; *complet, acheve; vollständig, vollende.*

Have a c. system; the work is incomplete; who is completing the book?; in c. harmony; you are completely wrong.

complex (un-), a., n. 'kɔmpleks; *complexe, compliqué; verwickelt, komplex, zusammengesetzt.*

(e) A system of unconscious desires and so on having an effect on a person's behavior; *complexe; Komplex.*

C. ideas; a c. form. A c. of parts. He has a c. about his father.

condition (-er, -ing, -ed), n. kən'diʃen; *état; Zustand.*

(e) Condition of an agreement (act); *condition; Bedingung.*

Living cc. are bad; a strange c. of mind; horses in good c.; conditioning a dog; a conditioned reaction. He made some cc.; a c. of the distribution.

  *On c. that.

connection, n. kə'nekʃən; *relation, liaison, lien, communication; Verbindung, Zusammenhang.*

  (e) Body of persons doing business with a given store and so on (freq. cc.).

  I do not see any c. between those statements; he has no c. with the business; the train cc. are bad. The music teacher has a good c.
  **In this c.

conscious (un-, -ly), a. 'kɔnʃəs; *conscient; bewusst.*

  The c. mind, a c. error; be unconscious; not consciously cruel.

  * (*C. of* something).

control (-ler, -ling, -led), n. kən'troul; *maîtrise, autorité, direction; Beherrschung, Kontrolle.*

  (e) Controlling apparatus; *régulateur; Kontroll-Apparat.*

  He has no c. over his son; his feelings are well under c.; take c.; controlling the work (army); a controlling interest; a well-controlled voice. The c. is not working.

  * (*C. of*).

cook (-er, -ing, -ed), n. kuk; *cuisinier(-ière); Koch.*

  -er, (s) Cooking apparatus; *fourneau; Kochherd, Kocher.*

  The c. made a cake; good cooking. A gas-cooker.

copper (-er, -ing, -ed), n. 'kɔpə*; *cuivre; Kupfer.*

  (s) Bit of copper money; *sou; Kupfermünze.*

  Get c. out of the earth; a c. pot; the box is coppered inside. Give the boy some cc.

copy (copies, -er, -ing, -ed), n. 'kɔpi; *copie; Kopie, Abschrift.*

  (e) Copy of a book; *exemplaire; Examplar.*

  Make a c. of a table; copying letters; copying someone's behavior. Printing more copies of the reading-book.

copyright, n. *Basic words.* Right to profits on a book.

cord (-er, -ing, -ed), n. kɔːd; *corde, ficelle; Schnur, (Bind-)Faden, Strick.*

  A whistle on a c.; the parcel had c. round it; a corded box.

cork (-er, -ing, -ed), n. kɔːk; *liege; Kork.*

  (s) Cork of a bottle; *bouchon; Korken.*

  Covered with c. Get the c. out; corking the bottle.

corkscrew, n. *Basic words.* Instrument for pulling out corks.

cotton, n. 'kɔtn; *coton; Baumwolle.*

(s) Cotton thread; *fil;* [*Baumwoll-*]*Garn.*

A field of c.; a c. dress. Take a needle and c.

cotton-wool, n. *Basic words.* Natural cotton before it is made into thread, a soft mass used medically and so on.

cough (-er, -ing, -ed), n. kɔf; *toux; Husten.*

(e) Tendency to coughing.

Give a c.; coughing in church. Have a bad c.

country (countries), 'kʌntri; *campagne; Land.*

(e) Division of the earth, political or other; *pays, patrie; Land, Vaterland.*

A farm in the c.; wooded c. The c. is at war; warm countries.

cover (-er, -ing, -ed), n. 'kʌvə*; *couverture; Decke.*

(s) Cover of box or pot; *couvercle; Deckel.*

(e) Something keeping from view; *abri; Deckung.*

A c. on the bed; covering his face with his hands; insurance covering damage by fire; hands covered with hair. The c. is off the box. The trees were c. for the army.

***Take c.*

cow, n. kau; *vache; Kuh.*

Milk from the c.; the cc. in the field.

crack (-er, -ing, -ed), n. kræk; *fente, crevasse; Sprung, Spalte.*

(e) Noise of cracking; *craquement; Krach, Knall.*

A c. in the place; cracking nuts. The c. of a whip.

credit (-or, -ing, -ed), n. 'kredit; *crédit; Kredit.*

(e) Good name: thing helping this; *honneur: honneur; Ansehen, Ehre: Ehre.*

Have c. at a bank; give c.; get c.; crediting one's account. His c. is high with his friends; crediting him with common sense. He is a c. to his father.

**On c.; to one's c.*

crime, n. kraim; *crime; Verbrechen.*

(e) Very bad, shocking, act or condition.

Go to prison for a c. Wasting your education is a c.

cruel (-ly), a. 'kruəl; *cruel; grausam.*

A c. man; a c. death; a c. thing to say; be acting cruelly.

crush (-er, -ing, -ed), n. krʌʃ; *écrasement; Quetschung, Zermalmen.*

(e) Mass of persons very near together.

Give the nut a c.; his hat was crushed by someone stepping on it; a crushing blow. In such a c., there was no room for dancing.

cry (-er, -ing, cried), n. krai; *cri; Schrei, [Aus-]Ruf.*

-**ing,** (e) Unhappy crying; *action de pleurer; Weinen.*

The c. of a street trader; a bird's c.; give a c. of pain; crying out that all is well. She was crying quietly.

cup, n. kʌp; *tasse; Tasse.*

The c. is broken; a c. of tea.

cupboard, n. *Basic words.* Box-like structure with doors and gen. shelves inside.

current, n., a. ˈkʌrənt; *courant; Strömung: aktuell, (um)-laufend.*

(s) Electric current; *Strom.*

Swimming against the c.; the c. of opinion was against him. Putting on the c. C. events.

curtain (-er, -ing, -ed), n. ˈkəːtn; *rideau; Vorhang, Gardine.*

(s) Theater curtain.

A c. over the window; part of the room was curtained off. Be at the theater before the c. goes up.

curve (-er, -ing, -ed), n. kəːv; *courbe; Krümmung, Kurve.*

The c. of an arm; a price c.; curving in the air; curving the metal; a curved knife.

cushion (-er, -ing, -ed), n. ˈkuʃən; *coussin; Kissen, Polster.* Resting on a c.; a cushioned seat.

cut (-ter, -ting, un-), a., n. kʌt; *coupé: coupure, entaille; geschnitten: Schnitt.*

-**ting,** (e) Bit cut out or off; *coupure; Ausschnitt.*

The cord is c.; a c. finger; a well-c. dress; cutting a bit off. A c. on the nose. A newspaper cutting.

*(Bread is c. up).

damage (-er, -ing, -ed), n. ˈdæmidʒ; *dommage, détriment, tort; Schaden.*

dd. = payment for damage; *dommages-intérêts, indemnité; Schadenersatz.*

Looking at the d. caused by the fire; the window was damaged by a storm; a damaging statement. Payment of dd.

*(Do d. to).

dance, dɑːns. *International word.*

danger, n. 'deindʒə*; *danger; Gefahr.*

    (e) Thing causing danger.

    The d. of walking on thin ice; be in d. of fire. He is a public d.; that machine is a d. to the workers.

dark, a., n. dɑːk, *sombre; dunkel.*

    A d. night; a d. color; dressed darkly. Fear of the d.

daughter, n. 'dɔːtə*; *fille; Tochter.*

    The d. of a poor man; have three dd.

daughter-in-law, n. *Basic words.* Woman one's son is married to.

day, n. dei; *journée: Tag.*

    (e) Opposite of night; time in history; *jour: jour.*

    A week has 7 dd.; d. and night; a bright d. In our d.

    *(All d.; by d.; d. by d.; from d. to d.; good-d.).

    **One d.; have one's d.

daylight, n. *Basic words.* The light of daytime.

daytime, n. The time when it is day.

dead, a., ded; *mort: [les] morts; tot: [die] Toten.*

    (e) Without feeling: gone out of use; *engourdi: perimé; abgestorben: tot.*

    A d. man; respect for the d. My foot is d. That idea is d.; d. languages.

dear (-ly), a., n. diə*; *cher; teuer.*

    (e) Loved (one); *cher: chéri; lieb: Liebe(r).*

    The goods are d. A d. friend; he was dearly loved. Come with me, my d.

    *(D. to the public).

death, n. deθ; *mort; Tod.*

    (e) Condition of death.

    His d. was a great blow; go to one's d.; come to one's d.; d. took him; the d. of his hopes. Beautiful in d.

    *(Put to d.).

debt, n. det; *dette; Schuld.*

    (e) Condition of having dd.

    A d. of £10; a d. to the past. Be badly in d.

decision, n. di'siʒən; *décision; Entscheidung.*

    (e) Power of making decisions; *Entschlossenheit.*

    Make a d.; the d. of this question. He has great d.

*(*Come to a d.*).

deep (-ly), a., adv. di:p; *profond; tief.*

(e) Going to the root (of a question); *à fond.*

D. water; a d. hole; be d. in debt; he was deeply moved. A d. book; a d. interest. Go d. into the earth.

degree, di'gri:; *degré; Brad.*

(e) Amount.

Two dd. under boiling-point; marking the dd. in red. A high d. of interest; a question only of d.

*(*By dd.*).

delicate (-ly), a. 'delikit; *délicat; zart, fein.*

(s) Readily made ill; *délicat; schwächlich.*

(e) Giving reaction to small details, using care: needing d. care; *sensible, délicat: fin; empfindlich; heikel.*

D. glass; the picture was delicately colored. A d. person. A d. instrument; d. tastes; a d. touch. D. work.

dependent (in-), a. di'pendənt; *dépendant; abhängig.*

A d. person; the country is now independent.

**D. on* (some thing or person).

design (-er, -ing, -ed), n. di'zain; *dessein, dessin; Muster, Entwurf.*

(e) What one has in mind to do; *projet; Plan.*

The d. on the curtain; a d. for a house; designing a dress. Dd. for a new organization; designing to get free.

**Have dd. on* (a person, his money, and so on).

desire (-er, -ing, -ed), n. di'zaiə*; *désir; Wunsch.*

A d. for food; a d. to go; give the desired answer.

destruction, n. dis'trʌkʃən; *destruction; Zerstörung. Ausrottung, Vernichtung.*

A substance for the d. of insects; the d. of one's hopes; go to one's d.; send him to his d.

detail (-er, -ing, -ed), n. 'di:teil; *détail; Einzelheit.*

(s) Unimportant detail.

The newspaper gives all the dd. of the crime; the dd. of her dress; detailing the events; a detailed account; go into dd. That is only a d.

**Story in d.*

development, n. di'veləpmənt; *développement; Entwicklung.*

(e) Outcome; *résultat.*

The d. of a new system (idea): the d. of man; go through a process of d. Interesting new dd.

did. See *do.*

different (-ly), a. 'difrənt; *différent; verschieden andere (-r, -s).*

Two d. sorts of fruit; a different man; viewing things differently.

digestion, n. di'dʒestʃən; *digestion; Verdauung.*

He has a good d.; d. is a slow process.

direction, n. di'rekʃen; *direction; Richtung.*

(e) Controlling: order; *gestion: instruction; Leitung: Anweisung.*

Birds coming from every d.; going in the d. of the town; the d. of the current. The d. of a business. Those were his dd.

dirty (dirtier, -ing, -dirtied), a. 'dəːti; *sale; schmutzig.*

(e) With a dirty suggestion; *indécent.*

The tablecloth is d.; make the floor d.; dirtying one's hands. A d. story.

discovery, n. dis'kʌvəri; *découverte; Entdeckung.*

(e) Thing uncovered by discovery.

He made an interesting d.; the year of the d. of America. May I see your d.?

discussion, n. dis'kʌʃn; *discussion; Erörterung.*

Have a d. about; the d. of details; deep in d.; the Peace D. in London.

* (An idea *under d.*).

** (*Come up for d.*).

disease, n. di'ziːz; *maladie; Krankheit.*

Get a d.; expert on dd. of the ear; a town full of d.

disgust (-er, -ing, -ed), n. dis'gʌst; *dégoût; Ekel, Abneigung.*

Have a d. for a person; go away in d.; disgusting facts; a disgusted person.

* (*Disgusted* (pleased, angry) *with*).

distance, n. 'distəns; *distance; Abstand, Entfernung.*

A d. of four feet; go a great d.; some d. away; in walking (hearing) d.; see from a d.

* (*At a* great *d.*).

distribution, n. distri'bjuːʃən; *distribution; Verteilung.*

(e) How things are placed; *répartition; Verbreitung.*

Make a d. of clothing; an unequal d. What is the d. of the disease (plants)?

division, n. di'viʒən; *division; Abteilung.*

(e) Space (wall) between: act of division: division of feeling (opinion); *cloison: séparation: divergence; Teilung: Teilung: Teilung.*

A d. of a school; a d. of the book. Put up a d. across the room; make a d. between the houses. The d. of the money; the boys are doing d. A d. of opinion among experts.

do (does, did, doing, done, doer), v., aux. v. duː; *faire, agir; tun, machen.*

(e) Be right, or enough, for a given purpose.

-ings, (e) Acts; *actes; Taten.*

D. a kind act; d. the right thing; d. the cleaning; d. music; d. nothing; d. wrong. This will d. for a curtain. I d. not keep dogs; he did not see me; d. you go to the theater?; I made an offer and so did he. Give an account of one's doings.

*The bricks will *d. damage to* the window; they *did well* (*badly*) in the test. (*D. one's best; have* nothing *to d. with*).

***How d. you d.?* I have *done with* the paper. *D. one's bit; d. trade in; d.* one *good*).

dog, n. dɔg; *chien; Hund.*

Take a d. for a walk.

dominion, do'minjən. *International name.*

door, n. dɔː*; *porte; Tür.*

Get the d. open; the d. into the room; at death's d.

***Out of dd.*

doorkeeper, n. *Basic words.* Person stationed at door of hotel and so on, to oversee incomings and outgoings.

doorway, n. *Basic words.* Opening for a door.

doubt (-er, -ing, -ed), n. daut; *doute; Zweifel.*

Have dd. about; be in d.; doubting a man (story).

***No d.*

down, prep., adv. daun; (*en*) *bas; herab, hinunter: unten.*

Go d. a mountain. The sun goes d.; put the pot d.; take d. words; the story has come d. from the past.

*He took a walk *d.* (*up*) *the street* (*road*); if you are good at fighting, that is no reason for *looking d. on* lovers of peace. (He *let* his friend *d.*).

°°(*Put one's foot d.* about something; *put* the smash *d. to* the wet road).

downfall, n. *Basic words.* Destruction, end.

drain (-er, -ing, -ed), n. drein; *égout, tuyau d'écoulement, drain; Abflussleitung, Entwässerungs-graben.*

-ing, (e) Process of making less or feebler; *affaiblissement; Verbrauchen.*

Put water down the d.; draining a bit of land. Draining away his power.

drawer, n. drɔː°; *tiroir; Schublade.*

Put away in a d.

dress (dresses, -er, -ing, -ed), n. dres; *robe; Kleid.*

(e) Clothing; *habit, habillement; Kleidung.*

-ing, (e) Cover put on wound: substance put on food; *pansement: asaisonnement, sauce; Verband: Sauce.*

She had a beautiful d.; their dresses were blue. A new form of d.; dressing oneself (the baby). Put a dressing on the leg; dressing the leg. A thick dressing on the meat.

°(*Dressing up*).

drink, n. driŋk; *boisson; Getränk.*

(s) Alcohol d.; *liqueurs fortes; (geistiges) Getränk.*

(e) (Amount of d. for) one act of taking d.; *coup de boire; Schluck.*

Tea is a good d. They had some d.; d. is his trouble. Have a d. of water; have a d. to him; give me another d.

°(*The worse for d.*).

driving (driver), n., a. draiviŋ; *action de conduire; Fahren, Führen.*

(e) Forcing; *action de pousser; Treiben.*

D. an automobile (cart), a good driver. Put the nail in by d. it with a hammer; the wind was d. the ship forward; a d. rain; you are d. me to drink.

drop (-per, -ping, -ped), n. drɔp; *goutte; Tropfen.*

(e) Fall: *chute; Fall.*

Dd. of rain on the window; a d. of blood from the wound. It is a long d. from the top of the wall; a d. in prices; dropping the plate.

dry (-er, -ing, dried), a. drai; *sec, arid; trocken.*

(e) Not interesting; *ennuyeux.*

A d. field (tongue, day); get d. in front of the fire; drying the linen; dried fruit. A d. discussion (book).

dust (-er, -ing, -ed), n. dʌst; *poussière; Staub.*

(e) Powder; *poudre.*

-er, (s) Cloth for taking off dust; *torchon; Staubtuch.*

There is d. on the books; get d. in his eyes; dusting the table (room). Chalk d. Cleaning the table with a duster.

dustman, n. *Basic words.* Man who goes round with cart for house waste.

dynamite*, 'dainəmait. *International word.*

ear, n. iə*; *orielle; Ohr.*

He put his e. to the key-hole; news comes to one's ee.

***An e. for* music; playing *by e.*

early, a., adv. 'ə:li; *de bonne heure, premier; früh.*

(e) Before the time; *prématuré; (zu) früh.*

It is e. in the day; the e. years. E. for the meal. Get up e.

ear-ring, n. *Basic words.* Ornament for ear.

earth, n. 'əθ:; *terre, sol; Erde.*

(e) The ball on which we are living; *terre.*

Put a seed in the e. The e. goes round the sun.

**Nothing *on e.*

earthwork, n. *Basic words.* Earth walls put up in war.

east, a., adv., s., i:st; *est; östlich: Osten.*

The e. side; an e. wind. Going e.; Germany is e. of France. The sun comes up in the e.; religions of the E.

edge (-er, -ing, -ed), n. edʒ; *bord, tranchant; Rand, Schneide.*

The e. of the sea (dress); the knife has a sharp e.; the collar is edged with blue.

education, n. edju(:)'keiʃən; *éducation, instruction; Erziehung, Bildung.*

Give a boy a good e.; the e. of the young; the experience will be a good e. for you.

effect (-er, -ing, -ed), n. i'fekt; *effet, résultat; Wirkung.*

A strange e. of light; his statement had no e.; get a snow e. by dropping paper; effecting a change.

*(Have *an e. on*).

***In e.; be of no e.; put into e.; take e.*

egg, n. eg; *œuf; Ei.*

This e. comes from the farm.

egg-cup, n. *Basic words.* Sort of cup used at table for an egg.

elastic (in-), a., n. i'læstik; *élastique; elastisch, dehnbar: Gummiband.*

(e) Readily stretched, changed.

An e. material. Very e. views. A bit of e.

electric (-ally), a. i'lektrik; *électrique; elektrisch.*

E. light (current); get an e. shock; the house is electrically heated.

embassy, embəsi. *International name.*

empire, 'empaiə*. *International name.*

encyclopaedia,* en'saiklo'pi:diə. *International word.*

end (-er, -ing, -ed), n. end; *fin, bout; Ende.*

-ing, (e) The end part of a story (word); *fin, terminaison; Endung, Ende.*

Come (get) to the e.; the e. of the street (story, work); a loose e. of thread; the day is ending. The ending '-ing.'

°In the e. (Put an e. [a stop] to).

engine, n. 'endʒin; *machine, moteur; Maschine, Motor.*

(s) Railway engine; *locomotive; Lokomotive.*

The automobile has a good e. The e. of the train is not strong enough.

engineer, 'endʒi'niə*. *International word.*

enough, adv., a., n. i'nʌf; *assez; genug.*

It is good e.; go far e. from danger. There is not e. time for the work. Have e.; you have said e.; get e. of.

°°Strangely e.

equal (un-, -ly), a., n. 'i:gwəl; *égal; gleich.*

E. amounts; take an e. pleasure in, the sides are unequal; this is e. to that; they are equally bad. A fight between ee.

error, n. 'erə*; *erreur; Irrtum.*

Make an e.; say in e.

even, adv. 'i:vən; *même; sogar, selbst.*

It is cold e. in the sun; e. though he was old, they made him go; he has no fear e. of death; the box was not e. open; he is e. happy; e. more interesting is the story of; e. if you have done it, I will still be your friend.

°°E. so.

event, n. i'vent; *événement; Ereignis.*

An e. has taken place; these strange ee.

**At all ee.; in the e. of.*

ever, adv. 'eve*; *jamais, toujours; immer, je(mals).*

If you e. see him, give him my love. Have you e. been?; it was e. the same; no man will go on living for e.

*It is as true *as* (truer *than*) e.

**(For e. saying the same thing).

evergreen, n., a. *Basic words.* Plant or tree which is green all the year.

every, a. 'evri; *chaque, tout; jede (-r, -s).*

E. word was true; he comes e. day; e. time he comes, I go; e. one of them became ill.

**There is e. reason why. (E. other day).*

everybody, n. *Basic words.* Every person.

everyday, a. *Basic words.* Common.

everyone, pron. *Basic words,* Every person.

everything, n. *Basic words.* Every thing.

everywhere, adv. *Basic words.* In (at, to) every place.

example, n. ig'zaːmpl; *exemple; Beispiel.*

(e) Thing (or person) rightly to be copied.

An e. of her work; an e. of false reasoning. He is an e. to us all.

exchange (-er, -ing, -ed), n. iks'tʃeindʒ; *échange; Tausch.*

(e) Money exchange between countries: money market; *change: Bourse; Wechsel: Börse.*

The e. of goods for money; exchanging hats (words). The e. is against us. The E. is doing no business.

*(In e. for).

existence, n. ig'zistəns; *existence; Vorhandensein, Dasein.*

(e) Condition, way, of living; *vie; Leben.*

Be in e.; the e. of a gas; come into e. An unhappy e.

*(Have e.).

expansion, n. iks'pænʃən; *dilatation, expansion, extension; Ausdehnung, Erweiterung.*

The e. of gases; the e. of a business; the e. of a theory; an e. of the sense of the word.

experience (-er, -ing, -ed), n. iks'piəriəns; *expérience; Erfahrung.*

(e) Event experienced; *aventure, épreuve.*

He has no e.; get some e.; experiencing a new feeling; an experienced person. My ee. in Russia.

expert (in-, -ly), 'ekspə:t; *expert, spécialiste; Fachmann.*

He is a great e. in that field; he put his questions expertly; her hair had been inexpertly waved. E. knowledge; e. work.

° (*E. at* doing; *e. on* a question).

eye (-er, -ing, -ed), n. 'ai; *œil; Auge.*

Keep one's ee. shut; eyeing the food; blue-eyed.

°*Keep an e. on; have an e. for* form.

°°*Make ee. at.*

eyeball, n. *Basic words.* The ball-like part of the eye.

face (-er, -ing, -ed), n. feis; *figure, visage; Gesicht.*

(e) Front; *face, façade, cadran; Vorderseite, Zifferblatt.*

-ing, (e) Looking straight at, meeting without fear; *affrontant, bravant; ins Angesicht schauend.*

Covering his f.; a smiling f. The f. of the clock (building); facing the church. Facing the facts.

°*Have the f. to; make a f.* (*at*). (*F. to f.*).

°°*To one's f.; on the f. of it.* (*Full f.*).

fact, n. fækt; *fait; Tatsache.*

The ff. about; it is a f. that.

° (*In f.*).

fall, n. fɔːl; *chute, baisse; Fall, Sturz.*

(e) Time of dropping leaves; *automne; Herbst.*

Have a f.; a f. of 10 feet; a f. in prices; a f. from power. Come to England in the f.

false (-ly), a. fɔːls; *faux; falsch.*

(e) Not true in feeling (acts); *perfide.*

A f. story; a f. idea of the place; f. teeth; he was falsely said to be away. Be f. to a person; a f. friend.

family, n. 'fæmili; *famille; Familie.*

(e) Offspring, son(s) and/or daughter(s): group like a f., specially naming a division of plants, animals.

One of that f.; he is of good f.; a f. hotel. She has a f. of three, two boys and one girl. A f. of languages; these plants are of the same f.

far (farther or further, farthest or furthest), adv., a. fɑː°; *loin: lointain; fern, weit: fern.*

Do not go f.; be sent f. away; I went no farther that day. This town is f. from London; the farthest star.

farm (-er, -ing, -ed), n. fɑːm; *ferme; (Bauern-)Gut, (Bauern-)Hof, Gehöft.*

Working on a f.; a good farmer; farming in Wales.

fat, a., n. fæt; *gras; dick, fett.*

(e) Thick; *gros; dick.*

A f. pig. A f. stick. Put some f. on the plate.

father, n. ˈfɑːðə°; *père; Vater.*

The f. of six boys; become a f.; my f. gave it to me.

father-in-law, n. *Basic words.* Father of man (woman) one is married to.

fatherland, n. *Basic words.* Country of one's birth.

fear (-er, -ing, -ed), n. fiə°; *peur, crainte; Furcht.*

F. is a cause of hate; be in f. of punishment; have ff. for him; fearing the future; he is feared by all.

° *(For f. of).*

feather (-er, -ing, -ed), n. ˈfeðə°; *plume; Feder.*

A bird without ff.; a feathered hat.

feeble (-ly), a. ˈfiːbl; *faible; schwach.*

(e) Without effect; *inefficace.*

A f. support; a f. mind; he was feebly crying out for help. Make a f. answer.

feeling (feeler), n., a. ˈfiːliŋ; *sensibilité, sensation; Gefühl.*

(s) Hate, love, and so on; *sentiment, émotion.*

-er, (s) Feeling part of insect; *antenne; Fühler.*

A f. of pain. Angry f. Be f. unhappy. The insect has two feelers.

female, a., n. fiːmeil; *féminin, femelle; weiblich.*

a f. voice; a f. animal. The cat is a f.

fertile (in-), a. ˈfəːtail; *fécond; fruchtbar.*

A f. field; a f. woman; infertile land.

° *Be f. in* (ideas and so on).

fiction, n. fikʃən; *fiction; Fiktion, Erfindung.*

(s) Stories as branch of letters; *[les] romans; Roman.*

Fact or f.; the f. that all men are equal. Hardy was a writer of f.

field, n. fiːld; *champ; Feld.*

(e) Range; *étendue, champ d'action.*

Cows in a f. F. of thought (work).

fight, n. fait; *combat, lutte; Kampf, Schlägerei.*

(s) Fight in a war; *bataille; Gefecht.*

Make a f. for equal rights; the two men had a f. A f. between two armies.

* (He *put up a f.*).

finger (-er, -ing, -ed), n. 'fiŋgǝ*; *doigt; Finger.*

A cut f.; fingering the goods; a two-fingered hand.

fingerprint, n. *Basic words.* Mark made by a finger.

fire (-er, -ing, -ed), n. 'faiǝ*; *feu; Feuer.*

(e) Mass of wood, coal, and so on (placed ready for) burning; event of destruction by f.: the going off of guns: free, moving, quality of feeling; *feu: incendie: feu: ardeur.*

Destruction by f. The f. is not lighted. On the night of the f.; firing the house. A burst of f. from the wood; firing his gun. His writing is without f.

* (*On f.; under f.; firing at* a bird).

***Take f.*

fire-arm, n. *Basic words.* Gun.

fire-engine, n. *Basic words.* Engine used to put out a fire.

fire-fly, n. *Basic words.* Sort of insect giving out light in the dark.

fireman, n. *Basic words.* Man who puts out fires.

fireplace, n. *Basic words.* Place for fire in room.

fireside, n. *Basic words.* Space round fireplace.

firework, n. *Basic words.* Plaything made of gunpowder.

first, a., n., adv. fǝːst; *premier: d'abord; erste (-r, -s): zuerst.*

(e) Best; *erste.*

The f. house in the street. Be f. in the school. The f. to come. Get there f.

* (*At f.; for the f.* (second, last, and so on) *time; at f.* (second) *hand*).

first-rate, a. *Basic words.* Very good, of the best.

fish (fish *or* fishes, -er, -ing, -ed), n. fiʃ; *poisson; Fisch.*

(s) Fishes as food.

Get a f.; birds and fish(es); fishing in the sea. Cooking f.

fishermen, n. *Basic words.* Man who gets fish from sea and so on.

fixed (un-, -ly), a. fikst; *fixe, fixé; fest, befestigt.*

(e) About which a decision has been made; *établi; festgesetzt.*

The rod is f.; f. to the wheel; eyes f. on the floor; a f. smile; looking at him fixedly. The day has been f.

*(Get *f. up*).

flag, n. flæg; *drapeau; Fahne.*

Put up a f.

flame, n. fleim; *flamme; Flamme.*

The f. of the match was blue; a house in ff.

flat, a., adv., s. flæt; *plat: appartement; platt: Wohnung.*

(s) F. and parallel with earth; *horizontal; wagerecht.*

A f. wall. F. country; keep the tray f. Put it f. down. Be living in a f.

flight, n. flait; *vol; Flug.*

(e) Quick going (away); *fuite; Flucht.*

A f. over London. His f. from the country.

*(The army is *in f.*).

**(*Put to f.*).

floor (-er, -ing, -ed), n. flɔː*; *plancher; Fussboden.*

(e) Level of a building; *étage; Stock(werk).*

Put the bags down on the f.; the room is floored with stone. His bedroom is on the second f.

flower (-er, -ing, -ed), n. 'flauə*; *fleur; Blume, Blüte.*

Get some ff.; the ff. have come out; the tree is flowering; a flowering plant; a flowered material.

**(*In f.*).

fly (flies), n. flai; *mouche; Fliege.*

A f. on the wall; the flies are biting the horse.

fold (-er, -ing, -ed), n. fould; *pli; Falte.*

-er, (e) Printed material for distribution: folded cardboard cover for papers; *prospectus (dépliant): chemise, portefeuille: (Falt-) Prospekt; Aktendeckel.*

Put a f. in the material; folding the paper; a folding seat. Send them a folder. Put the papers in a folder.

food, n. fuːd; *aliment; Speise, Nahrung.*

(e) Something acting like food; *nourriture; Nahrung.*

Take f.; have some f. A good nerve f.; f. for throught.

foolish (-ly), a. 'fuːliʃ; *bête, irréfléchi; töricht, närrisch.*

Say a f. thing; a f. person; be laughing foolishly.

foot (feet), n. 'fut; *pied; Fuss.*

   (e) Base; *bas.*

   Put one's f. forward; be on one's feet. The f. of the mountain.

   *On f.

   ***Under f.*

football, n. *Basic words.* Form of sport in which a ball is kicked; ball used in football.

footlights, n. *Basic words.* Lights edging theater stage.

footman, n. *Basic words.* Man servant for carriage, door, table.

footnote, n. *Basic words.* Note at the end (or foot) of page.

footprint, n. *Basic words.* Mark made by a foot.

footstep, n. *Basic words.* Sound made by a foot.

for, prep. fɔː*; *pour; für, auf, nach.*

   A place f. dancing; desire f. food; time f. thought; go f. the letters; put up f. offers; payment f. goods; acting f. another; A is f. apple; check f. £10; ready f. bed; need f. acting; noted f. wines; good enough f. him; timed f. to-morrow; be f. a person; waiting f. someone; sailing f. America; hoping f. peace; looking f. a letter; send f. him.

   *1. He has no *regret for* his acts.

   2. *For example,* he was cruel to his sister.

   3. He was *responsible for* her death.

   4. He went away *for this reason.*

   5. He kept away *for fear of* the law.

   6. He will go to prison *for the first* (*second* and so on) *time.*

   7. He will be there *for a long time.*

   8. There is no *cause for* protest.

   9. Every judge would say the same, *word for word.*

   10. Men are like animals, *but for* their brains.

   (We took *him* f. an expert; he *had a name* f. keeping on the right side of the law; *in exchange* f.; *as* f. *that; have an eye* f.; *the worse* f. *drink*).

   ***F. all that;* f. *ever* saying the same thing; f. it was untrue. (*F. my part;* f. *the most part; go in* f.; f. *short; come up* f. discussion; *an ear* f. *music; make things warm* f. a person; *put in* f.; *in time* f.).

force (-er, -ing, -ed), n. fɔːs; *force; Kraft, Stärke.*

   (s) Violent force; *violence; Gewalt.*

(e) Army (freq. ff.) or band of man: a power working for; *armée: puissance; Truppen: Macht.*

The f. of a blow; the f. of his arguments. F. will be necessary. Landing more ff.; the police f. A f. for good.

**Laws *in f.*

fork (-er, -ing, -ed), n. fɔːk; *fourche, fourchette; Gabel.*

(e) Point of branching, division into two arms; *bifurcation; Gabelung.*

Take food with a f.; a garden f.; forking the beds. A f. in the road; forking to the left; a forked stick.

form (-er, -ing, -ed), n. fɔːm; *forme; Form, Gestalt(ung).*

(e) Sort: fixed way of doing; *façon: formalité; Art: Formalität.*

The f. of the table is round; forming a ring. A new f. of art. Going through the necessary ff.

forward, adv., a. ′fɔːwəd; *en avant: avancé; worwärts, weiter: vordere, vorgeschritten, vorlaut.*

Go f.; put f. a suggestion; from this time f. The f. part of the ship; a f. boy; f. behavior.

* (They sent their boxes *carriage f.*).

** (*Looking f. to* the event).

fowl, n. faul; *poule; Huhn.*

The farmer keeps ff.

frame (-er, -ing, -ed), n. freim; *cadre; Rahmen.*

(e) Supporting structure; *charpente, armature; Gerüst.*

-ing, (e) Giving form to; *formant; form(ulier)end.*

A f. for a picture; framing the painting. The f. of a building (body). Framing an answer.

***F. of mind.*

framework, n. *Basic word.* Supporting structure.

free (-r, -ing, -d, un-), a. friː; *libre; frei.*

(e) Free from payment; *franco; umsonst.*

Make him f.; get f.; f. thought; you are f. to go; the prisoners have been freed. The drinks are f.; f. trade.

***Be f. with.*

free-hand, a. *Basic words.* (Of picture, outline) done without the help of instruments.

frequent (in-, -ly), a. ′friːkwənt; *fréquent; häufig.*

A f. event; his infrequent attempts; be frequently ill.

friend, n. frend; *ami; Freund.*

(e) Person who is kind to.

He is John's f.: I have no ff. A f. of the poor.

°°*Make ff. with.*

from, prep. from; *de, von, aus.*

Go f. a place; come back a year f. now; 10 miles f. London; letter f. a friend; away f. the point; free f. danger; get profit f. a business; a mark f. a blow; f. 10 to 20; it is clear f. the facts.

°The future will be *different f.* the past; his ideas took form *f. day to day (year to year).*

front (-er, -ing, -ed), n., a. frʌnt; *front, façade; Vorderseite, Front.*

(s) Front lines of an army at war; *front; Front.*

(e) Walk, road, gardens, on edge of town facing the sea; *digue, promenade; Strand-Promenade.*

The f. of a house; fronting the road; fronted with brick. News from the f. A walk on the f. The f. person; a f. view.

°*In f. of.*

fruit, n. fruɪt; *fruit; Frucht, Obst.*

(e) Outcome; *résultat; Frucht.*

Take f. off the tree; have some f. The f. of our work.

full (-ly), a. ful; *plein, au complet; voll.*

(e) Complete; *complet; völlig, vollständig.*

A f. vessel; get it f. The f. story; make f. use of; the f. moon; be fully conscious.

°(*F. of*).

°°*F. face; in f.; f. up.*

future, a., s. fjuːtʃə°; *futur; künftig: Zukunft.*

My f. work. No hope for the f.; be interested in the young man's f.

°°*In f.*

garden (-er, -ing, -ed), n. ˈgɑːdn; *jardin; Garten.*

A beautiful flower-g.; in the back g. is an apple-tree and produce for the table; he is a gardener; my father is gardening.

gas, gæs. *International word.*

gasworks, n. *Basic words.* Place where gas is made.

general (-ly), a. ˈdʒenərəl; *général; allgemein.*

(e) Wide in distribution, common; *commun; gewöhnlich.*

A g. rule; a g. idea of things; talking generally. The g. opinion is; blue eyes are very g.; he is generally right.

geography, dʒi'ɔgrəfi. *International name of science.*

geology, dʒi'ɔlədʒi. *International name of science.*

geometry, dʒi'ɔmitri. *International name of science.*

get (gets, got, getting), v. get; *obtenir, recevoir; bekomment, gelangen, lassen, machen.*

(e) Become; *devenir; werden.*

G. money; g. work; g. a disease; g. control (help); talk gets about; g. facts into one's head; g. a tooth out; g. a secret out of a person; g. over a disease; g. through money; he will g. the tree up with a spade; he got up a tree; getting up in the morning is hard for some; g. food ready; did he g. his book printed? G. married (tired).

*1. It was his hope to *get a book out* every year.

2. He said he would *get a play up* for advertisement.

3. But he did not *get on* (*well*) *with* the chief actor.

4. He *got* (himself) *into bad ways* through drink.

5. He *got* (himself) *out of doing* any more work.

(*G. on one's nerves; g. the better of*).

**Get at* the facts and so on; g. *to work* (*on* the work named).

(*G. clear of; g. off one's hands; g. a line on; g. up steam*).

girl, n. gə:l; *jeune fille; Mädchen.*

A good little g.; have two gg.; a g. to do the housework.

give (gives, gave, giving, given, giver), v. giv; *donner; geben.*

G. milk to the cat; g. time (attention) to work; g. the bell a push (pull, shake); g. an answer; the horse gave a kick; g. a talk; g. support; g. trouble; g. news about; g. away money; g. away a secret; g. off steam; g. out light; food was given round; the income for a given year.

*1. Mothers *give birth to* babies.

2. She *gave her word* to the family that she would take care of the little boy.

3. The wall *gave back* the sound of a strange voice.

4. They did not *give up* hope till the news was certain.

5. Newspapers are *given to* printing false statements. (Don't let them g. *way to* bad impulses).

**(*G. place to*).

glass (glasses), n. glɑːs; *verre; Glas.*

    (e) Drinking vessel.

    gg. (s) = eye-glasses; *lunettes; Brille.*

Windows are made of g.; a g. eye. A g. of water. Put your glasses on.

glasshouse, n. *Basic words.* Heated glass structure for plants.

glove (-er, -ing, -ed), n. glʌv; *gant; Handschuh.*

    (s) Fighting-glove.

Get one's gg. off; his father was a glover; a gloved hand. A fight with the gg.

glycerine*, glisə'riːn. *International word.*

go (goes, went, going, gone), v. gou; *aller, partir; gehen.*

    G. away from a person; g. after a rat; time goes by; they went for a swim; he did not g. into details; g. over accounts; g. through a room; g. through a story; roads g. to London; g. to work; the clock is going; the song goes like this; the books g. here; g. far; g. fishing; g. free; g. without food; everything has gone wrong.

    *1. The color of the walls did not *go with* my dress.

    2. An old man in the front had *gone to sleep.*

    3. Something (the gun) *went off* with a loud noise.

    4. The light (fire) *went out* in the middle of my talk.

    5. I am *going to* make a protest to the gas company.

    * (*Gone to seed; g. without* food).

    ***Let oneself g.; g. on a system; have a g. at; as far as it goes.*

    (*G. in for; g. out of business; g. smash*).

goat, n. gout; *chèvre; Ziege.*

    Milking a g.

gold, n., a. gould, *or, Gold.*

    (s) Gold money; *monnaie d'or.*

    (e) The color of gold.

Mining for g.; the exchange of goods for g.; a g. cup. A pocket full of g. The g. of the sun. G. paper.

goldfish, s. *Basic words.* Small fish the color of gold.

good (better, best), a., s. gud; *bon; gut.*

    gg. (e) = Things for marketing, property; *marchandises, biens; Güter, Waren.*

A g. day; the milk is g.; have a g. time; a g. idea; a g. bit of wood; a g. book; g. for the eyes; a g. man; g. weather. There is much g. in him; it is for your g.; do g. Transport of gg.

*G. morning (day, night); do one's best; get the better of. (G. at languages).

**It's no g. talking; you had better go; do one g.; 5s. to the g. (Make g.).

good-for-nothing, n. *Basic words.* Person of little value.

goodlooking, a. *Basic words.* Beautiful, pleasing the eye.

government, n. gʌvənmənt; *administration; Regierung.*

(e) Those in political authority: act of government; *gouvernement: gouvernement.*

A new form of g. One of the g.; the British G. made peace after a long war. Responsible for the g. of the country.

grain, n. grein; *grain; Korn.*

(e) Food grain; *céréale; Getreide.*

A g. of sand. G. for the birds.

grass, n. grɑːs; *herbe, gazon; Gras.*

Long g.; seated on the g.

**Put out to g.

gray, a., n. grei; *gri; grau.*

A g. sky. The g. of her eyes.

great (-ly), a. greit; *grand; gross.*

(e) Noted.

A thing of g. size; a g. dog; a g. amount; be greatly troubled. A g. man; living among the g.

green, a., n. griːn; *vert; grün.*

A g. coat; grass is g. G. is a good color.

grip (-per, -ping, -ped), n. grip; *prise, serrement; Griff.*

(e) Clear idea; *conception claire; Auffassung.*

-ping, (e) Keeping the attention; *passionnant; packend.*

He gave my hand a g.; the cord was slipping from his g.; gripping his arm; in the g. of a disease. He has a good g. of the political position. A gripping story.

**(Come to gg.).

group (-er, -ing, -ed), n. gruːp; *groupe; Gruppe.*

A g. of friends; the men were waiting in little gg.; the houses are grouped in fours.

growth, n. grouθ; *croissance, développement; Wachsen.*

(e) Thing produced by g.: diseased growth; *végétation, poussée: excroissance, tumeur; Wachstum: Gewäch.*

The g. of plants (ideas); the g. of the town has been very quick. A thick g. of low trees. A g. on his face.

guide (-er, -ing, -ed), n. gaid; *guide; Führer.*

(s) Person acting as a guide.

The light is a g.; guiding the men. A g. on the mountain.

gun, n. gʌn; *fusil, canon; Gewehr Geschütz.*

He has a g. on his back; the ship's gg.; firing a g.

gunboat, n. *Basic words.* Small, well-armed boat.

gun-carriage, n. *Basic words.* Wheeled support of great gun.

gunman, n. *Basic words.* Man using a gun in crime.

gunmetal, n. *Basic words.* Metal at one time used for guns.

gunpowder, n. *Basic words.* Firing material for guns.

hair, n. hɛə*°*; *cheveux, poil; Haar.*

(e) Hh. covering head or body.

Take out a h. Be brushing one's h.; the dog has long h.

hairspring, n. *Basic words.* Very thin spring in watch.

half-past, prep. *Basic words.* Half an hour past (some hour).

half-way, adv. *Basic words.* At or to half the distance (between).

hammer (-er, -ing, -ed), n. ′hæmə*°*; *marteau; Hammer.*

Using a h.; hammering a nail; hammered metal.

hand (-er, -ing, -ed), n. hænd; *main; Hand.*

(e) Handwriting; pointer; *écriture: aiguille; Handschrift: Zeiger.*

Take a book in one's h.; put one's h. on; hh. up!; handing round the plates; a note was handed to him; left-handed. Writing a good h. The h. of the clock.

°On the one (the other) h.; at first (second) hand; take in h.; make by h.

°°Have one's hh. full; get off one's hh.; ready to h.; be in someone's hh.; on h. (H. in h.).

handbag, n. *Basic words.* A woman's bag for money and so on.

handbook, n. *Basic words.* A guide book.

handcart, n. *Basic words.* Small cart pushed by hand.

handwriting, n. *Basic words.* Writing done by hand.

hanging (hanger), a., n. ′hæŋiŋ; *suspendu; hängend.*

(s) Putting to death by hanging; *action de pendre.*

-er (s) Dress-hanger: *portemanteau; Kleiderbügel.*

Be h. on a cord; h. up a curtain; a h. thread. Be h. a man. Give help in h. a picture. Put the dress on a hanger.

°°*Be h. about.*

happy (un-, -ly), a. 'hæpi; *heureux; glücklich.*

(e) Well placed (timed, said); *convenable.*

Make a person h.; a h. ending; she is very unhappy; they are happily married. A h. saying.

harbor (-er, -ing, -ed), n. 'ha:bə°; *havre, port; Hafen.*

Come into h.; harboring a friend (unkind feelings).

hard, a., adv. ha:d; *dur; hart.*

(e) Using much force; opposite of simple: not kind; *fort: difficile: dur; schwer: schwierig: hart.*

A h. wood. H. work; he gave the boy a h. blow. A h. question. A h. man. It is raining h.

°*Be h. on* a person.

°°*H. at work.*

harmony (harmonies), n. 'ha:məni; *harmonie, accord; Harmonie.*

(e) Harmony in music; *harmonie.*

H. in the family; living in h. The harmonies of music.

hat (-ter, -ting, -ted), n. hæt; *chapeau; Hut.*

Put on a h.; he is a hatter.

°°(*A touch of the h.*).

hate (-er, -ing, -ed), n. heit; *haine; Hass.*

(e) Strong feeling against.

H. is a bad feeling; he is hated by all. Have a h. for work.

have (has, had, having), v., aux. v. hæv; *avoir; haben.*

H. property; h. arms; h. a friend; h. a desire; h. a thought; h. control (of something); h. a drink; h. arguments ready; h. one's leg broken. He has done it; it has been done; I had done nothing.

°1. I *had a talk with* him this morning.

2. His arguments *had* no *effect on* me.

3. Our thoughts *have* no *existence* outside our heads.

4. They *have to* go into such questions because of their interest in history.

5. I will *have* nothing *to do with* foolish discussions.

(I h. *a good mind to* make; h. *the face to;* h. *a name for*).

°°(H. *a go at;* h. *one's day; you had better* go; h. *one's hands full;* h. *the heart to;* h. *reason to;* h. *in mind.*)

he (him, his; she, her, hers; it, its; they, them, their, theirs), pron. hi:; *il; er.*

H. is kind; I saw him yesterday; this is his house; it is h. She is his mother; give her this; her hat is black; the book is hers. It is a bird; its wing is broken; it is raining; it seems to me to be late; it may be so. They are wrong; take them away; their father has come; this may be theirs.

head (-er, -ing, -ed), n., a. hed; *tête; Kopf.*

(e) Head-like part, top, front: chief; *partie superieure: chef; Kopfende, Spitze: Haupt.*

-ing, (e) Writing at the top; *rubrique; Uberschrift.*

Turning my h. The h. of the bed (line); a silver-headed stick; headed by the guide. He is the h. of the business. The h. cook. The heading on a page.

° (They were almost *off their hh.*).

°°*Keep one's h.*

head-dress, n. *Basic words.* Something for covering the head.

headland, n. *Basic words.* High land going out into sea.

headline, n. *Basic words.* Heading of a newspaper story.

headstone, n. *Basic words.* Stone on resting-place of dead.

headway, n. *Basic words.* Forward development (motion).

healthy (un-, -ly), a. 'helθi; *sain; gesund.*

(e) Making or keeping healthy; *salubre; heilsam.*

A h. person; make the wound h.; they were healthily tired after their sport. A h. place; an unhealthy winter.

hearing (hearer), n., a. 'hiəriŋ; *action d'entendre; Hören.*

(e) Sense, power, range of hearing: hearing for purpose of judging: law hearing, *audience, audition: audience; Gehörouïe: Gehör, Audienz, Stimmprüfung: Verhör.*

Our ears are for h. with; his hearers were moved. His h. is bad; come into h.; be out of h. At the meeting they wouldn't give him a h.; after a h. the actor was given a part. The second h. Be h. a sound.

heart, n. haːt; *cœur; Herz.*

(e) Seat of the feelings.

His h. is not strong. Have a kind h.

° (*Have* his interests *at h.; get* words *by h.*).

°°*Have the h. to; take h.; take to h.*

heat (-er, -ing, -ed), n. hi:t; *chaleur; Hitze,* [*phys.*] *Wärme.*

    (s) High degree of heat; *chaleur; Hitze.*

    (e) Heat of feeling; *ardeur; Hitze.*

    A degree is a unit for measuring h. Be overcome by the h.; heating food; an electric heater. In the h. of the discussion; a heated argument.

he-goat, n. *Basic words.* Male goat.

help (-er, -ing, -ed), n. help; *aide, assistance; Hilfe.*

    (e) That which gives help; *secours.*

    Give h. to a person; helping the cook; have helpers. The suggestion was a great h.

    *(Of h.).

her. See *he.*

here, adv. hiə*; *ici; hier, hierher.*

    He is h.; come h.; h. is a book.

    *(There are houses) *h. and there.*

    **(*Here's to* him!).

hereafter, adv., n. *Basic words.* 1. After this. 2. Existence after death (frequently *the H.*).

herewith, adv. *Basic words.* With this.

herself, pron. *Basic words.* She, her (not any other person).

hiccup, n. *Onomatopoeic.* Sudden automatic jumping of throat muscles, with coughing sound.

high, a., adv. hai; *haut; hoch.*

    (e) High on a scale; *élevé.*

    A h. mountain; it is a mile h. A h. degree of heat; a h. position in the business; a h. opinion of himself. Go h. up.

    **On h.*

highlands, n. *Basic words. Mountain country.*

highway, n. *Basic words.* (Chief) road.

him, his. See *he.*

himself, pron. *Basic words.* He, him (not any other person).

hiss, n. *Onomatopoeic.* Noise (like that) of snake.

history (histories), n. 'histəri; *histoire; Geschichte.*

    (s) History of man or nations.

    The h. of the earth's development; this house has a long h.; the histories of the two families have much in common. They are learning h.; the teachings of h.

hole, n. houl; *trou; Loch.*

Make a h. in the wall (tooth).

hollow, a., n. 'hɔlou; *creux; hohl.*

The ball is h. Trees in a h.; the h. of his hand.

hook (-er, -ing, -ed), n. huk; *crochet; Haken.*

Put his coat on a h.; the hh. on the dress; fishing with a h. and line; hooking up the curtain; a hooked nose.

hope (-er, -ing, -ed), n. houp; *espoir; Hoffnung.*

(e) That on which hopes are fixed; *espérance.*

Have no h. of seeing her; go in the h. that she will be there; hoping for the best; the agreement which had been hoped for. He is the h. of his side.

horn, n. hɔːn; *corne; Horn.*

(e) Horn substance; music-horn; *corne: cor.*

The cow's hh. A vessel made of h. Playing on a h.

horse, n. hɔːs, *cheval; Pferd.*

Go on a h.

horseback, n. *Basic words.* Only 'on h.,' seated on a horse.

horseman, n. *Basic words.* 1. Man who goes on a horse. 2. Military man on horseback.

horseplay, n. *Basic words.* Rough behavior.

horsepower, n. *Basic words.* Measure of engine power.

horseshoe, n. *Basic words.* The iron put on the foot of a horse.

hospital, n. 'hɔspitl; *hôpital; Hospital, Krankenhaus.*

Go to a h.; be in the h.; a h. bed.

hotel, hou'tel. *International word.*

hour, n. 'auə*; *heure; Stunde.*

(e) Time (at which); *temps; Zeit.*

An h. from now; he did the work in two hh. In the h. of his need; at what h. will you come?

hourglass, n. Basic words. Glass instrument for measuring time with sand.

house (-er, -ing, -ed), n. haus; *maison; Haus.*

(e) Special building or sort of building.

Let a h.; a room housing a family of six; the housing question. A h. of religion; a store-h.; a fowl-h.

*(Keep h.)

houseboat, n. *Basic words.* Boat used as house.

housekeeper, n. *Basic words.* Woman looking after a house.

housework, n. *Basic words.* Work of keeping a house clean and so on.

how, adv. hau; *comment, combien: wie.*

   (e) To what degree; in what condition (sp. of persons).

   This is h. it is done; h. did you get in? We saw h. pleased he was; h. far (much) is it? I am going to see h. the wounded man is; h. are you, Mrs. X?

   °°H. good (*kind, bright* and so on) *of* you!

however, adv., conj. *Basic words.* In whatever degree (way); but.

humor (-er, -ing, -ed), n. ′hju:mə°; *humeur; Laune.*

   (e) Quality causing amusement; *humeur; Humor.*

   Be in a bad h.; a person with strange hh.; humoring an angry man. Say with h.; have a sense of h.; see the h. in.

hyena°, hai′i:nə. *International word.*

hygiene°, ′hai′dʒi:n. *International word.*

hysteria°, his′tiəriə. *International word.*

I (me, my, mine; we, us, our, ours), pron. ai; *je, moi; ich.*

   I am a boy; I am ill; it is I; give me your hand; that is my book; the other is not mine. We are ready; take us to the house; here are our bags; they are all ours.

ice (-er, -ing, -ed), n. ais; *glace; Eis.*

   (e) Iced sweet.

   Put food on i.; icing wine. Make an i.

idea, n. ai′diə; *idée; Begriff, Idee, Vorstellung.*

   Have no i. of a thing; be full of ii.; get the i. that; my i. of the animal is not very clear.

if, conj. if; *si; wenn, ob.*

   There will be room i. you come early; i. I am right, then you are wrong; see i. it is there; i. only I had a chance!; i. it is possible, come now; 10, i. not more, went.

   °(It seems *as i.*).

   °°(*I. possible*).

ill, a. il; *malade; krank.*

   He is i. in hospital.

imperial, im′piəriəl. *International name.*

important (un-), a. im′pɔ:tənt; *important; wichtig.*

   Be in an i. position; an i. discovery; unimportant detail.

impulse, n. 'impʌls; *impulsion; Impuls.*

    (e) Push forward; *Antieb.*

    Have a sudden i. to do. The agreement gave a new i. to trade.

    *Acting *on i.* is sometimes foolish.

in (-ner), prep., adv. in; *dans, en: dedans; in: herein.*

    (s) In or into power, the position in question.

    inner, a.; *intérieur; inner, inwending.*

    I. the pot; i. the water; i. the field; i. space; i. the year; i. trouble; i. the mind; be i. business; i. danger; i. doubt; i. thought; i. the summer; i. the light; dressed i. black; experienced i. crime; i. this book; i. China; i. bad condition; i. my opinion; i. my hearing; i. the hope that; i. comparison with; i. relaton to; i. bed; i. church; i. prison; he is i. authority here; the dog is shut i.; a work i. prose. A new government got i. The inner room.

    *1. The judge said the man was *in the right* (*wrong*).

    2. He took a tin tray *in exchange for* his picture.

    3. The picture itself was done *in metal* (*wood*).

    4. The head is turned *in a strange way.*

    5. Strange things are done *in the name of* art.

    6. He is *in love with* a woman who is not in love with him.

    7. The lift was *in motion* (the horse was *in flight*) when he got out.

    8. It will be *in operation* (*use*) again to-day.

    9. He gave the facts *in answer to* a question.

    10. Basic is a very good system *in fact* (and *in theory*).

    He *got into* bad *ways;* let her *into a secret; i. addition to this;* the cloth was *made into* trousers; a coat *i. bits;* a story *i. detail; i. the end; i. front of; i. memory of* him; *i. time* he got well; *have i. mind; put* (a person) *i. mind of; papers i. order;* right *i. part;* take *part i.;* the accounts *i. question;* things *i. request;* walking *i. step with; i. support of* this; words *i. good* (*bad*) *taste;* be *i. touch with; i. view of* this; *have a voice i.;* be *i. the way* (*of*); take *i. hand;* take *into account;* a cord *i. knots; i. store for;* something *i. common; fertile i.* ideas; *i. the belief* (*hope*) *that; i. one's interests;* have *belief i.* a story; he *i. his turn.*

    ***Arm i. arm* (*hand in hand*); come *i. a week;* make *an error i.* addition; *slow i. doing; i. flower* (*leaf*); go *i. for;* tricked (*surprised*) *into.* (*I. keeping with; put i.* (*words*); *put words into person's* *mouth; a baby i. arms; competition i.; i. this connection; i. effect; put into effect; i. the event of;* laws *i. force;* story *i. full; i. future; be i.* someone's *hands; be i.* someone's *light; come into line; i.* one's *line; long i. coming; i. the mass; i. some measure;* come *i. numbers; i. order to;* come *i. person; i. the first place; i. place of;* come *into play;* do *i. play;* get *i. position;* letter *i. the post; anything i. reason; i. receipt of* a letter; *i. the long run; a place i. the sun;* do *trade i.; put i. for; i. time for).*

income, n. *Basic words.* Amount of money a person has coming in every year.

increase (-er, -ing, -ed), n. 'inkri:s; *accroissement, augmentation; Vermehrung, Zunahme.*

    (e) Amount by which thing is increased; *Zuwachs.*

    An *i.* of money (interest); an *i.* in power; increasing the rate; on an increasing scale; an increased income. The *i.* was small.

indoor, a., **indoors,** adv. *Basic words.* (Placed, done) in the house and so on.

industry (industries), n. 'indəstri; *industrie, zèle, application; Fleiss.*

    (e) The producing of goods; a branch of producing; *industrie:* industrie; *Industrie: Industrie.*

    A person of great *i.* The development of trade and *i.* Trouble in the boot and shoe *i.*; the industries of the country.

inferno*, in'fə:nou. *International word.*

influenza, influ'enzə. *International word.*

ink (-er, -ing, -ed), n. iŋk; *encre; Tinte.*

    Writing with *i.*; inking a line.

inland, adv., a. *Basic words.* To or on land away from sea.

inlet, n. *Basic words.* Small arm of sea.

in(ner)most, a. *Basic words.* Farthest in.

insect, n. 'insekt; *insecte; Insekt.*

    A fly is an *i.* with wings.

inside, n., a., adv., prep. *Basic words.* (Of, in, to) the inner part.

instep, n. *Basic words.* Top of persons' foot.

instrument, n. 'instrumənt; *instrument; Instrument, Werkzeug.*

    (s) Instrument of music.

    (e) Thing or person used as an instrument; *moyen, agent; Mittel, Werkzeug.*

    A recording *i.*; using a sharp *i.* Playing on an *i.*; a stringed *i.* He made use of his friends as *ii.* for his purpose.

insurance, n. in'ʃuərəns; *assurance; Versicherung.*

Get i. for one's house; go to an i. company; he was late with his i. money.

interest (-er, -ing, -ed), n. 'intrist; *intérêt; Interesse.*

(e) Quality of causing interest; that which is to one's profit (freq. **ii.**): right to part of profits of a business: payment for use of money; *intérît: intérêt: participation: intérêt: Interesse: Interesse: Anteil: Zinsen.*

Take an i. in history; be interested in others; an interesting play. It has no i. for me. The agreement is against his ii. He has a small i. in the business. Get no i. for a year.

*Foolish acts are not *in one's ii.* (The *i. on* his money is high; these facts are *of i.*).

international, intə(ː)'næʃnl. *International word.*

into, prep. *Basic words.* To a position in.

invention, n. in'venʃən; *invention; Erfindung.*

(e) Act of invention.

The radio is a great i.; the story was an i. Working on the i. of a new process.

iron (-er, -ing, -ed), n. 'aiən; *fer; Eisen.*

(e) Iron for linen; *fer à repasser; Bügeleisen.*

The railing is made of i.; an i. rod; the i. industry. Using an electric i.; ironing linen.

is. See *be.*

island, n. 'ailend; *île; Insel.*

Living on an i.

it (its). See *he.*

itself, pron. *Basic words.* It (not any other thing).

jazz,* 'dʒæz. *International word.*

jelly (jellies), n. 'dʒeli; *gelée, gélatine; Gelee, Gallerte.*

(e) Any jelly-like substance.

Making j. from fruit; there were jellies and cakes on the table. Crushed to a j.

jellyfish, n. *Basic words.* Sea animal like a jelly.

jewel (-ler, -ling, -led), n. 'dʒuː(ː)əl; *bijou, joyau; Juwel.*

(e) Jeweled ornament; *bijou; Schmuck.*

A green j. in a ring; take a broken ring to a jeweler; a jeweled coat (hand). A j. with a blue stone.

join (-er, -ing, -ed), n. dʒɔin; *joint, jointure; Zusammen-fügung. Gelenk, Naht.*

   -er, (s) Woodworker; *menuisier; Tischler.*

   -ing, (e) Taking one's place with, becoming one of.

   The j. between the two boards; the j. of the arm; make a j. in the wood; joining two threads; with joined hands. Her son is a joiner. He is joining his friends in Paris to-morrow.

   ** *Joining up.*

journey (-er, -ing, -ed), n. 'dʒəːni; *voyage; Reise.*

   Take a long j.; the j. there and back; journeying from place to place.

   (Go on a j.).

judge (-er, -ing, -ed), n. dʒʌdʒ; *juge, arbitre; Beurteiler, Kenner.*

   (s) Law judge; *juge; Richter.*

   Be a good j. of horses; judging the distance; judging by his face. Come before a j.

jump (-er, -ing, -ed), n. dʒʌmp; *saut; Sprung.*

   Give a j. over the wall; make a bad j.; jumping from stone to stone.

keep (keeps, kept, keeping, keeper), v. kiːp; *garder, tenir; (be)halten.*

   (e) Have (take) care of (animals, sp. for profit), or be responsible for looking after (a place); go on (doing), do again and again.

   K. one's money; k. a secret; k. a person from doing; the rubber band keeps the pencils together; k. off the grass; k. to the point; he kept his thoughts back; they are keeping the fire burning. He keeps fowls; k. dogs; k. a store; one of the keepers in the museum (park); the keeper went out with a gun. He keeps coming to see me; the two girls kept talking.

   *1. She *keeps house* for her father.

   2. He has only her to *keep him company.*

   3. We *kept* the manager *on* though it was unwise.

   4. He *kept* his interest *up* all through the winter.

   5. I *kept up with* the changes in public opinion, and took his place.

   (K. one's word; k. an eye on; k. on (doing)).

   **K. something *to oneself; in keeping with. (K. clear of; k. one's head; k. one's mind on; k. time (with)).*

kettle, s. 'ketl; *bouilloire; Kessel.*

Put the k. on the fire; a k. of water.

key (-er, -ing, -ed), n. ki:; *clef; Schlüssel.*

(e) Scale of sound: guide to something: any of the parts of a piano, writing machine, or other instrument by which the fingers put it into operation; *ton: clef, clef; Tonart: Schlüssel: Taste.*

Turning the k. in the lock. This song is in a different k.; keying a piano. The k. to the question; go through the book with the k. The kk. of the piano are dirty; playing on the black kk. only.

keyhole, n. *Basic words.* Hole in lock for key.

keynote, n. *Basic words.* Note on which key (in music) is based.

keystone, n. *Basic words.* Middle stone in an arch.

kick (-er, -ing, -ed), n. kik; *coup de pied; Fusstritt.*

(e) Jump of an engine, gun; *retour d'allumage, recul; Rückstoss.*

Give the thing a k.; kicking the ball. The engine gave a k. when I was starting it.

kind (un-, -ly), a. kaind; *bon, bienveillant; gütig, freundlich.*

Be k. to animals; have a k. friend; unkind words; smiling kindly.

* (That *was* very *k. of* you).

king, kiŋ. *International name.*

kiss (-er, -ing, -ed), n. kis; *baiser; Kuss.*

Give her a k.; kissing his mother.

knee, n. ni:; *genou; Knie.*

(e) Knees as seat; *genoux.*

Go down on one's kk. A little boy seated on his father's k.

knife (knives, -er, -ing, -ed), n. 'naif; *couteau; Messer.*

Cutting meat with a k.; all the boys had knives; knifing a man.

knot (-ter, -ting, -ted), n. nɔt; *nœud; Knoten.*

(e) Knot in wood; *Knorren, Ast (im Brett).*

Put a k. in the thread; the wool is all knotted; knotting the cord. Planing down the kk. in the board.

*A fishing line *in kk.*

knowledge, n. 'nɔlidʒ; *connaissance; Kenntnis, Wissen.*

(e) Condition of having knowledge; *Kenntnis.*

I have no k. of it; talking with k.; a new bit of k.; a good k. of French. In the k. that; do it without their k.

***To my k.* he is not here.

land (-er, -ing, -ed), n. lænd; *terre; Land.*

(s) the country; *campagne.*

-ing, (e) Floor at top of steps; *palier; Treppenabsatz, Vorplatz.*

L. and sea; l. for building on; landing at Dover; landing a fish. Go back to the l.; working on the l. A bedroom opening onto the landing.

landmark, n. *Basic words.* Something marking a point (on the land or in history).

landowner, n. *Basic words.* Person who is an owner of land.

landslip, n. *Basic words.* The fall of a mass of land down a slope.

language, n. 'læŋgwidʒ; *langage, langue; Sprache.*

Suggestions for a new l.; talking a strange l.; using strong l.; dead ll.; the l. question; the power of l.

last, a., n., adv. lɑːst; *final: le dernier; letzte (-r, -s): zuletzt.*

(e) Latest up to now; *passé, dernier; vorige.*

This is my l. chance; his l. words. L. year he came earlier; at our l. meeting; the l. time I was there. He was the l. to go; that was the l. I saw of him. This comes l.

*(He came *at l.;* I have seen him *for the l. time*).

late, a., adv. leit; *tard; spät.*

(e) After the right time: now dead; *tardif, en retard: feu; (zu) spät: verstorben.*

It is getting l.; l. in the day. You are l. for the meeting. The l. George Smith. He came l.

**Come at 6 *at the latest.*

laugh (-er, -ing, -ed), n. lɑːf; *rire; Gelächter, Lachen.*

Have a good l.; he gave a loud l.; laughing about it.

*(*Laughing at* the boy).

laughing-gas, n. *Basic words.* Gas used medically for making person unconscious of pain when having teeth out and so on.

lava, 'lɑːvə. *International word.*

law, n. lɔ; *loi; Gesetz.*

(e) Natural law: system of laws: men of law; *loi: droit: hommes de loi; Gesetz: Recht: Gesetz.*

Make a new l. The l. about the attraction of bodies. In Roman l.; go to l. The opinion of the l.

lead (-er, -ing, -ed), n. led; *plomb; Blei.*

(e) Black substance used in pencils; *mine de crayon.*

A ball of l.; l. pipes; leaded windows. The l. of my pencil is broken.

leaf, n. li:f; *feuille; Blatt.*

(e) Flat bit: l. of paper forming 2 pages of book; *feuillet.*

A l. off a tree; the time of the fall of the leaves. A thin l. of wax. A l. has come out of the book.

**(Trees *in l.*).

learning (learner), n., a. 'lə:niŋ; *action d'apprendre, étude; Lernen.*

(e) Book-knowledge; *érudition; Gelehrsamkeit.*

He's not good at l. facts; a simple book for the learner. A person of great l. You are l. Basic English.

leather, n. 'leðə*; *cuir; Leder.*

The smell of new l.; a l. coat.

left, a., n. left; *gauche; linke (-r, -s).*

(e) Political group(s) desiring change, supporting workers (the L.).

The l. arm. On the l.; to the l. A government of the L.

left-handed, a. *Basic words.* Using left hand more than the right.

left-wing, a. *Basic words.* Politically of the Left.

leg, n. leg; *jambe; Bein.*

(e) Support or other thing like a leg; *pied.*

My left l.; the ll. of the table; one l. of his trousers.

less (least). See *little.*

let (lets, letting), v., aux. v. let; *laisser; lassen.*

(e) Give use of (building and so on) for payment; *louer; vermieten.*

I will l. the boys go to the woods to-day; she has l. down her hair; he came to the door to l. me in; l. the dog loose (free); l. it be done! I have l. my house for the winter. L, us go and see a play.

*1. The teacher *let* the boy *off* (punishment) when she saw how unhappy he was.

2. She will not *let* us *into* her *secret.*

3. She *let out* the skirt because it was tight.

4. A good man would not *let his friends down.*

5. Please *let* me (the machine) *be.*

**L. *me see.* (L. *oneself go*).

letter (-er, -ing, -ed), n. 'letə*; *lettre; Buchstabe.*

(e) Words in writing sent to a person; *Brief.*

ll. = books, writing.

Learning the ll.; lettering the cards. Send a l. to a friend. A man of ll.

level (-er, -ing, -ed), n., a. 'levl; *niveau: horizontal, plat; Niveau, Ebene: wagerecht.*

The l. of the water is lower than that of the field; a high l. of discussion; these are on a l. (with one another); leveling the road; a leveling tendency. L. country; keep the camera l.

library, n. 'laibrəri; *bibliothéque; Bibliothek.*

(e) Group of books; *Büchersammlung.*

Building a new l.; the town has three libraries. He has a good science l.

lift (-er, -ing, -ed), n. lift; *action de lever; Heben.*

(e) Lifting apparatus; *ascenseur; Fahrstuhl.*

A l. of the hand; lifting boxes; the clouds are lifting. Go up in the l.

light (-er, -ing, -ed), n., a. lait; *lumière: clair; Licht: hell.*

(e) Apparatus giving light; anything used as a match: new knowledge; *lampe: feu: éclaircissement; Leuchte: Feuer: Erleuchtung.*

The room is full of l.; the shutters keep out the l.; lighting the theater. Have electric l.; a wax l. Give him a l. for his pipe; lighting a match. The book gives new l. on the question. A l. color.

* (Facts *come to l.; the l. is on*).

**You are *in my l.*

lighthouse, n. *Basic words.* Tall structure with light for guiding ships.

like (un-), a., prep. laik; *comme, pareil à; gleich, wie, ähnlich.*

It is l. a flower; the two boys are very unlike (one another); they have l. tastes; I had a l. experience yesterday; fish-l. You are acting l. a baby.

***Not anything (nothing) l. as good (as).*

limit (-er, -ing, -ed), n. 'limit; *limite, borne; Grenze, Beschränkung.*

-ed, (e) Narrow; *étroit, borné; beschränkt.*

The town ll.; the ll. of our knowledge; his hate has no l.; limiting the amount; their power is unlimited. Limited views.

line (-er, -ing, -ed), n. lain; *ligne, trait; Linie, Zeile.*

(e) Line of things: rails for train: a cord; *file: voie, ligne: corde; Reihe, Zeile: Geliese: Leine.*

A l. on paper; a straight l. from A to B; a lined face. A l. of houses; a l. of men; a l. of thought; lining the streets. The train came off the l. A fish on a l.

°°*Come into l.;* something *in one's l.; out of l.; get a l. on.*

linen, n. 'linin; *toile de lin; Leinen.*

(e) Linen or cotton things for house; *linge; Wäsche.*

A square of l.; a l. dress. Send the bed-l. to the wash.

lip, n. lip; *lèvre; Lippe.*

(s) L.-like part; *bec; Rand.*

Biting his l.; she puts paint on her ll. The l. of the pot.

lipstick, n. *Basic words.* Stick of paint for the lips.

liqueur°, li'kjuə°. *International word.*

liquid, n., adj. 'likwid; *liquide; Flüssigkeit.*

Milk is a l. L. air; the butter has become l. in the heat.

list (-er, -ing, -ed), n. list; *liste; Verzeichnis.*

A l. of words; listing the names.

little (less, least), a., adv., pron., s. 'litl; *(un) peu (de); (ein) wenig.*

(e) Small in size; young; *petit; klein.*

There is l. food; please make less noise; this boy gave the least trouble. A l. house. When I was a l. boy. He is l. more than a boy; be a l. angry; he is less noted than his brother. I am able to do l.; he has the least. A l. goes a long way.

°*(Make l. of* a thing; *l. by l.* he got well again; there were *at least* 1,000 persons there.

living (liver), a., n. 'liviŋ; *vivant, demeurant, qui demeure; subsistence; lebend, wohnend: Unterhalt.*

A l. person; he is l. in a house (town); l. on a small income; put the l. before the dead. Get a l. by working; good l.

lock (-er, -ing, -ed), n. lɔk; *serrure; Schloss.*

The door has no l.; locking the door.

°*(The house is *locked up*).

lockout, n. *Basic words.* The shutting of a works by the owners for the purpose of forcing the workers to an agreement.

lockstitch, n. *Basic words.* Specially strong sort of stitch made by machine.

long, a. lɔŋ; *long; lang.*

(e) (As) measured from end to end; *de long.*

A l. distance; l. hair; a l. time. A snake 3 feet l.; l. measure.

*He *no longer* has peace.

***Before l.; l. before; be l. in* (coming); *so l. as* he goes. (*So l.!*).

look (-er, -ing, -ed), n. luk; *regard; Blick.*

(e) How a thing seems when looked at; *air, aspect; Ausdruck, Aussehen.*

Give a l. under the seat; looking for the book. A l. of regret came over his face; the l. of the house; looking sad.

*(*Looking at* the stars; *looking after* the house; *looking down on* teachers).

***On the l.-out; looking forward to* an event; *looking on; looking up to.*

looking-glass, n. *Basic words.* Glass backed with quicksilver for looking at oneself in.

look-out, n. *Basic words.* (Person, place for) keeping watch.

loose (-ly), a. luːs; *lâche, détaché, desserré; lose, locker.*

(e) (Of person, behavior) not controlled, having no respect for right rules: without care for facts, details; *relâché: irréfléchi; locker: achtlos, ungenau.*

A l. tooth; l. papers; her hair was loosely pinned up. A l. person. A l. statement.

loss, n. lɔs; *perte; Verlust.*

(e) Being unable to come across; *égarement; Abhanden-kommen.*

The l. of a position; his death was a great l. to her; he has had serious ll. in business. Troubled by the l. of one's papers.

*He was *at a l. for* words. (*A l. on* the business).

**(He kept the works going *at a l.*).

loud (-ly), a. laud; *fort, bruyant; laut.*

(e) In bad taste, forcing attention; *voyant; auffallend.*

Give a l. cry; a l. voice; say loudly. He is l. in his dress.

*(Say *out l.*).

love (-er, -ing, -ed), n. lʌv; *affection, amour; Liebe.*

(e) Thing for which one has love; pleasure in; *amour: amour.*

L. for one's son; loving a baby; he is her lover. She is his l. A l. for food; loving to do.

Make l. to a person. (His *l. of* animals; be *in love with* someone).

low, a., adv. lou; *bas; niedrig.*

(e) Placed far down; low on a scale; not upright.

A l. seat; a l. wall. The moon was l.; a l. branch. A person of l. birth; a l. opinion of. A l. trick. The airplane came l.

*macaroni**, mækə'rouni. *International word.*

machine (-er, -ing, -ed), n. mə'ʃiːn; *machine; Maschine.*

That work is now done by a m.; machining a dress.

madam, 'mædəm. *International word.*

make (makes, made, making, maker), v. meik; *faire, fabriquer; machen, veranfertigen.*

-er, (s) Owner of business making goods; *fabricant; Fabrikant.*

M. cloth; m. a law; m. a person go; m. money; m. a living; m. history; m. use of; m. an adjustment; m. observations; he is making trouble; m. an invention; that made him seem foolish; these walls m. a prison. The trade-mark of the maker is on the camera.

*1. He *made up* a story which was not quite true.

2. It was hard to *make out* the sense of his words.

3. He had *made* the material *into* trousers, in error.

4. She *made much* (*little*) *of* it.

5. Do not *make sport of* an old man.

*(*Made of wool; m. a face; m. certain; m. love to*).

**M. good; made up of. (*M. up for a loss; m. war on; m. eyes* at; *m. friends with; m. one's mark in society; m. a point* of; *m. things warm for a person; m. one's way*).

*malaria**, me'lɛəriə. *International word.*

male, a., n. meil; *mâle; männlich.*

A m. voice; a m. point of view. The cat is a m.

man (men, -ner, -ning, -ned), n. mæn; *homme; Mann.*

(e) Group name for men and women: one having strong qualities natural to a man. *Mensch: Mann.*

A m. with a future; a group of men; manning the boats. The history of m. The army will make a m. of him.

manager, n. 'mænidʒə*; *directeur, manager; Leiter.*

He is in the position of m.; the m. of the sports.

*mania**, 'meiniə. *International word.*

manhole, n. *Basic words.* Hole in floor (street) for man to go through to place under it.

map (-per, -ping, -ped), n. mæp; *carte, plan; [Land-, See-]Karte, Plan.*

A m. of the country; mapping a journey.

mark (-er, -ing, -ed), n. mɑːk; *marque; Zeichen.*

(s) Mark as sign; *marque; Zeichen.*

(e) School mark; *note; Zensur.*

-ed, (e) Noted down for punishment; strong, clear, readily noted; *repéré: marqué, accentué; gebrandmarkt, gezeichnet: bemerklich, ausgeprägt.*

A m. on a dress; a page marked by a dirty finger; she is marking the linen with her name. A m. over the letter; his last resting-place is marked by a stone. Get good mm. Become a marked man. A marked interest in.

**A man *of m.;* be *wide of the m.; make one's m.*

market (-er, -ing, -ed), n. 'maːkit; *marché, halle; Markt.*

(e) Persons or organizations ready to give money in exchange for certain goods; *debouché; Absatz.*

There is a m. in the town square; take pigs to m. There's no m. for pictures; the cotton m.; marketing produce.

married (un-), a. 'mærid; *marié; verheiratet.*

He is m. to my sister; we are going to get m.; a m. woman; an unmarried girl.

mass (masses, -er, -ing, -ed), n. mæs; *masse; Masse, Haufen.*

(e) Amount of material in a body; *Masse.*

mm. = the workers; *masses; Massen.*

A m. of jelly; a m. of persons; a m. meeting; massing the things together. The m. of a body is not the same thing as its weight. Government by the masses.

**Good *in the m.*

match (matches), n. mætʃ; *allumette; Streichholz.*

Lighting a cigarette with a m.; a box of matches.

material, a., n. mə'təriəl; *matériel; stofflich: Stoff.*

(e) With thoughts on things of the earth; *materiell.*

A m. substance. A very m. view. Using good m.

*(*Make* the m. *into* trousers).

mathematics, mæθi'mætiks. *International name of science.*

may (might), aux. v. mei; *pouvoir; mögen, dürfen, können.*

(s) Be free to, be let (do and so on).

It m. be true; if that took place, you might be worse off than you are; they said they might come. He m. have my seat; you m. go now.

me (*my*). See *I.*

meal, n. miːl; *repas; Mahlzeit.*

(e) Powdered grain; *farine; Mehl.*

Have a good m. M. mixed with water.

measure (-er, -ing, -ed), n. 'meʒə*; *mesure; Mass.*

(e) Measuring-scale or instrument.

Get its m.; measuring the top. Using a steel m.; a m. of heat.

**In some m.

meat, n. miːt; *viande; Fleisch.*

Get the m. cut up.

medical (un-, -ly), a. 'medikəl; *médical; ärztlich.*

Go to a m. man; a m. substance; a m. school; the plant is used medically.

meeting, n., a. 'miːtiŋ; *rencontre; Begegnung.*

(s) Group meeting; *assemblée; Versammlung.*

(e) Persons at a meeting; *assemblée; Versammlung.*

Have a m. with a friend. A m. of a society. Put it before the m. I am m. the train.

memory (memories), n. 'meməri; *mémoire; Gedächtnis.*

(e) Memory picture; *souvenir; Andenken, Erinnerung.*

I have a bad m. Have happy memories of Rome.

**In m. of* his father.

metal, n. metl; *métal; Metall.*

Silver is a white m.; a m. plate.

* (The picture was done *in m.*).

mew, s. Onomatopoeic. Sound of a cat.

middle, n., a. 'midl; *centre, milieu: moyen; Mitte: mittel.*

(e) Position between; *intermédiaire.*

The m. of a circle; the m. of the day. I was in the m., with a man on my right, and man on my left. The m. point.

might. See *may.*

military (un-), a., s. 'militəri; *militaire; militärisch.*

A m. event; m. dress; his air is quite unmilitary. The m.

milk (-er, -ing, -ed), n. milk; *lait; Milch.*

Have a glass of m.; milking a cow.

mind, n. maind; *intelligence; Verstand, Sinn.*

(e) Memory; *mémoire; Gedächtnis.*

He has an interesting m.; the idea is still in her m. It went out of my m.

**I have in m.* the picture; it *puts* me *in m. of* you; I *have a* (*good*) *m. to* get it.

***Keep one's m. on. (Frame of m.).*

mine (-er, -ing, -ed), n. main; *mine; Bergwerk.*

(e) Place and so on which has great store (of something): mine used in war; *puits: mine; Fundgrube: Mine.*

Get gold out of a m.; mining coal; be a miner. A m. of knowledge. Put down mm.; the ship was mined.

minute, n. 'minit; *minute; Minute.*

(e) A very short time; *moment: Augenblick.*

Put it in water for two mm.; it is five mm. to one; at that m. someone came into the room. I will come in a m.

Miss, International name.

mist, n. mist; *brouillard, brume; Nebel.*

There was a m. over the town; a m. came up from the sea.

mixed (un-), a. mikst; *mêlé; gemischt.*

(e) Of different sorts: not clear; *mélangé: embrouillé; gemischt: durcheinander.*

Two powders m. together; get the paints well m.; pleasure unmixed with regret. A m. group of women. He has got his ideas very m.

***M. up.*

money, n. 'mʌni; *argent; Geld.*

Give m. to a person; make m.; put m. into a business.

money-order, n. Basic words. Post-office check.

monkey, n. 'mʌŋki; *singe; Affe.*

The m. took a nut.

month, n. mʌnθ; *mois; Kalender-Monat.*

(e) A space of 4 weeks; *mois; Monat.*

March is the third m. Come a m. from now; the work took three mm.

moon, n. muːn; *lune; Mond.*

(e) Body going round a moving star.

There is no m. tonight. Jupiter has 4 mm.

more (most). See much.

moreover, adv. Basic words. In addition to this.

morning, n. 'mɔːniŋ; *matin; Morgen.*

(e) Early part of the day; *matinée; Vormittag.*

After 12 at night it is m. The m. has gone quickly.

*(*Good m.*).

mother, n., a. 'mʌðe*; *mère, natal, naturel; Mutter,* Geburts-.

    She became a m.; a m. bird; English is my m. tongue.

mother-in-law, n. *Basic words.* Mother of the man (woman) one is
  married to.

motion (-er, -ing, -ed), n. 'mouʃən; *mouvement; Bewegung.*

    (s) Motion of part of the body as a sign; *geste, signe; Körper-*
bewegung, Wink(en).

    (e) Suggestion put to a meeting; *motion; Antrag.*

    The quick m. of the airplane. Make a m. with the hand; motion-
ing him to come. Put a m. to the meeting.

    *(The train is *in m.*).

mountain, n. 'mauntin; *montagne; Berg.*

    Go up a m.; a m. range.

mouth (-er, -ing, -ed), n. mauθ; *bouche; Mund, Maul.*

    (e) Opening: mouth of a river; *orifice, embouchure; Öffnung,*
Mündung.

    His m. was open; the cat has a bird in its m.; he has a way of
mouthing his words. The m. of the bag. Near the m. of the river.

    *(By word of m.).

    **(Put words into someone's m.).

move (-er, -ing, -ed), n. muːv; *action de bouger, déplacement, dé-*
ménagement; Bewegung.

    (e) Step, act; *démarche; Schritt.*

    -ing, (e) Causing strong feeling; *émouvant; rührend.*

    Make a m.; moving the train forward. Make a foolish m. A
moving play; the hearers were much moved.

Mr., International name.

Mrs., International name.

much (more, most), a., adv., pron. mʌtʃ; *beaucoup; viel: sehr.*

    Have m. food; she took more trouble than her brother. Fruit is
m. cheaper here; this book is more interesting than that, but this
other is the most interesting of the three; it isn't raining m. Have
m. to do; he gave more than I did; most of what he said is true.

    *(Make m. of a fact; there were at *most 100* persons).

museum, mju(ː)'ziəm. *International name.*

muscle, n. 'mʌsl; *muscle; Muskel.*

    The eye is moved by 6 mm.; this work makes one's arm mm.
strong.

music, n. 'mjuːzik; *musique; Musik.*

(e) Pleasing group of sounds: pages of music; *musique: cahier de musique; Musik: Noten.*

They were playing beautiful m. The m. of the wind in the trees. He came without his m.

myself, pron. *Basic words.* I, me (not any other person).

nail (-er, -ing, -ed), n. neil; *clou; Nagel.*

(e) Finger or toe nail; *ongle.*

Hammering a n. into the wood; nailing a board across the window. Cleaning her nn.

name (-er, -ing, -ed), n. neim; *nom; Name.*

(e) Name for being (or doing); *réputation; Ruf.*

Give the n. of a person (thing); naming the baby. The business has a good n.

*Have a n. for kind acts. (Done *in the n. of* religion).

narrow, a. 'nærou; *étroit; eng.*

(e) Limited; *borne; beschränkt.*

A n. opening. Take a n. view; be n.-minded.

nation, n. 'neiʃən; *nation; Nation, Volk.*

Italy was made into a n.; an agreement between nn.

natural (un-, -ly), a. 'nætʃrəl; *naturel; natürlich.*

(e) Not surprising; not self-conscious, straightforward.

We have to keep our n. impulses under control; he has a n. love of music; have an unnatural desire for food; the girl is naturally good-humored. Make a very n. error; his interest in the boy is quite n.; naturally he was angry. She is very n. in her behavior.

near (-er, -est), adv., prep., a. niə*; *près: proche; nahe.*

Come n.; they got nearer and nearer to him. They are n. here; we are n. the time of the test. The town is quite n.; the nearest hospital.

necessary (un-, -ly), a. 'nesisəri; *nécessaire; notwendig.*

Food is n. for all; take the n. steps to get him free; a n. effect; your trouble was quite unnecessary; his statement is not necessarily true.

neck, n. 'nek; *cou; Hals, Nacken.*

(e) Narrow (joining) part; *col; Hals, Landenge.*

Have a collar round one's n.; turning one's n.; a dress with a square n. The n. of a bottle; a n. of land.

need (-er, -ing, -ed), n. niːd; *besoin, nécessité; Notwendigkeit.*

(s) Being without what is necessary for existence; *dénuement; Not.*

(e) Thing needed; *besoin; Bedürfnis.*

There is n. for him to go; we are needing help. A person in great n. His nn. are simple.

**Have *n. of.*

needle, n. 'niːdl; *aiguille; Nadel.*

Stitching with a n.; threading the n.

needlework, s. *Basic words.* Stitching done by hand.

nerve (-er, -ing, -ed), n. 'nəːv; *nerf; Nerv.*

A pain in the n. of a tooth; nerving oneself to do.

Get on one's nn.

net (-ter, -ting, -ted), n. net; *réseau; Netz.*

(e) Net material; *filet.*

Put a n. over one's hair (the trees); a fishing-n.; netting fish. A hat made of n.; a n. bag.

network, n. *Basic words.* Complex system of lines and so on, like the threads in a net.

never, adv. *Basic words.* N(ot) ever.

new (-ly), a. njuː; *nouveau, frais; neu.*

(e) Newly got or made; *neuf.*

These n. houses are interesting; go to a n. country; a n. form of art; that is n. to me. She had on a n. dress; n. bread is bad for the digestion; is that old table in your living-room n.? They are newly married.

news, n. njuːz; *nouvelle; Nachricht, Neuigkeit.*

Give them the n.; get into the n.

newsboy, n. *Basic words.* Boy with newspapers for distribution.

newspaper, n. *Basic words.* Printed paper giving news and so on regularly.

nickel, nikl. *International word.*

nicotine,* nikə'tiːn. *International word.*

night, n. nait; *nuit; Nacht.*

(e) The early part of the night; *soir; Abend.*

Some were working all the day, others all the n.; have a good night's rest. A n. at the theater.

(All n.; come by n.; go to bed at n.; good n.).

nightfall, n. *Basic words.* End of daylight.

no, a., adv., int. nou; *non, pas; nein, kein, nicht.*

There is n. money; I have n. knowledge of the crime; I saw n. one; this is n. time for talking; that is of n. use; it's n. trouble. N. less than 100; say n. more. N., I will not go.

* (*N. longer*).

** (It's *n. good* talking; *n. doubt*).

nobody, pron. *Basic words*. No person.

noise, n. nɔiz; *bruit; Lärm.*

(e) Sound; *son; Geräusch.*

They made a n. when the teacher went out; the papers are making a great n. about his play. The n. of a rat.

normal (un-, -ly), a. 'nɔːməl; *normal; normal.*

A n. person; a n. number; he is not acting normally.

north, a., adv., n. nɔːθ; *nord; nördlich: Norden.*

A n. window; a n. wind. We went n.; France is n. of Africa. The n. of the island is flat; the cold N.

nose, n. nouz; *nez, museau; Nase.*

Breathing through the n.; the dog's n. is cold.

***Under one's n.*

not, adv. nɔt; *ne . . . pas; nicht.*

I do n. see it; he was ordered n. to go; n. one of them went; the play was n. good; she did n. say if she would come or n.

* (He is *n. at all* interesting).

note (-er, -ing, -ed), n. nout; *note; Notiz, Anmerkung.*

(e) Short letter: unit of sound in music: sign for a music note: bit of paper money; *billet: ton: note: billet; [Kurzer] Brief: Ton: Note: [Bank-]Note.*

-**ed**, (e) With a public name; *connu; berühmt.*

Make a n. of it; noting down ideas. Send him a n. Hearing the nn. Playing without looking at the nn. The money was all in nn. A very noted man.

**Take n. of.*

notepaper, n. *Basic words*. Writing paper.

nothing, n. *Basic words*. No thing, not anything.

now, adv. nau; *maintenant; nun, jetzt.*

I will go n.; n. is the time; we are n. going; they have done nothing up to n.; from n. on he will come every day.

***N., my point is.*

nowhere, adv. *Basic words.* In (to, at) no place.

number (-er, -ing, -ed), n. 'nʌmbə*; *nombre, chiffre; Zahl, Ziffer, Nummer.*

(e) Amount of units: group of units: one printing of a paper; *nombre: nombre: numéro; Anzahl: Anzahl: Nummer.*

Writing down a n.; numbering the doors. That was the n. present. A n. of books. A new n. of the paper.

**Come *in nn.*

nut, n. nʌt; *noix; Nuss.*

(e) Nut for screw; *écrou; Schraubenmutter.*

Their food is nn. Put the n. on tightly or the screw will come out.

nutcrackers, n. *Basic words.* Instrument for cracking nuts.

observation, n. 'ɔbzə(ː)'veiʃən; *observation; Beobachtung.*

(e) Statement based on o.; power of observation; *commentaire: observation; Bemerkung: Beobachtungsgabe.*

He got his facts by o.; keep a man under o. Make an interesting o. about. He has no o.

of, prep, ɔv; *de; von.*

A bit o. cake; a day o. the month; a representative o. the government; a group o. friends; a copy o. a picture; a noise o. voices; a waste o. time; an example o. art; the power o. doing; take any o. these; be o. good family; words o. love; a tin o. milk; a cake o. soap; a house o. wood; shoes o. the same size.

*1. Do not go *out of* the room so quickly.

2. You were *talking of* writing a book.

3. I am *full of* good ideas.

4. These facts may be *of use* (*value, help, interest*) *to* you.

5. Clothing *made of* wool is best in a cold country.

6. The Englishman's *love* (*care, control*) *of* animals (the boy's *grip of* the facts) is surprising.

7. A man *of* 50 (*years*) is not old.

8. In the future, we may be *conscious of* events at a distance.

9. Basic is the best system *because of* its simple rules.

10. That was very *kind of* you; and your last point is a good example of advertisement.

(*Make much o.; make sport o.; in front o.; in memory o.; put in mind o.; take note o.; point o. view; in support o.; in view o.* these facts; *in the name o.* the King; be *in the way o.* the horses; *by word o. mouth; get the better o.; get tired o.; get out o.* doing; *be out o. touch* with).

**A touch o. the hat.* (*Made up o.; on account o.;* get (keep) clear o.; be o. no effect; in the event o.; on the face o. it; frame o. mind; a man o. mark; wide o. the mark; o. some size; have need o.; on the part o.; make a point o.; in receipt o.; be short o.;* send *word o.* something; *what has become o.* it?; *stopping short o.; going out o. business*).

off, prep., adv. ɔf; *de; von . . . weg: ab, weg.*

(e) Away, at or to a distance.

Take a cover o. a box; you are getting o. the point; a street o. the square; put a person o. doing. Take your coat o.; there is a bit cut o.; the table leg was broken o. Keep the dogs o.; the man went o. whistling.

*It was clear from their strange behavior that they were almost *o. their heads;* his experience in the war did not put him *o. his balance.* (The gun went o.; he put o. the meeting; the teacher let the boy o. [punishment]).

***Badly o.; time o.* (*See* a person *o.; get o. one's hands*).

offer (-er, -ing, -ed), n. 'ɔfə*; *offre; Anerbieten, Antrag.*

(s) Price offer made in competition; *enchère; Angebot.*

-ing, (e) Something given; *offrande, cadeau; Opfer, Gabe.*

Make an o. to do the work; offering him a cigarette; no help was offered. What oo.? He gave an offering to the Church.

office, n. 'ɔfis; *bureau; Bureau.*

Working in an o.

offspring, n. *Basic words.* Sons and daughters.

oil (-er, -ing, -ed), n. ɔil; *huile; Öl.*

Put o. in the machine; oiling a gun.

oilman, n. *Basic words.* Man trading in oil.

oilskin, n., a. *Basic words.* (Coat of) cloth put through oil process to keep out water.

old, a. ould; *vieux; alt.*

(e) Of, coming down from, the past; *ancien, vieux.*

He is an o. man now; my coat is o. That's an o. story; in the o. days; we are o. friends.

*I am 20 years o.

olive*, *'ɔliv. International word.*

omelette*, *'ɔmlit. International word.*

on, prep., adv. ɔn; *sur, dessus; auf, über, an.*

(e) On the line of a given direction, forward; *en avant; fort, weiter.*

O. the top; o. a certain day; be o. one's feet; o. the list; o. a line; hanging o. the wall; goods o. the market; put shoes o. one's feet; they were all o. my side; the sailors went o. land; put a tax o. goods; trouble o. his mind; the story is based o. facts; put a value o. jewels. The house is farther o. Put a record o.; put a hat o.

*1. The light (water, gas, play) is now *on*.

2. The pictures are *on view*.

3. I came *on purpose* to see them.

4. This design is *on a great (small) scale*.

5. I have a friend *on the committee*.

6. He is an *expert on* old prints.

7. He has gone *on a journey* to get some more.

8. The *profit (loss, interest) on* his business is chiefly through insurance.

9. Look! The house is *on fire!*

10. Let us *go (keep) on putting* water on it. We will *go on with* the fight till the firemen come.

(*Keep* the manager *o.; put money o.* a horse; *get on* (well, badly) *with* a person; have an *effect o.; looking down o.;* acid *acting o.* material; goods *o. approval; o. condition that;* goods *o. credit; designs o.* her money; acting *o. impulse;* put *o. record; take o. one side; working o.* a book; *keep an eye o.;* go *o. foot; o. the one (other) hand; get o.* one's nerves; *o. watch;* be *dependent o.;* be *hard o.* a person; *and so o.;* an *attack o.* a man).

***O. coming* here; have it *o. good authority; make war o.* (*Go o. a system; take o.* a servant; goods *o. account; o. no account; o. account of;* come *o. business;* come *o. the chance that;* a check *o. the bank; nothing o. earth; o. the face of it;* work *o. hand; o. high; o. the look-out; looking o.; keep one's mind o.* work; *o. the part of; play o. words; o. the radio;* a *run o. the bank; smiling o.; o. the telephone; o. second thoughts; trading o.* one's name; make a statement *o.* one's *word; o. receipt of; get a line o.*).

oncoming, a. Basic words. Which is coming on.

one (*one's*), a., n., pron. *Basic number-word.* 1. *un, une; ein,* (*-e.*).

   (e) Any person; *on; man.*

   Have only o. sock. O. is the lowest number. The blue o. is cheap. Butter makes o. fat.

   *(*O. another; on the o. hand*).

oneself, pron. *Basic words.* Anyone himself or herself.

onlooker, n. *Basic words.* Person watching, not taking part in, an event.

only, adv., a. 'ounli; *seulement, ne . . . que; nur, erst: einzig.*

   I have o. one pencil; he is o. a boy; he came o. one time; I was o. playing; it was not o. dark but raining; if o. you were here. He is an o. son.

onto, prep. *Basic words.* To a position on.

open (*-er, -ing, -ed, un-, -ly*), a. oupən; *ouvert; offen.*

   (e) Not shut in: keeping nothing secret: about which no decision has been made; *plein: franc: franc; frei: offen: offen.*

   -ing, (e) Hole: start(ing); *ouverture: début; Öffnung: Beginn.*

   An o. door; get the tin o.; opening a letter; the box has been opened. O. country. Please be o. with me; he said openly he would not go. It is still an o. question. Go through an opening. I am opening the discussion; the play has a good opening.

   *(Question *o. to* argument).

   **Opening up* a country.

open-work, n. *Basic words.* Design with openings as in net.

opera, 'ɔpərə. *International word.*

operation, n. ɔpə'reiʃən; *opération, action, fonctionnement; Tätigkeit, Verfahren.*

   (s) Medical operation on the body; *opération; Operation.*

   Bank oo.; the o. of milking; two men are needed for the o. of the machine. Do an o. on a person; he had an o. on his leg.

   *(The lift is *in o.*).

opinion, n. ə'pinjən; *opinion; Meinung.*

   Give us your o.; I have no o. about it; in my o. you are wrong.

opium,* 'oupjəm. *International word.*

opposite, a., prep., s. 'ɔpəzit; *opposé, contraire: vis-à-vis* (*de*); *entgegengesetzt: gegenüber: Gegenteil, Gegensatz.*

   O. points of view; on the o. side of the street; they went in o. directions. We are o. the house. Green is the o. of red.

or, conj. ɔː*; *ou; oder.*

You o. I will go; living o. dead; two o. three; Is it true o. not?;
the foot, o. base, of a mountain; o., you may say.

orange, n., a. 'ɔrindʒ; *orange; Apfelsine.*

(e) Orange color; *Orangenfarbe: orangenfarbig.*

Take an o. off the plate. The door is painted light o. The book
has an o. cover.

orchestra, 'ɔːkistrə. *International word.*

order (-er, -ing, -ed), n. 'ɔːdə°; *ordre; Ordnung.*

(e) Word of authority: highest division but one of plants, animals:
organization of persons living together in the name of religion:
public reward; *commandement, commande: classe, ordre: ordre:
décoration; Befehl, Bestellung: Klasse: Orden: Orden.*

Put the letters in a certain o. The chief gave an o.; send an o.
to the store for goods; he was ordered to go; ordering a coat. Ants
and worms are in different oo. She is joining an o. He was rewarded
with an o.

°Accounts kept *in o.* (No smoking, *by o.*).

°°Goods *made to o.; in o. to;* the lift is *out of o.*

organization, n. 'ɔːgənai'zeiʃən; *organisation; Organisation.*

(e) Persons grouped together by o.; act of o.

The school has no o. An o. for helping persons who have been
in prison. The o. of an army is a very complex business.

ornament (-er, -ing, -ed), n. 'ɔːnəmənt; *ornement; Verzierung,
Schmuck, Nippsache, Zierde.*

An o. on the shelf (hat); ornamenting the room with flowers.

other, a., pron. 'ʌðə°; *autre; andere (-r, -s).*

He came to a stop and the o. man did the same; have you any
o. suggestion?; come some o. time; was anyone there o. than you.
Others may see us; take one or the o. of the books.

°Talking to *one another.* (I, *on the o. hand,* went to Paris).

°°*Every o.* day; *the o. day.*

our. See *I.*

ourselves, n. *Basic words.* We, us (not any other persons).

out, adv. aut; *hors, dehors; aus, hinaus.*

outer, a. *extérieur; äuszer.*

Let us go o.; flowers come o.; breathing o.; I had a tooth o. today.
An outer cover; the outer door is open.

°Say *straight o.;* be reading *o. loud;* get *worked o.* (*Get o.* a

book; the light (fire) *went o.; let o. the skirt; make o.* the sense;
go *o. of* the room; *be o. of breath; o. of touch with;* put *o. of the
way; get o. of* doing).

***Stamping (rubbing) o.*; men *come o.* (Go *o. of business; o. of
doors; put o. to grass; o. of line;* be *on the look-o.; o. of order; o. of
pocket; o. of the question;* walking *o. of step; tired o.; o. of turn;
turning o. well; washing o.* clothing).

outburst, n. *Basic words.* A sudden bursting out of sound or feeling.

outcome, n. *Basic words.* What comes from events.

outcry, n. *Basic words.* Loud noise, protest.

outdoor, a. *Basic words.* In the open air, not in a house.

out(er)most, a. *Basic words.* The farthest out.

outgoing, a. *Basic words.* Which or who is or are going out.

outhouse, n. *Basic words.* Building in connection with a house but
separate from it.

outlaw, n. *Basic words.* Person who is put outside the care of the law.

outlet, n. *Basic words.* Way out for force or substance.

outline, n. *Basic words.* 1. Line round a form. 2. A statement of chief
points to give a general idea of something.

outlook, n. *Basic words.* 1. Way of looking at things. 2. View.

output, n. *Basic words.* Amount of work done in a given time.

outside, n., a., adv., prep. *Basic words.* (Of, in, to) the outer part.

outsider, n. *Basic words.* Person outside, not one of, a given group.

outskirts, n. *Basic words.* The outer edge (of town).

outstretched, a. *Basic words.* Fully unfolded, (of arms and so on)
put out.

oven, n. 'ʌvn; *four;* (*Brat-, Back-*) *Ofen.*

Put meat in the o.

over, prep., adv. 'ouvə*; *au dessus: restant; über: übrig.*

(e) More than: at an end: down from edge or upright position.

A cover *o.* the meat; have authority *o.* a person; there is a
window *o.* the door; the airplane is *o.* a house; get *o.* a wall; jumping *o.* the water; a change came *o.* him; get *o.* a disease. Go *o.* to
the other side. An apple for everyone and two *o.*; he is *o.* 21. The
war is *o.* The boy was pushed *o.*

*The page is *turned o.; say* the words *o.*

**(*Straight o. there; turning it o. in one's mind*).

overacting, n., a. *Basic words.* Overdoing the acting (on the theater stage).

overall, n. *Basic words.* Work dress put on over other clothing.

overbalancing, n., a. *Basic words.* Undergoing loss of balance.

overcoat, n. *Basic words.* Coat put on over other clothing.

overcome, v. *Basic words.* Get the better of.

overdo, v. *Basic words.* Do more than is wise or necessary.

overdressed, a. *Basic words.* Loud in one's dress.

overfull, a. *Basic words.* More than full.

overhanging, a. *Basic words.* (Of roof, part of mountain and so on) coming out over.

overhead, a., adv. *Basic words.* Up, in the sky (air).

overhearing, a. *Basic words.* Hearing the talk of others without their knowledge.

overland, a., adv. *Basic words.* (Going) over the land as opp. by sea or air.

overleaf, adv. *Basic words.* On the other side of the page.

overlooking, a. *Basic words.* 1. In a position giving a view over. 2. Not seeing; not taking into account.

overpowering, a. *Basic words.* Over-great in degree.

overseas, a., adv. *Basic words.* Across the sea.

overseer, n. *Basic words.* Person in authority over workers.

overshoe, n. *Basic words.* Rubber shoe put on over others to keep out wet.

overstatement, n. *Basic words.* Statement in which more is said than is true.

overtake, v. *Basic words.* Come up with (and go farther than).

overtaxed, a. *Basic words.* Taxed more than is right.

overtime, n., adv. *Basic words.* (Work) after normal working hours.

overturned, a. *Basic words.* Pushed over, upside-down.

over-use, n. *Basic words.* More use than is right (necessary).

overvalued, a. *Basic words.* Given more than right value.

overweight, n., a. *Basic words.* More than the right weight.

overwork, n. More work than is wise.

owner, n. 'ounə°; *propriétaire, possesseur; Eigentümer.*

He is the o. of a newspaper (a dog).

page (-er, -ing, -ed), n. peidʒ; *page; Seite.*

(e) Leaf of book or writing-paper; *Blatt.*

A book of 100 pp.; paging the book. Writing on one side of the p. only.

pain (-er, -ing, -ed), n. pein; *douleur; Schmerz.*

-ed (-ing) (e) Wounded in one's feelings; *peiné; verleizt.*

His tooth gives him p.; he is in p.; my hand is paining me. She has a pained look on her face.

paint (-er, -ing, -ed), n. peint; *peinture; Farbe.*

(s) Face-paint; *fard; Schminke.*

-ing, (e) painted picture; *peinture; tableau; Malen; Gemälde.*

Put p. on the wall; a box of pp.; painting the house; making (pictures) with p.; a painter and builder. She puts p. on. Painting a picture; he is a noted painter. A painting of ships.

paper (-er, -ing, -ed), n. 'peipə*; *papier; Papier.*

(s) Newspaper; *journal; Zeitung.*

(e) Bit of writing about some question; *traité; Aufsatz.*

Put p. round the meat; put down on p.; papering a room. Writing for a p. Reading a p. on Basic English.

paper-knife, n. *Basic words.* Knife for cutting pages.

paper-weight, n. *Basic words.* A weight for keeping loose papers in place.

*paradise**, 'pærədais. *International word.*

paraffin, 'pærəfin. *International word.*

parallel (un-), a., n. 'pærəlel; *parelléle; parallel.*

(e) Of like sort, value; *semblable, pareil; gleichartig.*

P. lines. The questions are not p. There is an interesting p. to this in history.

parcel, n. 'pɑːsl; *colis, paquet; Paket.*

Make a p. of the shoes; put the food into a p.; send it by p. post.

park, pɑːk. *International word.*

part (-er, -ing, -ed), n. pɑːt; *portion, partie; Teil.*

(e) Part in a play (or undertaking); *rôle; Rolle.*

ing, (e) Division in hair: separating; *raei: séparation; Scheitel: Trennung.*

He gave me p. of the field; go p. of the way; the heart is a p. of the body; 2 pp. of acid and 5 of water; parting the animals. Be acting a small p. Your parting is not straight. A sad parting.

°*In p.* because he was ill; *take p. in* a play.

°°I, *for my p.; for the most p.; on the p. of.*

passport, 'pɑːspɔːt. *International word.*

past, a., prep., adv., n. pɑːst; *passé: aprés; vergangen, früher: nach,. über: vorbei: Vergangenheit.*

His p. crimes; my p. experience; my best years are p. It is ten minutes p. six; I was taken p. my station. They went p. slowly. Events in the p.

°The train goes at *half (a quarter) p. one.*

paste (-er, -ing, -ed), n. peist; *pâte; Teig.*

(s) Sticky paste; *colle; Kleister.*

The p. is ready to go in the oven. Put the paper on the walls with p.; pasting two pages together.

patent, 'peitənt. *International word.*

payment, n. 'peimənt; *paiement; Zahlung.*

(e) Giving of a payment; *acte de payer; Bezahlung.*

The first p. is £5; his p. was a kind word. Attempting the p.. of his debts; he made p. of the full amount.

peace, n. piːs; *paix; Friede.*

(e) Condition of rest; *tranquillité; Ruhe.*

Make p. with a country. The p. of night; p. of mind.

° (The nations are *at p.*).

peacemaker, n. *Basic words.* One who makes peace.

pen (-ner, -ning, -ned), n. pen; *(porte-) plume; Feder.*

Writing with a p.; penning a long letter.

pen-name, n. *Basic words.* Name used by a writer.

pencil (-ler, -ling, -led), n. 'pensl; *crayon; Bleistift.*

The point of my p. is broken; a penciled note.

penguin,* 'peŋgwin. *International word.*

person, n. 'pəːsn; *personne; Person.*

Every p. in the room; an important p.; young pp.

°°Come *in p.*

phonograph, 'founəgræf. *International word.*

physical (un-, -ly), a. 'fizikəl; *physique; physikalisch.*

(s) To do with the body; *körperlich.*

Our knowledge of p. things. Have great p. force; physically he is like his father.

physics, 'fiziks. *International name of science.*

physiology, fizi'ɔlədʒi. *International name of science.*

piano, 'pjænou. *International word.*

picture (-er, -ing, -ed), n. 'piktʃə°; *image, tableau; Bild, Gemälde.*

(s) Motion picture; *film; Film:*

(e) Picture in words or in the mind; *image; Bild.*

Painting a p. of the girl. The p. takes 2 hours. Give a p. of events; picturing things to oneself.

° (*Take a p.* with a camera).

pig, n. pig; *porc; Schwein.*

He keeps pp.

pigtail, n. *Basic words.* Hair on head twisted together and hanging down like a tail.

pin (-ner, -ning, -ned), n. pin; *épingle; Stecknadel.*

(e) Something p.-like in form or purpose; *cheville; Bolzen.*

Put a p. in the cloth; pinning two bits together. A strong metal p. in the machine.

pincushion, n. *Basic words.* Small cushion for pins.

pipe (-er, -ing, -ed), n. paip; *tuyau, conduit; Rohr.*

(s) Music-pipe; *flûte; Pfeife.*

(e) Smoker's pipe; *pipe; Pfeife.*

Send water through the p.; piping the house. Playing notes on a p. He has no tobacco in his p.

place (-er, -ing, -ed), n. pleis; *place, lieu, endroit; Ort, Stelle.*

(s) Space: *place; Platz.*

(e) Position (as worker); *place; Stellung.*

This is the p. where I saw the animal; go from one p. to another; take one's p.; the p. where the story gets sad; placing the cake on the table; we are well placed here for seeing the stage. Here is a p. for you. She has a good p. in a store.

° (Events) *take p.*

°°*In the first p.; give p. to; in p. of.* (*A p. in the sun*).

plane (-er, -ing, -ed), n. plein; *rabot; Hobel.*

(e) Flat level stretch of space or substance, for example that forming 2 wings of airplane: level of development or existence; *plan: plan; Fläche: Ebene.*

Make the board smooth with a p.; planing the wood. The points A, B, and C are all in the same p.; a circle is a p. form; the tail p. of the airplane came off. A different p. of thought.

plant (-er, -ing, -ed), n. plɑːnt; *plante; Pflanze.*

(e) Works and/or machines for industry; *outillage, usine; Betrieb-sanlage, Fabrik.*

A garden p.; planting trees. An electric-light p.; needing new p.

plate (-er, -ing, -ed), n. pleit; *assiette; Teller.*

(e) Flat bit; *plaque; Platte.*

Put food on a p. Making steel pp.; on the door was a brass p.; some cameras take pictures on glass pp. A silver-plated tray.

platinum*, 'plætinəm. *International word.*

play (-er, -ing, -ed), n. plei; *récréation, jeu; Spiel.*

(e) Stage play; *piéce de theâtre; Schauspiel.*

-ing, (e) Playing a music instrument; *action de jouer; Spielen.*

The boys' p. was rough; he is playing with a ball; playing football. Put a p. on (the stage). Playing a piano.

*(*Get a p. up; at p.*).

***Come into p.; do in p.; a p. on words; playing a trick.*

plaything, n. *Basic words.* Thing for playing with, sp. for small boys and girls.

please (-ing, -ed), int. pliːz; *s'il vous plaît; bitte.*

P. give me some money; may I p. come?; yes, p. do; I was pleased by the play; a pleasing face.

*(Be *pleased with*).

pleasure, n. 'pleʒə*; *plaisir; Vergnügen, Freude.*

(e) Thing giving pleasure.

There is no p. in getting wet; take a p. in gardening; the p. of doing good work. Writing is a p. to him; the pp. of the town; simple pp.

***Come and go at p.*

plow (-er, -ing, -ed), n. plau; *Charrue; Pflug.*

The p. is pulled by a horse; plowing a field; the ship was plowing through the waves.

plowman, n. *Basic words.* Man who does plowing.

pocket (-er, -ing, -ed), n. 'pɔkit; *poche; Tasche.*

(e) Hollow, bag; *Beutel, Behälter.*

Take money out of one's p.; a drain on one's p.; pocketing the profits. A p. of poison gas.

***He is out of p. through this business.*

pocket-book, n. *Basic words.* Small leather folder for notes and papers.

pocket-money, n. *Basic words.* Money for small needs.

point (-er, -ing, -ed), n. pɔint; *pointe; Spitze.*

(e) Small mark as made by a p. on paper; position in space or time looked on as such a p.; chief purpose or idea; *point; point; essentiel; Punkt: Punkt: Hauptsache, Point.*

The p. of the pencil; a pointed end; pointing to the man; the pointer of the instrument. Four p. five (4.5); boiling-p. Put a stick in at this p. My p. in coming; the p. of the argument; make a good p. A p. in space.

*A p. of view. (Your answer is not *to the p.; pointing at* the men).

***Make a p. of.*

poison (-er, -ing, -ed), n. 'pɔizn; *poison; Gift.*

Give the rats p.; poisoned by taking bad meat.

police, po'liːs. *International word.*

policeman, n. *Basic words.*

polish (-er, -ing, -ed), n. 'pɔliʃ; *vernis, cirage; Politur, Wichse.*

(e) Bright, smooth quality; smooth quality of behavior, writing, and so on; *poli: élégance; Glanz: Schliff.*

Rubbing with p. Get a good p. on the shoes; polishing with a duster. A person with p.; polished writing.

political (un-, -ly), a. pə'litikəl; *politique; politisch.*

The two countries have different p. systems; his outlook is quite unpolitical; politically he is very expert.

poor, a., n. puə*; *pauvre; arm.*

(e) Of low quality; unhappy; *pauvre, médiocre: pauvre, malheureux; gering, schlecht: arm.*

The family is very p.; the country is p. in water. The ink is p.; the table is poorly made. The p. man has been sent to prison. Food for the p.

porter, n. 'pɔːtə*; *porteur, facteur; Gepäckträger.*

(e) Door-keeper at hotel and so on; *portier; Portier.*

The p. took the bags. The p.'s place is by the door.

position, n. pə'ziʃən; *situation; Lage, Stellung.*

(e) Place as worker; position of body; *emploi: position; Stelle, Amt: Stellung.*

This is the p. of my house; the coal-owners are in a strong p. I have a p. at the bank. Seated in a strange p.

***In p.*

possible (im-, -ly), a. 'pɔsəbl; *possible; möglich.*

A p. event; it is p. to get there today; I may possibly go; such a thing is impossible.

**Come *if p.*

post (*-er, -ing, -ed*), poust. *International word.*

postcard, n. *Basic words.* Card for sending by post.

postman, n. *Basic words.* Man whose work is taking the letters to and from the post-office.

postmark, n. *Basic words.* Mark stamped on letters giving name of post-office and time of posting.

post-office, n. *Basic words.* Organization or building to do with post.

pot (-ter, -ting, -ted), n. pɔt; *pot; Topf.*

-ter, (e) Maker of earth pots; *potier; Töpfer.*

Put the p. on the fire; potted meat; potting a plant. The potter's wheel.

potash,* 'pɔtæʃ. *International word.*

potato (potatoes), n. pə'teitou; *pomme de terre; Kartoffel.*

Give me one p. with my meat, please; get potatoes up with a spade.

powder (*-er, -ing, -ed*), n. 'paudə*; *poudre; Puder.*

(s) Medical powder; *Pulver.*

She put p. on her face; powdering one's hair; powdered sugar. He took a p. for his cold.

power, n. 'pauə*; *pouvoir; Vermögen.*

(s) Work force produced by muscles or machines; *force; Kraft.*

(e) Authority over: important country; *autorité: puissance; Macht: Macht.*

Have the p. to do; great pp. of mind. I have no p. in my arm; water-p. is used for driving the machine; electric p. Have p. over; be in p. One of the great pp.

power-house, n. *Basic words.* Works making electric or other power.

present, a., n. 'preznt; *actuel, présent; gegenwärtig: Gegenwart.*

(e) At the place and so on in question; *présent; zugegen.*

The p. position of the country. All were p. at the meeting. Living in the p.

*Happy *at p.*

present-day, a. *Basic words.* Of the present time.

president, 'prezidənt. *International name.*

price (-er, -ing, -ed), n. prais; *prix; Preis.*

The p. of the house is high; get it at a low p.; the dress is priced at £ 10; we are pricing goods.

prince, prins. *International name.*

princess, prin'ses. *International name.*

print (-er, -ing, -ed), n. print; (*caractère d'*) *imprimerie; Druck.*

(s) A printed picture; *gravure;* [*Kupfer-,* *Stahl-*]*Stich, Holz-schnitt, Graphik.*

(e) Mark made by a thing; print of camera picture; *empreinte, impression: épreuve; Abdruck, Spur: Abzug.*

The p. is very small; his verses are in p.; printing a book; directions for the printer. An old p. of London. There is a p. in the sand. Give me a p. of that picture.

prison (-er, -ing, -ed), n. 'prizn; *prison; Gefängnis.*

-er, (e) Person kept (as) in prison; *prisonnier (-ière); Gefangener.*

Be kept in a dark p.; p. made him bitter; be sent to p.; be in p.; prisoning her hand. The prisoners are happy.

**Take (a person) *prisoner.*

private (-ly), a. 'praivit; *personnel, particulier, privé; privat, persönlich.*

(e) Safe from observation; *secret; heimlich, zurüchgezogen.*

Send a p. letter; one's p. views; this is not a store, it is a p. house. The garden is very p.; they saw one another privately.

probable (im-, -ly), adj. 'prɔbəbl; *probable; wahrscheinlich.*

A p. event; it seems p. that he will come; you are probably right; the story is improbable.

process (processes, -er, -ing, -ed), n. 'prouses; *cours, processus; Verfahren, Verlauf.*

(s) Law process; *procès; Prozess.*

(e) P. used to give goods some special form; *procédé; Verfahren.*

Waving hair is a delicate p.; the processes of growth; go through the p. of being washed. There will be a long law p. if the agreement is broken. The discovery of a new p.; processed cheese.

produce (-er, -ing, -ed), n. 'prɔdjuːs; *produit; Erzeugnis(se).*

-er, (s) Theater producer; *metteur en scène; Regisseur.*

The p. from the farm; producing goods for the market; this effect is produced by the sun. The producer of the play.

profit (-er, -ing, -ed), n. 'prɔfit; *profit, bénéfice; Gewinn.*

(e) Value, help; *avantage; Vorteil.*

The business made a small p. What p. was it to him?; profiting by his knowledge.

* (The *p. on* the business was high).

** (*At a p.*).

program, 'prougræm. *International word.*

propaganda, 'prɔpə'gændə. *International word.*

property, n. 'prɔpəti; *propriété; Eigentum.*

(s) Land property; *biens immeubles, propriété; Besitz[tum].*

(e) Quality; *propriété; Eigenschaft.*

That book is my p. He has a p. in the country. It has not the pp. of an acid.

prose, n. prouz; *prose; Prosa.*

Writing good p. is as hard as writing verse.

protest (-er, -ing, -ed), n. 'proutest; *protestation (contre); Protest.*

-ing, (e) Making a statement with force; *protestant (de); Beteuern.*

He made a p. against the noise; the teachers were protesting about what had been done. He went to prison protesting that he had not done the crime.

**He did it *under p.*

psychology, psai'kɔlədʒi. *International name of science.*

public (-ly), a., n. 'pʌblik; *public; öffentlich; Publikum.*

(e) Open to general observation.

He gave a p. talk in a p. place. Let us go where it is less p.; he made the statement publicly. He has a small p. for his books; putting ideas before the p.

pull (-er, ing, -ed), n. pul; *action de tirer; Zug.*

(e) Better chance than others have; *avantage; Beziehungen.*

Give the cord a p.; have a p. at the boot; pulling the cat's tail. He had a p. with the authorities.

pump (-er, -ing, -ed), n. pʌmp; *pompe; Pumpe.*

Get water from the p.; pumping air into a cushion.

punishment, n. 'pʌniʃmənt; *punition; Strafe.*

(e) Act of giving punishment; anything looked on as punishment; *châtiment: châtiment; Bestrafung: Strafe.*

He was sent to be bed as a p. for crying. The p. of the men took place at night. His p. was the loss of his friends.

purpose (-er, -ing, -ed), n. 'pəːpəs; *but, intention; Zweck, Absicht.*

He had a p. in coming; he was purposing to do it.

*(He came *on* p. to see you).

**He did it *to no (some)* p.

purr, n. *Onomatopoeic.* Sound made by a happy cat.

push (pushes, -er, -ing, -ed), n. puʃ; *poussée; Stoss, Schub.*

(e) Driving-power: *énergie; Stosskraft.*

Give the table a p.; their pushes had no effect on the door; pushing a hand-cart. Good businessmen have p.

push-cart (-carriage), n. *Basic words.* Cart (carriage) for pushing by hand.

put (puts, putting), v. put; *mettre; setzen, legen, stellen.*

P. water in a bottle; p. a story into words; p. an idea forward; p. a man in prison; he has p. money into the business; if the government puts a tax on land; I am putting such thoughts out of my head; p. a person out of doubt; p. away doubts; p. things together; p. a question; p. the clock back an hour; p. work before play; p. others against him; p. him off doing.

*1. A common way of *putting* an idea (suggestion) *across* is by advertisement.

2. He *put up an argument (fight)* when the trainer said the horse had been poisoned.

3. Someone had made an attempt to *put it to death.*

4. They *put* the discussion (talk, meeting) *off* till the morning.

5. The chances are generally against you if you *put* money *on* a horse (event).

(*p. up with* troubles; *p. in mind of; p. a stop to*).

**P. *one's foot down* about something; *p. in* (words in talk); *p. in for; p. words into person's mouth; p. to the test (to flight); p. it down to; p.* an undertaking *through.* (*P. into effect; p. out to grass*).

pyjamas*, pəˈdʒɑːməz. *International word.*

pyramid*, 'pirəmid. *International word.*

quack, n. *Onomatopoeic.* Sound of water-bird.

quality (qualities), n. 'kwɔliti; *qualité; Eigenschaft, Beschaffenheit.*

(e) Quality of a person; *Eigenschaft.*

(e) Degree of value; *Qualität.*

The hard q. of the stone. He has a number of good qualities. The cloth is of the best q.; a good q. shoe.

queen, kwiːn. *International name.*

question (-er, -ing, -ed), n. 'kwestʃən; *question, interrogation; Frage.*

(e) Something for decision or discussion: doubt; *question, proposition, sujet; doute.*

Put a q. to him; questioning a person. The q. of what to do now; it is a q. of organization; the peace q.; I am not questioning his word; there is no q. that he took the money.

*The accounts in *q.*

**Out of the *q.*

question-mark, n. *Basic words.* Mark put at end of a question in writing.

quick (-ly), a. kwik: *vif; raseh, schnell.*

(e) Quick to see or make a point; *vif, intelligent; flink.*

A q. train; have a q. journey; a q. move; talking quickly. He has a q. tongue (mind).

*(*Q.* at languages).

quicksilver, n. *Basic words.* Hg.

quiet (un-, -ly), a., s. 'kwaiət; *tranquille, calme; ruhig, still.*

(e) Not violent; *calme, paisible; ruhig.*

A q. place; the night is q.; make them be q.; she was crying quietly. A q. horse; have a q. day; a q. color; an unquiet mind. In the q. of the night.

*quinine**, kwi'niːn. *International word.*

quite, adv. kwait; *tout à fait; ganz.*

(e) To a somewhat high degree; *assez; ziemlich.*

I am q. ready; not q. the right color. He is q. kind; q. a good book.

radio, 'reidiou. *International word.*

**On the *r.*

*radium**, 'reidiem. *International word.*

rail (-er, -ing, -ed), n. reil; *barre, barreau; Geländer.*

(e) (One rail of) train line; (*rail de*) *chemin de fer; Schiene, Eisenbahn.*

-ing, (e) Wall of rails; *grille; Gitter, Einzäunung.*

A r. round the tree; railing off the flowers. The train came off the rr.; go by r. A railing round the field.

railway, n. *Basic words.* 1. Rails for train. 2. Train system.

rain (-er, -ing, -ed), n. rein; *pluie; Regen.*

Wind and r.; it is raining; blows were rained on him.

rainfall, n. *Basic words.* Amount of rain in a given time.

range (-er, -ing, -ed), n. ɹein(d)ʒ; *chaîne, rangée; [Berg-]Kette.*

(e) Group formed of different sorts, degrees: field of operation; *assortiment, variété: portée; Reihe: Ausmass, Reichweite.*

Across a r. of mountains; ranging the books on the shelf; the boys were ranged before him. A r. of goods; ranging from black to white. A narrow r. of thought; the r. of a gun.

rat, n. ræt; *rat; Ratte.*

Put down poison for the rr.

rate (-er, -ing, -ed), n. reit; *taux; Verhaltnis, Mass.*

(s) Rate of motion; *vitesse; Geschwindigkeit.*

The r. of interest is 5%; the birth-r. is going down; the r. of exchange is low; rating her qualities high. The r. of the train was increasing.

At any r.

ray (-er, -ing, -ed), n. rei; *rayon; Strahl.*

(e) Form like a r.

Sending out a r. of light; rr. from the fire; raying its heat in all directions; a r. of hope. The rr. of a flower.

reaction, n. ri(ː)'ækʃən; *réaction; Reaktion.*

(s) Sudden change of feeling; *Gegenwirkung, [Gefühls-]Umschlag.*

(e) Tendency, specially political, to go back to old ideas: chemical effect; *Reaktion: Reaktion.*

The natural r. to a loud noise is to give a sudden jump. He had a r. against his old way of living. A time of political r. The r. of the acid with the metal is violent.

reading (reader), n., a. 'riːdiŋ; *lecture; Lesen.*

(s) A public reading; *lecture, communication; Vortrag.*

(e) Sense given to words; *interprétation; Auffassung.*

-er, (e) Book for teaching r.; *livre de lecture; Lesebuch.*

She is getting on well with her r.; a note to the reader. He gave a r. of his verses. My r. of that line is different. Readers with colored pictures. I am r. an interesting book.

ready (un-, -ly), a. 'redi; *prêt; fertig, bereit.*

(e) Quick; *prompt; prompt.*

Get r. to go out; the meal is r.; he was r. to do whatever was necessary. Give a r. answer; have a r. tongue; be unready to give his approval; they readily made room for us.

°° (The book is *r. to hand*).

reason (-er, -ing, -ed), n. 'riːzn; *raison; Grund.*

(e) Power of thought: *raisonnement; Vernunft.*

I have a r. for going. Do animals have r.?; reasoning about a question; reasoning with a boy; a reasoned answer.

° (He went away *for this r.*).

°°*Anything in r. Have r. to.* (There is *every r. why*).

receipt (-er, -ing, -ed), n. ri'siːt; *reçu, quittance; Quittung.*

Give a r. for the goods (payment); receipting an account.

°°I am *in r. of* your letter; I will do it *on r. of* your check.

record (-er, -ing, -ed), n., a. 'rekɔːd; *procès-verbal, archives, enregistrement; Protokoll, Aufzeichnung, Leumund.*

(s) Phonograph record; *disque; Schallplatte.*

(e) Best recorded attempt; *record; Rekord.*

Make a r. of the agreement; his past r. is good; recording one's experiences. Make a r. of his playing. He made a r. for the high jump; the r. is broken again. Do it in r. time.

°The facts are *on r.*

record-player, n. A machine by which sounds recorded on records may be given back as sound.

red, a., n. red; *rouge; rot.*

Waving a r. flag; getting r. in the face. R. is the wrong color for this.

referendum°*, refə'rendəm. *International word.*

regret (-ter, -ting, -ted), n. ri'gret; *regret; Bedauern, Reue.*

Feeling r. that one was unkind; have no r. about the past; regretting the loss of his watch.

° (He has no *r. for* his acts; *to my r.* it is still there).

regular (ir-, -ly), a. 'regjulə°; *régulier; regelmässig.*

(e) Taking place regularly.

The lines are r.; a r. rhythm; her teeth are very irregular. Get r. work; a r. event; he sees her regularly.

relation, n. ri'leiʃən; *relation, rapport; Verhältnis, Beziehung.*

(e) Family relation; *parent; Verwandte.*

The r. between being good and being happy; this is small in r. to that; our rr. with that country have never been good. She is one of his rr.

Have sex rr. *with*.

religion, n. ri'lidʒən; *religion; Religion.*

(e) Thing taken as seriously as a religion; *culte; Kultus.*

Take up a new r.; they are not interested in r. They make a r. of sport.

representative, n., a. 'repri'zentətiv; *représentant: représentatif; Vertreter, Abgeordneter: vertretend, repräsentativ.*

(e) Person acting for others; *représentant, député.*

This may be taken as a r. of the group. Send a r. to the meeting. A r. selection; r. of all shades of opinion.

request (-er, -ing, -ed), n. ri'kwest; *demande; Bitte.*

Make a r. for some more; requesting him to come.

*His books were much *in r*.

**The song was given *by r*.

respect (-er, -ing, -ed), n. ris'pekt; *respect, estime; Achtung.*

The boy has no r. for his teachers; the old man is respected by all; respecting the opinions of others.

responsible (ir-, -ly), a. ris'ponsəbl; *responsable; verantwortlich.*

(e) Looked on as having the care of something: who may safely be made responsible; needing such a person; *responsable: digne de confiance; de responsabilité; verantwortlich: verantwortungsvoll; verantwortungsvoll.*

If the meat is bad, the heat is r. The law makes the owner r. Put it in the hands of a r. person; she is quite irresponsible; he will do his part responsibly. A r. position.

*(He was *r. for* her death).

rest (-er, -ing, -ed), n. rest; *repos; Ruhe.*

(e) The other things (parts, persons); *reste; Rest.*

-ing, (e) Being supported; *s'appuyant; ruhend.*

Have a r. on the bed; take a r. from work; resting one's eyes. The r. of the books will come later. His arm is resting on the table.

*(His mind was at r.).

restaurant, 'restərɔːŋ. *International word.*

reward (-er, -ing, -ed), n. ri'wɔːd; *récompense; Belohnung.*

(s) Special reward offered; *prix; Preis.*

He got no r. for the trouble he took; rewarding him with a smile.
A r. is given to the person who does best in the competition.

rheumatism°, 'ru:matizm. *International word.*

rhythm, n. 'riðm; *rythme; Rhythmus.*

Dancing to the r. of the music; the r. of the heart.

rice, n. rais; *riz; Reis.*

Put r. in the pot; working in the r. fields.

right (-ly), a., n. rait, *droit; recht.*

(e) Opposite of in error: good, opp. bad, wrong: (angle) of 90°:
what one may do or have in agreement with law or r. (freq. **rr.**);
correct: juste: droit: droit; richtig: recht: recht: Recht, Vorrecht.

the R. Political group opposite the Left.

His r. eye is smaller than his left. That answer was r. Do what
is r.; he was rightly angry. A r. angle. Keep to the r.; a knowledge
of r. and wrong. Have the r. to do something. He has gone over to
the R.

°Everything seems *all r.* (The prisoner was *in the r.*).

°°**R.***!* I will come; *cut r. through.*

right-handed, a. *Basic words.* Using the right hand more than the left.

right-wing, a. *Basic words.* Of the Right politically.

ring (-er, -ing, -ed), n. riŋ; *anneau, cercle; Ring.*

(s) Finger ring; *bague.*

(e) Business ring; *cartel; Kartel.*

Put rr. on the curtain; the house is ringed with trees. She has rr.
on her fingers; a ringed hand. A r. formed by the ship-owners.

river, n. 'rivə°; *rivière, fleuve; Fluss.*

(e) Mass of moving liquid; *ruisseau; Strom.*

Have a swim in the r. A r. of blood.

road, n. roud; *route chaussée; (Fahr)Strasse, Weg.*

Walking in the r.; go by r.

rod, s. rɔd; *baguette, triangle; Stange.*

Put a r. up for the curtain; a fishing-r.

roll (-er, -ing, -ed), n. roul; *action de rouler; Rolle.*

(e) Act of rolling: roll of bread; rolling motion; *roulement: petit
pain: roulis; Walzen: Semmel: Rollen, Schlingern.*

-er, (s) Turning structure of roll-like form; *cylindre, rouleau;
Walze.*

Take down a r. of cloth. Give the ball a r.; the cart was rolling down the slope; rolling up the paper. Have coffee and rr. The r. of the sea; the ship is rolling. Go over the earth with a roller; be rolling the grass.

roof (-er, -ing, -ed), n. ruːf; *toit; Dach.*

(e) Top of room; roof of mouth; *plafond: palais; Decke: Gaumen.*

Put a r. on the house; a building roofed with tin. The room has a low r. Put your tongue against the r. of your mouth.

room, n. rum; *chambre, pièce d'une maison; Zimmer.*

(e) Space; *place; Platz, Raum.*

A house with five rr. There is r, for another box.

root (-er, -ing, -ed), n. ruːt; *racine; Wurzel.*

(e) Cause, base; *fondement.*

The tree has deep rr.; rooted in the earth. The r. of the trouble.

*The tree *took r.* in the earth.

rough (-ly), a. rʌf; *rugueux; rauh.*

(e) Incomplete, not polished; rough in behavior; *ébauché, grossier: brutal, rude; roh: grob.*

R. cloth; a r. road. A r. copy; a roughly cut stone. A r. man; be r. with the boy.

round, a., adv., prep. raund; *rond: autour de; rund: ringsum: um . . . herum.*

A r. button; a r. ball. The wheels of the cart go r. The girls are going r. the tree.

**All the year r.; r. the other side; come r.* after an operation.

roundabout, a. *Basic words.* Not going straight to the place (point).

royal, 'rɔiəl. *International name.*

rub (-ber, -bing, -bed), n. rʌb; *frottement; Reiben, Abreibung.*

-ber, (e) (Bit of) substance of that name; *caoutchouc, gomme; Gummi.*

-bed, (s) Damaged by rubbing; *écorché; abgerieben, abgescheuert.*

Give the table a r.; give his back a r.; rubbing the silver. A bit of rubber; a rubber sponge. Take the marks off the paper with a rubber. The horse got badly rubbed by the leather.

**(Rubbing (stamping) out).*

rule (-er, -ing, -ed), n. ruːl; *règle; Regel, Vorschrift.*

(e) Straight-edged or measuring rule: control of a ruler; *règle: règne; Lineal, Zollstock: Herrschaft.*

-er, (s) Ruler of a country; *souverain; Herrscher.*

Make new rr. for the society. Make your lines with a r.; ruling lines. Under the r. of John. The ruler of the country; ruling a country well.

***As a r.*

rum*, rʌm. *International word.*

run, n. rʌn; *course; Lauf.*

Have a r.; go for a r.

***A r. on the bank; in the long r. (At a r.).*

runaway, n., a. *Basic words.* 1. (Person) running away from authority. 2. (Horse and so on) out of control.

sad (-ly), a. 'sæd; *triste; traurig.*

Have a s. face; a s. story; a s. man; he said it sadly.

safe (un-, -ly), a., n. seif; *sauf, en sécurité: coffre-fort; sicher, gefahr-los: Geldschrank.*

Put the money in a s. place; keep the jewels s.; it is unsafe to go; they got back safely. The s. has been broken open.

sail (-or, -ing, -ed), n. seil; *voile; Segel.*

(e) Journey in sailboat; *promenade à la voile; Segelfahrt.*

-or, (s) Seaman; *marin, matelot; Seemann, Matrose.*

Put up the s.; sailing a ship in the North Sea. Go for a s. The sailors are cleaning the ship.

salad*, sæləd. *International word.*

salt (-er, -ing, -ed), n. sɔlt; *sel; Salz.*

(e) Chemical salt (freq. **ss.**).

Put s. in the food; salting the meat. When you have stomach trouble, take ss.; the ss. of copper are blue.

same, a., pron. seim; *même; gleich, selb. derselbe.*

The two friends went to the s. place; they have the s. walk; these pictures are the s. He says the s.

***All the s. (At the s. time).*

sand, n. sænd; *sable; Sand.*

ss. = stretch of sand by the sea.

Put s. on the floor. Playing on the s(s).

sardine*, saːdiːn. *International word.*

saw. See *see.*

say (says, said, saying), v. sei; *dire; sagen.*

-ing, (e) Thing commonly said; *diction; Ausspruch.*

S. words; s. something to the man; s. to oneself; s. no to his sug-gestion; it says in the book that it is so; "Yes," he said; the book says. An old saying.

  * (S. the words *over; that is to s.*).

scale (-er, -ing, -ed), n. skeil; *échelle; Masstab, Skala.*

  (s) Music scale; *gamme; Tonleiter.*

  ss. = Apparatus for measuring weight; *balance; Wage.*

The first degree on the s.; the s. is an inch for a mile. She is playing ss. on the piano. Put another weight on the ss.

  * (The design is *on a great (small) s.*).

  **Little ships *made to scale.*

school (-er, -ing, -ed), n. sku:l; *école; Schule.*

  (e) Group united by an idea.

The s. by the church; go to s.; schooling oneself to undergo pain. A new s. of thought (painting).

  *The boys were *at s.*

science, n. 'saiəns; *science; Wissenschaft.*

  (s) The physical sciences taken together.

Art and s.; botany is a s.; the new s. of psychology; there is no s. of government. New discoveries in s. are changing these industries completely.

scissors (scissors), n. 'sizəz; *ciseaux; Schere.*

  Cutting with s.; this store keeps scissors.

screw (-er, -ing, -ed), n. skru:; *vis; Schraube.*

  The board is fixed to the wall with ss.; screwing a top on a bottle.

  **He was *screwing up* the box.

screwdriver, n. *Basic words.* Instrument for putting in screws.

sea, n. si:; *mer; Meer.*

  A ship on the s.; go to s. in a boat.

  **The boats are *at s.*

seaman, n. *Basic words.* Sailor.

seaside, n., a. *Basic words.* (Place) by the sea.

seat (-er, -ing, -ed), n. si:t; *siege; Sitz.*

  (e) Where something has its place; *Place.*

A hard s.; take a s. by the fire; the s. of his trousers; seating one-self on the floor. The s. of the trouble.

second, a., adv., n. 'sekənd; *second, deuxième; zweite (-r, -s).*

(e) ⅟₆₀ of a minute; *seconde; Sekunde.*

The s. man in the line; give it a s. thought. Put him s. He was the s. to get there. I was a s. late.

* (Facts *at s. hand*).

secondhand, a. *Basic words.* Not new, used.

secret (-ly), a., n. 'si;krit; *secret; geheim: Geheimnis.*

A s. store of gold; have a s. agreement; they are meeting secretly. It was a s. between them.

* (*Let him into the s.*).

secretary (secretaries), n. 'sekrətri; *secrétaire; Sekretär.*

The work has been done by my s.; the s. of an important organization; he has three secretaries.

see (sees, saw, seeing, seen), v. si;; *voir; sehen.*

I s. the sun; if he sees you there he will be angry; she saw me; have you seen the point?; please go and s. who is at the door; I have to s. the manager about my account.

**S. a person *off; s. to* a thing.

seed (-er, -ing, -ed), n. si;d; *graine; Samen, Saat.*

(e) Start (of idea); *germe; Saat.*

Put a s. in the earth; plants come from s(s).; the plants are seeding; a black-seeded flower. The ss. of the new learning.

*These flowers have *gone to s.*

seedsman, n. *Basic words.* Person trading in seeds.

seem (seems, seemed, seeming), v. si;m; *sembler; scheinen.*

You s. to be angry; he seems uncertain; it seemed right to go; it seems to me that there is no hope.

selection, n. si'lekʃən; *sélection;* (*Aus-*)*Wahl.*

(e) Group got by selection; *choix; Auslese.*

Make a s. They were a good s.

self, n. self; *soi-même, moi, individu; Selbst.*

Some say that all knowledge is only of the s.; we all have our worse and our better selves.

* (Be *by oneself*).

self-conscious, a. *Basic words.* Conscious of the effect one is having on others, not natural in behavior in company.

self-control, n. *Basic words.* Keeping control of oneself.

self-interest, n. *Basic words.* Care for one's private profit.

self-respect, n. *Basic words.* Respect for oneself.

self-starter, n. *Basic words.* Electric apparatus for starting an automobile.

send (sends, sent, sending, sender), v. send; *envoyer; senden, treiben.*

S. a letter by post; s. goods by train; s. him news; s. out a smell; the plant is sending out roots; the girl was sent away; war sends prices up; give the sender's name.

*Sending a stone *at* (*firing a gun at*) the window.

**(He *sent word of* his doings).

sense (-er, -ing, -ed), n. sens; *sens, Sinn.*

(e) Sense which words have: common sense: feeling; *sens: bon sens: sensation, sentiment; Bedeutung: Verstand: Empfindung, Sinn.*

The use of one's five ss.; s. experience. Your words have no s. She had the s. to get a medical man. A s. of right and wrong; sensing danger.

*(It was hard to *make out the s.* of what he said).

**(*Come to one's ss.*).

separate (-or, -ing, -ed, -ly), a. 'seprit; *séparé, distinct, isolé; getrennt, gesondert, einzein.*

Get the stones s. from the sand; the boys have s. rooms; the gas is separated from one liquid by a special process; separating the two dogs; the farmer has a separator; he saw them separately.

serious (-ly), a. 'siəriəs; *grave, sérieux; ernst* (*haft*).

(e) Giving reason for serious thought (feeling); *ernst.*

A s. person; take a s. interest in art; be talking seriously. S. news; a s. wound.

servant, n. 'sə:vənt; *domestique, serviteur; Diener, Dienstbote.*

(e) Person working for another; *serviteur, employé; Diener, Angestellte.*

An old family s. The manager is a s. of the company.

**(*Take on* a s.).

sex (sexes), n. seks; *sexe; Geschlecht.*

(e) Sex group.

A talk about s. What is the s. of the newest baby?; the relations between the sexes.

**(*Have s. relations with*).

shade (-er, -ing, -ed), n. ʃeid; *ombre, ombrage; Schalten.*

(e) Shade of color: dead person walking on earth; *nuance: fantôme; Schattierung: Schatten, Gespenst.*

In the s. of the tree; shading his eyes with his hand. A s. of blue. His s. is walking.

shake, n. ʃeik; *secousse, tremblement; Schütteln.*

Give oneself a s.; give his hand a s.

shame (-er, -ing, -ed), s. ʃeim; *honte; Scham.*

(e) Thing which is wrong, a cause of shame; *honte; Schande.*

He had a feeling of s. for what he had done; shaming them with his words. It was a s. to take the money.

sharp (-ly), a. ʃɑːp; *affilé! scharf, spitz.*

(e) With a quick mind: narrow (angle), sudden (turn, slope): angry (words): sudden, violent (pain); *intelligent: aigu: mordant: vif; aufgeweckt: scharf: scharf: heftig.*

The pin had a s. point; get the knife s. He's a s. boy. A s. turn in the pipe; the road goes sharply up at this point. She said something s. A s. pain in the head.

she. See *he.*

she-goat, s. *Basic words.* Female goat.

sheep (sheep), n. ʃiːp; *mouton; Schaf.*

The man had a s. in his arms; the sheep were together in the field.

shelf (shelves), n. ʃelf; *étager, rayon; Brett.*

Put the book on the s.; there were shelves for cups and plates.

ship (-per, -ping, -ped), n. ʃip; *bateau, navire; Schiff.*

Get on a s.; shipping the goods to Canada.

shirt, n. ʃəːit; *chemise; Hemd.*

He was dressed in a s. and trousers.

shock (-er, -ing, -ed), n. ʃɔk; *choc; Schlag, Stoss, Erschütterung.*

(e) Thing acting like a shock to one's feelings, sense of right and wrong.

-ed (**-ing**), (e) Shocked by something as in bad taste; *choqué; entseizt.*

The s. of steel meeting steel; the s. of getting into cold water; an electric s. The news gave me a s.; I was shocked to see him crying; a shocking crime. Her mother was shocked by her short skirt.

shoe (-er, -ing, -ed), n. ʃuː; *soulier; schuh.*

(e) Curved iron for horse's foot; *fer à cheval; Hufeisen.*

Put your ss. on. The horse's s. came off; shoeing a horse.

short, a. ʃɔːt; *court; kurz.*

(e) Opp. tall; *petit; klein.*

A s. line; go a s. way; take a s. time. He is a s. man.

**Be *s. of* food; *be s. with* a person; £ s. d. *for s.;* stopping s. of.

shortcoming, n. *Basic words.* Bad quality or point.

shorthand, n. *Basic words.* Short way of writing.

shut (-ter, -ting), a., n. ʃʌt; *fermé; geschlossen.*

-ter, (s) Outer cover for window; *volet; Fensterladen.*

The door is s.; shutting her eyes. The shutters are down.

*(The house is *s. up*).

side (-er, -ing, -ed), n. said; *côte, bord; Seite.*

(s) Side of the body.

(e) Angle, view of a thing; *côte.*

At the s. of the house; a s. view; siding with the army. A wound in his s. A different s. of the question.

*Walking *s. by s.* (*with* her); *take on one s.*

sideboard, n. *Basic words.* Side-table for plates.

sidelight, n. *Basic words.* Light on some question and so on got in connection with some other thing.

sidewalk, n. *Basic words.* Side of road for persons on foot.

sideways, adv. *Basic words.* In a side-to-side direction.

sign (-er, -ing, -ed), n. sain; *signe; Zeichen, Schild.*

(s) Language sign; *symbole; Zeichen.*

(e) Something pointing to a fact; *trace; Spur, Zeichen.*

-ing, (e) Writing one's name at the end of, putting one's name to; *action de signer; Unterzeichnen.*

He made a s. with his hand; a road s.; signing to the automobile to come on. This is the s. for a stop. There's no s. of it. Signing a check (a newspaper story, one's name).

signboard, s. *Basic words.* Board on the outside of country hotel (beer-house, store) giving its name.

silk, n. silk; *soie; Seide.*

(s) Silk thread; *fil de soie; Nähseide.*

A dress made of s.; s. gloves. Stitching with s.

silver (-er, -ing, -ed), n., a. ˈsilvə*; *argent; Silber.*

(s) Silver money; *monnaie d'argent.*

(e) Color of silver.

A ring made of s.; silvering a tea-pot; a s. tray. Give me s. for this note. Clouds touched with s. A s. sea.

simple (-ly), a. 'simpl; *simple, einfach.*

(e) Needing little trouble: without art or airs, inexperienced; *facile: simple; ernfach: schlicht.*

A s. animal; simply dressed. It is quite s. to make; the answer is s. A s. country girl.

sir, sə:*. *International word.*

sister, n. 'sistə*; *sœur; Schwester.*

She is John's s.

sister-in-law, n. *Basic words.* Sister of the person one is married to.

size, n. saiz; *taille, grandeur; Grösse, Umfang.*

What is the s. of the box?; the s. of the house is important; we have different ss. of socks.

** *(Of some s.).*

skin (-ner, -ning, -ned), n. skin; *peau; Haut, Schale.*

A man with a dark s.; take the s. off the fruit; dressed in ss.; skinning an animal.

skirt (-er, -ing, -ed), n. skə:t; *jupe; [Frauen-]Rock.*

Lifting up her s. in the wet; skirting the town.

* *(Let out a s.).*

sky (skies), n. skai; *ciel; Himmel.*

There are clouds in the s.; Turner is noted for his skies.

sleep, n. sli:p; *sommeil; Schlaf.*

Talking in his s.; have a good s.

* *(He had gone to s.).*

slip (-per, -ping, -ped), n. slip; *action de glisser, faux-pas; (Aus-) Gleiten.*

(e) Error; *faux pas, lapsus; Versehen.*

Her foot gave a s.; they were slipping on the ice; the note was slipped into his pocket by someone. Make a s. in writing.

slope (-er, -ing, -ed), n. sloup; *obliquité, pente; Abhang.*

(e) Sloping land; *pente [colline]; Anhöhe.*

The s. of the roof is sharp; a sloping line. The house is on the top of a s.

slow (-ly), a. slou; *lent; langsam.*

(s) With a slow brain; *benêt, lourd; schwerfällig.*

It is a s. journey; they are s. workers; the train was going slowly. The slowest boy in the school.

* *(He is s. at learning).*

°°(S. *in* doing).

small, a. smɔːl; *petit; klein.*

(e) On a s. scale: unimportant.

A s. girl; a s. amount; say in a s. voice. A s. trader. A s. error.

°°He has some s. *change* for the porter.

smash (smashes, -er, -ing, -ed), n. smæʃ; *action de briser, fracas; Krach, Zerschmettern.*

(s) Smash caused by running into something; *accident, collision; Zusammenstoss.*

(e) Downfall (of business); *faillite; Zusammenbruch.*

The sound of a s. of cups; smashing the stones. There were two smashes on the railway today. The business had a s.

°°The business *went* s.

smell (-er, -ing, -ed), n. smel; *odeur; Geruch.*

(e) Act of smelling; *action de sentir; Riechen.*

There was a strong s. of cooking; the nose is for smelling with; a sweet-smelling oil. The dog had a s. at the meat.

smile (-er, -ing, -ed), n. smail; *sourire; Lächeln.*

A s. on her face; he gave a quick s.; they were all smiling.

°°*Smiling on* everyone.

smoke (-er, -ing, -ed), n. smouk; *fumée; Rauch.*

(e) Act of smoking tobacco; *action de fumer; Rauchen.*

smoking, (e) Getting meat, fish, and so on dried in s.; *fumer, sécher à la fumée; Räuchern.*

A cloud of s. came from the fire; the fire is smoking. Let us have a s.; smoking a pipe; this carriage is for smokers. His business is smoking fish; a tin of smoked meat.

smooth (-er, -ing, -ed, un-, -ly), a. smuːð; *lisse; glatt.*

(e) Untroubled: polished; *facile: poli; geebnet: glatt.*

The walls are s.; the ship was sailing smoothly over the sea; smoothing his hair. The way is s. for her; all has gone smoothly up to now. A s. way of talking.

snake, n. sneik; *serpent; Schlange.*

There is a s. in the grass.

sneeze (-er, -ing, -ed), n. sniːz; *éternuement; Niesen.*

Give a s.; sneezing violently.

snow (-er, -ing, -ed), n. snou; *neige; Schnee.*

There is s. on the roof; it is snowing.

so, adv., pron., conj. sou; *si, ainsi; so, auch: also.*

I am s. tired that I am going to bed. If it is s.; quite s.; I was wrong and s. were you; he says s.; please do s. I will come, s. you may go.

*S. *as to* get it done; eggs, fruit, *and* s. *on; s. that* in the end he was right.

**S. *long;* be s. tired. (*Even s.*).

soap (-er, -ing, -ed), n. soup; *savon; Seife.*

There is water here for washing but no s.; soaping his hands.

society (societies), n. sə'saiəti; *société; Gesellschaft.*

(s) Those with a high position in society; *le monde.*

(e) Organization; *société; Verein.*

Crime is a disease of s.; different societies have different ways. She is not in s. Forming a university s.

sock, n. sɔk; *chausette; Socke.*

He had a hole in his s.

soft (-ly), a. sɔft; *mou; weich.*

(e) With little force: not loud; *doux: tranquille; sanft: leise.*

Resting on a s. bed. A s. touch on his face; a s. wind. A s. voice; the band was playing softly.

solid (un-, -ly), a., n. 'sɔlid; *solide; fest: fester Körper.*

(e) With much substance; *solide, massif; solide: gediegen.*

Wood is a s. substance. A s. wall; a s. book; the snow was solidly massed against the door. The geometry of ss.

some, a., pron. sʌm; *quelque; etwas, irgend ein (-e), einige.*

(e) An unnamed (person, thing).

Here are s. apples; I have s. butter; he went away s. time back; s. cows have no horns. He was with s. other person; s. day I will come and see you. S. of these are ready; have s. more.

**Of s. *size.* (*In s. measure*).

somebody, pron. *Basic words.* Some person.

somehow, adv. *Basic words.* In some way.

someone, pron. *Basic words.* Some person.

something, n. *Basic words.* Some thing.

sometimes, adv. *Basic words.* At some times.

somewhat, adv. *Basic words.* To some degree.

somewhere, adv. *Basic words.* In (at, to) some place.

son, n. sʌn; *fils; Sohn.*

They are ss. of the same father.

son-in-law, s. *Basic words*. Man one's daughter is married to.

song, n. sɔŋ; *chant; Gesang, Lied.*

(e) Sounds like a song: words (as) of song; *chant: chanson.*

The sound of a s. came through the window; he gave a s. The s. of a bird. These verses are a s. to spring.

sort (-er, -ing, -ed), n. sɔːt; *sorte, espèce; Art, Sorte.*

A strange s. of fruit; sorting letters; sorted into groups.

sound (-er, -ing, -ed), n. saund; *son; Laut, Klang, Schall.*

A s. of laughing came to her ears; the s. of feet; sounding a bell; sounding happy.

soup, n. suːp; *potage, soup; Suppe.*

Take s. with a spoon.

south, a., adv., n. sauθ; *sud; südlich: Süden.*

A s. wall; a s. wind. Go s.; Spain is s. of the Pyrenees. In the s. of France; the ice wastes of the S.

space (-er, -ing, -ed), n. speis; *espace, intervalle; Raum, Zwischen-raum.*

(s) Room (for); *place; Platz.*

(e) Where there is no substance; *espace; Raum.*

Come to an open s.; a s. of time; there is a s. between the beds; spacing the houses well. There is s. for another person here. The earth is moving in s.

spade, n. speid; *bêche; Spaten.*

Get roots up with a s.

spadework, n. *Basic words*. Hard work with attention to details, sp. as necessary at the start of an undertaking.

special (-ly), a. 'speʃəl; *spécial, particulier; besondere(-r, -s), extra.*

He has no s. reason for going; a s. drink; a s. train; be specially interested in art.

sponge (-er, -ing, -ed), n. spʌndʒ; *éponge; Schwamm.*

Get the s. full of water; sponging the wound.

sponge-cake, n. *Basic words*. Cake of a sponge-like substance.

spoon, n. spuːn; *cuiller; Löffel.*

Put the s. in the pot.

sport, spɔːt. *International word.*

spring, n. spriŋ; *ressort; Feder.*

(e) Spring of water: time of year between winter and summer; *source: printempts; Quelle: Frühling.*

The s. of the watch is broken. Water from the s. Birds come in the s.

spring-board, n. *Basic words.* Elastic jumping-off board from which to take a jump into the water.

square (-er, -ing, -ed), e., adj. skwçɛ; *carré; Quadrat: viereckig.*

(s) Square open space with houses round; *place; Platz.*

(e) Of a number, x, the amount produced by $x \times x$.

A s. of cloth; a s. has 4 equal sides; squaring the edges; squared paper. Living in Russell S. The s. of 2 is 4; 5 squared is equal to 25. A s. box. S. measure.

stage (-er, -ing, -ed), n. steidꝫ; *estrade, échafaudage; Gerüst.*

(s) Theater stage; *scène; Bühne.*

(e) Point of development: theater work; *phase, étape: théâtre; Stufe, Studium: Bühne.*

The painters put a s. round the house. Put a play on the s.; staging a play. At a later s. An interest in the s.

stage-manager, n. *Basic words.* Person who oversees the putting on of a play.

stamp (-er, -ing, -ed), n. stæmp; *timbre, estampille; Stempel.*

(s) Post Office stamp; *timbre-poste; Briefmarke.*

(e) Instrument for stamping; stamp of foot; *instrument pour timbrer: action de frapper du pied; Stempel: Stampfen.*

The maker's s. is on the metal; stamping the form. The letter has no s. A rubber s. Put one's foot down with a s.; give a s.

°°(*Stamping (rubbing) out*).

star (-rer, -ring, -red), n. stɑ:°; *etoile; Stern.*

(o) Star like form; *astérisque.*

Moon and ss.; flowers starring the grass. A printer's s.; a starred word.

starfish, n. *Basic words.* Sea-animal of star-like form.

start (-er, -ing, -ed), n. stɑ:t; *commencement; Anfang.*

Make a s. now; at the s. of my talk; starting a book.

statement, n. steitmənt; *constatation, déclaration; Aussage.*

(e) Making a statement; *exposition; Darlegung.*

Make a s. about. The art of clear s.

station (-er, -ing, -ed), n. 'steiʃən; *gare; Bahnhof.*

(e) Place used as a branch by army or other organization; *poste; Station.*

The train came into the s. Be sent to a s. in Africa; a police s.; he is stationed in Malta.

steam (-er, -ing, -ed), n. st:m; *vapeur; Dampf.*

-er, (s) Steamship; *bateau à vapeur; Dampfer.*

-ing, (e) Cooking by steam; *cuire à la vapeur; Dämpfen.*

The water gave off s.; the pot is steaming. Go by steamer; steaming into harbor. Steaming fish.

**Get up s.

steamship, n. *Basic words.* Ship moved by steam-power.

steel (-er, -ing, -ed), n. sti:l; *acier; Stahl.*

A rod made of s.; a s. ship; steeling oneself to go.

stem, n. stem; *tronc, tige; Stengel, Stamm.*

(e) Long, thin, stem-like part of anything; *tige; Stiel.*

The flower has a long s.; the tree has a straight thick s. with no low branches. The s. of his pipe is broken.

step (-per, -ping, -ped), n. step; *pas; Schritt.*

(e) Stage; structure for stepping from one level to another: act; *démarche: marche: mesure; Schritt: Stufe: Schritt.*

ss. (e) Structure formed of ss. which may be taken from place to place; *échelle; Stufenleiter.*

Take a s. forward; a dance s.; stepping into a carriage. We are a s. farther forward with the work. Go down a stone s. Ss. will be taken to put the apparatus right. Put the ss. near the window.

*Walking *in* s. (*with*).

**He was *out of* s. (*with* the man at his side).

stick, n. stik; *canne, tige; Stock.*

(e) Thin stick-like bit of anything; *bâton; Stange.*

Walking with the help of a s.; make a fire of ss. A s. of sugar.

sticky, a. 'stiki; *gluant, collant; klebrig.*

Liquid sugar is s.

stiff (-ly), a. stif; *raide; steif.*

(e) Stiff in behavior: (of body) giving pain when moved: not moving freely; *guinde: raide: dur; steif: steif: hart.*

Put the picture on card or s. paper; a s. collar; the jelly is not s. enough. He was very s. with me. I am s. after such a long swim. The lock is s.; he is walking stiffly.

still, adv. stil; *encore; noch.*

He is s. a boy.

**S., it's not bad.

stitch (stitches, -er, -ing, -ed), n. stitʃ; *point, maille; Stich, Masche.*

-ing, (e) Line or design of ss. used as ornament.

Make a s.; take out the stitches; stitching a skirt. A brown bag with white stitching.

stocking, 'stɔkiŋ; *bas; Strumpf.*

Have shoes and ss. on.

stomach, n. stʌmək; *estomac; Magen.*

He has no food in his s.; a man with a fat s.

stone (-er, -ing, -ed), n. stoun; *pierre, caillou; Stein, Kiesel.*

(e) Thing hard like a stone, sp. a jewel or a fruit-stone; *pierre précieuse, noyau; Edelstein, Kern.*

A house of s.; s. steps; a road covered with ss.; seated on a s.; the dog was stoned by boys. A s. has come out of her ring; take the ss. out of the fruit; stoning fruit.

stop (-per, -ping, -ped), n. stɔp; *arrêt, pause; Halt, Pause.*

(s) Being, living, in place for a time; *séjour; Aufenthalt, Anhalten.*

(e) Sign for a stop; *point; Punkt.*

-per, (s) Cork; *bouchon; Stöpsel.*

-ping, (e) Substance put in a hole in a tooth; *plombage; Füllung.*

Working without a s.; stopping work; stopping the machine. Make a s. in New York; she is stopping with the baby. There is a s. after the word. Put a stopper in the bottle. The stopping has come out of my tooth.

*Put a s. (end) *to* this talking. (The train *came to a s.;* drains get *stopped up*).

stopwatch, n. *Basic words.* Watch which may be started and stopped as desired for timing runs and so on.

store (-er, -ing, -ed), n. stɔː*; *magasin; Laden.*

(e) Amount of anything kept for use when needed: *réserve; Vorrat.*

Get goods at a s.; keep a s. A s. of oil; storing wine.

*Trouble was in s. (for him).

storekeeper, n. *Basic words.* Person keeping a store.

story (stories), n. 'stɔːri; *histoire; Geschichte, Erzählung.*

(s) Work of fiction; *conte; Erzählung.*

The s. of his experiences in the war. A writer of short stories.

straight (un-), a., adv. streit; *droit; gerade: direkt.*

(e) Straightforward; *droit, honnête.*

Make a s. line. He's a s. person. Go s. to the point.

*He got tired of it *s. away.* (Say *s. out*).

**It's *s. over there.*

straightforward, a. *Basic words.* 1. Open, true (of person, behavior).

2. Simple (of process).

strange (-ly), a. streindʒ; *étrange; seltsam, eigenartig.*

(e) Of which one has no knowledge; *inconnu; fremd.*

His behavior was very s.; she was looking at me strangely. The
writing was s. to me.

** (*Strangely enough*).

street, n. striːt; *rue; Strasse.*

A narrow s.; there are no houses on that side of the s.; a s. fight.

*(Go *up* (*down*) *the s.*).

stretch (stretches, -er, -ing, -ed), n. stretʃ; *étendue; Strecke, Fläche.*

(e) Expansion; *extension;* (Aug-) *Dehnung, Erweiterung.*

-er, (e) Bed for transporting ill persons; *brancard; Tragbahre.*

A wide s. of sea; she saw nobody for long stretches of time. Give
the elastic a s.; a s. of sense; stretching himself. Take him away on
a stretcher.

strong (-ly), a. strɔŋ; *fort; stark.*

(e) With force: having great effect on senses; *vigoureux: fort;
kräftig: stark.*

Have s. muscles. Make a s. protest; they were pulling strongly.
S. tea; a s. smell.

structure, n. 'strʌktʃə*; *structure, construction; Bau.*

(e) Organization of parts.

Put up a s. of wood. The body has a complex s.

substance, n. 'sʌbstəns; *substance; Stoff.*

(e) Solid quality, true or material existence; *Substanz; Stoff.*

Put a rubber s. on the road. Shades have no s.; there is no s. in
these stories.

such, a., adv., pron. sʌtʃ; *tel; solche (-r, -s.).*

S. stories as these make me angry; there is no s. thing as a winged snake; s. an event is very uncommon; he had s. a shock that it made him ill. We had s. happy hours together; this is not s. a bad book as that. S. is the story.

suchlike, n., a. *Basic words.* Such as these.

sudden (-ly), a. 'sʌdn; *soudain; plötzlich.*

I was surprised at the s. change of opinion; the end came suddenly.

sugar (-er, -ing, -ed), n. 'ʃugə*; *sucre; Zucker.*

I do not take s. in my tea; sugaring the cake.

suggestion, n. sə'dʒestʃən; *suggestion; Vorschlag, Anregung.*

(e) Power of controlling a person's mind; *hypnotisme; Suggestion.*

Make a s. about the work; the s. was that I had done it. Make a person do things by s.

summer, n. 'sʌmə*; *été; Sommer.*

We have fruit in the s.; a s. dress.

sun (-ner, -ning, -ned), n. sʌn; *soleil; Sonne.*

(e) Any fixed star with stars moving round it.

The s. is covered by clouds; sunning oneself on a wall. There are ss. of which we have no knowledge.

**He was given *a place in the s.*; nothing *under the s.* was good enough for him.

sunburn, n. *Basic words.* Burn or brown color of skin caused by the sun.

sun-down, n. *Basic words.* Time when the sun goes down.

sunlight, n. *Basic words.* The light of the sun.

sunshade, n. *Basic words.* Umbrella to keep off the sun.

sun-up, n. *Basic word.* Time when the sun comes up.

support (-er, -ing, -ed), n. sə'pɔːt; *soutien; Stütze.*

(e) A living; help; *soutien, aide; Unterhalt; Unterstützung.*

-er, (e) Person on the side of; *partisan; Anhänger.*

This is a s. for the roof; supporting a great weight. Do nothing for one's s.; supporting one's mother. Give s. to an organization. A supporter of the view.

In s. of this statement.

surprise (-er, -ing, -ed), n. sə'praiz; *étonnement; Uberraschung.*

(e) Thing causing surprise; *surprise.*

I had no feeling of s.; a surprise event; surprising his friends. The news was a s.

*(He was *taken by* s.; there was s. *at* their words; *to my* s. he
was not there).

**(*Surprised into*).

sweet (un-, -ly), a., n. swiːt; *doux: plat sucré, bonbon; süss: süsse
Speise, Bonbon, Süssigkeit.*

(e) Pleasing; *agréable.*

Sugar is s. A s. song; be smiling sweetly. Have a s. at the end
of the meal; a box of ss.

sweetheart, n. *Basic words.* Lover.

swim, s. swim; *action de nager; Schwimmen.*

Have a s.; go for a s.

system, n. 'sistim; *système; System.*

(s) The body as a working s.; *organisme; Organismus.*

(e) Reasoned, ordered, way of doing; *système; System.*

The railway s. of the country; a s. of ideas; a s. of pipes. Get
poison into the s. A s. of farming; he has no s. in his work.

table, n. 'teibl; *table; Tisch.*

(e) Ordered list; *tableau; Tafel, Tabelle.*

The food is on the t. A t. of weights and measures.

**They were *at* t. when the news came.

tableland, s. *Basic words.* Level country higher than country round it.

tail, n. teil; *queue; Schwanz.*

(e) Anything like a tail; *extrémité.*

Cats have long tt. The t. of the airplane.

tail-coat, n. *Basic words.* Man's coat cut away in front with long back
parted in the middle.

take (takes, took, taking, taken), v. teik; *prendre; nehmen.*

(e) Have certain reaction to (event and so on).

T. money; the dog will not t. food; building takes time; t. a
chance; t. a look at the picture; I took down his words; t. a dog
for a run; t. 5 from 35; t. a pleasure in helping others; t. off
clothing; t. over a business; t. trouble with one's work; t. a breath;
t. a position; t. a suggestion; t. a walk; t. a house; t. a rest after a
day of hard work; the play has taken his mind off his troubles; did
you t. in the sense of what he said? He took the bad news well.

*1. He *took up* the question (painting) with great interest.

2. He did not *take into account* all the details.

3. He said he would *t. a picture* but he had no camera.

4. We *took* him *for* an expert.

5. The news *took* us *by surprise.*

(*T. note of; t. care of; t. part in* an event; the meeting *takes place* at 4.0; I *took him on one side; t. in hand;* the tree had *taken root* there).

**I *t. it that* you are coming; *t. on* servants (work); he *took it on himself* to go; the nations *took up arms; be taken up with* one's thoughts. (*T. cover; t. effect; t. fire; t. to heart; t. heart from* my words; *t.* (a person) *prisoner; t. turns* at the wheel; *t. the trouble* to go).

talk (-er, -ing, -ed), n. tɔːk; *action de parler, conversation; Sprechen, Gespräch.*

(e) Public talk; *discours; Ansprache, Vortrag.*

Hearing their t. in the train; talking about his invention. Give a t. about the latest developments in science; an interesting t.

*(I *had a t. with* him about it; *be talking of* doing).

**(*It's no good talking*).

tall, a. tɔːl; *haut, grand; lang, gross, hoch.*

(e) Measured from feet to head.

A t. person; t. buildings. He is 6 feet t.

*tapioca**, tæpi'ouke. *International word.*

taste (-er, -ing, -ed), n. teist; *goût; Geschmack.*

(e) Act of tasting: sense of taste: direction of feelings of approval: small amount of food (for tasting); *action de gouter: goût: goût: soupçon; das Kosten: Geschmack: Geschmack: Kostprobe.*

The fruit has a good t. Give the meat a t.; tasting the soup. There is something wrong with his t. Bad t. in pictures. Give me a t. of your soup.

*The words were (not) *in good t.* (The music is not *to my t.*).

**Put in salt *to t.*

tax (taxes, -er, -ing, -ed), n. tæks; *impôt, taxe; Steuer.*

Put a t. on beer; they say nothing is certain but death and taxes; taxing amusements (storekeepers).

taxi, 'tæksi. *International word.*

tea, tiː. *International word.*

teaching (teacher), n., a. 'tiːtʃiŋ; *enseignement, instruction; Lehre, Unterricht.*

(e) View put across by person or group (freq. **tt.**); *doctrine;*
Lehre.

Be good at t. the young. The tt. of the early Christians. He is t.
in a school; a history teacher.

tea-room, n. *Basic words.* Restaurant for tea and small meals.

telegram (*telegraph*), 'teligræm (-graːf). *International word.*

telephone, 'telifoun. *International word.*

**He is *on the t.*

tendency (tendencies), n. 'tendənsi; *tendance; Richtung, Tendenz,*
Neigung.

Have a t. to be late; the development of early tendencies.

terrace, 'terəs. *International word.*

test (-er, -ing, -ed), n. test; *épreuve, essai, expérience; Probe.*

(s) Knowledge test; *examen; Prüfung.*

Put a machine through a t.; testing his statement. Be given a
science t.

**(*Put to the t.*).

than, conj. ðæn; *que; als.*

I am a better man t. he is; she came more readily t. her sister;
he does less work t. he might.

*(The weather is better *t. ever*).

that (those), a., pron., conj. ðæt; *ce*(*tte*) . . . (*là*): *cela: que; jene*
(*-r, -s*), *das: dass.*

T. man there. T. is a tree; t. is not true; who was t.? He was so
angry t. he gave me a blow; I said t. he was wise.

*T. *is to say.* (*So t.*).

**(*For all t.*).

the, a. ðiː; *le, la, les; der, die, das.*

T. man in the black coat; t. gold question; t. one thing needed;
t. poor are ever here; London is on t. River Thames.

**T. *quicker* he goes t. *better* for him.

theater, 'θiətə*. *International word.*

themselves, n. *Basic words.* They, them (not any other persons).

then, adv., conj. ðen; *alors: donc; damals: also, fölglich.*

(e) After that; *puis; dann.*

It was different t.; he was t. 10 years old. T. I will see you
tomorrow. T. he got angry; we came first to a field and t. to a
wood.

**Do it, *t.*

theory (theories), n. 'θiəri; *théorie; Theorie.*

Put forward a t. of how the crime was done; a t. of values; Einstein's two theories.

* (*In t.*).

there, adv. ðɛə*; *là, y; da, dort, dahin.*

He was not t. at the time of the smash; t. is the place; are you t.? I am in agreement with you t.

*T. *is* time for a meal. (*Here and t.* you come across a man with money).

**T.!

these. See *this.*

they (*them, their*). See *he.*

thick (-ly), a. θik; *épais, gros; dick.*

(e) Measured from front to back or from top to under side; having great number of units in a small space; (of liquid and so on) not clear, thick in substance; *d'épaisseur: épais: trouble; dick: dicht, dick.*

Building a t. wall. The board is 2 inches t. Your hair is very t.; country thickly covered with trees. A t. mist; t. soup.

thin (-ly), a. θin; *maigre, mince; dünn.*

(s) (Of person, animal) without much fat.

(e) Widely spaced: thin in substance; *clair, semé: clair.*

A t. book. A t. person. The grass is t. T. blood; thinly clothed.

thing, n. θiŋ; *chose; Ding, Sache.*

It is quite a small t.; a t. for making holes; get tt. for the house; do a number of tt.; the t. is on my mind; how are tt. going?; take control of tt.

***The great t.* is to be healthy; *poor t.!*

this (these), a,, pron. ðis; *ce* (*tto*) . . . (*ci*). *ceci; diese* (*-r, -s*).

T. house here is mine; t. time we will go together; come t. week.

T. is my room; who is t.?; t. makes us equal; my point is t.

those. See *that.*

though, conj. ðou; *quoique; obgleich.*

The road is wet t. it is not raining; t. old, he is strong.

thought, n. θɔ:t; *pensée; Gedanke.*

(e) Act of thought; *action de penser; Denken.*

Put tt. into words; have no t. of going; troubled by the t. of death. Give t. to the question; be deep in t.

***On second tt.,* I will not go.

thread (-er, -ing, -ed), n. θred; *fil; Faden.*

(e) Line of connection.

There is a t. on your coat; get some red t.; threading a needle; threading one's way through the trees. The t. of the argument.

throat, n. 'θrout; *gorge; Kehle.*

Have a dry t.; take food down one's t.; he put his hands round her throat.

through, prep., adv. θruː; *à travers, par; durch.*

(e) With the help of; *par l'intermédiaire de.*

Go t. the hole; come t. the door; all t. the day; breathing t. one's nose; a hole t. the wall; see t. a trick; get t. money (work). Do it t. a representative. Get t.

thumb (-er, -ing, -ed), n. θʌm; *pouce; Daumen.*

Gripping it between his finger and t.; thumbing the pages.

thunder (-er, -ing, -ed), n. 'θʌndə*; *tonnerre; Donner.*

(e) Loud noise.

There is t. about; it is thundering. The t. of the guns; the police were thundering on the door.

ticket (-er, -ing, -ed), n. 'tikit; *billet, étiquette; (Fahr-)Karte, Zettel.*

Get a t. for the journey (theater); the price t.; ticketing the books.

ticket-office, s. *Basic words.* Place where one gets tickets.

tight (-ly), a. tait; *serré, ferme, étroit; fest, eng, straff.*

(e) Stretched.

In a t. grip; his hands were chained tightly together; a t. dress; a t. knot. Get the cord pulled t.

till, prep., conj. til; *jusqu'à; bis.*

Waiting t. tomorrow; she did not come back t. 10. He was unhappy t. they came.

time (-er, -ing, -ed), n. taim; *fois, temps; Mal, Zeit.*

(s) A point of time (as by the clock); *heure, fois; Uhr, Mal.*

(e) One taking place of an event: music time; *temps; Tempo.*

We have no t. for a meal; give t. to work; the process takes a long t.; at one t. the sea came up here; in the t. of Caesar; the meeting is timed for 10; timing an event. The t. is 4.30. I went three tt.; four tt. three is 12. The band's t. was wrong.

*In t. his wound became serious. (At tt. he seemed quite well).

**He came *in t. for* the meeting; they came three *at a t.; at the same t.* this may be said; *keep t.* (*with*). (*T. off*).

time-table, n. *Basic words.* Ordered list giving times of trains or doings.

tin (-ner, -ning, -ned), s. tin; *étain, fer blanc; Zinn, Blech.*

(e) Tin box or pot; *boîte* [*en fer blanc*]; *Blechbüchse.*

A flat bit of t.; a t. plate. Keep cake in a t.; tinning fish; tinned milk.

tin-opener, n. *Basic words.* Instrument for opening tins.

tired (un-, -ly), a. 'taiəd; *fatigué: müde.*

(e) Having had more than enough of; *lassé.*

He gets t. quickly; after dancing till 2, she was quite untired; they were walking tiredly down the road. The music makes me t.

*I get t. *of* his talk.

**She was t. *out* after the walk.

to, prep. tu:; *à, vers; zu, an, nach, für.*

Go t. the theater; an addition t. the family; give it t. me; give attention t. details; he has a right t. the property; an answer t. a question; a help t. the memory; the street is parallel t. the river; that is equal t. this; a danger t. the public; in debt t.; she is married t. an American; be kind t. animals; a wound t. one's feelings.

*1. That music is not *to my taste.*

2. They are *dancing to* the radio.

3. The question is not *open to argument.*

4. They have 2 machines *face to face* (*back to back*).

5. Your answer is not *to the point.*

6. *To my surprise* and *regret,* it is still going on.

7. Bad music is *dear to* the public.

8. The chances are 10 *to* 1 that it will be better in the future.

9. Most of us are slow to get *used to* new forms of art.

10. I was *able to* make this last use clear earlier.

(They *came t. an agreement;* the train *came t. a stop;* facts *came t. light;* he *got into bad ways;* she *gave birth t.* a son; newspapers *are given t.* printing wrong facts; she had *gone t. sleep;* I am *going t.* come; I *have t.* go; I *have nothing t. do with* her; she *let us into her secret;* I *made* the material *into* a dress; she said that *in answer t.* his question; this may be *of use t.* you; he's *about t.* go; it was changing *from day t. day; that is t. say; so as t.* get it right; *in addition t.* this; his coat had *come t. bits;* it was *t. his credit; have a good mind t.* say so; he made ships t. scale; I *put a stop t.* it; he *gave way t.* his feelings; I kept my *word t. him;* the boxes were *at right angles t.* one another; he *had the face t.* say; the flowers had gone t. seed; *as t. that*).

***Here's t. him!* (They *came t. blows* about it; *come t. grips;* she *came t. her senses* again; *it comes t. this; get t. work on;* he *kept* the secret t. *himself;* she *put the words into my mouth;* they were *put t. the test* (*t. flight*); I will *see t.* the food; he was *tricked into* doing it; she was *walking up t.* him; a person *answering t.* your account; you *have no business t.* do it; *put* the design *into effect;* he said it *t. my face;* 5s. *t. the good;* the horse *was put out t. grass;* have *ready t. hand; have the heart t.; take it t. heart; t. my knowl-edge* it was not so; I am *looking forward t.* the meeting; *looking up t.* authority is right; these boots were *made t. order;* I came *in order t.* see you; I *gave place t.* a younger man; it was all *t. no purpose;* I have *reason t.* say so; put in salt *t. taste;* soft *t. the touch; put it down t.*).

toast*, toust. *International word.*

tobacco, tə'bækou. *International word.*

today, n., adv. *Basic words.* (On or in the space of) this day.

toe, n. tou; *orteil; Zehe.*

    (e) Toe-part; *bout;* [*Fuss-*]*Spitze.*

    His tt. have come through the sock. The t. of his shoe.

together, adv. tə'geðə*; *ensemble; zusammen.*

    We went out t.; they all did it t.; put things t.; let us get t.; this t. with that is very surprising.

tomorrow, adv., s. tə'mɔrou; *demain; morgen.*

    I will go t. T. is the day of the test; the day after t.

tongue, n. tʌŋ; *langue; Zunge.*

    (e) Language; long t.-like bit; *Sprache: Zunge.*

    Put out your t. Talking a strange t. The t. of the shoe has come off; they are out on that t. of land; tt. of flame.

tonight, n., adv. *Basic words.* (On or in the space of) this night.

tooth (teeth), n. tuːθ; *dent; Zahn.*

    (e) Toothlike form; *denté, à dents.*

    I have a hole in a t.; she has very white teeth. The t. of a wheel.

toothbrush, n. *Basic words.* Brush for cleaning the teeth.

toothpaste, n. *Basic words.* Paste for cleaning the teeth.

top (-per, -ping, -ped), n. tɔp; *haut, sommet; Spitze, oberer Teil.*

(s) Cover; *couvercle; Deckel.*

(e) Best position; *sommet; Spitze, Höhepunkt.*

Go to the t. of the mountain; the t. of the table; the t. card; there is a church topping the slope; a snow-topped wall. Put the t. on the bottle. He is at the t. of the business; topping a list.

torpedo*, tɔː'piːdou. *International word.*

touch (-er, -ing, -ed), n. 'tʌtʃ; *touche(r), contact; Berührung, Tasten.*

(s) Way of touching; *touche(r); Anschlag.*

(e) Quality experienced by touch; *toucher; Berührung.*

-**ing,** (e) Moving the softer feelings; *émouvant; rührend.*

She gave her hair a t.; learning by t.; touching the flowers; the wires are touching. A good t. on the piano. The smooth t. of the polished wood. A touching story.

*He was *out of* (not *in*) t. *with* the authorities. (The camera picture was *touched up*).

**A cat is soft *to the t.* (*A t. of the hat*).

town, n. taun; *ville; Stadt.*

Have a house in the t.

trade (-er, -ing, -ed), n. treid; *commerce; Handel.*

(e) Industry: way of making a living; *industrie: métier; Industrie: Gewerbe.*

Taxes are bad for t.; do t. with a country; trading with one another. The linen t. His t. is making shoes.

**He does *t. in* horses; he was *trading on* his name.

trade-mark, n. *Basic words.* Special mark of maker on goods.

tradesman, n. *Basic words.* Storekeeper.

train (-er, -ing, -ed), n. trein; *train; [Eisenbahn-]Zug.*

(e) Line of things; *suite; Zug.*

-**ing,** (e) Education; *entraînement, practique, éducation; Ausbildung.*

Take the t. to Durban; go by t. A t. of carriages. Give him a good training as a builder; training a horse; a trained secretary; he is an animal trainer.

transport (-er, -ing, -ed), n. 'trænspɔːt; *transport; Transport.*

A ship for the t. of goods; the t. business; damaged in t.; transporting machines from Birmingham to India.

tray, s. trei; *plateau; Tablett.*

Put the drinks on a t.

tree, n. triː; *arbre; Baum.*

(e) Family tree or other such map; *arbre généalogique: Stamm-baum.*

The t. gives shade; an apple t. Make a t. of the family.

trick (-er, -ing, -ed), n. trik; *tour, manière de faire; Kniff.*

(s) Stage-trick; *artifice, tour d'addresse; Kunststück.*

(e) False behavior; *ruse, tricherie; Kniff.*

This is the t. of opening it. He does tt. with cards; the dog does a balancing t. He got the money by a t.; tricking his friend.

** (*Tricked into; playing a t.*).

trouble (-er, -ing, -ed), n. 'trʌbl; *troubles; Schwierigkeit, Mühe, Unruhe.*

(s) Trouble of mind; *ennuis; Sorge.*

(e) Thing causing trouble; *ennui; Plage.*

There is t. in India; have t. with the boys; get into t. with the authorities; he took no t. with his work; troubling the teacher with questions. A person in great t.; troubling news. The flies are a t. to him.

***Take the t.* to go.

trousers (trousers), n. 'trauzəz; *pantalon; Hose.*

He put on his t.; some of his trousers have holes in them.

true (un-, -ly), a. tru; *vrai; wahr.*

(e) With unchanging feelings; *fidéle; treu.*

A t. story; it is not a t. monkey; what he says is quite untrue. Be t. to a person; have a t. heart; yours truly.

*Her fears *came t.*

turn (-er, -ing, -ed), n. 'təːn; *tour, action de tourner; (Um-) Drehung, Wiendung.*

(e) A person's time to do something in order after another person or other persons; *tour; Reihe.*

-ing, (e) Changing; (*se*) *changeant; Umwandlung.*

Give the key a t.; make a t. to the right; she is turning her face away; his trousers are turned up; turning the wheel. Waiting for one's t. The milk is turning into butter; the men were turned into pigs.

*He, *in his t.,* became ill. (The page is *turned over.*).

**The card was played *out of t.;* they *took tt. at* going; *turning it over in one's mind; turning out well (badly)*.

turnover, n. *Basic words.* Amount of business done, measured by money taken.

turn-table, n. *Basic words.* Any table-like part or apparatus which goes round, used, for example, for turning train-engines.

twist (-er, -ing, -ed), n. twist; *action de tordre; Drehung.*

(s) Twist damaging muscle; *entorse; (Ver-)Zerrung.*

(e) Turn of sense: *déformation; Verdrehung.*

-er, (e) Person who is not straightforward; *escroc; Verdreher, Gauner.*

The pig's tail has a t. in it; twisting the threads together; a twisted mouth. Give one's leg a t. You give a t. to everything I say. The man is a twister and full of tricks.

umbrella, n. ʌm'brelə; *parapluie; (Regen-) Schirm.*

She put her u. up in the rain.

under, prep, 'ʌndə*; *sous; unter.*

(e) Less than.

U. the table; the water u. the earth; be u. a cloud; he has the machine u. control; u. his rule the nation became great; he is u. the head teacher. She is still u. 21.

*An idea *u. discussion;* an army *u. fire.*

**(Wet *u. foot;* the book is there *u. your nose; u. protest;* nothing *u. the sun* will make me different).

underclothing, n. *Basic words.* Clothing put on under dress.

undercooked, a. *Basic words.* Not cooked enough.

undergo, v. *Basic words.* Have the experience of.

undergrowth, n. *Basic words.* Low growth of plants, trees.

undermined, a. *Basic words.* Damaged from the base.

undersigned, n., a. *Basic words.* (Person) whose name is signed at the foot (of the paper).

undersized, a. *Basic words.* Smaller than normal.

understatement, n. *Basic words.* Statement in which amounts or facts are made to seem less, or less important, than they are.

undertake, v. *Basic words.* 1. Take in hand (work). 2. Say one will do (something).

undertaking, n. *Basic words.* 1. Work, business (to be) undertaken.

2. Statement that one will do something, word (e).

undervalued, a. *Basic words*. With less than the true value put on it, viewed as of less value than it is.

undo, v. *Basic words*. 1. Get open or loose (parcel, coat). 2. Do something to take away the effect of what has been done.

unit (-er, -ing, -ed), n. 'juːnit; *unité; Einheit.*

-ed, (-ing), (e) Joined together; *uni; vereinigt, einig.*

A note is a u. of sound; a second is a u. of time. United by their interest in education; a united family; make a united attempt.

university, ju(ː)ni'ʌːsiti. *International word.*

up, prep., adv. ʌp; *en haut; hinauf, auf.*

Go u. a mountain; u. a scale; u. a river; get u. a tree. Get a tree u.; go u. to the top; come u. to one's hopes; building u. a business; get u. from one's seat; get u. in the morning.

°1. At school, *dressing up* was one of my greatest pleasures.

2. Now, it is hard even to get my overcoat *buttoned up*.

3. In a cold country, all one's force is *used up* in the attempt to keep warm.

4. Bread has to be *cut (broken) up* for the birds.

5. Even if your house is *shut (locked) up,* the rain may get in.

6. Yesterday there was ice in the bath and the drains got *stopped up*.

7. Get the pipes *fixed up* again before the spring!

8. The wet places on the walls have to be *touched up*.

9. There is no need to get *worked up* about it.

10. In England, we have to *put up with* small troubles of this sort.

(He *got u.* the play in a week; the manager *gave u. hope* completely; the actors *kept u. their interest;* I *kept u. with* the developments; he *made u.* the play himself; they *took it u.* seriously; he was *walking u. (down) the street; put u. an argument*).

°°He saw someone *walking u. to* him; he had been *making u. for* a loss. (The question *came u. for discussion; getting u. steam; made u. of* men; they did not *take u. arms;* they were *taken u. with* thoughts about trade; they were *cleaning u.* the prisons; *full u.;* there were men *joining u.* at the army-station; the army is much *looked u. to; mixed u.* in your ideas; *opening u.* a country; *screwing u.* boxes is simple; *washing u.*).

upkeep, n. *Basic words.* (Price of) keeping in good condition.

uplift, n. *Basic words.* The process of getting thoughts lifted to higher things, or teaching and so on which does this.

upright, a. *Basic words.* 1. Straight up. 2. Good (in behavior).

upside-down, a., adv. *Basic words.* Turned over with the under side up.

uptake, n. *Basic words.* (Power of) getting the idea (point) of something.

us. See *I.*

use (-er, -ing, -ed), n. juːs; *usage, emploi; Gebrauch, Anwendung.*

    (e) Use-value; *utilité; Nutzen.*

    -ed, (s) Used up; *épuisé; aufgebraucht, benutzt.*

    Before the u. of electric power; using one's brains. This apparatus has an important u.; make u. of. A used match; all the butter has been used.

    °(The machine is *in u.;* these facts may be *of u.;* you will get *used to* them; my force is *used up*).

value (-er, -ing, -ed), n. ˈvælju; *valeur; Wert.*

    (s) Market-value.

    His opinion has no v.; that is the v. of his writing; valuing one's friends. The picture has a v. of £1,000; valuing the spoons at a very high price.

    °(*Of v.*).

vanilla°, veˈnilə. *International word.*

verse, n. vəːs; *poésie; Vers.*

    (e) Division, unit of verse; *strophe; Strophe.*

    He is writing v. That line is in the second v.

very, adv., a. ˈveri; *très: même, juste; sehr: derselbe.*

    I am v. happy; do v. badly: You are the v. person I am looking for; this drink is the v. thing for a warm day.

    °°(V. well).

vessel, n. ˈvesl; *récipient; Gefäss.*

    (e) Ship; *vaisseau; Schiff.*

    Get the milk in a v.; one group of blood vv. takes the blood to the heart, the other group takes it from the heart. The harbor is full of vv.

view (-er, -ing, -ed), n. vjuː; *vue; (Uber-)Sicht.*

    (s) Wide, sp. beautiful, view of country; *vue; Aussicht.*

(e) Range of seeing; opinion; *vue; opinion; Schweite; Ansicht.*

You will get a better v. of the stage from here; viewing the room from the door. A house with a beautiful v.; the v. from the bridge. The town was at last in v.; the tree kept him from my v.; the men came into v. I am in agreement with your vv.; viewing the question differently.

In v. of these facts. (*On v.; point of v.*).

viewpoint, n. *Basic words.* Point of view.

violent (-ly), a. 'vaiələnt; *violent; heftig, gewalttätig.*

Give a dog a v. blow; a v. man; be violently angry.

violin*, vaiə'lin. *International word.*

visa*, viːzə. *International word.*

vodka*, 'vɔdkə. *International word.*

voice (-er, -ing, -ed), n. vɔis; *voix; Stimme.*

(s) Voice for song; *voix, ton.*

There was a note of pleasure in his v.; voicing the opinions of others. He has a very good v.

*He *has a v. in* his friend's business.

volt*, voult. *International word.*

waiting (waiter), a., n. 'weitiŋ; *attendant, qui attend: attente; war-tend: Warten.*

waiter, (e) Man acting as table servant in hotel and so on; *garçon; Kellner.*

I am still w. here. I am tired of w. for her. The man is a waiter in a restaurant; w. at table is hard work.

walk (-er, -ing, -ed), n. wɔːk; *marche, promenade; Spaziergang.*

(e) Place where one goes for a walk; way of walking; *promenade: démarche; [Spazier-]Weg: Gang.*

Go for a w.; take a w.; we were walking in a wood; walking the horse on the road. A w. between trees. She has a strange w.

** (*Walking up to* a person).

wall (-er, -ing, -ed), n. wɔːl; *mur; Wand, Mauer.*

Get over a w.; a w. of ice; a walled garden.

war, n. wɔː;*; *guerre; Krieg.*

(e) Fight; *lutte; Kampf.*

Go to w. with; have a long w. The w. against disease.

*(The country is *at w.*).

** (*Make w. on*).

warm (-ly), a. wɔːm; *chaud; warm.*

(e) Keeping one w.: strong (of feeling); *chaud: chaleureux, ardent; warm: innig, warm.*

A w. day; be feeling w.; get w.; be warmly dressed. W. clothing; a w. fire. A w. love for his daughters.

°°*Make things w. for* a person.

warship, n. *Basic words.* Armed ship used in war.

was (*were*). See *be.*

wash (-er, -ing, -ed), n. wɔʃ; *lavage, ablution, lessive; Waschen.*

(e) (Place of) washing clothing: waves from moving ship; *blanchissage: sillage; Wäsche: Kielwasser.*

Have a w.; washing the baby. Send a dress to the w. In the w. of the ship; a stretch of sand washed by the waves.

°*Washing out* the clothing; *washing up* the tea things.

washerwoman, n. *Basic words.* Woman who does washing.

wash-leather, n. *Basic words.* Soft leather which may be made wet and used for washing windows and so on.

waste (-er, -ing, -ed), n. weist; *gaspillage; Vergeudung.*

(e) Waste material: waste land; *déchet: désert, friche, terrain vague; Abfall: Einöde, Ödland.*

-er, (s) Good-for-nothing; *vaurien; Taugenichts.*

-ing, (e) Getting less in size; *dépérissement; Schwund.*

Going to the pictures is a w. of time (money); you are wasting the wine. Put all the w. in the bucket. A w. of sand; w. land. The boy is a waster. A wasted arm; she is wasting slowly away.

waste-paper-basket, n. Basket (or other vessel) used for dropping waste paper into in office and so on.

watch (-er, -ing, -ed), n. wɔtʃ; *montre: Taschenuhr.*

(e) Observation: persons watching; *voillo, attention. veille; Bewachen, Zuschauen: Wache.*

What is the time by your w.? Watching the house; watching the play. He is one of the night w.

°He was *on w.* by the fire.

water (-er, -ing, -ed), n. 'wɔːtə°; *eau; Wasser.*

There is not much w. in the river now; a drink of w.; watering the flowers; my eyes are watering.

waterfall, n. *Basic words.* The water of a river and so on falling over a sudden drop in the land.

watermark, n. *Basic words.* Trade-mark in writing paper.

water-tight, a. *Basic words.* Not letting water through.

wave (-er, -ing, -ed), n. weiv; *onde; Welle, Woge.*

(s) Sea wave; *vague; Welle, Woge.*

(e) Wave of the hand: hair-wave; *signe: ondulation; Winken: Welle.*

The wind makes ww. in the grass. The ship goes through the ww. He gave a w. of his hand; waving to her friends. A w. in her hair; she is having her hair waved.

wax (-er, -ing, -ed), n. wæks; *cire; Wachs.*

Put w. on the parcel; waxing the thread.

waxwork, n. *Basic words.* Copy of a person made in wax.

way, n. wei; *chemin; Weg.*

(e) Way of behavior (doing): regular behavior; *manière: coutume; Art, Weise, Hinsicht: Art und Weise.*

This is the w. to New York. The best w. to make it clear is to give a picture of it; the school is now better in some ww. The dog has a w. of not looking where it is going; the men in that country have strange ww.

He gave w. to his impulse; he *got in (out of) the w.* of the law. (She *got into bad ww.; by the w.,* what did she do?; she went *straight away*).

**He *made his w.* to the house; he was *working his w.* through school.

we. See *I.*

weather (-er, -ing, -ed), 'weðə*; *temps; Wetter.*

-ing, (e) Getting safely through (trouble and so on); *resistant à; widerstehend, überstehend.*

We are having good w.; the weathering of mountains; weathered stone. We saw a ship weathering the bad sea.

weather-glass, n. *Basic words.* Apparatus for seeing what the weather is going to be.

week, n. wi:k; *semaine; Woche.*

Get the work done in a w.; have a w. of rain; do nothing for a w.

**(Come *in a w.*).

weekday, n. *Basic words.* Any day but Sunday.

weekend, n. *Basic words.* Saturday and Sunday.

weight (-er, -ing, -ed), n. 'weit; *poids; Gewicht.*

(e) Thing for measuring weight: something troubling: quality of being important; *poids: fardeau: importance.*

The w. of the ball is 2 lbs.; weighting the cart down. Put a w. on the scales. It's a w. on his mind. A person of w. on the committee; his opinion has no w.

* (This system *has w. with* the authorities).

well (better, best), adv., a. wel; *bein: en bonne santé; gut wohl: gesund.*

Do a thing w.; you may w. say so; a w.-polished table; w. over 40. Get w.; be quite w.

*He has horses *as well (as* cows). (He *did w.* in the test).

***Very w.* then; *w., why not?*

well-being, n. *Basic words.* A condition of comfort, happy feeling.

well-off, a. *Basic words.* Having a great amount of money.

went. See *go.*

west, a., adv., n. west; *ouest; westlich: Westen.*

The w. door; a w. wind. Sailing w.; America is w. of England. The sun is low in the w.; the science of the W.

wet (-ter, -ting, -ted), a., n. wet; *mouillé, humide, pluvieux; nasse, feucht, regnerisch.*

The grass is w.; w. weather; wetting the material is part of the process. Go out in the w.

what. See *who.*

whatever, pron., a. *Basic words.* All or any which.

wheel (-er, -ing, -ed), n. wiːl; *roue; Rad.*

The ww. are going round; wheeling a small cart; the baby was wheeled out in its carriage; a 4-wheeled carriage.

when, conj., adv. wen; *quand; wenn, als.: wann.*

I was in bed w. the news came; w. I am ready I will go; the days w. we were young; he did not say w. the meeting was. w. did he come?

whenever, adv. *Basic words.* At whatever time, every time that.

where, conj., adv. weə*; *où, wo, wohin.*

The street w. his house is; this is w. you went wrong; I don't see w. the dog has gone. W. is the house?; w. did you come from?

whereabouts, n., adv. *Basic words.* Roughly where a thing is; about where?

wherever, adv. *Basic words.* In (at, to) whatever place.

which. See *who.*

whichever, pron., a. *Basic words.* The one(s) or any which.

while, conj. wail; *pendant que; während.*

He is happy w. he is here; do it w. there is time.

whip (-per, -ping, -ped), n. wip; *fouet; Peitsche.*

Give the horse a blow with the w.; a whipped dog; whipping
eggs for a cake.

whipcord, n. *Basic words.* Thin, tightly twisted cord.

whisky, 'wiski. *International word.*

whistle (-er, -ing, -ed), n. 'wisl; *siffet; Pfeife.*

(e) Sound made by a whistle or like sound made with the mouth;
sifflement; Pfiff.

Playing on a w. Give a long w.; whistling for the dog.

white, a., n. wait; *blanc; weiss.*

The paper is w. W. is a good color for summer clothing.

whitewash, n. *Basic words.* Chalk and water used as paint.

who (whom, whose; which, what), pron., a. huː; *qui; wer, welche*
(*-r, -s*).

The boy w. came; I did not see w. went; the girl whom you saw;
w. is there?; whose son is he?; which of them is right?; the river
which is there; a play in which I took part; this is what you said;
what did you see?; do what is possible; what is he to me? Which
way do we go?; what time is it?; what books did you get?; I did not
see which way he went.

**What* a strange thing!; *what's more.*

whoever, pron. *Basic words.* Any one or every one who.

why, adv. wai; *pourquoi; warum.*

There is a reason w. it is necessary; she is ill, that is w. I am here;
w. did you come?

wide (-ly), a. waid; *large; breit.*

(e) Measured from side to side: not limited; *weit.*

The door is w.; his writings are widely noted. A band 2 inches
w. A person with w. views; a w. education.

**She was *w. awake* at 4.0. (*W. of the mark.*)

will (would), aux. v. wil; *werden, wollen.*

I w. go tomorrow; they w. not be ready; he said he would be
there; you would be happier if you had a better position; I put
the money where nobody would see it.

wind, n. wind; *vent; Wind.*

The sound of the w. in the trees; at sundown a w. got up.

windfall, n. *Basic words.* 1. Fruit sent down by the wind. 2. Unlooked-for profit.

window, n. 'windou; *fenêtre; Fenster.*

Get the w. open; be looking through the w.

windpipe, n. *Basic words.* Pipe in throat through which air goes.

wine, n. wain; *vin; Wein.*

Put w. in the glass; a bottle of red w.

wineglass, n. *Basic words.* Glass for wine.

wing, n. wiŋ; *aile; Flügel.*

(e) Wing-like structure: wing of a building.

The bird is moving its ww. An airplane with two ww. The building has a new w.

winter, n. 'wintə*; *hiver; Winter.*

W. is the coldest time of the year in England; they have fires in the houses in the w.

wire (-er, -ing, -ed), n. 'waiə*; *fil métallique; Draht.*

A hat with a w. round the edge; telegraph ww.; a roll of copper w.; wiring the house for electric light; a w. net.

wise (un-, -ly), a. waiz; *sage, sensé; klug, weise.*

A w. man; a w. suggestion; he wisely said nothing; your outburst was very unwise.

with, prep. wið; *avec; mit.*

The apples are w. the oranges; a man w. a hat; a woman w. wide interests; wine mixed w. water; have an argument w.; be rough w.; the table is covered w. flies; he gave it a blow w. his hand; what do you do w. this instrument?; he got away w. the help of a friend; be experienced w. dogs.

*A simple system *has weight w.* experts; be *angry (pleased, disgusted) w.* persons. (That color does not *go w.* your hair; I *had a talk w.* him; I *have nothing to do w.* her; walking *in step w.;* I was *in touch w.* them; animals *w. young* are violent; *put up w.*).

**(He was taken up w. his thoughts; make friends w.; be short w. (a person); he has done w. school for ever; be free w.).

without, prep., adv. *Basic words.* Not having (any).

*Go without (food and so on).

woman (women), n. 'wumén; *femme; Frau, Weib.*

The w. has three sons; he has no women friends.

wood, n. wud; *bois; Holz.*

(e) Number of trees together (freq. **ww.**); *Wald.*

Get w. for the fire. A house in the ww.

woodcut, n. *Basic words.* Print from picture cut in wood.

woodland, a., s. *Basic words.* (Of) land covered with trees, woods.

woodwork, n. *Basic words.* (Making) things, parts, of wood.

wool, n. wul; *laine; Wolle.*

(s) Wool thread; *fil de laine; Wollgarn.*

Sheep give w.; a w. coat. Get some w. for making stockings.

word (-er, -ing, -ed), n. wɔːd; *mot; Wort.*

(e) Serious statement that one will, or will not, do (has, or has not done) something; *parole (d'honneur).*

-ing, (e) Words used; *rédaction; Wortlaut.*

He put his thoughts into ww.; his request was worded strangely. His w. was doubted. The wording of the letter is important.

°I had the story *by w. of* mouth; I *kept my w.* to him. (She *gave her w.* she would go; he said the same, *w. for w.*).

°°He *sent w. of* it; he made the statement *on his w.* (He *put the ww. into* her mouth; a *play on ww.*).

work (-er, -ing, -ed), n. wəːk; *travail; Arbeit.*

(s) What a man does for a living; *travail; Arbeit.*

(e) Thing produced; *œuvre; Werk.*

-ing, (e) in operation, in order; *en mouvement, en bon ordre; in Betreib.*

ww. = Working parts of a machine: work-place in industry; *méchanisme: usine; Getriebe: Werk.*

It was hard w. to get the house clean; farm w.; brain w.; working for an hour; working a machine. What is his w.? The picture is a great w. The machine is working; the system is working well. The ww. are in need of oil. Send goods back to the ww.; a gas ww.

°I am *working on* a book. (The men are *at w.;* there is no need to get *worked up* about it; the details have been *worked out; working at* languages).

°°(He is *working his way* through school; *get to w. (on).* Make up the *w.* you did not do; *take on* new *w.*).

workhouse, n. *Basic words.* Public place where the poor are housed and given work to do.

workman, n. *Basic words.* Man working with his hands.

worm (-er, -ing, -ed), n. wəːm, *ver; Wurm.*

There are ww. in the garden; my dog has ww.; worming one's way into a secret.

worse (worst). See *bad.*

would. See *will.*

wound (-er, -ing, -ed), n. wuːnd; *blessure; Wunde.*

Have a w. in the hand; her words were a w. to his feelings; the gun went off, wounding a man; a wounded animal.

writing (writer), n., a. 'raitiŋ; *action d'écrire; Schreiben.*

(e) Putting stories, ideas, and so on into words in writing: book, work of letters: marks made by writing; *composition littéraire: écrit: écriture; Verfassung, Schriftstellerei: Schrift: Schrift.*

She is teaching him w.; a quick writer. W. for the newspapers is hard work; good at letter w.; a noted writer. All his ww. have been put into a book. The w. is very clear. I am w. letters.

wrong (-ly), a., n., adv. rɔŋ; *erroné, faux: tort: mal, de travers; falsch, verkehrt, im Irrtum; Unrecht.*

(e) Bad; *mal; unrecht.*

Go the w. way; say the w. thing; give the w. answer; he was wrongly sent to prison. They had w. desires. There is a clear line between right and w.; a w. had been done to him. Go w.

* (The judge said he was *in the w.*).

wrongdoer, n. *Basic words.* Person who does wrong.

X-ray, n. *Basic words.* Röntgen ray.

year, n. jəː*; *an(née); Jahr.*

The work will take a y.; in the y. of my birth; I was there for some yy.

*A man *of 50 (years);* (I am 20 *yy.* old).

** (*All the y. round*).

year-book, n. *Basic words.* Book of facts put out every year.

yellow, a., n. 'jelou; *jaune; gelb.*

Butter is y. The y. on the walls is not dark enough.

yes, int. jes; *oui; ja.*

Y., I will come; she will say y.

yesterday, adv., n. 'jestədi; *hier; gestern.*

I went y. Y. is gone; the day before y.

you (your, yours), pron. ju; *tu, vous; du, Sie, ihr.*

(e) Any person; *on; man.*

Y. are a young man; y. are foolish; it was y. whom I saw; this is your pen; the other one is not yours. If y. go north y. come to Iceland.

young, a., n. jʌŋ; *jeune; jung.*

(e) Young family, offspring (of animal); *petits; die jungen.*

The y. tree is bent by the wind; keep y. by working hard. The y. have more need of sleep than the old. The bird is getting food for her y.

*When these animals are *with y.* they make a bed of leaves and grass for the coming family.

yourself, pron. *Basic words.* You (not any other person).

zebra, 'ziːbrə. *International word.*
zink, ziŋk. *International word.*
zoology, zou'ɔlədʒi. *International name of science.*

NOTE

In Basic as in other international languages no attempt is made at covering a complete system of measuring, such as would be necessary for complex work in science or mathematics. The simpler forms for numbering, however, and the chief divisions of time are given their place in Basic English, in a separate list of 50 words. Of these, 12 are the names of the months in the year, 7 are for the days of the week, and the rest are Basic number-words. These last words are not necessary in writing, because the number signs, for which most of these words are sounds, are themselves international.

Here are the 50 words:

The months of the year: *January, February, March, April, May, June, July, August, September, October, November, December.*

The days of the week: *Monday, Tuesday, Wednesday, Thursday, Friday, Saturday, Sunday.*

Number-words: *One, two, three, four, five, six, seven, eight, nine,*

ten, eleven, twelve, thirteen, fourteen, fifteen, sixteen (16) . . .
twenty (20), *twenty-one* . . . *thirty* (30), *forty* (40), *fifty* (50)
. . . *hundred* (100), *thousand* (1,000), *million* (1,000,000).

once (one time), *twice* (two times).

half (½), *quarter* (¼).

third (number 3 in order), *fourth* (number 4), *fifth* (number 5).

Examples

Examples

The chief questions about the theory and purpose of Basic have now been answered; an account of the way in which the system came into existence has been given; and the structure of the system itself, with most of the details necessary for learning and teaching it, has been made clear. Section Two of this volume and more than half of Section One were all in Basic, so there is little doubt that the 850 words will say everything necessary about language and its behavior. The examples to which we now come are designed to let us see Basic in operation in other important fields.

PART ONE

Government

1. The Gettysburg Address

ABRAHAM LINCOLN

Seven and eighty years have gone by from the day when our fathers gave to this land a new nation—a nation which came to birth in the thought that all men are free, a nation given up to the idea that all men are equal. Now we are fighting in a great war among ourselves, putting it to the test if that nation, or any nation of such a birth and with such a history, is able long to keep united. We are together on the field of a great event in that war. We have come to give a part of that field as a last resting-place for those who went to their death so that that nation might go on living. It is in every way right and natural for us to do this. But in a wider sense we have no power to make this place an offering in their name, to give any mark of our respect, any sign of our belief. Those men, living and dead, who had no fear in the fight, have given it a name far greater than our poor power to make additions or to take away. The future will take little note of what we say here; will not long keep it in mind. But what they did here will never go from memory. It is for us, the living, to give ourselves here to the work which is not ended, which they who were in the fight have taken forward to this point so well.

It is for us to give ourselves here to the great work which is still before us, so that from these dead who are in our hearts we may take an increased love of the cause for which they gave the last full measure of their love; so that we may here come to the high decision that these dead will not have given themselves to no purpose; so that this nation, under the Father of All, may have a new birth in the hope to be free; and so that government of all, by all, and for all, may not come to an end on the earth.

2. The Atlantic Charter, and the Prime Minister's Statement on Basic English of March 9, 1944; in their original form, and in Basic English, for purposes of Comparison

Presented by the Prime Minister to Parliament
by Command of His Majesty, March 1944

THE ATLANTIC CHARTER

ORIGINAL VERSION

The President of the United States and the Prime Minister, Mr. Churchill, representing His Majesty's Government in the United Kingdom, being met together, deem it right to make known certain common principles in the national policies of their respective countries on which they base their hopes for a better future for the world.

First, their countries seek no aggrandisement, territorial or other.

Second, they desire to see no territorial changes that do not accord with the freely expressed wishes of the peoples concerned.

BASIC ENGLISH VERSION

The President of the United States and the Prime Minister, Mr. Churchill, acting for His Majesty's Government in the United Kingdom, being now together, are of the opinion that it is right to make public certain common ideas in the political outlook of their two countries, on which are based their hopes for a better future for all nations.

First, their countries will do nothing to make themselves stronger by taking more land or increasing their power in any other way.

Second, they have no desire for any land to be handed over from one nation to another without the freely voiced agreement of the men

and women whose interests
are in question.

Third, they respect the right
of all peoples to choose the
form of government under
which they will live; and they
wish to see sovereign rights
and self-government restored
to those who have been
forcibly deprived of them.

Third, they take the view
that all nations have the right
to say what form of government they will have; and it is
their desire to see their self-
government and rights as independent nations given back
to those from whom they
have been taken away by
force.

Fourth, they will endeav-
our, with due respect for their
existing obligations, to further
the enjoyment by all States,
great or small, victor or van-
quished, of access, on equal
terms to the trade and to the
raw materials of the world
which are needed for their
economic prosperity.

Fourth, they will do their
best, while respecting their
present undertakings, to make
it possible for all nations,
great or small, whichever side
they were on in the war, to
take part in the trade, equally,
with others, and have the
materials which are needed
for the full development of
their industry.

Fifth, they desire to bring
about the fullest collaboration
between all nations in the
economic field, with the object of securing for all improved labour standards, economic advancement and so-
cial security.

Fifth, it is their desire to
get all nations working together in complete harmony
in the field of trade and industry, so that all may be
given better working conditions, have greater material
well-being, and be certain of
the necessaries of existence.

ORIGINAL VERSION

Sixth, after the final destruction of Nazi tyranny, they hope to see established a peace which will afford to all nations the means of dwelling in safety within their own boundaries, and which will afford assurance that all the men in all the lands may live out their lives in freedom from fear and want.

Seventh, such a peace should enable all men to traverse the high seas and oceans without hindrance.

Eighth, they believe all of the nations of the world, for realistic as well as spiritual reasons, must come to the abandonment of the use of force. Since no future peace can be maintained if land, sea or air armaments continue to be employed by nations which threaten, or may threaten, aggression outside of their frontiers, they believe, pending the establishment of a wider and permanent system of general security, that the disarmament of such nations is essential. They will likewise aid and encourage all other

BASIC ENGLISH VERSION

Sixth, after the complete destruction of the Nazi rule of force, it is their hope to see a peace made which will keep all nations safe from attack from outside, and which will make certain that all the men in all the lands will be free from fear and need through all their days.

Seventh, such a peace will have to make it possible for all men to go freely everywhere across the sea.

Eighth, it is their belief that all the nations of the earth, for material reasons no less than because it is right and good, will, in the end, give up the use of force. Because war will come again if countries which are, or may be, ready to make attacks on others go on using land, sea, or air power, it is their belief that it is necessary to take away all arms from them till a wider system of keeping the general peace, more solid in structure, comes into being.

They will, further, give their help and support to all

|

practicable measures which will lighten for peace-loving peoples the crushing burden of armaments.

other possible steps which may make the crushing weight of arms less for peace-loving nations.

PRIME MINISTER'S STATEMENT ON BASIC ENGLISH ON MARCH 9, 1944

|

The Committee of Ministers on Basic English, after hearing a considerable volume of evidence, have submitted a Report which has been approved in principle by His Majesty's Government. The Committee, in their report, distinguish between the use of a system such as Basic English as an auxiliary international language, and as a method for the teaching of ordinary English. In this latter field, several very promising methods, other than Basic, have been developed in recent years, which make use of progressively increasing vocabularies based on analysis of the words most frequently used in conversational and literary English. In foreign countries,

The Committee of Ministers on Basic English, after hearing the views of a great number of experts, have made a statement on the question which has been given general approval by His Majesty's Government. It is pointed out by the Committee in their statement that the use of a system such as Basic English as an international second language is something quite separate from its use for the teaching of normal English. In this second field, two or three other systems which give signs of working very well have been produced in the last five or ten years. These make use of selections of words, increasing by stages, which are based on observation of the

ORIGINAL VERSION

the method used in the teaching of English will naturally be matter for the decision of the Departments of Education of those countries, and, where teaching is conducted in British Institutes, it will be a matter for the free decision of those who direct the teaching of English whether they employ any of these methods or the Basic method. There is no reason why His Majesty's Government should support one method rather than another. So far, however, as concerns the use of Basic English as an auxiliary international language, His Majesty's Government are impressed with the great advantages which would ensue from its development not in substitution for established literary languages, but as a supplement thereto. The usefulness of such an auxiliary language will, of course, be greatly increased by its progressive diffusion.

His Majesty's Government have, therefore, decided on the following steps to develop

BASIC ENGLISH VERSION

words most frequently used in talking and writing English. In other countries, the system used in the teaching of English will naturally be a question for the decision of the Education Offices in those countries, and where teaching is given in British Institutes, those in control of the teaching of English will be free to make use of any of these systems or of the Basic system. There is no reason for His Majesty's Government to give more support to one system than to another.

So far, however, as Basic English is offered as an international second language, His Majesty's Government take the view that much good would come from its development not in place of languages rooted in history and used by great writers, but as an addition to them. The value of such a second language will naturally be increased if it is more and more widely used.

For this reason His Majesty's Government have come to the decision to take these

ORIGINAL VERSION

Basic English as an auxiliary international and administrative language:—

(1) The British Council will include among its activities the teaching of Basic English, so far as may be practicable, in any area where there may be a demand for instruction in Basic for its specific purpose as an auxiliary medium of international communication. This will be in addition to, and not in substitution for, the Council's more general activities in promoting the teaching of English for its own sake.

(2) Diplomatic and commercial representatives in foreign countries will be asked to do all they can to encourage the spread of Basic English as an auxiliary language.

(3) It is also intended to arrange for the translation into Basic English of a wider range than is at present available of literature—scientific, technical and general—both

BASIC ENGLISH VERSION

steps for the development of Basic English as a language for international use and for purposes of government:—

(1) The British Council, in addition to its other work, will undertake the teaching of Basic English, so far as may be possible, in any place where there may be a desire for a knowledge of Basic for its special purpose as a second language for international use. This will be in addition to, and not in place of, the Council's more general work of helping forward the teaching of English as an end in itself.

(2) Foreign Office and trade representatives in other countries will be requested to do everything possible to get Basic English more widely used as a second language.

(3) In addition, our purpose is to have a wider range of books on science, on special arts and processes and on general questions put into Basic English from normal

ORIGINAL VERSION

from ordinary English and from foreign languages and also to increase the supply of manuals of instruction in Basic English.

(4) Some Colonial Governments will be invited to experiment by the issue in Basic English of handbooks for colonial peoples on agriculture, hygiene, etc., and by the use of this simplified language as the medium for some administrative instructions issued by the Government.

(5) The British Broadcasting Corporation has been asked to consider a recommendation to include the use and teaching of Basic English in appropriate overseas programmes. The Corporation has already expressed its willingness to make experiments on these lines within the limits imposed by special war-time responsibilities and conditions. It is recognised that such developments as may be practicable must pro-

BASIC ENGLISH VERSION

English and from other languages, at the same time increasing the number of handbooks for teaching Basic English.

(4) The suggestion will be made to the Governments of some of our Colonies that they take part in the testing of Basic by getting out handbooks in Basic English on farming, on how to keep healthy, and so on for their Colonies, and by using this simple language for some of their orders in connection with government business.

(5) The British Broadcasting Corporation has been requested to give its attention to a suggestion for the teaching and use of Basic English in overseas programmes where this might be of value. The Corporation has said that it is ready to put the system to the test on these lines inside the limits made necessary by war-time undertakings and conditions. It is clear that such developments as may be possible will have

ceed in parallel with the
steps to be taken by other
agencies.

It will be seen that several
Departments are concerned
in these measures. It has been
decided, however, that primary responsibility for questions affecting Basic English,
and for giving effect to
the recommendations of the
Committee of Ministers,
should rest with the Foreign
Office, through the British
Council. The British Council
will, of course, keep in close
contact with the Foreign Office and with the other Departments concerned, and
an inter-Departmental committee has been established
for this purpose, under a
chairman who will be nomi-
nated by the British Council.

to go forward parallel with
the steps taken by other
bodies.

It will be seen that more
than one Government Office
will have a part in the pro-
gramme outlined. The de-
cision has been made, however, that the Foreign Office,
through the British Council,
will be chiefly responsible for
questions to do with Basic
English and for giving effect
to the suggestions of the
Committee of Ministers. The
British Council will naturally
keep in touch all the time
with the Foreign Office and
with the other Government
Offices which are interested.
For this purpose, a Committee made up of representatives of these Offices has been
formed and its head will be a
person named by the British
Council.

3. The Rights of Man

H. G. WELLS

H. G. Wells (1866–1946) had been dead for more than two years when most of the nations in the United Nations organization gave their approval to the "Universal Declaration of Human Rights," that is to say, the agreement about the rights of persons. Though less is covered by the "Declaration" than Wells had been hoping, it might not have come into existence at all but for his work, from 1939 on, in putting before an international public the idea that such an agreement had to be part of any attempt at building a better earth-wide society. "The Rights of Man" was put into Basic English by C. K. Ogden with Wells's help and approval in 1941.

GENERAL NOTE

In little more than a hundred years a complete change has taken place in the material conditions of existence. Invention and discovery have made it possible for men and news to get so much more quickly round and about the earth that the distances which kept nations and governments separate have almost been overcome. At the same time there has been such a great development of machine-industry, freeing men for work in other directions, that our powers of working with or against one another, and of using, wasting, or increasing the fruits of the earth are on a new scale, and it is hard even to make a comparison with earlier times. All through the past thirty years the rate of this

5

al5 382 BASIC ENGLISH

process of change has been increasing and it is now not far from a danger-point.

The greater dangers and chances of these new conditions have made adjustments necessary in our ways of living and in the structure of society. We are being forced to the organization of harmony among the separate governments which have so far been the instruments of man's political purposes.

At the same time, in economics, we have to keep the good things of the earth safe from the waste and destruction which have been caused by the sudden expansion of business undertaken for profit and by the increasing power of money over men and things.

Public control in the political field, in trade, in industry, and in society generally, is being forced on us.

Our reaction to these new conditions is without direction; chances of greater well-being are being wasted for ever.

Government is getting into the hands of one group which takes power from the rest, or is being given over to organizations in trade or industry which have been strong enough to put an end to competition.

Religion, education, and the newspapers are ruled by groups and persons who are not representative of public opinion, while men of science and letters, and a number of other workers in the arts of peace, which have so far had a free and natural development, are experiencing the effects of this massing of power.

Governments and the great organizations of industry and banking, as we now see them, were not designed to have such powers; their growth was the outcome of the needs of earlier times.

Under the new conditions, men have the feeling that they are less safe and there is an increase in the wrong or cruel use of authority; we become less free, specially in thought and in public talk. By slow degrees those badly-working Governments and controls are limiting that free use of the mind which keeps men happy and able to do their work well.

By acting quickly and secretly, controlling organizations are for a time in a position to get things done at the price of a deep and ever more serious undermining of the structure of a good society.

When men and nations no longer have the feeling that they are free and responsible, they first let themselves be crushed by their rulers and then give way to violent outbursts against law and order. Belief in a good future and the power to make balanced decisions give place to loss of self-control, loss of interest, and work of poor quality.

Everywhere war becomes more serious in its effects and the grip of the money-makers becomes stronger, so that those very same increases of power and chances of further development which have given men the idea of an unlimited future, with more than enough of the good things of the earth for all, may go under again, possibly for ever, in a violent destruction of society ending all hope of better things.

It becomes clear that this process will only be stopped by a new order of society, stretching to the ends of the earth, in which political, trade, and business interests are united for a common purpose.

All men would do well to give attention to the history of the nations of the West.

In the past, whenever it has been necessary to put power into the hands of one man or a small group of men, it has been the way of what are named the Democratic or Parliamentary countries to make once again a strong and clear statement or Declaration of the rights of man.

Never before has the need for such a Declaration been so important as at present.

We of the Parliamentary countries are clear that an organization of society based on control by all in the interests of all is necessary and will come about, but, as in the past, we put forward that belief together with a Declaration of Rights, so that as the outcome of the great changes now taking place we may get not an attempt made in the dark to put things straight, but a reasoned design for the future, worked out in the full light of day.

To that instrument then, which has been marked out by history for the purpose, a Declaration of Rights, we now come back once more, but on a scale which will take in all the countries of the earth.

1. RIGHT TO EXISTENCE

The word 'man' in this Declaration is used for every living person, young or old, male or female.

Every man is a part-owner of all the goods and natural materials, and of the powers, inventions, and chances of development which have come down to us from the men of earlier times.

Inside the limits of what there is for distribution, all men of every sort or color, whatever their beliefs or opinions, have the right to the food, cover, and medical care needed for the full development of mind and body from birth to death. However different and unequal their qualities may be, all men are to be looked on as completely equal in the eyes of the law, and as having an equal right to the respect of other men.

2. CARE OF THE YOUNG

The right and natural persons to be responsible for those who are not old enough to take care of themselves are their fathers and mothers.

Where it is not possible for this care, or any part of it, to be given, society, taking into account the family conditions of the boy or girl, will be responsible for their safe-keeping by other persons.

3. WORK FOR SOCIETY

It is the business of every man not only to have respect for the rights of all other men in every part of the earth, but to give those rights his support and take steps to put them into effect.

In addition, it is his business to do his part of any necessary work, which the rewards in operation in a free society do not take into account, so as to make certain that such work gets done.

It is only by taking part in such work that a man is able to make clear his right to a place in society.

No man is to be forced to undertake military or other work which is against his sense of right and wrong, but he who does no work whatever for society will be without political rights and under the control of others.

4. RIGHT TO KNOWLEDGE

It is the business of society to give every man enough education to make him of as much use to others, as interested in his work, and as free as his powers make it possible for him to be; to put all knowledge before him; and to let him have whatever special education may be needed to give him the same chance as others for the development of his special powers as an instrument for helping his brother-men. The authorities are to see that he is able to get quickly and readily at all facts necessary for forming an opinion on current questions and events.

5. THOUGHT AND RELIGION

Every man will have the right to be quite free in talking and writing, in discussion, in joining with others, and in religion.

0. RIGHT TO WORK

So long as the needs of society are taken care of, a man may freely take up any work which is not against the law, and get payment in relation to the value of his work to society or to the desire of any private person or persons for his produce, his acts, or his further work.

He is to get payment for his work, and may make suggestions about the sort of work which, in his opinion, he is able to do.

A man may get profit from work done by himself. He may get

payment for transporting, or giving news about, goods to others. But he may not do business so that he gets payment or profit through 'speculation'—that is to say, not for work of any sort but simply because he has come between the worker or workers and those others who are in need of what the workers do or make.

7. RIGHT IN PRIVATE PROPERTY

In using his private property, if it is his by law, a man has the right to be kept safe from violent acts public or private; what is his may not be taken away from him, and he may not be forced, by fear or in any other way, to give it up.

8. RIGHT OF MOVING ABOUT

A man may go freely about the earth, if he makes all the necessary payments himself.

But only such persons as have been given authority by the law may go without the owner's approval into a private house or into any more or less limited space which has been shut off for his use. So long as in moving about he does not go on to the private property of any other man, and does not do any sort of damage to what is not his or make it of less use, and does not seriously get in the way of others, he may come and go anywhere, by land, air, or water, over any sort of country, mountain, waste land, river, inland water, or sea, and all the wide spaces of this, his earth.

9. RIGHT TO BE FREE

If a man has not been said by a medical authority to be a danger to himself or to others through not being right in his mind—and any such statement will have to be supported by another authority after not more than seven days and then be looked into at least once a year—he is not to be kept under control for more than twenty-four hours without hearing what he has done which, in the eyes of the authorities, is against the law, and is not to be sent back to prison while the facts are further looked into for more than eight days without his agreement, or kept in prison for more than three months without being judged.

Before he is judged, he is to be given a statement in writing of what will be said against him, in time to make use of it.

At the end of three months, if he has not been judged by the normal process of law and given punishment or made free, he is to go free.

No man may be judged more than once for the same act.

Though the opinions which others have of any man may be given freely, he will have the necessary power of answering or going to law about any false statement which may be the cause of pain or damage to him.

Secret records, or 'dossiers,' may not be taken into account in law.

Such record is only a note for the use of the authorities; it is not to be used in law if a public statement is not made of the facts on which it is based.

10. VIOLENT ACTS

No man is to be made to undergo any operation on, or damage to, his body without his agreement freely given, or to be attacked or controlled by force when he himself is not being violent against others, or to be given punishment in the form of pain, by blows or any other physical act.

No man is to be made to undergo pain of mind greater than that caused by being in prison, or to be put in any prison which is dirty or has been made unhealthy by animals, disease, or any other cause, or to be put into the company of persons with body-animals or diseases which he may get from them.

But if he himself has a disease of this sort, so that he is a danger to others, he may be made clean or free from it, or be put in a separate place, or controlled so far as may be necessary to keep others safe from him.

It is clear that no one may be given punishment by the selection of others (as 'hostages'), by their being put in prison, or by any sort of act against them.

11. RIGHT OF LAW-MAKING

Society is based on the rights named in this Declaration; they may not be given or taken away.

In questions of everyday control, or those about which there is general agreement, but in no others, it is clearly necessary for certain of these rights to be limited.

(For example, in such questions of general agreement as the rule of the road or laws against the making of false money, or in such questions of control as the organization of town and country building, or public hygiene.)

No man or group in society is to be forced to keep any law of this sort if it has not been made openly by a decision of the greater number of those interested or by the greater number of their representatives publicly sent to take their place in a body made responsible by law for government.

These representatives are to be the highest authority responsible for all laws made by organizations under their control and for detailed rulings on how the laws are to be given effect.

In questions of general agreement and decisions taken in the interests of any group or nation, men are to be ruled by the views of the greater number as fixed by the system of representative government, which gives effect to the desires of the different persons who make up a society. All laws are to be open to public discussion, and may be changed or put an end to by a representative government.

No international or other agreements may be made secretly in the name of any nation or nations or other groups of men with a common government.

Those responsible for making laws in a free society are all the men who make up that society, and because existence is handed on to new bodies of men and never comes to an end, no one body may give up or give away the power of making and changing laws, or any part of this power; such power now being necessary to man's well-being for all time.

PART TWO

Science

Science is one of the key interests in the development of Basic, and at the same time it is the greatest international force in existence. Through science, which has given us the radio and television, the talking-picture, and the telephone, it is possible for a knowledge of Basic to become general in a very short time; and science itself might go forward with greatly increased power if Basic was used for papers and meetings.

Earlier in this book [1] something has been said of the value of Basic in connection with science, and of the further word-lists which have been designed for covering this field. Some examples of science-writing in Basic have been given, and now, in this division are grouped five more, all but the last taken from Basic printed books. The first of these is from *The Basic Dictionary of Science*, which is designed to be used by persons whose knowledge of English is limited to Basic, and so is itself limited to Basic. The second and third, the purpose of which is simply to give the Basic learner interesting reading-material, in the same way do not make use of any of the science lists. The fourth, though equally interesting to the general reader, may be looked on as more for those taking up science, and for this reason words from the General Science List have been freely used in it. In the last, we see in operation the full apparatus of Basic for the man

[1] See pp. 75–81 and 236.

of science. Notes at the front of the Examples will make clearer
the different ways of working with material at different levels.

The reader of this book, however, will not for the most part
be an expert in science, and it is not desired to make a knowledge of the Basic Science Lists a condition of his getting any
pleasure from these examples. So the senses of all the special
science words used in Example 4, and of anything which might
be a cause of trouble in Example 5, are given there. Our only
desire in giving examples using the lists is to let him see the system at work. For the same reason, we give here the complete
General Science List of 100 words, and two of the special science
lists of 50—that for Physics and Chemistry and that for Biology.
Anyone desiring more light may get it from *Basic for Science,*
where further lists are given, with examples of the use of all of
them in material for the expert. Such high-level examples have
not been put in here, because the material needing the special
lists is generally not of a sort to give pleasure to the general
reader—as we may see from Example 5.

General Science List

absorption
age
application
arc
area
arrangement
ash
axis
break
bubble
capacity
case
cell
column
component
compound
cross
decrease
deficiency
deposit
determining
difference
difficulty
disappearance
discharge
disturbance
elimination
environment
equation
evaporation
experiment
explanation
focus
friction

fusion
generation
groove
guard
hinge
impurity
individual
interpretation
investigation
joint
latitude
layer
length
link
longitude
mean
melt
mixture
nucleus
origin
path
pressure
projection
proof
reference
reproduction
resistance
rigidity
rock
rot
rotation
screen
seal
section

sensitivity
shadow
shear
shell
similarity
solution
spark
specialization
specimen
stimulus
strain
strength
stress
substitution
supply
surface
swelling
thickness
thrust
tide
transmission
tube
valve

active
adjacent
alternate
continuous
direct
exact
relative
successive
transparent

Physics-Chemistry List

adsorption	fume	reflux
beaker	funnel	repulsion
buoyancy	furnace	residue
charge	grating	solvent
circuit	image	stream
clip	insulator	suspension
coil	lag	switch
collision	lens	tongs
combination	medium	trap
conductor	oxidation	valency
conservation	particle	vapour
corrosion	pendulum	vortex
density	plug	wedge
dilution	porcelain	
dissipation	radiation	reversible
explosion	reagent	saturated
flask	receiver	stable

Biology List

abdomen
appendage
bark
beak
bud
cartilage
cavity
claw
climber
creeper
domesticating
duct
ferment
fertilizing
fiber
fin
germinating

gill
gland
hoof
host
inheritance
jaw
juice
kidney
liver
lung
metabolism
parent
petal
pollen
sac
scale
secretion

sepal
skull
slide
soil
stain
stalk
stamen
sucker
thorax
tissue

degenerate
fresh
mature
vascular
vestigial
wild

1. From *The Basic Dictionary of Science* [1]

determi′nation, n. Measuring, getting clearly fixed, the value or amount of anything, or the place of something in a system. [Biol.] The process by which, in the development of a plant or animal, the future of every part is fixed at an early stage. de′termine, v.t. de′termined, a. de′termining, a., n.

de′terminism, n. The theory that all events in material existence take place by necessary law.

′detonate, v.t. and i. (Make) EXPLODE [1] very violently and suddenly. deto′nation, n. Sp. violent EXPLOSION; in an INTERNAL-COMBUSTION engine, the sudden taking fire of gas through overheating, causing loss of power and a sharp sound. ′detonating, a. ′detonator, n. Substance or apparatus effecting detonation.

de′torsion, n. Untwisting, or twisting in opposite direction, sp. [Med.] making a twisted part of body normal again. [Zoo.] Twisting in opposite direction to that at start.

de′tox-icate, -ify, vv.t. [Med.] Take away poison or effect of poison from. de′toxi′cation. n.

de′trition, n. [Geol.] Natural rubbing or washing away of stone by wind and water.

de′tritus, n. [Geol.] Loose material, broken stones, mixed with earth, sand, etc., produced by DETRITION.

detu′mescence, n. [Med.] The going down of a swelling.

′deuteran′omaly, n. [Optics, Psych.] A form of DEFECTIVE COLOUR VISION in which a person, though normal in being TRICHROMATIC, sees the green part of the SPECTRUM more feebly than a normal person.

′deuteran′opia, n. [Optics, Psych.] A form of DICHROMATISM in which a person is unable to see different CHROMATIC colours in the red-yellow-green part of the SPECTRUM but in which, as opp. PROTANOPIA, the LUMINOSITY of all parts of the spectrum is almost the same as for a normal person (earlier named *′green blindness′*). ′deuteranope, n. Person having d.

deu′terium, n. [Chem.] An ISOTOPE of H with at. wt. 2.00147, sign D, MASS NUMBER 2, having a NEUTRON as well as a PROTON in the NUCLEUS—commonly named *heavy hydrogen.*

′deuter(o)-. Second or SECONDARY.

deute′rogamy, n. [Bot.] Any process which takes the place of normal FERTILIZATION.

[1] In this Dictionary, only the 850 words of the general Basic list are used to give the senses. No use is made of the Basic Science lists or of the words judged to be international for the science expert. But any word in the Dictionary may, naturally, be used in giving the sense of another, the only condition being that, if it is not Basic, it has to be put in the special print we see here (EXPLOSION).

deutero'genic, a. [Geol.] (Of ROCK) formed of material from older rock.

'deut(er)on, n. [Chem.] NUCLEUS of D ATOM.

deut(o)-. Second, or SECONDARY.

de'velop, v.t. and i. (Make) undergo development. [Photog.] Put (a camera PLATE or FILM on which a picture has been taken) through the chemical process, gen. the changing of silver SALTS to silver metal, by which the effect which the light has had on it is made clear in the form of a picture, or get (picture) formed on a plate, etc., in this way. **de'-veloper,** n. Sp. [Photog.] Any chemical substance used for developing a camera picture.

de'velop'mental me'chanics. [Zoo.] Science of the chemical and physical processes causing development of the different parts of an animal before birth.

devi'ation, n. Change of direction of anything in motion, as light. **d. of the 'compass.** Regular error of ship's MAGNETIC COMPASS caused by the magnetic effect of the iron in the structure of the ship.

de'vitrify, v.t. and i. [Geol.] Get changed from a glass-like into a CRYSTALLINE condition. **de'vitri-fi'cation,** n.

de'vocalized, a. DEVOICED.

de'voiced, a. [Phonet.] Said of a VOICELESS sound put in the place of a VOICED sound in ASSIMILATION.

De'vonian, n. [Geol.] System of ROCKS forming part of the PALAEOZOIC group.

'Dewar flask or **'vessel.** Glass vessel with an outer and an inner wall between which there is no gas so that heat is not able to get through, used for keeping any-thing which has to be kept unchanged by heat or cold, for example, liquid air.

dew, n. [Meteor.] The water which is put down onto solid things by the air in the night. **'d.-point.** The TEMPERATURE at which a given mass of wet air becomes SATURATED, so producing d.

'dextral, a. Of or to the right; right-handed.

'dextrin, n. [Chem.] Any of certain GUM-like substances formed when STARCH is broken down.

'dextro(o)-. To the right. [Chem.] DEXTROROTATORY.

'dextro'gyrate, a. DEXTROROTATORY.

'dextroro'tatory, a. Turning in direction of hands of clock, sp. [Optics] of the turning of the plane of POLARIZED light by a substance. **'dextroro'tation,** n.

'dextrorse, a. [Biol.] Twisting from left to right from the point of view of a person looking at it, opp. SINISTRORSE.

'dextrose, n. [Chem.] DEXTROROTATORY GLUCOSE, the sugar present in fruit.

d-'glucose, n. DEXTROSE.

'di-. Two, twice.

Di. Sign for DIDYMIUM.

dia-. Through, between, across.

'diabase, n. [Geol.] ROCK, commonly named 'greenstone,' made up of PLAGIOCLASE, MAGNETITE, AUGITE, and sometimes OLIVINE.

dia'betes, n. [Med.] Any of certain diseased conditions marked by an over-great output of URINE, sp.: **d. 'mellitus.** D. in which over-much sugar is present in the blood and URINE, caused by not enough INSULIN being produced by the PANCREAS, and marked by serious loss of weight and a great desire for food and drink.

'nitrogen, n. Chemical ELEMENT, at. no. 7, at. wt. 14.008, sign N, a gas without colour or smell not readily taking part in chemical reactions, forming more than 75% of air, and present, united with other substances, in earth and in all living substance. n. 'cycle. The process by which N in some form is taken from the air, earth, and sea and made into more complex substances by plants, then goes into the bodies of animals in the form of food, is given back to the earth in the form of animal waste or dead bodies, and in the end is again changed into free N going back to the air, or into INORGANIC material forming part of earth and sea, by the operation of BACTERIA. n. fi'xation. The producing of N COMPOUNDS from free N for purposes of industry; the producing of ORGANIC N compounds from the N of the air by certain BACTERIA in the earth. n. 'fixers, 'n.-'fixing bacteria. Any of the sorts of BACTERIA having the power of n. fixation. ni'trogenous, a.

nitro'glycerin(e), n. [Chem.] Any NITRATE of GLYCEROL, sp. C_3H_5-$(ONO_2)_3$, an oil made by the reaction of H_2SO_4 and HNO_3 with GLYCERINE, not SOLUBLE in water, becoming solid when cold, burning quietly in the open air, but EXPLODING with great force when given a blow or heated quickly in a shut vessel.

ni'trophilous, a. [Bot.] Living in NITROGENOUS earth.

ni'troso compounds. [Chem.] Complex substances having in them the group —NO.

'nitrous, a. [Chem.] To do with, having in it, producing, N, sp.

used of complex substances in which N has one of its lower VALENCIES. n. 'acid. HNO_2, forming substances having in them the group —NO_2, but itself having existence only in a SOLUTION of $Ba(NO_2)_2$ in H_2SO_4. n. 'oxide. N_2O, a gas used as an ANAESTHETIC, sometimes named 'laughing gas.'

ni'vation, n. [Geol.] The effects produced by NÉVÉ on ROCKS, etc.

'noble gas. [Chem.] INERT GAS.

'noble 'metal. Any metal, such as silver and gold, which is not readily united with non-metals or attacked by acids or the O of the air.

nocti-. Night.

nocti'lucent, a. [Zoo.] Giving out light at night. nocti'lucence, n.

noc'turnal, a. To do with, taking place in, the night. [Zoo.] Sleeping in the day and coming out, getting food, etc., at night.

node, n. A meeting or joining-point, or the middle point of a system. [Geom.] Point where a curve goes across itself, that is, point common to two parts of a curve. [Biol., Med.] A hard round mass or place on something, as on a diseased JOINT; a point of narrowing between two wider parts. [Bot.] The place on a stem where a branch or leaf is joined to it. [Phys.] The point, line, or plane in a VIBRATING body where little or no motion is taking place, a point of least AMPLITUDE in a system of STATIONARY WAVES. [Astron.] One or other of the two points where the way taken by a PLANET etc. is cut by the ECLIPTIC. [Radio] A point in a CIRCUIT where the current is greatest and the VOLTAGE least. 'nodal, a. 'nodal point.

[Radio] Node. 'nodal points (of a lens). [Optics] Two points on the AXIS of a LENS or system of lenses such that a ray sent in through one will come out as a parallel ray through the other.

'nodical month. [Astron.] The time between the moon's being at a NODE and coming round to it again.

'nodose, a. [Biol.] Having small, round, knot-like outgrowth. no-'dosity, n.

'nodule, n. [Biol., Med.] A small round outgrowth or thick place, sp. [Bot.] such a structure on the root of a plant where BAC-TERIA have their living-place. [Astron.] GRANULE. 'nodu-l(at)ed, aa. nodu'lation, n. 'nodular, a. nodu'liferous, a. 'nodulose, a.

noe'genesis, n. [Psych.] The development of knowledge by the mind, ranging from conscious experience to the point of producing new ideas, the highest operation of the mind.

no'esis, n. [Psych.] The operation of the mind in becoming conscious of things not given to it by sense, for example, ABSTRACT relations, sp. at first view, without any process of reasoning;

more generally, the working of the mind or reason as opp. the conscious experiencing of things outside, which is the first stage in the development of knowledge. no'etic, a. To do with n. or the higher powers of mind, not a part of sense experience.

noise, n. [Elec.] Undesired effect caused in any ELECTRONIC CIRCUIT, chiefly by the heat motion of ELECTRONS.

'noma, n. [Med.] A serious ULCERATION of the side of the face in young boys and girls who have become very feeble, sp. after an INFECTIOUS disease.

'nomenclature, n. System of naming.

-nomy. System of knowledge or rules.

non-. Not:— n.-e'lectrolyte, n. [Chem.], n. -'viable, a. [Biol. etc.].

non(a)-. Nine.

nona'gesimal, n. [Astron.] The middle point (90°) of the half of the ECLIPTIC limited by the HORIZON.

'nonagon, n. [Geom.] Plane form having 9 straight sides and 9 angles.

non-'arcing, a. [Elec.] (Of a metal) not readily keeping up an electric ARC.

2. From *Possible Worlds* [1]
by J. B. S. Haldane

ON SCALES

"The unending quiet of those unending spaces," said Pascal, looking at the stars and between them, "puts me in fear," and this fear, which has little enough reason in it, has been sounding on in men's minds for hundreds of years.

It is common to say that one is unable to get any idea of the distance even of the nearest fixed stars, and to make no attempt to get an idea of the number of *atoms* [2] in one's thumbnail. This tendency makes it quite unnecessarily hard for the man in the street to get clear in his mind about the chief discoveries of present-day science; a great part of which are quite straightforward, but for the fact that the numbers they are based on are of some size. Pascal's feeling, in fact, has nothing to do with science, or with religion. "I will be over the top of him in a short time," said Sir Thomas More, when he took his last look at the sun before his head was cut off; and in the view of the present-day expert in astronomy the sun is a somewhat small but more or less representative star.

There is no reason for the belief that outer space is unlimited. Very probably all space is of fixed size, and certainly the distances to all the stars we see are not outside the range of man's mind. To be unlimited is a property of mind and not of material things. We have the power of reasoning about what is unlimited

---

[1] Taken from the Basic of W. Empson in *The Outlook of Science*.
[2] Words in italics have been made clear earlier in *The Outlook of Science*.

but not of seeing it. As for the quiet of outer space, one would be unable to go on living in it, and so would be unable to say if it was quiet or not. But if one was shut up in a steel box in it, like the men in Jules Verne's book who went to the moon, there would probably come to one's ears quite frequently, at any rate when near a star, the sound of a very small bit of dust moving at a very great rate and coming up against the box.

The common man frequently makes the protest that he is unable to get any idea of the eighteen million million miles which is the unit used in astronomy in connection with the fixed stars, and is named a *parsec* because the parallax of a star at that distance seems to be a second; in other words, the circle the earth makes round the sun would take up an angle of two seconds at that distance, or seem the size of a halfpenny three thousand yards away. Naturally one is unable to see a parsec in one's mind. But one may have thoughts about it, quite clear ones.

Every person of education has got used to a process which is most complex, and makes necessary a quite surprising change of scale. That process is map-reading. Our smallest unit for everyday use is about a centimeter, or two-fifths of an inch. It is not necessary for most of our normal measuring to make less error than this. Now if we take a look at a map of the earth on a ball measuring 16 inches round, we are using something on a scale of one in a hundred million (10^{-8}), and the common man is able to see its purpose and make use of it. An Englishman hearing that his son is going to New Zealand has only to take a look at the map to see that letters will take longer to come from there than from his other son in Newfoundland. But though we are quite happy with this scale (a scale of 1,000 kilometers, or about six hundred miles, to a centimeter) so long as we keep to the earth, the normal person has still not got used to the fact that on the same scale the sun is a mile off and about the size of a church.

Our sons' sons will have got used to the opposite trick, that is to say, they will be happy working with things on a scale of a hundred million to one. On this scale the common sorts of atom are seen as less than an inch across, and *molecules* of quite complex substances from living bodies are a foot or so long. The *electrons* in these atoms and the *nuclei* which, on the present view, they go round, would be so small as not to be seen, but the way they go might be marked out, as railway lines are on a map, though only by making them wider than they would in fact be. It is to be doubted if there would be any purpose in having a greater scale than this. When we come to events inside the atom it is no longer possible to give an account of them in space and time; or at any rate the properties of space and time in very small amounts are so unlike those of common-sense space and time that scale-copies are not of much value. On the other hand scale-copies of molecules, based on X-ray discoveries about *crystals*, are of great use as guides, and are taking us forward to a new stage of chemical discovery.

Let us now take a second step in the opposite direction, and make a scale-copy such that in it the ball will be made as much smaller as the earth was made to get it down to the size of the ball. That is to say, our copy will be on a scale of one in ten thousand million million (10^{-16}). This would, in fact, do very little for us, because not only the earth, but the circle it makes round the sun, would be so small that we would be unable to see it, and even the circle made by Neptune would go with comfort on a pin's head, which would at the same time give the size of the greatest star we have knowledge of. But unhappily, even on this scale the nearest fixed star would be four yards away, and only about a hundred would be less than thirty yards off. The *Galaxy* would be a good day's walk across. Light would go much more slowly than a *snail*, but quicker than the growth of most plants!

There would probably be some purpose in taking a third step in the same direction. If we again made our scale smaller by a hundred million times, the Galaxy would be so small that we would be almost unable to see it at all, the nearer 'spiral *nebulae'* would be only a small part of an inch away from it, and probably all the 'spiral nebulae' which we are able to see with the best instruments would be less than half a mile away. It is not clear that we would be able to do the operation a fourth time. Because the general theory of *Relativity* seems necessarily to take us to the belief that space is limited, and that to go straight on in any direction would in the end take one back to the starting-point. An attempt to make a copy on this scale would possibly give an outcome as false as that got when, by Mercator's system, we make an attempt at copying all the earth on one plane. On the fourth-order scale the size of all space might be as small as one hundred thousandth part of a solid measuring a millimeter long and a millimeter wide, though this is a lower limit.

We have now seen that it is possible, and frequently of use, to make copies of things up to a hundred million times their true size and down to a scale of about a million million million millionth. Outside these limits space does not have the properties given to it by common sense, and it is no use attempting to get pictures of things. We have to go into the mathematics of the *Quantum Theory* at the small end and of Relativity at the other end. But long before that is necessary, the normal man's powers of thought have come to a stop, from a fear, it seems, of the word 'million.' This is because it is generally used for things like a million bits of gold or a million years, which it is hard for us to get an idea of, though in fact a quite normal room would take a hundred million bits of gold money, as long as the floor did not give way. But it would be a good thing for us to get into the way of using millions by keeping in mind that our bath every day has about ten million drops of water in it, and that we have frequently done ten million millimeters in a day, walking.

It is to be regretted that outside India one has no chance of seeing a million men and women, because such numbers only come together for the great Hindu journeys for purposes of religion, and very interesting they are. Sometimes three million men and women may be seen at the Kumbh Mela, a public event which takes place every twelve years (it last took place, if my memory is right, at Allahabad in January 1930). Anyone who is unable to get an idea of a million would do very well to go and see it. And it is said, by the way, that by going to it you get out of two or three million future births.

In science we get used to these great numbers. The astronomer quite happily goes from measuring the distance of a star in *kiloparsecs*—light takes 3,000 years to go a kiloparsec—to measuring how long the waves of its light are, with an error much less than an 'Angström' unit, which is a hundred-millionth of a centimeter. And there is a certain shock of pleasure when the outcome of a mathematics operation in which one has made use of hundreds of millions, comes out at one or two—when up till the last minute it seemed as if it might have been anything from a million to a millionth—and so gives you a simple theory. I have in mind, for example, the great discovery of Eddington as to why stars have so little weight (not one of those whose weight has been measured is as much as a hundred times the weight of the sun). Starting from the facts of physics he got at the degree of heat inside the stars; and because waves of heat or light give a push to the material they come against he was able to see by mathematics what part of the weight of a star of given mass was supported by the waves of the heat or light produced in the star itself. The part which is supported in this way is so small as to be unimportant for stars of less weight than the sun, but comes up to half the weight in a star about five times the sun's weight, and a star with much more weight is in danger of bursting. In this way, through a waste of millions, we come to a clear account of why all stars have about the same weight.

In the same way Gorter and Grendel, and Fricke and Morse, have made it clear by quite different tests that the thin skin of oil round a red blood-cell is two molecules thick. Gorter got the oil separate from the blood-cell and put it on water so that a thin skin was formed; Fricke took the measure of the power of the blood-cells as *condensers* by putting blood in a very quickly changing electric field. They made use of such numbers as the five thousand million blood-cells in a milliliter and the six hundred thousand million million million atoms in a gram of hydrogen (H_2), but the answer at the end was 'two' for Gorter and 'one or two' for Fricke. It is the agreement of such processes which makes it necessary for a person trained in science to put belief in the numbers on which they are based.

3. From *The Sea and Its Living Things* by H. Stafford Hatfield

In the book from which this third example is taken, no use is made of any of the science lists or of international science words, and the senses of the small number of working words which are used in addition to the 850 are given as they come in. There are, however, a great number of names of sea-plants and sea-animals of which it is hard to give the sense in a small number of words, and which have, for this reason, been made clear in a different way—by picturing the plants and animals and, in addition, by giving their Latin names in footnotes. The pictures have not been printed here, but notes pointing to them have been kept to let the reader see the system of the book.

FOOD OF SEA PLANTS AND ANIMALS

The first business of all living things is to get food. The great division between plants and animals is dependent on this food question. Plants are able to make use, as food, of very simple chemical substances. In theory, they are not dependent on animals for their existence. In what is named 'tank culture,' [1] com-

[1] A 'tank' is a box-like or basin-like vessel, frequently of great size, and 'culture' is 'producing, causing growth of' (plants or animals).

mon food-plants are produced from seed put into wood dust
(of no use to them as food) wetted with water having in it
certain simple chemical salts. The plant has the power of building up the chemically complex substances out of which it is
made from the element carbon (C) (a small amount of which is
present in the air as carbon dioxide, CO_2), from ammonia (NH_3)
or other substances having nitrogen (N) in them, and from salts
present in almost all water. For these chemical reactions the
plant makes use of light; our chemical knowledge is, so far,
quite unequal to producing them in this or any other way.

However, plants are in fact dependent for their existence
on animals, because but for these, the carbon of the air would
long have been used up. Plants have, from far back in the
past, been building up great stores of carbon, stores which
now have the form of coal, and which, till we get the coal out of
the earth for burning, are no longer of use for plants or animals.
We get heat and power by burning this coal, and in the process
the carbon gets back into the air as carbon dioxide. This same
process goes on in the bodies of all animals, but what is 'burned'
by them is not coal but the substance of plants taken by them
as food, or that of the bodies of other animals, themselves living
on plant food. In making use of these substances, animals give off
carbon dioxide into the air, as we ourselves do in breathing.
This same exchange of materials between plants and animals
takes place in the sea and in fresh water. If fish kept in an
'aquarium' (a glass vessel in which observation of them is possible) are to be healthy, it is necessary to have in the water
enough plants of the right sort, and to put the aquarium where
it will get enough light. The plants then take in carbon dioxide
and give off oxygen; the animals make use of the oxygen for
breathing, and give off carbon dioxide. If this exchange between
plants and animals is not possible, it is necessary to have a current of air going through the water all the time.

On land we have a great number of all sorts of plants, forming the food of some animals which themselves are food for others. Very important is the fact that the waste material from the bodies of animals, and these bodies themselves after death, gi·'e back to the earth a number of chemical substances necessary to plants, such as sulphur (S), phosphorus (P), and nitrogen, these substances, naturally, being equally necessary to animals. Animals get them as part of the complex food material of plants, the plants themselves get them from the substances forming the earth, or from the air, in addition to what they get from animal waste. In the sea, we have in some places a strong growth of plants used as food by animals, but it is clear that this is far from equal to supporting the very great number of animals present in the sea, most of them a long way from the shores where these sea plants, or 'seaweeds,' [2] are. The fact is that the plants of the sea on which much the greater part of its animals are dependent are very small. The only sign of their existence is the fact that the water is not quite clear.

In some places, specially in the warmer seas, sea-water is very clear; we are able to see to a depth of ten or even more meters. In others, it is not so; the water seems dirty yellow or green, not a clear blue. It is in such water that fish are present in great numbers, the reason being that in it there is a very great number of these small plants, and of small animals living on them as food. This mass of living things is the necessary base for the existence of all greater sea animals, in the same way as, on land, the grass and other plants with the insects living on them, and other small and simple living things, are the necessary food for the greater and higher animals.

This mass of small food is named the 'plankton,' and it is generally made up of a great number of different sorts and sizes of plants and animals.[3] By using a net of silk, such as a stocking, anyone may get enough of these little things in a minute or two

[2] See Picture II.
[3] See Picture III.

to keep him at work for a long time with a strong glass, or better, a microscope,[4] making out their strange and interesting forms.

Chief of the plant forms are the diatoms,[5] very small glass-like boxes, having all sorts of beautiful forms, and full of green plant substance. The green coloring of plants is responsible for their power of using light for their chemical work. There are thousands of sorts of diatoms, and we commonly come across a great number together in any one place. Their beautiful little shells, falling to the bed of the sea on their death, make a thick cover of soft mud over great stretches of its deepest parts.

Again, there are certain 'peridinians' (Peridiniales) which have the power of motion, having two whip-like tails. These take in solid food, and so may possibly be looked on as animals, but some have green coloring, and the power of living as plants do.

These and other very small plants are the food of a great number of plankton animals of different sizes—a plankton animal being one which, though it may have the power of motion, is so small and slow that it is transported from place to place by the water currents, and not by the operation of swimming or walking, as other animals are. Among the most important animals are the 'copepods,' a division of the greater division of land and sea animals named Crustacea. Some sorts of copepods are as much as a centimeter or more long, but most of them are very much smaller. The commonest copepod in the colder waters of the north is *Calanus finmarchicus,* which, though only about a millimeter long, is one of the most important animals in the sea, being the chief food of the herring,[6] the commonest and cheapest of all food fish, and of a number of other important food fish. The copepods are quite complex animals, with heads and legs and eyes, but other much simpler animals, the 'radiolarians'

[4] Apparatus for looking at very small things, through which they are seen as greatly increased in size.
[5] Sorts of algae of the order Bacillariales.
[6] *Clupea harengus* (Picture IV).

(Radiolaria) and 'globigerinas' (Globigerinidae) are very important as food for greater animals. The greater 'crustaceans,' such as shrimps,[7] prawns,[8] lobsters,[9] and crabs,[10] are used as food by man.

The animals of which we have been talking are the most important of those living from birth to death in the plankton. But a great number of other water animals, even of the fishes, go through an early stage of living in the plankton. When they come out of the egg they are very small, and quite unable to make any headway against tides and currents. They come up near the surface and are there transported by the motion of the water, possibly to places where there is more room and food for them. While undergoing growth, they have food enough in the plankton, though, naturally, they themselves may come to an early end as food for others. A great number of sea animals, such as shell-fish (a 'shell' is a hard outer cover), are fixed to the sea-bed when their growth is complete, and others get about only very slowly. The young animals in the plankton are quite different in structure, as a rule, from their fathers and mothers; in fact, such young animals have not infrequently at first been taken for separate sorts of animals, their relation to the older animal being a later discovery. The common crab (Cancer pagurus), for example, goes through two separate stages, in which it has quite a different structure, before it is ready for our tables.

Though men make use of animals for food, the land animals in question are, almost all, those themselves living on plants. Their meat has a better taste; and anyhow, such animals are common everywhere, even in natural conditions unchanged by man. On the other hand, almost all the fish used for food are those living on other smaller fish; only one or two, such as the lobster, take

[7] *Crago.*
[8] *Peneus* and like groups (Picture V).
[9] *Homarus* (Picture V).
[10] *Cancer* and other groups of Brachyura (Picture V).

anything they are able to get, like rats on land. Some good-sized fish get their food from seaweeds, but these in turn have masses of small animals living on them, which are more important to the fish than the weed itself; they are the butter on its bread.

One of the strangest facts about the sea is the distribution of the plankton. As we have seen, its starting-point is plants, which, as on land, are building up simple substances, with the help of light, into the complex materials necessary for animal food. Now, on land, the growth of plants is greatest where there is most sun; this is of use for giving not only light, but heat. Plant growth on land is helped by heat; this is why glass-houses are used. But in the sea, the plankton is present in much greater amounts in the colder parts. So in the warmest parts of the earth the land (if there is enough rain) is thickly covered with plants and trees of all sorts, but the sea is very poor in fish. In the north and south seas, on the other hand, we have very great numbers of fish of all sizes, but the land is poor in plants. The Mediterranean is badly off in plankton, and so in fish. The North Atlantic and the North Sea are well stored with plankton, and so with fish.

In the English Channel, the amount of plankton diatoms has been roughly measured. Strangely enough, the weight of the fishes' plant food produced in one square kilometer of sea is a little greater, if anything, than the weight of our chief plant food, the potato, produced on an equal measure of good land. The fishes have to get on with potatoes only a small part of a millimeter in size, but then, only very little fish make use of this uninteresting food. The surprising thing is that the only sign we get of this great mass of produce, on which our fish food is in the end dependent, is the fact that the water round our islands is not clear. The range down into the earth of potatoes in a field is only about half a meter; that of the plankton down into the sea is about 50 meters. However, plankton plants, needing light for growth, have to keep quite near the surface. For the same reason, seaweeds are present only in shallow water. There are no plants on the bed of the deep seas.

There is no limit to the number of different and beautiful forms to be seen among plankton plants and animals. The delicate structure of diatoms is used as a test for our microscopes. An account of this side of sea science is, however, only possible with the help of a great number of pictures. Though it has little to do with the everyday work of the fisherman, it is very important when it comes to a discussion of the reasons for the changes in the amount and position of our food fish. The fisherman has need of direction as to where good fishing is to be had, and when. There are changes from year to year, and it would be a great help if he had early news of what changes are probable. The reader will see that the plankton may well be a guide of much value, when we have enough knowledge to say, from its properties and amount, what it is doing in the way of growth and so on.

For this reason tests of the plankton at a number of different places are now made regularly, and it is to be hoped that in time the number of these regular observations of the condition of the sea will be greatly increased. As with the weather, the greater the number of observation stations, the more certain the answers which science is able to give to questions which are important not only to science but to industry and trade. It is, however, not a simple business to make a true test of the plankton at a given place; what is needed is a knowledge not only of the sorts, but of the numbers, of the different plants and animals present. Some of these are so small that they will get through any net which readily lets water through; and it is necessary to get them all out of a measured amount of water, representative of the sea at the point under observation to a depth of about a hundred meters or more. At present, no simple way of effecting this has been worked out. In addition, a very expert eye is needed for looking at the mass of material taken by a net or other apparatus, there being hundreds and thousands of possible forms to be noted.

It is the smallest plants and animals which give us the greatest trouble. They are the food for other and greater animals, some very much greater. How do these get them out of the water? One of the commonest structures for this purpose makes use of 'cilia.' Cilia are short, very thin, hair-like bodies with the power of waving in such a way as to put any liquid round them in motion, driving it in the desired direction. They are used by almost every animal in one form or another; some of the pipe-like structures in our bodies have their inner sides covered with them. A sponge, which is a network of pipes in which an animal is living, is all the time sending a current of water through them with the help of the cilia coating their insides, and so getting its food from whatever bits of solid substance may be in the water. In some animals these solid bits are gripped by a sticky substance on the skin to which the cilia are fixed; in others, they are taken in a net of some sort, with very small holes, which is got clear by the operation of special cilia. Two common shell-fish, oysters [11] and mussels,[12] make use of the first system, the structure being commonly named the 'beard,' because it is somewhat like the beard, or growth of hair, on a man's chin. The food is sorted out; naturally, not all the solid material in the water is of use to the animal, and some of it has to be let go again from time to time.

One of the plankton animals, *Oikopleura*, has an even stranger way of getting food. It has the power of building round itself a 'house' of jelly-like material, with a quite complex structure. By waving its tail, it sends water through the house, taking it in through openings covered with a network stopping all but the very smallest bits of solid. These bits are then kept back by a net with much smaller holes inside the house, and are pulled off this from time to time by the help of cilia. This house is not of use for long; the nets get stopped up in an hour or two, but the animal is able to make a new house in half an hour.

Some of the smaller Crustacea have their legs covered with hairs, acting as a net when the leg is moved through the water.

[11] *Ostrea* (Picture V).
[12] *Mytilus*.

Their food is kicked into their mouths! In others, such as the common copepods, the legs in swimming are all the time producing a current of water between them; this goes through a sort of net by which the food is kept back to be pushed into the mouth.

The sea-cucumber [13] has a simpler system. It sends out long, sticky feelers, waving them about till bits of food become fixed to them, and then, pushing them into its mouth, makes a meal in much the same way as some cats do by letting their tails down into a bottle of milk and then taking it off with their tongues.

As on land, a great number of the smaller animals in the sea get their food by attacking other animals. There is no doubt about the use a fish makes of its mouth when this is armed with strong, sharp teeth, but nothing is more surprising than the power of attacking other animals seen in some of the most beautiful and delicate living things in the sea, for example, the anemones [14] and jellyfish. [15] These have long delicate feelers, every one armed with sharp needles and little bags of poison; an animal gripped by such a feeler has no chance of getting away, because power of motion is taken away by the poison. The starfish [16] is able to get the shell of an oyster open by gripping it and pulling; it is not strong enough to overcome the oyster's muscle straight away, but the oyster gets tired first. The shell then comes open, and though the starfish is unable to get the oyster into its mouth, and so into its stomach, by pushing out its stomach it gets it round the body of the oyster. After doing its work of digestion, the stomach goes back into place

[13] Name given to animals of the division Holothurioidea, specially the group *Cucumaria* (see Picture II).

[14] Flower-like animals of the order Actiniaria, branch *Coelenterata* (Picture II).

[15] Animals with jelly-like bodies, frequently umbrella-like in form, of the same branch as the anemones, but free-swimming (Picture II).

[16] Any of a number of different animals, roughly starlike in outline, forming the division Asteroidea, of the branch *Echinodermata* (Picture II).

ready for another oyster. The 'bivalves,' animals which, like the
oyster, have two shells shutting together, are a food as much
desired by other sea animals as by man. We get them open with
a knife; in the sea, one animal has a way of cutting a hole in the
shell, another makes the shell soft by putting on it a strong
acid, a third, waiting quietly by till the animal inside is opening
the shell, gets the edge of its shell between the two halves of the
other by a sudden quick motion. Others, again, get the edges of
the bivalve's covering broken by forcing them together.

On land, all living things have a fight for existence, but, in a
general way, conditions are simpler. A great number of animals,
among which are some of the highest, make use only of plant
food—we ourselves are able to do without animal food—but the
number of animals living only on animal food is not important.
In the sea, on the other hand, much the greater number of
animals take no food but other animals, so that between some
of them and the diatoms, the chief plant food, there may be
quite a long chain. The porpoise,[17] an air-breathing animal living only in the sea, and only on fish, is dependent on such as
are of a good size; the fishermen have no love for him. A great
part of this fish food is, however, dependent on other, smaller
fish, and on crustaceans, 'molluscs,' [18] worms, most of which,
again, make use of animals smaller than themselves. A number
of fish, however, such as the herring, mackerel,[19] and shad,[20]
have 'filters' in their gills—networks such as we gave an account
of in connection with smaller and simpler animals. Some of these
are small enough to keep back diatoms; the sardine,[21] for example, takes in this way plant and animal food. Strangest of all,
certain whales, the greatest of all sea animals, get their food
in the same way, using a filter made of 'whalebone,' an elastic,

[17] *Phocaena.*
[18] Mollusca, see Picture V.
[19] *Scomber scombrus,* an important food fish in America and Europe.
[20] *Alosa sapidissima,* etc., an American food fish.
[21] The young of *Sardinella pilchardus,* the tinning of which in oil when
very small is a great industry in Europe.

horn-like substance which is of value to man for a number of purposes needing thin, strong springs. One of its uses is for 'boning' parts of women's dress to make them stiff; unlike steel, whalebone is not attacked by water. But women's dress (and behavior!) is much less stiff than in past times, so whalebone is no longer so much in request.

However, as we have said, a very great number of animals in the sea are far from getting their food in this quiet sort of way; they get it by going after and attacking others, and there is no end to the different sorts of apparatus with which they are armed for this purpose. Naturally, together with this development of apparatus for attack, there has been a development of ways of meeting attack, of 'defense.' In the sea, as on land, one of the commonest forms of defense is the property of being, or becoming at need, so like the things round—stones, plants, sand, and so on—that the animal is not readily seen by its attacker. On land, this natural copying of other things—the leaves or stems of plants, the color of the earth, and so on—is common, specially among insects, but generally the animal has no power of changing its looks. A great number of animals are so marked that, at a distance, it is hard to see them against the plants among which they are living. But they are, as a rule, unable to make any change in themselves when they go from one place to another where the plants are different in form and color. Some fish—in fact, a great number of different sorts—are able to do this, however. We will give a more detailed account of this very interesting process later.

Almost everyone will at times have seen the sea giving out a bright light wherever its surface is cut through by a ship, a stick, or the hand. This 'phosphorescence' is produced by certain of the plankton animals. Now, light-giving animals are quite uncommon on land; fire-flies and glow-worms [22] are the only ones

[22] The first name is given to a number of winged insects, chiefly of the family Lampyridae, which give out light; the second to the light-giving unwinged females of certain sorts.

frequently seen. But in the sea, this light-giving power has undergone much greater development. It is, no doubt, based on much the same chemical reactions, though the range of color produced is greater. We are completely at a loss to say how it is done. As with most other chemical powers of living things, the best which science is able to do is very poor in comparison. Much the greater part of the electric or other power used in lighting our streets and houses is wasted. Our eyes are acted on by only a very short range of waves, but we are quite unable to make apparatus limited to producing these only; we get in addition a great range of waves, of the same sort as light, having no effect on the eyes, but producing only unnecessary heat. The fire-fly or glow-worm, on the other hand, is producing no light-waves other than those acting most strongly on the eye; it is wasting no power. No doubt this is true of fish and all other animals which are light-givers. Strangest of all, these animals make their light by burning a substance, that is, by a chemical reaction between it and the oxygen of the air. We, however, are able to do this only with oil or wax or other like substances, which give out much more heat than light in burning. The animal makes a special substance, 'luciferin,' which in burning gives out only light. That it *is* burning, in the chemical sense of uniting with oxygen, is made clear by the fact that no light is given out when air is kept away from the animal.

Some of the simplest of all living things, bacteria,[23] are able to give out light; it is a common experience that bits of dead fish do so, and this is the effect of the growth of bacteria on them. Sometimes growth of bacteria may take place on living animals. It would be of the greatest value if we were able to get enough of them living on our bodies to be of help to us in getting about in the dark. The phosphorescence in the sea is commonly caused by equally simple plankton animals. We will have more to say further on about the structures producing light. Here we are interested in the use of this property to the animal, and this is a very complex question.

[23] *Schizomycetes,* the simplest of plants, seen only under a microscope.

One way of getting fish out of the sea is by using a line and hook, on which is a 'bait,' that is, something, having an attraction for the sort of fish we are after—most commonly, food, but sometimes simply a bright, or brightly colored, bit of other substance. Now, this idea is much older than man; it is used in a number of ways by certain fish. These angler fish [24]—so named from the 'angler,' or fisherman, we see waiting for long hours with his rod over the river for the fish which do not come— have a 'baited' rod like the fisherman's, with something interesting-looking, and sometimes a light, on the end of it. The rod is quite short, about ten or twenty centimeters, and the strange thing is that the fish itself has a great mouth armed with sharp teeth, which it keeps open all the time. No fish is more cruel-looking; it might well put fear into the strongest man. But the little fish seem to see nothing but the bait. It is clear that little fish have little sense.

By some angler fish, then, light is used as a bait. Strong light has an attraction for fish; in some places, the fishermen take with them to sea high-powered lights. In other fish, apparatus for producing light clearly has the purpose of helping them, in the deep waters where there is no daylight, to the discovery of their food. But it is hard to see what use this light-producing power is to some of the simpler animals. Probably not any. This sort of question comes up in connection with a great number of animals. For example, there are fish of the most beautiful forms and colors, looking as if they had been designed by man. For what purpose? There is here no question of sex selection, which is said to be the reason for the beautiful colors of male birds and insects.

In the sea, as on land, some animals have taken to a very unpleasing way of supporting themselves, by becoming 'parasites' living on or in, and getting their food from, the bodies of other animals. Some make their living-places on the outside, others on the inside, of their 'host,' their hotel-keeper. Some of

---

[24] Fish of the order Pediculati, specially *Lophius piscatorius*, and the deep-sea angler fishes (Ceratioidea), which have a lighted bait (Picture VI).

them have kept the structure and powers of independent animals, moving about freely but using the blood of the host as
their food; others have given up all attempt at working for
their living, and become fixed to the body of the host. They are
then able to do without the process of digestion; in fact, there
may be a complete loss of structure but for the parts necessary
for producing offspring. One strange example of such a parasite is *Sacculina*, living on crabs, and looking at full growth like
a little bag with roots going into the body of the unhappy host.
But from its eggs, which it sends out into the sea, comes a small
animal, named a 'nauplius,' forming part of the plankton, and
swimming freely with its six legs. It is, in fact, like the early
stage of a crab. After a time, a change of form gives it no less
than twelve legs, which have to be used quickly for the discovery of a crab host. It gets into the blood of the crab, letting
its legs go in the process. Then it puts its roots out, and, last of all,
when the crab is changing its shell for a new and greater one
(as crabs have to do to make room for growth), it takes up a
position on the outside of the new shell and from there the eggs
are sent out.

As on land, there is in the sea 'symbiosis,' the living together
of animals, or animals and plants, which are necessary to one
another. This is not at all the same relation as that of parasite
and host. As a stage on the way to symbiosis itself, in which
the two beings are dependent on one another, we have examples
of animals living with others which are a help in keeping off
danger, and which in exchange are helped to food by the friend
profiting by their power of defense. Crabs make use of anemones
in this way. The anemone, an animal with long feelers which
give it the look of a flower, is dependent on food coming to it,
being itself fixed to a stone. Its feelers, however, are poisoned
as a defense. A crab, on the other hand, gets it food broken up
by its strong 'claws,' and naturally, some of it is wasted, specially
the smallest bits. Some crabs have taken to living with anemones.
The poison feelers of the anemone are a defense to the crab,

and the anemone gets the little bits of food from the crab's meal. Another crab gets anemones fixed to its claws, pushing them forward when attacked, and taking out of them, for its use, the food they get a grip of. This may seem a loss to the anemone, but probably it does better when transported from place to place by the crab than it would have done hanging on to one stone all the time, and waiting for food to come to it.

The commonest form of symbiosis, common on land and in the sea, is that of the green alga,[25] a very simple plant, and an animal. Here we have the most complete example of that necessary adjustment of plants to animals and animals to plants. . . . The algae make complex materials from the simplest chemical substances, so producing food for the animal, which in turn lets them have back the waste produced by its living processes, to be worked up again. The eggs of some animals take little bits of alga with them when the female lets them go, so that the offspring is quite certain of not being without its necessary friend. The offspring of other animals are dependent on chance for meeting algae, but these are so common that there is no danger of not doing so under natural conditions. Such an animal is the worm *Convoluta*, living in the sand on the shore of Brittany and the Channel Islands. It is seen in the form of bright green masses on the yellow shore, suddenly coming up out of the sand after the tide has gone out, and going down into it again a short time before the tide comes back. The green color is that of the algae with it. Though when young it is able, like other worms, to make use of smaller animals for food, it quickly becomes completely dependent on the algae, and its power of digestion, being no longer used, is then a thing of the past. The alga has need of daylight for its work as a plant, so the worm has to come out from its safe cover in the sand, taking the chance of destruction by other animals. In the end, the worm gets tired of living in this uninteresting way, and makes a meal of the algae

[25] Algae, the general name for thousands of different sorts of very simple plants of the branch Thallophyta.

themselves, going white from the tail up in the process. Death is the only possible outcome of this foolish behavior, but the worm makes good use of this last meal by producing eggs in great numbers, so the family goes on. The offspring, never having seen their mother, have naturally no idea of how she came to her early death, and so go on, in time, to make the same error themselves.

As we have said, symbiosis is only a special example of the general fact that living beings are dependent on one another. Over a given range of natural conditions in the sea or on the land, we have a most complex network of relations between the animals and plants, by which, among other things, the number of them is limited. If any one sort undergoes a great change in numbers, the natural balance of the organization may get so much out of order that all sorts of other changes take place. Examples of this are more readily seen on land than in the sea, where we have much less chance of getting a complete knowledge of what is going on. One point is of special interest. In symbiosis, we have two living things helping one another. Against this, we have everywhere living things attacking one another. It might seem that any animal would be better off without its attackers, its 'enemies.' But this is not necessarily so. In a certain wide stretch of country, covered with woods, there were living a number of animals kept in more or less natural conditions for purposes of sport. The sportsmen went after them with guns, and the payment made to the owner of the land for this amusement was naturally dependent on the number of animals of the desired sort, chiefly deer.[26] Now these deer were not troubled by sportsmen only, but by a number of animal enemies of no value for this sort of sport, specially the fox,[27] and

[26] Animals of the family Cervidae, noted for their powers of running and for the fact that the males have branching horns which come off every year.
[27] Sorts of dog-like animal of the group *Vulpes*, having a sharp-pointed nose and a long thick tail.

it seemed to the owners of the land that it would be a good thing to put an end to all the foxes and other enemies of the deer, so that the valued animals would be safer. This was done, and naturally, there was at first a great increase in the numbers of the deer. But in a short time it became clear that these animals had undergone a great loss of quality, and from year to year they became poorer and feebler. The reason was simple. The foxes, in the past, had kept them moving, which had the effect of making them stronger and quicker; in addition, the feebler ones were put to death by these enemies, so that offspring were produced chiefly by the stronger, those able to get away from the foxes. We see from this example how its enemies may be of value to an animal or plant by keeping its quality high.

Though the number of different living forms seems almost without end, we keep on meeting with the same sort of structure or process again and again, in a lower or higher stage of development. An eye may be anything from a point on the body simply having the power of reaction to light and dark, to a very complex apparatus such as we have in our heads. There are good reasons for the belief that the complex structures of plants and animals are the outcome of the slow development, through thousands or millions of years, of simpler structures, which have been of value to their owners.

It is for this reason surprising that, of all living things on land or in the sea, only two fish are able to give electric shocks strong enough to be a danger to small animals, and even to man. The apparatus in the fish named the torpedo or electric ray,[28] by which electric shocks are produced, is naturally very complex. To be of use, it has to give out a current of some hundreds of units ('volts'), and though very feeble electric currents are produced by muscles and nerves when acting normally, only the most delicate instruments give us any sign of them. They would have to be a thousand times stronger to be a danger even to the smallest animal, and we have never come across any simple

[28] *Torpedo torpedo,* a great flat fish of the order Hypotremata (Picture VI).

form of shock-producing apparatus, such as might have been an earlier stage in the development of the one present in the electric ray. It is, in fact, hard to see of what use a low-powered apparatus would be. Electric shocks are only a danger to animals with a very complex nerve-system, and these are of such a size that a strong shock is necessary.

The last word has not been said on the question of how these 'inventions' with which living beings are armed come into existence. Some are like our inventions, ways of using, or even making things out of, natural materials. Others are the development of parts of the body in such a way as to get an effect which is of value to the plant or animal. The present theory is that such inventions come about by 'natural selection.' Any small change in the structure of a plant or animal which is of use to it gives it a better chance of living on and producing offspring. These offspring will themselves probably have the same point of structure; some may have it in an even better form than before. For example, those fish with bodies best formed for moving through the water are the quickest swimmers, and so have the best chance of getting food by overtaking other fish, and of keeping out of danger from greater fish. Now, of the same *sort* of fish, some of those living at any one time will have bodies a little better formed than others; no two living things are ever completely the same in every way. Of the young fish produced at this time, probably much the greater number will come to an early end in the stomachs of other fish; it is the quickest swimmers which will have the best chance of living on and producing offspring. So a natural selection of quick swimmers takes place, like the selection made by man in producing horses, when he takes care that the quickest runners become the fathers and mothers of the young horses to be trained later as runners. The effect of man's selection has been the beautiful lines seen in our best horses, and there is little doubt that the operation of natural selection has had much to do with the development of those structures and processes which are of value to different sorts of plants and animals. But we frequently come across forms, as in the electric ray, which seem to have no earlier stages, and where it is hard to see how development by degrees has been possible.

4. From *The Growth of Science*
by A. P. Rossiter

The account to which we now come is an example of science writing in which free use is made of the words in the General Science List and of words which are international in science. The words of the second group are put in italics with ° after them, and may be taken as not needing to be made clear to anyone with any knowledge of science. Those in the first group which come into these pages (and are marked out by being put between single quotes) are listed after this with their senses in Basic, in the order in which they come in.

rock	(great natural mass of) stone or stone-like material; any special sort of solid material present in great amounts in the earth
shell	hard outer cover of certain sea and land animals
deposit	solid material put down, specially by water, on some other body; *depositing*—the process of putting down material in this way
solution	substance, specially a liquid, having another substance (solid, liquid, or gas) so mixed with it that there is a regular distribution of the *molecules* of the one among those of the other, and the mixed substance gives no sign of the separate existence of the two; the condition of being so mixed in a liquid and so on
age	time for which anything has been in existence, how old it is; great stretch of time, division of history
generation	the act or process of producing offspring; the group of offspring produced by a given plant, animal, or group; one stage or level in a family-tree
environment	place and other outside conditions in which a living thing has its existence and development

mean   condition, quality and so on equally far from two opposites, coming between them, specially as taken to be representative of what is most normal, generally come
across

EVOLUTIONS

The idea of 'Evolution,' or the development of different sorts
of things from simpler forms by natural processes, was not new
in the year 1859.[1] Not only had such ideas come to the Greeks
(probably from Egypt); but a general uncertain belief that
some such process was responsible for the different forms of the
living things on Earth had been 'in the air' for 70 or 80 years.
And, what is more important, a theory of the evolution of the
'rocks' of the Earth had taken a strong position with the printing
of Charles Lyell's *Principles of Geology* in 1830–33.

To make a connection with the past, we will go back to the
theories of Buffon, if only because they are signs and records
pointing to one special tendency. They put the authority of the
Bible on one side: they gave an idea of the Earth's past history,
in comparison with which all the records of Man's past were
like notes on the last two or three pages of a great shut book,
at the broken edges of which a sign might here and there be
seen. It was in this way that John Michell (1760) saw the rock-
beds of England; though no reading of the signs, and no decision
about the true order of the leaves, was possible till the time of
William Smith (1769–1839).

At quite an early stage the Italian experts Vallisneri (1721),
Marsilli, and Moro (1740) had seen that *fossils** were grouped
in certain rocks; and in his expansion of Moro's theories,
Generelli (1749) had made it his design to give reasons for the
structure of the Earth "without unnatural changes, without
fictions, without hypothesis.[2] His general theory, like that of

[1] When Darwin's *Origin of Species* came out.
[2] 'Hypothesis' is theory based on reasoning from observation to what seems
possible.

Hooke before him, was that the rocks had been formed under the sea, and lifted by earth-shocks. Donati had seen how 'shells' were being put down in the Adriatic in groups like those seen by Spada, Schiavo, and Marsilli in the rocks; and the fact that earth-shocks were not uncommon in Italy, and that a new island had been sent up by one in 1707 made this theory of sudden change seem very probable.

Attempts had been made to put the rocks into groups in the order in which they were formed. Lehmann in Germany (1756) and Arduino some three years later in Italy had made three divisions: (i) the first, or 'Primary' Rocks, coming from the Creation [3] (and so with no fossils); (ii) the second or 'Secondary' Rocks produced by destruction of these; and (iii) the third, or Tertiary Rocks formed by later 'depositing,' possibly or probably by the Flood.[4] Theories not unlike those of Moro were put forward in Germany by Gesner (1758) and Raspe (1763), after the groupings had been made clearer by Fuchsel (1762, 1773). But almost all these workers were limited in their discoveries by two chief troubles: the need to get their theories into agreement with the Bible-story; and the very limited distribution of ideas at this time. Had this not been so, the good work of Guettard (1715–86) and Desmarest (1725–1815) in France might have made a great change; though the wall of authority was still very strong even after Lyell's great work. On this point, the trouble was put very clearly by Gesner in 1758, though it was not very different from what had kept Steno's mind back a hundred years earlier. It was clear from measurings of the rate of depositing in the Baltic that at least 80,000 years would be necessary for forming such mountains as the Apennines. But the range of time given by working from the Bible was not more than one-twentieth of this. There was no doubt that the Bible was right; so that it was clear that the

[3] The word 'creation' = act of making, and 'the Creation' is the making of the earth by God.
[4] A 'flood' is the over-running of land by water, and 'the Flood' is the covering of the earth in this way as recorded in the Bible.

Earth had been made by God, using natural forces, possibly, but certainly using them in ways which were no longer natural.

What was needed was a general uniting of knowledge into an ordered structure of theory, taking in all the facts. But when a great mind came to do this, the effect was to keep back the growth of the science for 50 years of bitter argument. Abraham Gottlob Werner (1749–1817) was a great teacher with a surprising power over the minds of other men, and a very German love of system. He made his name by a well worked-out grouping of *minerals** and by discoveries in Crystallography which have every right to a respected memory. But in his theory of the Earth he went from a limited knowledge of Saxony and Hesse to the widest and most general views (dependent on Leibnitz and Lehmann in some degree) with little or no knowledge of the structure of any other part of Europe. His greatest error was to take over from the past the idea of the Great Deep (or *Universal** *Ocean**) by which the earth had been covered at the Creation, and say that the earliest rocks were chemically deposited from it at a time when there were no living things. Rocks had been formed, he said, all over the Earth at the same time, and under like conditions, and there had been no far-ranging violent changes from the time of the Flood.

Now in France, the work of Guettard and Desmarest had made it quite certain that *volcanoes**, commonly taken to be fire-mountains, had sent liquid rock over, through, and between water-formed beds, in a way which made any theory of chemical depositing from 'solution' quite impossible. And these rocks were very like some of the 'primaries' in a number of ways. Werner, however, had only seen the *basalts** round Freiburg; flat tables on the mountain-tops which had the same form as the common *strata** or parallel beds formed by water. So though Desmarest had been able to make comparisons with rocks in other places, and to see that the Freiburg basalts, like those of Staffa, were 'igneous' rock, that is, rock formed at great heat, this had no authority with the "Neptunian School," as it was named: after Neptune, the Roman sea-god.

In the year 1788 James Hutton (1726–1797) first made public his theory, later printed with additions (1795) and given a wider public in the more pleasing prose of his friend Playfair's *Illustrations of the Huttonian Theory* (1802). The uniting purpose of these was to give an account of the earth's structure based only on observations of fact; that is to say, on reasoning from changes of the sort still going on. Hutton was attempting to do for the structure of the Earth what Laplace had made complete for the motions of the stars: to give a reading of the Past and Future based only on reasoning from present observation. Great changes, said Hutton, had gone on very slowly in very great time. The earliest rocks were igneous, the later ones chiefly water-formed; but from time to time there had been great outbursts of heated rock (producing the basalts and the Scots *granites**) which had been forced through earlier strata. Everywhere there was to be seen the destruction of past earths, from which, when the broken bits were taken to the sea by rivers, the building of future rocks would be started, till the sea-beds were lifted, and a new land took the place of the old; then that again would go through the same unending process of change and destruction under the rains and snows of a far-off future. Looking back into the great uncertain ranges of past time, he saw "no sign of a start, no sign of an end."

These very Pythagorean views of the Vulcanists (as they were named, possibly not without humor, after Vulcan, the Roman fire-god) were taken as an attack on religion; and this put expert opinion completely against them. Here the outlook of society had an important effect. The French 'Revolution' [5] of 1789 was full of political danger to the other governments of Europe. Somewhere at the back of the Revolution were the ideas of Voltaire and the Encyclopaedists, who had made frequent attacks on the Church and the Bible; so that there was a natural chain of half-unconscious suggestion joining thoughts about 'Jacobinism' (being a supporter of the Revolution), about questioning the Bible, and about having no belief in God. Against

[5] A violent overturning of the government of a country.

this general feeling all Playfair's attempts to make it clear that
Hutton had never said there was no God had not the smallest
effect. Though Sir James Hall, using a development of De Saus-
sure's tests on minerals, made it certain that rock heated till
liquid gave something with a structure very like basalt, this did
not have any weight with those who saw that the Wernerian
theory gave room for a Creation and a Flood, the Huttonian did
not.

This was the position till 1830–1833, when the *Principles of
Geology* of Charles Lyell (1797–1875) was first put before the
public. What Werner might have done for Geology, Lyell did:
putting together a beautifully ordered structure from the great
and ever-increasing mass of observations, in a clear and
balanced prose which of itself gave weight to his views. The
great number of experts in geology before and after Lyell make
hard reading: as if they did their work hammer in hand. Not so,
Lyell, whose knowledge of Gibbon had given him more, possibly, than he got from Hutton and Playfair. The art of writing
a prose at once strong and delicate, balanced and natural, with
all the force of a great mind, is not common enough among men
of science for this side of Lyell's work to be overlooked. His
theory went farther than Hutton, his facts came from a wider
field; and the full force of his argument was on the side of an
evolutionary view of the Earth's history. What was named the
"Uniformitarian theory" gave an account of the evolution of the
rocks by slow and regular ('uniform') changes, of the sort still
seen acting, working unendingly through a time so long that in
its great stretch the buildings of old Egypt were no older and
for no longer than last night's snow-fall.

Against this view there was not only the school of Freiburg,
but that of the 'Catastrophists,' who had a belief in a past of
sudden and violent changes ('catastrophes'), among which the
Flood might be put. Here there was a connection with the
sciences of living things: in France, De Lamarck (1744–1829)
and Cuvier (1769–1832) took opposite views of the past history

of the animals, the first having a belief in change by a sort of self-adjustment to natural conditions, while the second was a supporter of the old belief in the sudden general destruction of living forms, after which there came a new stage of development. There was no doubt by this time that a number of *species**, or sorts, of animals had come completely to an end; while others seen at the present day seemed not to have been in existence in the past (though this was naturally less certain, the chances of getting the fossils being small). Lamarck's theory was that animals had a power of self-development by something like conscious attempts, the blood and 'living forces' being given a special direction to any parts used in a special way (as, for example, the cow-family makes use of its head in fighting, or the horse-family of its legs in running); and that these developments were given by the animal to its young. (It is this last idea, that changes in the living animal may have an effect on its offspring, which is now commonly named Lamarckism.)

In this there was an idea of Evolution, as opposite to the belief that God made the animals at the Creation, one and all in their present forms. A number of arguments for change in species had been put forward by Erasmus Darwin in his Zoönomia (1796) and in notes to his works in verse; but (then as now) the writer of *The Loves of the Plants* was not taken very seriously. Earlier again, Robert Hooke had had an idea of the possible effects of living-conditions, seen the different forms of the same species in the animals kept by man (dogs, sheep, etc.), and made the suggestion that small regular changes in what were at first only different examples of the same species might, in time, give lines of offspring so different that they would not be judged to be of the same species.[6]

A strong argument, first put forward by Erasmus Darwin and used later by Charles, came from Cuvier's work on Anatomy,

[6] *Posthumous Papers of R. Hooke* (1702), pp. 327–28, 435. Hooke's idea of an evolution-theory has been generally overlooked. See *Nature*, January, 1936. (Notes by W. N. Edwards and the present writer.)

in which it was seen that the species grouped together commonly had structures with a general design, as if there were only a certain number of forms, which had undergone special adjustments for their special conditions and behaviors. This seemed to make it necessary to say that God's powers of invention were somewhat limited: an improbable way out of a hard question.

Here a short note may be given on the past history of Zoology and Botany, and specially on this question of grouping, or *classification**. In 1660 John Ray had made his system of plants, in which those with one seedleaf (*Monocotyledons*) were first grouped separately from those with two (*Dicotyledons*); and in 1676 Nehemiah Grew, another Fellow of the Royal Society, had taken the first steps in the discovery of the sex-*organs** in plants. This work was taken farther by Rudolf Camerarius (1665–1721) and Geoffroy, till Carl von Linné, or Linnaeus (1707–1778) put forward his complete system of groupings. Like Ray, Linnaeus went on from plants to animals, and it is from his work that we get our system of international names in the Latin form. His observations made it clear that the place of Man in the system was with the Apes, or higher monkeys; and from about 1770 playing with the idea that the two were relations was one of the amusements of men of learning with a taste for something out of the common. Discoveries of fossil Man, however, are not very frequent; so that even in Lyell's time it was possible to say that no signs of his existence had been seen in any but the newest orders of rocks.

In England, William Smith (1769–1839) had put into effect Hooke's uncertain idea of a time-scale of the rocks, using the fossil groups as guides. The wide observation and detailed geological maps produced by this great worker had been the mark of a new stage in the science. In 1808 Cuvier and Brogniart had done the same work with the rocks of the Paris Basin, when the first had put together the fossil bones of a number of animals no longer seen anywhere on earth, some of them of a quite shockingly improbable size. Work of the same sort was done later by Saint-Hilaire (1772–1844), who was a strong supporter of the theories of Lamarck. In 1844 there was printed a book named *Vestiges of Creation,* by Robert Chambers (1802–1871), though he did not put his name to it. This, like the writings of Herbert Spencer (1820–1903), had in it a general idea of evolution, though there was still no ordered basework of detailed facts, and no suggestion of a process less uncertain and generally improbable than Lamarck's. These were the conditions under which Darwin's theory was put forward; and strong as was the position of the Bible in England, great though the dangers were of openly making a suggestion that its account was false, the very fact that belief was so important made this the most probable country to be the heart of the latest great war between Science and 'Religion,' that is to say, the Churches.

Like most of the great theories, Darwin's is simple. His special quality was that of being able to take a far-ranging and detailed mass of facts and give it an order and design, much as Newton had done with the facts of motion. Only—and it is an important point—there was here no question of using the clear and certain authority of numbers. Like Geology, the sciences of living things are necessarily based on reasoned argument about what seems probable. Where time is all-important, the only possible base for theory is argument from the little which *may* be seen to the much which *might* be.

The uniting idea of the theory seems to have taken form at different times in the minds of Darwin and A. R. Wallace as the effect of reading the same book: Malthus's *Essay of Population* (1798), which Darwin had seen in 1838, and Wallace 20 years later, though before Darwin had made his theory public. Malthus's theory was that there was a natural tendency for the number of living persons (the 'population') to go on increasing till there was not enough food; when the condition was only balanced again by war, disease, or some other cause of a high death-rate (such as need of food). Darwin and Wallace saw

that under these conditions there was a tendency for those who
were 'better' in some way to keep themselves from death; if not
as far as the natural limit, at least long enough for them to have
more offspring than those who were 'worse.' This is "the survival of the fittest": a *formula* * of words which has from the first
been a general cause of error.[7] The sense of 'survival' is simply
the one we have given ('going on living long enough to have offspring'); but that of 'fittest' ('best able to go on living in the
conditions') was taken to have a suggestion of 'necessarily better' about it (the 'better' being measured in some less simple
scale of values) which is unsupported by Darwin's use and by
the facts. The Thread-worm is not 'better' than the Mammoth
(*Elephas primigenius*) in any but the sense that thread-worms
are still among us, while mammoths are not.

Darwin's theory of "natural selection" said that in any group
of offspring no two would be quite the same in every smallest
detail. Under changing conditions (of weather, food, the attacks
of other animals) some of these small details might be a great
help in the general competition for the needs of existence which
had been named "the struggle for existence." [8] If conditions were
hard enough, this small detail might have 'survival-value'; so
that this one animal had offspring, while his brothers and sisters
did not, or had less. In the family produced by this animal (in
the second 'generation,' that is) there might again be two or
more with the special qualities which had given their father a
better chance of 'survival'; so that in time the number of that
species with what had at first been an uncommon quality would
be increased till what had been 'uncommon' was now 'normal'
among that group. This process of automatic adjustment to
living-conditions was "natural selection."

Competition between animals of the same sort, taken as sex-
groups, is part of the 'conditions.' In general, the males will be in
competition for the females: so that being able to keep up the

[7] The formula was Herbert Spencer's. See *Origin of Species,* III.
[8] "The (unending) struggle for room and food" (Malthus III).

fight against weather, need of food, etc., is only part of the war. 'Environment,' or the living-conditions, then, is not a simple thing: it takes in everything which may have an effect on offspring-producing in numbers greater than the 'mean.'

Taking the argument the other way, into the past, it becomes clear that this process of adjustment gives a reason for the *general* design to be seen in animals of the same great groups (Mammals,[9] Fish, Birds, Insects, and so on) and for the *special* qualities seen in the species. A species is a development of one general design which has gone through a long process of adjustment to special environments. Whales,[10] for example, are mammals which have gone through a process of adjustment to fish-like conditions: the ostrich,[11] emu,[12] and cassowary [13] are birds which have gone through a process of increase of weight and power of running, and loss of the power of flight; and so on. But all these special forms seem to be developments of a small number of simpler designs; so that there has been a process of development in time from simple to complex, as an effect of natural selection, which is the 'cause' of the different species. Going back farther, there was at some time deep in the past some one First Living Thing, the Adam of the plants and animals; and from it all things have been produced by this process of evolution of complex from simple, under the ever-present forces of change and destruction.

Darwin's theory was supported by facts from all fields of observation; and it gave ideas as widely as it took. In Geology it gave a most clear and certain reason for the distribution of the fossils in the different beds, and made it clear why the higher forms of living things were never seen in any but the newest

[9] The group of warm-blooded, milk-producing, *Vertebrata* (back-boned animals) more or less covered with hair, and producing their young from the body in a late stage of development.
[10] Great sea mammals of the order Cetacea.
[11] Sorts of bird of the genus *Struthio*.
[12] Sorts of bird of the genus *Dromiceius*.
[13] Sorts of bird of the genus *Casuarius*.

beds, while in the older and deeper rocks only the simplest
forms were seen. It gave a new authority to Smith's time-scale,
and made Palaeontology [14] less the natural history of the past
than a science of the causes of the present. To all questions
about the order of fossils, there was no answer but Darwin's.[15]
Evolution put together the facts from Geology and Palaeontology, those from Comparative Anatomy and Morphology (the
structure of animal forms), the observations used in grouping,
the special knowledge got from producing the animals in common use among men, and made it clear that through this theory
these were all in agreement with one another, and with what
might be seen to take place among animals or plants under
natural conditions, and with the facts of their distribution in
different parts of the earth. In addition to all this, it gave a
reason for the existence of signs of parts which seemed to be
of no use (those of leg-bones in one form of snake, the tail-
structures in the Apes and in Man, and the wings of running-
birds, never used in flight): feeble, unused, and incomplete
structures for which the theory of Special Creation (as in the
Bible story) was able to give no reason at all. Again, the theory
had the support of Embryology, in which a sort of fossil behavior had been seen in the development of the embryo [16] of
the higher animals, a tendency for certain parts to go through
stages in which they were like those of simpler animals. (In
fishes, for example, there is a worm-stage; in mammals, a fish-
stage.) This had been noted in the brain by Tiedemann, and
made the base of a theory of Embryology by Meckel (1781–

[14] The science of the animals of the past.
[15] A suggestion was, however, made that God put the fossils in the rocks
as a test of belief. A strange idea of God! Another writer said that when
God made the Earth it was clearly going to have a *Future,* and for that
reason it was necessary for it to have a *Past;* so God kindly gave it signs
of one. It would be hard to give a better example of the effect of language on thought.
[16] The general name for the living thing in the development-stages, before
it has a free existence: in the seed, the egg, or the mother's body.

1833). It gave Darwin an important parallel to the fossil-record, in which there was the same order of simple-to-complex; and, again, it was not very clear why there was any need for animals made by Special Creation to go through these roundabout stages.

The effect of the *Origin of Species* on the general current of thought was greater than that of any theory from the time of Copernicus. It was, it might be said, an effect of the same sort. Copernicus had taken away the Earth from the middle of the Universe,[17] and put it among the other stars: Darwin had put Man among the animals, and made living things the outcome of their physical conditions. But where Newton's system had given comforting suggestions of an unlimited care in the adjustment of parts to purpose, Evolution seemed at first to take all sense and value from the idea of purpose: to make Man no more than a chance-formed Higher Ape, looking on for a time at the unresting currents of change by which he had been forced into being, and by which he would, in time, be sent the way of the Pterodactyl, the Ichthyosaurus, and the Mammoth, a man of stone among the fossils of the ice-cold rocks.[18]

The reaction was quick and violent. Society was ready to have a belief in the effects of environment: the desire for wider education is a sign of it, and this was common talk long before Darwin's time. It was ready to see that 'everything had a use,' and that competition was a 'law of existence'; but it was less ready to see that men might not be completely responsible for their qualities, and not ready at all to have anything to do with a theory which said that the story of Creation was untrue, that Man was a somewhat less indelicate form of Monkey, and that he was not under the guiding hand of God, but part of an un-

---

[17] Everything in existence, looked on as a complete system; here, specially the system of suns and stars of which our earth is a part.
[18] Though printed nine years before Darwin's book, Tennyson's *In Memoriam* is an unequaled record of the deeper effects of the new outlook on men's minds.

ending round of changes and destructions without purpose or design, with no reason for his existence, and no reward at the end of it. About a great number of these things Darwin had said nothing; but it was in this form that the theory came before the minds of the public, and was attacked by the newspapers, by the churches, by political authorities, by private letters; by almost every sort of man with a low opinion of the monkey and a high one of himself. Unlike the wave-theory of light or the laws of Thermodynamics, this was a question in which everyone seemed (to himself) to be a good judge.

For a number of years Darwin and T. H. Huxley and their supporters were kept fighting for the theory, till the churchmen had taken to reading science, and had made the surprising discovery that the hand of God might be as clearly seen in the long and complex process of evolution as in the unnatural industry of the Third, Fifth, and Sixth Days. On science the effect was like that of a fixed bright light; but while some branches underwent a new stage of growth, Biology went almost to sleep for forty years, in which Natural Selection seemed to have given the first, last, and only formula.

In Geology, the great work of Lyell had given so much order that the Uniformitarian theory was the baseline from which almost all future developments were made. The systems of beds under (and older than) the Old Red Sandstone had been slowly worked out by the discoveries of Adam Sedgwick (1785–1873) and Sir Roderick Murchison (1792–1871); American geology, started by William Maclure in 1807, became important with the work of J. D. Dana (1813–1895); and by 1900 the *formations*** in almost all countries had been worked out by the discoveries of an army of experts using the fossils in what was, at root, Smith's way, and working by a general theory which was Lyell's in design. Knowledge of the conditions and effects of 'ice-ages' had been started by Agassiz in 1840; and though not given full attention till the work of Sir Archibald Geikie (1863) and his son James (1874), was then seen to be an important addition to theory.

The details of the discovery of the different systems and their working-out have no place in a general history; but in all this work, the evolution theories of the building of the Earth and the development of the animals and plants took on an authority like that of the Newtonian system in physics. Observations which seemed to give results not in agreement with the theory were not taken as a sign that it might be false, but as making it certain that if the order of guide-fossils was not regular, then the strata had been violently overturned or twisted in some way, after the fossils were bedded in them. Here Darwin's work is a first step in the direction of later discoveries about the age of the Earth.

It is not hard to see that there is a *method** in common between the work of Hutton and Lyell, Wallace and Darwin: one in which Past and Present are seen as united parts of an unbroken and regular process. To put it simply, the method is that of History: only History on a greater scale, and with Man at a different level. When Darwin's later books and Huxley's *Man's Place in Nature* (1863) had taken their place among valued works of science, this method had taken discovery into some completely new fields. Science took a new and important line when Man was seen as the outcome of his natural conditions.

5. Basic English
and the British Standards Institution

The example to which we now come is of interest less for its material than because it lets us see Basic at work in a field where clear statement is specially important. What the British Standards Institution is, and to what use Basic was put by it is given under this, and it seems unnecessary to say that such a use by such a body is something for the supporters of Basic to be very pleased about.

Only a small part of the 'specification' is here given, because it has, naturally, to go into a great amount of very dry detail, which not only does not make interesting reading but which is not readily taken in without the help of pictures and tables which would be out of place here. In such work the writer will certainly be free to make use of the General Science List together with any Special Science List having a connection with his material, and of all international science words. In addition to about ten of these, there are, in the bit here given, five or six more science words, which are listed with their senses at the end.

The following is an extract from the aims and objects of the British Standards Institution:

STANDARD ENGLISH	BASIC ENGLISH
AIMS AND OBJECTS	PURPOSES

The British Standards Institution is the national organisation for the promulgation of British Standard terms, definitions, codes of practice and specifications for materials, articles, etc., and methods of test. It is governed by a General Council, the constitution of which is given on page 2.

The British Standards Institution is the organisation in this country for making public British Standard words, the senses in which they are to be used, systems for working, and details for materials, goods, and so on, and ways of testing. It is controlled by a General Council, the structure of which is given on page 2.

The underlying principles covering the preparation of British Standards are: (a) that they shall be in accordance with the needs of industry and fulfil a generally recognised want; (b) that the interests of both producer and consumer shall be considered; (c) that periodic review shall be undertaken.

The guiding rules for framing British Standards are: (a) that they are to be in agreement with the needs of industry while meeting those of the general public, (b) that the interests of producer and user are to be taken into account, (c) that from time to time any necessary adjustments are to be made.

A translation of the British Standard Portland Cement *Specification* (B.S. 12:1940) will be available shortly, price 2s. The

British Standards Institution is in debt to the Orthological Institute for putting this specification into Basic English. This is the first example of a British Standard printed in Basic. It gives all the facts and nothing has been cut out or changed.

B.S. 12:1940 (Basic)

BRITISH STANDARD *SPECIFICATION* [1]
FOR
COMMON PORTLAND AND
RAPID-HARDENING PORTLAND CEMENTS

NOTE. The name 'rapid-hardening' is used in this specification because it has become the common name in Britain. It is the equivalent of 'high early strength,' which is used in other countries, and it is not the same as 'quick-*setting*.' It will be seen from section 12 that rapid-hardening cement (if not specially requested) is not quick-setting.

Composition of Cement and Method of Making

1. The cement, common or rapid-hardening, is to be made by mixing well together substances having calcium carbonate ($CaCO_3$) in them, such as chalk, and substances having silica (SiO_2), alumina (Al_2O_3), and iron oxide (Fe_2O_3) in them, such as clay, then heating them to a *clinkering* temperature and crushing the *clinker* into powder so that a cement in agreement with this specification is produced.

No addition of any substance is to be made after heating other than calcium sulphate ($CaSO_4$), or water, or the two together.[2]

Specimens for Testing and by Whom to Be Taken

2. A specimen or specimens for testing may be taken by the person who has given the order for the cement or his representa-

[1] Words whose sense is given in the 'special word list' at the end are put in sloping print the first time they are used.
[2] No cement which has an addition of *slag* or which is a mixture of Portland cement and slag, is to be taken as covered by this specification. For a specification of cement with slag in it, see B.S. 146 'Portland blast-furnace cement.'

tive, or by any person who has been put in control of the works
for the purpose of which the cement is needed, or by his representative, or by any expert *analyst* under the direction of the
person giving the order or by his representative, or by any
person in control of the works or by his representative.

Specimens for Testing and How to Be Taken

3. A specimen for testing is to be a mixture of equal amounts, as
near as possible, taken from at least 12 different positions in the
mass or masses when the cement is loose, or from not less than
12 bags, *casks,* or other parcels when the cement is not loose,
or where there is a smaller number than 12 different bags, casks,
or other parcels, then from every bag, cask, or other parcel. All
possible care is to be taken in the selection, so that a representative specimen is taken. The weight of the specimens when complete is to be at least 10 lb. (4·54 kg.).

Taking Specimens of Great Amounts

4. When specimens are to be taken of more than 250 tons (560,-
000 pounds—254,012 kg.) of cement at one time, separate specimens are to be taken by the method given in section 3, from
every 250 tons or part of such amount.

The cement is to be stored in units of not more than 250 tons,
these units being kept separate from one another so that specimens may be taken from them by the method given in this
section and section 3. If more than 250 tons are kept in one
store, every 250 tons or part of 250 tons is to be kept separate,
so that specimens may be taken at different places from every
specimen.[3]

[3] As there are stores in existence which take more than 250 tons, and in
which it would not be possible to put divisions without danger to the structure, specimens may be taken from such stores if the person ordering, or
his representative, gives his agreement and is certain that a good and
representative specimen may be taken of every 250 tons put into the store.
Such specimens may be taken from holes made for this purpose in the walls

Taking and Marking Specimens

5. The supplier [4] is to give the person taking the specimens for testing, men and materials for taking them, putting them into bags, and marking them, together with any other help which is necessary.

Payment for Tests, Analyses, and Specimens

6. The payment for the tests and analyses given in sections 7 to 13, but not in section 15, will be made by the person ordering the cement if there are no special conditions about this in the agreement between the person ordering the cement and the supplier, but no payment is to be made to the supplier for the cement used for specimens or for the carriage of them.

Tests

7. The specimen or specimens are to be tested by the methods given under for:

    a. Screen analysis
    b. Chemical composition
    c. Strength
    d. Setting time
    e. Maximum expansion

Screen Analysis

8. One puts 100 g. (or say 4 ounces) of cement onto a B.S. Laboratory Test Screen Number 170, shaking it continuously for 15 minutes.

of the store, or may be taken by an automatic apparatus at the point where the cement is put into the store.

In the event of any such specimen of a 250 ton unit not being in agreement with this specification, the person ordering or his representative may say he will not take cement from any part of the store from which the specimen came.

Whenever possible, however, every 250-ton unit is to be kept separate.

[4] The 'supplier' in this specification is the trader, who may or may not be the maker of the cement.

SPECIAL WORD LIST

specification   detailed account of how something is to be made and what properties it is necessary for it to have

rapid-hardening   becoming *hard* very quickly, as against 'quick-setting,' which is 'starting to become *solid* very quickly'

setting   (of cement) early stage in the process of becoming hard

clinker   mass of hard unburned material formed in the process of burning the materials to make cement

clinkering   forming clinker

analyst   person doing an *analysis* (International word)

cask   great, round, flat-ended, wood vessel

slag   hard stone material from iron works

PART THREE

The Bible

The examples here printed are taken from *The Bible in Basic English* which came out in 1949 (though the New Testament had been in print since 1941). In addition to the general 850, the Basic Bible makes use of 100 words for reading verse:

angel, arrow, beast, bow, breast, bride, brow, bud, child, cross, crown, curse, dawn, delight, dew, dove, dream, eagle, evening, evil, faith, fate, feast, flock, flow, fountain, fox, glory, God, grace, grape, grief, guest, hawk, heaven, hell, hill, honey, honor, image, ivory, joy, lamb, lark, life, lion, lord, meadow, melody, mercy, passion, perfume, pity, pool, praise, prayer, pride, priest, rapture, raven, robe, rock, rose, rush, search, shower, sorrow, soul, spear, spirit, storm, stream, strength, sword, thief, tower, travel, valley, veil, vine, violet, virtue, vision, wandering, wealth, weariness, weeping, wisdom, wolf, wonder.

blind, calm, eternal, fair, gentle, glad, holy, noble, purple, shining.

And 50 special words for reading the Bible:

altar, ark, ass, ax, baptism, blessing, captain, cattle, circumcision, deceit, disciple, envy, flesh, forgiveness, generation, herd, heritage, husband, kingdom, leaven, leper, locust, master, neighbor, oath, ox, people, pillar, preaching, prophet, revelation, righteousness, saint, salvation, saviour, scribe, sin, spice, tent, testament, thorn, tribe, virgin, widow, wife, witness, world, worship, wrath, yoke.

1. Opening Note from *The Bible in Basic English*

The form in which the Bible is given here is not simply another
example of the Bible story put into present-day English. The
language used is Basic English.[1]

Basic English, produced by Mr. C. K. Ogden of the Orthological Institute, is a simple form of the English language which,
with 850 words,[2] is able to give the sense of anything which may
be said in English.

Working with the Orthological Institute, a Committee under
the direction of Professor S. H. Hooke, Professor Emeritus of
Old Testament Studies in the University of London, has been
responsible for a new English form of the Bible made from the
Hebrew and the Greek.

In this undertaking, the latest ideas and discoveries in connection with the work of putting the Bible into other languages
were taken into account, and when the Basic form was complete
it was gone over in detail by a Committee formed by the Syndics
of the Cambridge University Press.

The Basic Bible, which in this way was watched over by two
separate groups of experts through its different stages, is designed
to be used wherever the English language has taken root.

Frequently, the narrow limits of the word-list make it hard to
keep the Basic completely parallel with the Hebrew and the
Greek; but great trouble has been taken with every verse and
every line to make certain that there are no errors of sense and
no loose wording. It is only natural that, from time to time, some
of the more delicate shades of sense have not been covered; on
the other hand, it is well to keep in mind that in the Authorised

---

[1] The language of this *Note*.
[2] By the addition of 50 Special Bible words and the use of 100 words listed
as giving most help in the reading of English verse, this number has been
increased to 1000 for the purpose of putting the Bible into Basic.

Version the power and music of the language sometimes take so much of the reader's attention that these more delicate shades are overlooked.

In fact, the Basic expert is forced, because of the limited material with which he is working, to give special care to the sense of the words before him. There is no question of the Basic work taking the place of the Authorised Version or coming into competition with it; but it may be said of this new English Bible that it is in a marked degree straightforward and simple and that these qualities give it an independent value.

2. The Making of the Earth

GENESIS, 1

1. At the first God made the heaven and the earth.

2. And the earth was waste and without form; and it was dark on the face of the deep: and the Spirit of God was moving on the face of the waters.

3. And God said, Let there be light: and there was light.

4. And God, looking on the light, saw that it was good: and God made a division between the light and the dark,

5. Naming the light, Day, and the dark, Night. And there was evening and there was morning, the first day.

6. And God said, Let there be a solid arch stretching over the waters, parting the waters from the waters.

7. And God made the arch for a division between the waters which were under the arch and those which were over it: and it was so.

8. And God gave the arch the name of Heaven. And there was evening and there was morning, the second day.

9. And God said, Let the waters under the heaven come together in one place, and let the dry land be seen: and it was so.

10. And God gave the dry land the name of Earth; and the

waters together in their place were named Seas: and God saw
that it was good.

11. And God said, Let grass come up on the earth, and plants
producing seed, and fruit-trees giving fruit, in which is their
seed, after their sort: and it was so.

12. And grass came up on the earth, and every plant producing
seed of its sort, and every tree producing fruit, in which is its
seed, of its sort: and God saw that it was good.

13. And there was evening and there was morning, the third
day.

14. And God said, Let there be lights in the arch of heaven,
for a division between the day and the night, and let them be
for signs, and for marking the changes of the year, and for days
and for years:

15. And let them be for lights in the arch of heaven to give
light on the earth: and it was so.

16. And God made the two great lights: the greater light to
be the ruler of the day, and the smaller light to be the ruler
of the night: and he made the stars.

17. And God put them in the arch of heaven, to give light on
the earth;

18. To have rule over the day and the night, and for a division
between the light and the dark: and God saw that it was good.

19. And there was evening and there was morning, the fourth
day.

20. And God said, Let the waters be full of living things, and
let birds be in flight over the earth under the arch of heaven.

21. And God made great sea-beasts, and every sort of living
and moving thing with which the waters were full, and every
sort of winged bird: and God saw that it was good.

22. And God gave them his blessing, saying, Be fertile and have
increase, making all the waters of the seas full, and let the birds
be increased in the earth.

23. And there was evening and there was morning, the fifth day.

24. And God said, Let the earth give birth to all sorts of living things, cattle and all things moving on the earth, and beasts of the earth after their sort: and it was so.

25. And God made the beast of the earth after its sort, and the cattle after their sort, and everything moving on the face of the earth after its sort: and God saw that it was good.

26. And God said, Let us make man in our image, like us: and let him have rule over the fish of the sea and over the birds of the air and over the cattle and over all the earth and over every living thing which goes flat on the earth.

27. And God made man in his image, in the image of God he made him: male and female he made them.

28. And God gave them his blessing and said to them, Be fertile and have increase, and make the earth full and be masters of it; be rulers over the fish of the sea and over the birds of the air and over every living thing moving on the earth.

29. And God said, See, I have given you every plant producing seed, on the face of all the earth, and every tree which has fruit producing seed: they will be for your food:

30. And to every beast of the earth and to every bird of the air and every living thing moving on the face of the earth I have given every green plant for food: and it was so.

31. And God saw everything which he had made and it was very good. And there was evening and there was morning, the sixth day.

3. Saul Is Put Down by God

I SAMUEL, 15

1. And Samuel said to Saul, The Lord sent me to put the holy oil on you and to make you king over his people, over Israel: so give ear now to the words of the Lord.

2. The Lord of armies says, I will give punishment to Amalek for what he did to Israel, fighting against him on the way when Israel came out of Egypt.

3. Go now and put Amalek to the sword, putting to the curse all they have, without mercy; put to death every man and woman, every child and baby at the breast, every ox and sheep, every *camel* and ass.

4. And Saul sent for the people and had them numbered in Telaim, two hundred thousand footmen and ten thousand men of Judah.

5. And Saul came to the town of Amalek and took up his position in the valley secretly.

6. And Saul said to the Kenites, Go away, take yourselves out from among the Amalekites, or destruction will overtake you with them: for you were kind to the children of Israel when they came out of Egypt. So the Kenites went away from among the Amalekites.

7. And Saul made an attack on the Amalekites from Havilah on the road to Shur, which is before Egypt.

8. He took Agag, king of the Amalekites, prisoner, and put all the people to the sword without mercy.

9. But Saul and the people did not put Agag to death, and they kept the best of the sheep and the oxen, and the fat beasts and the lambs, and whatever was good, not desiring to put them to the curse; but everything which was bad and of no use they put to the curse.

10. Then the Lord said to Samuel,

11. It is no longer my pleasure for Saul to be king; for he is turned back from going in my ways, and has not done my orders. And Samuel was very sad, crying to the Lord in prayer all night.

12. And early in the morning he got up and went to Saul; and word was given to Samuel that Saul had come to Carmel and put up a pillar, and had gone from there down to Gilgal.

13. And Samuel came to Saul; and Saul said to him, May the

blessing of the Lord be with you: I have done what was ordered by the Lord.

14. And Samuel said, What then is this sound of the crying of sheep and the noise of oxen which comes to my ears?

15. And Saul said, They have taken them from the Amalekites: for the people have kept the best of the sheep and of the oxen as an offering to the Lord your God; all the rest we have given up to destruction.

16. Then Samuel said to Saul, Say no more! Let me give you word of what the Lord has said to me this night. And he said to him, Say on.

17. And Samuel said, Though you may seem little to yourself, are you not head of the tribes of Israel? for the Lord with the holy oil made you king over Israel;

18. And the Lord sent you on a journey and said, Go and put to the curse those sinners, the Amalekites, fighting against them till every one is dead.

19. Why then did you not do the orders of the Lord, but by violently taking their goods did evil in the eyes of the Lord?

20. And Saul said, Truly, I have done the orders of the Lord and have gone the way the Lord sent me; I have taken Agag, the king of Amalek, and have given the Amalekites up to destruction.

21. But the people took some of their goods, sheep and oxen, the chief of the things which were put to the curse, to make an offering of them to the Lord your God in Gilgal.

22. And Samuel said, Has the Lord as much delight in offerings and burned offerings as in the doing of his orders? Truly, to do his pleasure is better than to make offerings, and to give ear to him than the fat of sheep.

23. For to go against his orders is like the sin of those who make use of secret arts, and pride is like giving worship to images. Because you have put away from you the word of the Lord, he has put you from your place as king.

24. And Saul said to Samuel, Great is my sin: for I have gone against the orders of the Lord and against your words: because, fearing the people, I did what they said.

25. So now, let my sin have forgiveness, and go back with me to give worship to the Lord.

26. And Samuel said to Saul, I will not go back with you: for you have put away from you the word of the Lord, and the Lord has put you from your place as king over Israel.

27. And when Samuel was turning round to go away, Saul took the skirt of his robe in his hand, and the cloth came away.

28. And Samuel said to him, The Lord has taken away the kingdom of Israel from you this day by force, and has given it to a neighbor of yours who is better than you.

29. And further, the Glory of Israel will not say what is false, and his purpose may not be changed: for he is not a man, whose purpose may be changed.

30. Then he said, Great is my sin: but still, give me honor now before the heads of my people and before Israel, and come back with me so that I may give worship to the Lord your God.

31. So Samuel went back after Saul, and Saul gave worship to the Lord.

32. Then Samuel said, Make Agag, the king of the Amalekites, come here to me. And Agag came to him shaking with fear. And Agag said, Truly the pain of death is past.

33. And Samuel said, As your sword has made women without children, so now your mother will be without children among women. And Agag was cut up by Samuel, bone from bone, before the Lord in Gilgal.

34. Then Samuel went to Ramah; and Saul went up to his house in Gibeah, in the land of Saul.

35. And Samuel never saw Saul again till the day of his death; but Samuel was sorrowing for Saul: and it was no longer the Lord's pleasure for Saul to be king over Israel.

4. The Testing of Job

JOB, 1

1. There was a man in the land of Uz whose name was Job. He was without sin and upright, fearing God and keeping himself far from evil.

2. And he had seven sons and three daughters.

3. And of cattle he had seven thousand sheep and goats, and three thousand *camels*, and a thousand oxen, and five hundred she-asses, and a very great number of servants. And the man was greater than any of the sons of the east.

4. His sons regularly went to one another's houses, and every one on his day gave a feast: and at these times they sent for their three sisters to take part in their feasts with them.

5. And at the end of their days of feasting, Job sent and made them clean, getting up early in the morning and offering burned offerings for them all. For Job said, It may be that my sons have done wrong and said evil of God in their hearts. And Job did this whenever the feasts came round.

6. And there was a day when the sons of the gods came together before the Lord, and the Satan came with them.

7. And the Lord said to the Satan, Where do you come from? And the Satan said in answer, From wandering this way and that on the earth, and walking about on it.

8. And the Lord said to the Satan, Have you taken note of my servant Job, for there is no one like him on the earth, a man without sin and upright, fearing God and keeping himself far from evil?

9. And the Satan said in answer to the Lord, Is it for nothing that Job is a god-fearing man?

10. Have you yourself not put a wall round him and his house and all he has on every side, blessing the work of his hands, and increasing his cattle in the land?

11. But now, put out your hand against all he has, and he will be cursing you to your face.

12. And the Lord said to the Satan, See, I give all he has into your hands, only do not put a finger on the man himself. And the Satan went out from before the Lord.

13. And there was a day when his sons and daughters were feasting in the house of their oldest brother,

14. And a man came to Job, and said, The oxen were ploughing, and the asses were taking their food by their side:

15. And the men of Sheba came against them and took them away, putting the young men to the sword, and I was the only one who got away safe to give you the news.

16. And this one was still talking when another came, and said, The fire of God came down from heaven, burning up the sheep and the goats and the young men completely, and I was the only one who got away safe to give you the news.

17. And this one was still talking when another came, and said, The Chaldaeans made themselves into three bands, and came down on the camels and took them away, putting the young men to the sword, and I was the only one who got away safe to give you the news.

18. And this one was still talking when another came, and said, Your sons and your daughters were feasting together in their oldest brother's house,

19. When a great wind came rushing from the waste land against the four sides of the house, and it came down on the young men, and they are dead; and I was the only one who got away safe to give you the news.

20. Then Job got up, and after parting his clothing and cutting off his hair, he went down on his face to the earth, and gave worship, and said,

21. With nothing I came out of my mother's body, and with nothing I will go back there; the Lord gave and the Lord has taken away; let the Lord's name be praised.

22. In all this Job did no sin, and did not say that God's acts were foolish.

JOB, 2

1. And there was a day when the sons of the gods came together before the Lord, and the Satan came with them.

2. And the Lord said to the Satan, Where do you come from? And the Satan said in answer, From wandering this way and that on the earth and walking about on it.

3. And the Lord said to the Satan, Have you taken note of my servant Job, for there is no one like him on the earth, a man without sin and upright, fearing God and keeping himself far from evil? And he still keeps his righteousness, though you have been moving me to send destruction on him without cause.

4. And the Satan said in answer to the Lord, Skin for skin, all a man has he will give for his life.

5. But now, if you only put your hand on his bone and his flesh, he will certainly be cursing you to your face.

6. And the Lord said to the Satan, See, he is in your hands, only do not take his life.

7. And the Satan went out from before the Lord and sent on Job an evil disease, covering his skin from his feet to the top of his head.

8. And he took a broken bit of a pot, and, seated in the dust, was rubbing himself with the sharp edge of it.

9. And his wife said to him, Are you still keeping your righteousness? Say a curse against God, and put an end to yourself.

10. And he said to her, You are talking like one of the foolish women. If we take the good God sends us, are we not to take the evil when it comes? In all this Job kept his lips from sin.

11. And Job's three friends had word of all this evil which had come on him. And they came every one from his place, Eliphaz the Temanite, and Bildad the Shuhite, and Zophar the Naamathite. So they came together to a meeting-place, in order that

they might go and make clear to Job their grief for him, and
give him comfort.

12. And lifting up their eyes when they were still far off, it did
not seem that the man they saw was Job because of the change
in him. And they gave way to bitter weeping, with signs of grief,
and put dust on their heads.

13. And they took their seats on the earth by his side for seven
days and seven nights: but no one said a word to him, for they
saw that his pain was very great.

5. The Birth of Christ

MATTHEW, 2

1. Now when the birth of Jesus took place in Bethlehem of
Judea, in the days of Herod the king, there came wise men from
the East to Jerusalem,

2. Saying, Where is he who is King of the Jews by birth? We
have seen his star in the East, and have come to give him worship.

3. And when it came to the ears of Herod the king, he was
troubled, and all Jerusalem with him.

4. And he got together all the chief priests and scribes of the
people, questioning them where the birth-place of the Christ
was to be.

5. And they said to him, In Bethlehem of Judea: because this
is in the writings of the prophet,

6. You, Bethlehem, in the land of Judah are not the least among
the princes of Judah; out of you will come a ruler, who will be
the keeper of my people Israel.

7. Then Herod sent for the wise men privately, and put a question to them about what time the star had been seen.

8. And he sent them to Bethlehem, and said, Go and make
certain where the young child is; and when you have seen him,

let me have news of it, so that I may come and give him worship.

9. And they did as the king said, and went on their way; and the star which they saw in the East went before them, till it came to a stop over the place where the young child was.

10. When they saw the star, they were full of joy.

11. And they came into the house, and saw the young child with Mary his mother, and went down on their faces and gave him worship; and they took from their boxes things of great price, and gave him gold and perfumes.

12. And it was made clear to them by God in a dream that they were not to go back to Herod; so they went into their country by another way.

13. And when they had gone, an angel of the Lord came to Joseph in a dream, saying, Get up, and take the young child and his mother, and go into Egypt, and do not go from there till you get word from me; because Herod will be looking for the young child to put him to death.

14. And he got up, and took the young child and his mother by night, and went into Egypt.

15. And was there till the death of Herod; so that what the Lord said by the prophet might come true, Out of Egypt I have sent for my son.

16. Then Herod, when he saw that he had been tricked by the wise men, was very angry; and he sent out, and put to death all the male children who were in Bethlehem, and in all the parts round about it, from two years old and under, acting on the answers given to him by the wise men.

17. Then that came about which Jeremiah the prophet had said,

18. In Rama there was crying, weeping and great trouble, Rachel weeping for her children, and she would not be comforted, because they are not.

19. But when Herod was dead, an angel of the Lord came in a dream to Joseph in Egypt,

20. Saying, Get up, and take the young child and his mother, and go into the land of Israel: they are now dead who were attempting to take the young child's life.

21. And he got up, and took the young child and his mother and came into the land of Israel.

22. But when it came to his ears that Archelaus was ruling over Judea in the place of his father Herod, he had fear of going there: and being made conscious of the danger by God in a dream, he went out of the way into the country parts of Galilee.

23. And he came and made his living-place in a town named Nazareth; so that what the prophets said might come true, He will be named a Nazarene.

6. Jesus Goes to Jerusalem

MARK, 11

1. And when they came near to Jerusalem, to Beth-phage and Bethany, at the Mountain of Olives, he sent two of his disciples,

2. And said to them, Go into the little town opposite: and when you come to it, you will see a young ass with a cord round his neck, on which no man has ever been seated; let him loose, and come back with him.

3. And if anyone says to you, Why are you doing this? say, The Lord has need of him and will send him back straight away.

4. And they went away and saw a young ass by the door outside in the open street; and they were getting him loose.

5. And some of those who were there said to them, What are you doing, taking the ass?

6. And they said to them the words which Jesus had said; and they let them go.

7. And they took the young ass to Jesus, and put their clothing on him, and he got on his back.

8. And a great number put down their clothing in the way;

and others put down branches which they had taken from the fields.

9. And those who went in front, and those who came after, were crying, Glory: A blessing on him who comes in the name of the Lord:

10. A blessing on the coming kingdom of our father David: Glory in the highest.

11. And he went into Jerusalem into the Temple; and after looking round about on all things, it being now evening, he went out to Bethany with the twelve.

12. And on the day after, when they had come out from Bethany, he was in need of food.

13. And seeing a *fig*-tree in the distance with leaves, he went to see if by chance it had anything on it: and when he came to it, he saw nothing but leaves, for it was not the time for the fruit.

14. And he said to it, Let no man take fruit from you for ever. And his disciples took note of his words.

15. And they came to Jerusalem; and he went into the Temple, and sent out those who were trading there, overturning the tables of the money-changers and the seats of those who were offering doves for money;

16. And he would not let any man take a vessel through the Temple.

17. And he gave them teaching, and said to them, Is it not in the Writings, My house is to be named a house of prayer for all the nations? but you have made it a hole of thieves.

18. And it came to the ears of the chief priests and scribes, and they took thought how they might put him to death; being in fear of him, because all the people were full of wonder at his teaching.

19. And every evening he went out of the town.

20. And when they were going by in the morning, they saw the fig-tree dead from the roots.

21. And Peter, having a memory of it, said to him, Master, see, the tree which was cursed by you is dead.

22. And Jesus, answering, said to them, Have God's faith.

23. Truly I say to you, Whoever says to this mountain, Be taken up and be put into the sea; and has no doubt in his heart, but has faith that what he says will come about, he will have his desire.

24. For this reason I say to you, Whatever you make a request for in prayer, have faith that it has been given to you, and you will have it.

25. And whenever you make a prayer, let there be forgiveness in your hearts, if you have anything against anyone; so that you may have forgiveness for your sins from your Father who is in heaven.

27. And they came again to Jerusalem: and while he was walking in the Temple, there came to him the chief priests and the scribes and those in authority:

28. And they said to him, By what authority do you do these things? or who gave you authority to do these things?

29. And Jesus said to them, I will put to you one question; give me an answer, and I will say by what authority I do these things.

30. The baptism of John, was it from heaven or from men? give me an answer.

31. And they gave thought to it among themselves, saying, If we say, From heaven; he will say, Why then did you not have faith in him?

32. But if we say, From men—they were in fear of the people, because all took John to be truly a prophet.

33. And they said in answer to Jesus, We have no idea. And Jesus said to them, And I will not say to you by what authority I do these things.

PART FOUR

Fiction

The Examples in this division are again taken from Basic books, though *Little Women* has not so far come out. But it has been used because it and *Treasure Island* go well together, being noted and well-loved stories, one American and one English, which the learner of English will have a special interest in reading, and those whose language is English a special interest in seeing in their Basic dress. On the other hand, these two books are as different from one another in material and outlook as they are from the third example, taken from *Arms and the Man*. The three together seem to make up a well-balanced selection from what might be named 'Basic for Pleasure.' *Arms and the Man* was put into Basic some time before Shaw's death, and was seen and given approval by Shaw himself before it was printed.

1. From *Little Women* by Louisa May Alcott

THE DANCE

"Jo! Jo! Where are you?" came Meg's cry from the foot of the narrow steps going up to the top floor of the house.

"Here!" said a voice from overhead, sounding strangely thick, and running up, Meg saw her sister with an apple in her hand and a warm coat round her, crying over a book on an old three-legged seat under the window. This little room right under the roof was where Jo went most frequently to be by herself; and here her happiest hours went by, with six or seven apples, a good book, and the company of a rat living there, which by this time was used to her and had no fear of her at all. When Meg came in, Scrabble went quickly into his hole, and Jo, brushing the drops from her eyes, put down her book, waiting for the news.

"Only see! A note from Mrs. Gardiner for tomorrow night!" said Meg, waving a bit of paper in the air, and then reading out loud in a pleased voice: "Mrs. Gardiner would be happy to see Miss March and Miss Josephine at a little dance on New Year's *Eve*.[1] Marmee says we may go. Now what dresses are we going in?"

"What's the good of saying that when we've only got one dress which will do?" said Jo with her mouth full.

"If only I had a silk one!" said Meg, sadly. "Mother says possibly I may have one when I'm eighteen, but two years is such a long time off."

"The ones we have are almost like silk, and they're good enough for us. Yours is as good as new, but there's the burn and the hole in mine. Whatever am I to do? The burn is very bad and nothing will take it out."

"You'll have to keep seated as much as possible, so that your back's not seen. The front is all right. I'll have a new silk band for my hair, and Marmee will let me have her little silver pin; and my new dancing-shoes are beautiful, and my gloves will do, though they aren't as good as they might be."

"Mine got marked by some fruit-drink or something, and I'll not be able to get any new ones, so I'll have to go without," said Jo, who was never much troubled about her dress.

"You'll *have* to have gloves, or I won't go," said Meg with decision. "Gloves are the most important thing. No one ever goes dancing without them."

[1] The 'Eve' of any day is the day before it. "New Year's Eve" is the day before "New Year's Day"—the first day of the New Year.

"Then I'll be an onlooker. Company dancing isn't my idea of amusement anyhow. It's so stiff and slow. Give me something with a bit of a spring in it."

"It would be wrong to let Mother get you new ones. They're so dear, and you don't take any care of them. She said when they were damaged that she wouldn't get you any more this winter. Is there nothing to be done with them?" said Meg, looking troubled.

"I might be able to keep them all crushed up in my hand, so that nobody sees the marks, that's all. No! I have a better idea. This is what we'll do. You put on one good glove and keep the other in your hand and I'll do the same—don't you see?"

"Your hands are wider than mine and my glove will be badly stretched," said Meg, whose gloves were specially important to her.

"Then I'll go without. It's nothing to me what anyone says." And Jo took up her book.

"Oh you may have the glove, you may! Only don't get any marks on it and do be on your best behavior. Don't put your hands together at your back, or keep looking fixedly at the same person, or say 'Christopher Columbus!' will you?"

"Don't get worked-up about me! I'll be as polished as a plate and not do anything wrong—that is to say, I'll do my best. Now go and get your note answered and let me get on with this story."

So Meg went off to say how pleased they would be to go, and to get her dress ready, while Jo got through her story and her four apples, and had a good time playing with Scrabble.

On New Year's Eve there was no one in the living-room because the two younger girls were waiting on their sisters, who had no time now for anything but the important business of 'dressing for the dance.' Though their dresses were very simple, this process was the cause of much running up and down, laughing, and talking, and at one point of a strong smell of burning in every part of the house. This last came from the fact that

Meg had a great desire to have the hair round her face waved, and Jo had undertaken to do this with some heated irons.

"Is it all right for there to be quite so much smoke?" said Beth from her seat on the bed.

"What a strange smell! It's like burning feathers," said Amy, touching *her* soft waves with a little air of being pleased with herself and them.

"There! Now I'll take off the papers and you'll see a cloud of beautiful waving hair," said Jo, putting down the irons.

She did take off the papers, but no cloud of beautiful waves came into view, because the hair came with the papers, and the shocked hairdresser put down a line of little black twists on the dressing-table in front of her unhappy sister.

"Oh, oh, oh! What *have* you done? It's all gone wrong. I won't be able to go! My hair! Oh my hair!" and Meg, crying bitterly, gave one long look in the glass at the burned ends of hair round her face.

"Oh dear! Oh dear! If only you'd never made the suggestion! Whatever I do goes wrong, every time! The irons were over-heated, that's the trouble," said poor Jo, crying in her turn over the little black rolls.

"It's not hard to put right," said Amy, comforting them. "You have only to put your band on so that the ends are turned under, Meg, and your hair will be quite like the way they are doing it now. I've seen numbers of girls with it like that."

"If anyone is responsible, it's me, for attempting to be beautiful," said Meg. "If I had had any sense I'd have gone with it as it was, without touching it."

"If only you had! It was so smooth and soft. But it will be quite all right again before very long," said Beth, taking her turn at comforting, and she gave Meg a kiss.

After one or two other, smaller troubles, Meg was dressed at last, and, by the hard work of all the family, Jo's hair was got up and her dress on. They made a very pleasing picture in their simple dresses. Meg was in silver-gray, ornamented with some delicate white open-work and her mother's silver pin, and had a blue band round her hair. Jo was in red-brown, with a stiff linen collar, almost like a man's, and a white flower or two for her only ornament. They put on one clean new glove, and took the other up in one hand, and everybody said that the general effect was 'quite natural and pleasing.' Meg's shoes had high *heels* [2] and were very tight, and they were giving her some pain, though she would not say so; and Jo's nineteen hairpins all seemed to be going straight into her head, which was not her idea of comfort. But let us be beautiful for once at any price!

"Have a good time, dears," said Mrs. March, watching the two sisters stepping delicately down the front garden. "If the meal is late, don't take very much, and come away at eleven, when I send Hannah for you." And as they were going through the garden door, her voice came again from one of the windows: "Girls, girls! Have you got clean pocket-*handkerchiefs*,[3] the two of you?"

"Yes, yes, beautifully clean, and Meg has some *Cologne* [4] on hers," Jo made answer, and they went on, Jo saying with a laugh, "Marmee would be crying that question after us if we were all running out of a burning house."

"It is one of the marks of her good taste, and quite right. The most important parts of a lady's dress are her shoes, gloves, and handkerchief," said Meg, who had quite a number of these little ideas about what was good taste and what was not.

"Now, you *will* do your best to keep the burn on your dress from being seen, won't you, Jo? Is my band all right? And does my hair seem *very* bad?" said Meg, turning from the glass in Mrs. Gardiner's dressing-room after a long, hard look.

"It's certain to go right out of my head later. If you see me

[2] *heel:* The part of a shoe placed under, and acting as a support for, the back of the foot.
[3] *handkerchief:* Square of linen and so on, kept in pocket for blowing nose on and such uses. (Made clear earlier in the book.)
[4] *Cologne:* A sweet-smelling liquid made in Cologne.

doing anything wrong, make a face at me, will you?" said Jo,
giving her collar a little pull, and her hair a quick brush.

"No, I won't. That would be very bad behavior. I'll give you
a look if anything is wrong, and a smile if you are all right.
Now, keep your back straight, and take short steps; and don't
give your hand to anyone when meeting them for the first time;
it isn't the right thing to do."

"How *do* you get your knowledge about all these little details? I never have any. Isn't that music bright?"

Down they went, feeling a little self-conscious, because they
did not go out very frequently, and even this small dance was
an event to them. Mrs. Gardiner, who was old and had the air
of a great lady, said something kind to them and then put them
in the care of the oldest of her six daughters. Meg was one of
Sallie's friends, and so before long was talking quite naturally
and happily. But Jo, who didn't take much interest in other girls
and their doings, kept where she was with her back against the
wall, feeling as much out of place as a young horse in a flower-
garden. Five or six light-hearted boys were talking about *skates* [5]
in another part of the room, and she had an impulse to go over
to them, because skating was one of her greatest pleasures. She
sent a questioning look to Meg, looking first at the boys and
then giving signs of joining them, but her sister's face was so
shocked that she made no move from where she was. Nobody
came up to say anything to her, and one by one the group near
her went away, till she was by herself. It was impossible for her
to go walking about, because of the burn in her dress; so she
kept her place, looking on at everybody a little sadly, till the
dancing was started. Meg was in request straight away, and
the tight shoes seemed so quick and carefree that nobody had
any idea of the pain their smiling owner was feeling. Jo saw a
tall young man with red hair coming in her direction, and, fearing that he was coming to make a request for a dance, took

[5] *skates:* Steel blades fixed under shoes for moving smoothly over level ice.
Using skates for this purpose is named 'skating.'

the chance of slipping into a little curtained space near-by, so that she would be able to go on watching in peace. But another self-conscious person with the same idea had come across this small secret place before her, and, turning from pulling the curtains across after her, Jo came face to face with 'the Laurence boy.'

2. From *Arms and the Man* by George Bernard Shaw

ACT I

Night: A Woman's bedroom in Bulgaria, in a small town near the Dragoman Pass, late in November in the year 1885. *Through an open window with a little railed walk outside, a mountain-top in the Balkan range, strangely white and beautiful in the starlight and snow, seems quite near at hand, though it is in fact miles away. The inside of the room is not like anything to be seen in the West of Europe. It is half good Bulgarian, half cheap Viennese. Over the head of the bed, which is placed against a little wall cutting off an angle of the room, is a painted wood structure, blue and gold, with a white Christ, and a light in front of it in a metal ball with a hole through it hanging by three chains. The chief seat, placed near the other side of the room and opposite the window, is a long Turkish one. The outer cover and the curtains of the bed, the window curtains, the little floor covering, and the bits of material used for ornamenting the room are of the East and very beautiful: the paper on the walls is of the West and poor in design. The washing-place, against the wall on the side nearest the long seat and the window, is made up of a painted iron basin with a bucket under it in a painted metal frame, and one linen cloth on the rail at the side. The dressing-table between the bed and the window is a common wood table, covered with a cloth worked in a number of different colors, and on it is a very good looking-glass. The door is on the side nearest the bed: and there is a chest-of-drawers between. The chest-of-drawers, like the dressing-table, is covered by a brightly-colored cloth of Bulgarian design; and on it there are some paper-backed books of fiction, a box of soft* chocolates, and in a frame resting on a support like those used for painter's canvases, a camera-picture of some size of a very good-looking man in military dress. Even in the picture he has an important air, and one is conscious of the attraction of his eyes. There is a wax-light on the chest-of-drawers, and another on the dressing-table with a box of matches by the side of it.

The window is made like a door and is wide open. Outside, two wood shutters may be seen open. On the railed walk a young woman, very conscious of the strangely beautiful quality of the night, and of the fact that, being young and beautiful, she is part of it, is looking at the snow-topped Balkans. She is in her nightdress, well covered by a long loose coat of skins which is, at the very least, about three times the value of the things in her room.

Her thoughts are broken into by her mother, Catherine Petkoff, a woman over forty, of great force and authority, with beautiful black hair and eyes, who seems as if she might be married to a mountain farmer, but is doing everything in her power to be like a Viennese of good birth, and for that purpose goes about in a tea dress of the latest design.

CATHERINE [coming in quickly, full of good news]: Raina! [She says 'Rah-eena,' with the weight on the 'ee']. Raina! [She goes to the bed, in the belief that Raina is there]. Why, where—? [Raina is now looking into the room]. My dear girl! Are you out in the night air, and still not in bed? You'll get such a cold. Louka said you were sleeping.

RAINA [her thoughts far away]: I sent her away. I had a desire to be by myself. The stars are so beautiful! What's wrong?

CATHERINE: Such news! There has been a fight.

RAINA [her eyes wide open]: Ah! [She comes quickly to Catherine].

CATHERINE: A great fight at Slivnitza! We overcame the Serbians! And it was all because of Sergius.

RAINA [with a cry of pleasure]: Ah! [Running into her mother's open arms] Oh, mother! [Then, with sudden fear] Is father safe?

CATHERINE: Naturally; he sends me the news. Sergius is the great man of the hour, a second Napoleon in the eyes of his men.

RAINA: Go on, go on. How was it? [*Overcome by her feelings*] Oh, mother, mother, mother! [*Pulling her mother onto the long seat; they give one another a rain of kisses*].

CATHERINE [*more and more moved by her story*]: You have no idea what a fight it was. An attack by the horsemen! What a thought! He went against the authority of our Russian generals [1]—did it without orders—made himself responsible for the attack—heading it himself—was the first man to go through their guns. Don't you see it all, Raina: our good Bulgarians with their blades and eyes flaming, thundering down like a mass of snow over a mountain slope and driving the poor Serbs and their Austrian chiefs in every direction like leaves in a wind. And you! You kept Sergius waiting a year before you would take his ring. Oh, if you have a drop of Bulgarian blood in your body, you will go down on your knees to him when he comes back.

RAINA: What attention will he give to my poor little love after he has had an army of strong men at his feet? But that's not important: I am happy—so uplifted at the thought of him! [*She gets up, walking about very much moved*]. It makes it clear that all our ideas were right after all.

CATHERINE [*angrily*]: Our ideas right! What are you talking about?

RAINA: Our ideas of what Sergius would do. Our love of country. Our high purpose. Sometimes I had a fear that they might be simply thoughts without substance. Oh, what false-hearted little things girls are! When I put on Sergius's blade he seemed so great, so good; I was not true to my love for him when I had the thought that he might not come up to our hopes, or that he might make us seem foolish or do the wrong thing.

[1] Some of the names marking a man's position in the army are used in this play. The highest of those named is a *field-marshal*, after which come, in order of authority, *general, major-general, colonel, major, captain*.

But—but—[*suddenly seating herself again*] Give me your word you'll never say anything to him about this.

CATHERINE: I'll not give my word till I am certain what I'm undertaking.

RAINA: Well, it came into my head while I was in his arms and he was looking into my eyes, that possibly we only had these high ideas because we are so given to reading Byron and Pushkin, and because we were so taken out of ourselves by the opera that winter at Bucharest. Common existence is not generally like that!—in fact, it had never been, so far as my experience went then. [*With regret*] How foolish I was, mother—to have doubts about him: I was not certain if all his great qualities and his military knowledge might not go up in smoke when he went into his first fight. I had a troubling fear that he might seem a little cheap there by the side of all those expert Russians.

CATHERINE: Seem cheap! Shame on you! The Serbs have Austrians over them who are quite as expert as our Russians: but even so we have got the best of them in every fight.

RAINA [*laughing and resting happily against her mother*]: Yes. I was a feeble-hearted little thing to let myself be overcome by the fears of common sense. Oh, to have the knowledge that it was all true—that Sergius is every inch as good and great as he seems—that the earth is truly a beautiful place for women who have eyes to see it and men who are able to make it so! How happy I am! What a flowering of all my hopes! Ah!

At this point Louka comes in. She is a good-looking girl, in the dress of a Bulgarian country woman, with an overskirt and a cloth round her head. She has a good opinion of herself, and has such an air of questioning all authority that though her behavior to Raina is that of a servant there is little respect in it. She has some fear of Catherine, but even with her goes as far as possible.

LOUKA: Please, madam, all the windows are to be shut, and the shutters fixed. They say there may be firing in the streets. [*Raina and Catherine get up together in fear*]. The Serbs are being sent back through the Dragoman Pass; and they say they may come into the town. Our horsemen will be after them; and you may be certain our men will be ready for them now they are running away. [*She goes out on the railed walk, pulling the outside shutters together: then comes back into the room*].

CATHERINE [*businesslike, her housekeeping impulses awake*]: I will have to see that everything is made safe in the lower part of the house.

RAINA: Why are our countrymen so cruel? How is one any better off for putting unhappy runaways to death?

CATHERINE: Cruel! When they would be ready to put you to death—or worse?

RAINA [*to Louka*]: Let me have the shutters open a little, and I will get them shut if any noise comes to my ears.

CATHERINE [*in a voice of authority, turning on her way to the door*]: No, no, dear: you are to keep them shut. You would be certain to go off to sleep with them open. Put them together, Louka.

LOUKA: Yes, madam. [*She gets them shut*].

RAINA: Have no fear about me. The minute the sound of a gun comes to my ears, I will put out the lights and get the bed things rolled round me with my ears well covered.

CATHERINE: Quite the wisest thing to do, my love. Good night.

RAINA: Good night. [*Her feeling comes back for a minute*]. Keep me in your thoughts [*They give one another a kiss*]. This is the happiest night of my existence—if only there are no runaways.

CATHERINE: Go to bed, dear; and don't give them a thought. [*She goes out*].

LOUKA [*secretly to Raina*]: If you would be happier with the shutters open, give them a push like this [*she gives them a push: they come open: she puts them together again*]. One of them is generally fixed at the base; but the pin has gone.

RAINA [*with authority, protesting*]: It is very good of you,

Louka; but we have to do what we are ordered. [*Louka makes a face*] Good night.

LOUKA [*untroubled*]: Good night. [*She goes out, looking very pleased with herself*].

Raina, now by herself, takes off her coat and puts it on the long seat. Then she goes to the chest-of-drawers, stopping before the picture with feelings which she is unable to put into words. She does not give it a kiss, or put it against her heart, or make any sign of physical love; but she takes it in her hands, lifting it up, as if moved to some act of religion.

RAINA [*looking up at the picture*]: Oh, I will never be less than you have made me in your thoughts, ruler of my heart— never, never, never. [*She puts it back again with great respect. Then she takes a work of fiction from the books on the table. After turning the leaves over with a far away look on her face, she comes to her page, at which she puts the book down inside out; then, with a happy little cry, she gets into bed, and is all ready for reading herself to sleep. But before giving herself up to fiction, she takes a look up aagin, her mind full of the beautiful present, and says in a low voice*] My Sergius! my great Sergius!

The quiet of the night outside is broken by a gun in the distance. She gives a jump, all attention; then come two more sounds, much nearer, putting such fear into her that she gets quickly out of bed, and puts out the light on the chest-of-drawers. Then, with her fingers in her ears, she goes running to the dressing-table, puts out the light there, and goes quickly back to bed in the dark, nothing being seen but the feeble light in the ball hanging in front of the Christ, and the starlight through the cracks in the shutters. The firing is starting again: there is a sudden burst of it quite near at hand. While the sound is still in the air, the shutters go from view, pulled open from outside, and for a minute the square of white starlight is suddenly seen with the form of a man outlined in black upon

*it. The shutters are pulled together straightaway and the room
is dark again. But the quiet is now broken by the sound of
quick, hard breathing. Then there is a small noise; and the
flame of a match is seen in the middle of the room.*

RAINA [*making herself as small as possible on the bed*]: Who's
there? [*The match is out in a second*]. Who's there? Who is
that?

A MAN'S VOICE [*in the dark, quietly, but with a note of danger
in it*]: Sh—sh! don't make a noise; or you'll be fired at. Be good;
and you'll be quite safe. [*There is a sound of her getting out of
bed, and going to the door*]. Take care: it's no use attempting to
get away.

RAINA: But who—.

THE VOICE [*with a note of danger*]: Now then; if you make a
noise, my gun will go off. [*With authority*] Get a light and let me
see you. Is that clear? [*It is quiet and dark for another minute
while she goes back to the dressing-table. Then she puts a match
to a wax-light, and all becomes clear. He is a man of about
35 in a shocking condition, covered with wet earth and blood
and snow, the leather band round his body and that of his
gun-cover keeping together the bits of the blue coat of a Serbian gunner. All which the light and his unwashed, dirty condition make it possible to see is that he is not very tall and not
specially interesting-looking, that he has a strong neck and back;
a round, thick-looking head, covered with short, stiff brown
waving hair, clear quick blue eyes, good mouth and front part
of head, an impossibly common-sense nose like that of a strong-
minded baby, a military walk and quick way of talking, and has
all his senses about him, though he is in such a tight place; even
seeing the humor of it, without, however, the least suggestion
that he is not being serious or is giving away a chance. He gets
a rough idea of what Raina is like from one look at her: how old
she is, her position in society, her general qualities, and the
degree of her fear—and goes on, less roughly, but still with great
decision*] It is with great regret that I put you in this position;

but you see what my dress is—Serb! If I am taken I will be put to death. [*Darkly*] Is that clear to you?

RAINA: Yes.

THE MAN: Well, I'm not going to be put to death if I have anything to do with it. [*Even more darkly*] Is that clear to you? [*Quickly but quietly he gets the door locked*].

RAINA [*A note of disgust in her voice*]: There's no doubt about that. [*Pulling herself up very straight, and looking him in the face, she says slowly and in a cutting voice*] It is true that some military men have a fear of death.

THE MAN [*with unsmiling good-humor*]: All of them, dear madam, all of them, take my word for it. It is our business to go on living as long as we are able. Now, if you make a noise—

RAINA [*cutting him short*]: You will let off your gun at me. Why are you so certain that *I* have a fear of death?

THE MAN [*with design*]: Ah, but if I don't let off my gun, what will be the outcome? A number of your horsemen will come bursting into this beautiful room of yours and put me to death here like a pig; because I'll put up a hard fight: they're not going to get me into the street for their amusement: I've seen what they are. Are you ready for that sort of company in your present undressed condition? [*Raina, suddenly conscious of her nightdress, has an impulse of shame, and puts it more tightly about her neck. Watching her, he says, unkindly*]: Not quite, eh? [*She goes in the direction of the long seat. He puts his gun up in a second, and says loudly*] Stop! [*She comes to a stop*] Where are you going?

RAINA [*quietly, with self-control*]: Only to get my coat.

THE MAN [*going quickly to the seat and suddenly taking the coat*]: A good idea! No; I'll keep the coat; and you will take care that nobody comes in and sees you without it. This is a better instrument than the gun. [*He puts the gun down on the seat*].

RAINA [*disgusted*]: It is not the instrument which a self-respecting man would make use of!

THE MAN: It's good enough for a man who has only you between him and death. [*While they are looking at one another for a minute, Raina feeling shocked that even a Serbian is able to be so coldly self-interested as this and to have so little respect for women, a sharp outburst of firing in the street gives them a sudden sense of danger. The cold feeling of death near at hand makes the man's voice quiet while he says*] Have you got that straight? If you are going to let those dogs in on me they will see you as you are.

A great noise. The military in the street give violent blows on the door of the house, crying out "Get the door open! Get the door open! Get up, will you!" *A man servant's voice says to them angrily from inside* "This is Major Petkoff's house: you mayn't come in here"; *but after another outburst of noise, and rain of blows on the door, he lets down a chain with a sharp sound, after which loud footsteps quickly come nearer and there are further cries, but these sounds are overcome at last by the voice of Catherine saying angrily to the man who is in authority,* "What is this, sir? Have you any idea where you are?" *The noise suddenly comes to an end.*

LOUKA [*outside, giving blows on the bedroom door*]: Madam! madam! Come quickly and get the door open. If you don't it will be broken down.

The runaway puts up his head with the motion of a man who sees that there is no hope for him, dropping the behavior he has been putting on to keep Raina in fear of him.

THE MAN [*kindly and with true feeling*]: No use, dear: there is no hope for me. [*Sending the coat across to her*] Quick! put it round you: they're coming.

RAINA: Oh, how good of you. [*She puts it round her, feeling very much happier*].

THE MAN [*between his teeth*]: Not at all.

RAINA [*troubled*]: What will you do?

THE MAN [*unsmilingly*]: The first man in will get my answer. Don't come near; and keep your head turned away. It will not take long; but it will not be delicate. [*He takes out his blade, turning to the door and waiting*].

RAINA [*acting on impulse*]: I'll give you help. I'll keep you safe.

THE MAN: There is nothing to be done.

RAINA: There is. I'll put you out of view. [*Pulling him in the direction of the window*] Here! At the back of the curtains.

THE MAN [*giving way to her*]: There's half a chance if you keep your head.

RAINA [*pulling the curtain in front of him*]: S—sh! [*She goes in the direction of the long seat*].

THE MAN [*putting out his head*]: Keep this in mind—

RAINA [*running back to him*]: Yes?

THE MAN:—nine military men out of ten have no brains.

RAINA: Oh! [*pulling the curtain in front of him angrily*].

THE MAN [*looking out at the other side*]: If they see me, I give you my word there'll be a fight: a great fight.

She gives a stamp with her foot. He goes from view quickly. She takes off her coat and puts it across the foot of the bed. Then, with a tired, troubled air, she gets the door open. Louka comes in, very full of something.

LOUKA: One of those pigs of Serbs has been seen getting up the water-pipe to your window. Our men have come after him; and they are the worse for drink, and so angry and violent. [*She goes in the direction of the other side of the room to get as far from the door as possible*]. Madam says you are to get dressed this minute, and to— [*She sees the gun on the long seat, and comes to a stop, cold with fear*].

RAINA [*as if angry at being troubled*]: They will not come in here. Why have they been let in?

CATHERINE [*coming in quickly*]: Raina, dearest: are you safe? Have you seen anyone? Has any sound come to your ears?

RAINA: Only the firing. The military will not come in here, will they?

CATHERINE: By a happy chance there is a Russian among
them: he is a friend of Sergius. [*Talking through the door to
someone outside*] Sir: will you come in now. My daughter will
see you.

*A young Russian, in Bulgarian military dress, comes in, blade
in hand.*

THE RUSSIAN [*with a soft cat-like air and stiff military walk*]:
Your servant, dear madam. It is with regret that I come into
your room like this; but there is a Serb who has got onto the
walk outside your window. Will you and madam your mother
please go out while we have a look?

RAINA [*with bad humor*]: How foolish, sir: you may see for
yourself that there is no one outside. [*She gets the shutters wide
open, keeping her back to the curtain, where the man is, and
pointing to the railed walk in the moon-light. Two guns are fired
from under the window: and the glass opposite Raina is broken
to bits. Raina, taking a quick breath and shutting her eyes, keeps
where she is, while Catherine gives a cry, and the Russian with
a loud 'Take care' goes quickly outside the window*].

THE RUSSIAN [*outside the window, crying angrily down to the
street*]: No more firing down there, you fatheads: no more firing
I say. [*He is seen angrily looking down for a minute; then turning to Raina, he makes an attempt to put on his polished air
again*]. Would it be possible for anyone to have got in without
your knowledge? Were you sleeping?

RAINA: No, I have not been in bed.

THE RUSSIAN [*bad-humoredly, coming back into the room*]:
The persons living round here have their heads so full of runaway Serbs that they see them everywhere. [*With respect*] Dear
madam: a thousand regrets. Good night. [*Sets his head bent low
as a sign of respect, in a stiff military way, and Raina coldly does
the same. He does the same to Catherine, who goes out after him*].

*Raina gets the shutters fixed. Turning, she sees Louka, who has
been watching it all with interest.*

RAINA: Keep by my mother, Louka, till the military go away.

Louka gives a look at Raina, at the long seat, at the curtain; then, screwing up her lips as if she had a secret and laughing openly, she goes out. Raina, very angry at this behavior goes to the door, shutting it after her with a loud noise, and locking it violently. The man quickly comes out from the back of the curtain, pushing his blade back in its cover, then putting the danger from his mind in a businesslike way, he comes over to Raina.

THE MAN: A narrow chance; but all is well. Dear madam: your servant to the death. My one regret now, in your interests, is that I did not go into the Bulgarian army in place of the other one. I am not a Serb by birth.

RAINA [*stiffly*]: No: you are one of the Austrians who gave support to the Serbs in the hope that they would put an end to our existence as a free nation, and are controlling their army for them. They are hated here.

THE MAN: Austrian! Not I. You've no reason for hating me, dear young woman. I am a Swiss, fighting only for a living. I went in with the Serbs because they came first on the road from Switzerland. Be kind: you have completely got the better of us.

RAINA: Have I not been kind?

THE MAN: More than kind! Without a thought of self! But I am still not safe. This present wave of fighting will be quickly over; but they will be after the runaways all night on and off. I will have to take my chance to get away when it's quiet for a little. [*Smiling at her*] You will not be troubled by my waiting a minute or two, will you?

RAINA [*putting on her smoothest society air*]: Oh, not at all. Do take a seat.

THE MAN: With pleasure. [*Seating himself at the foot of the bed*].

Raina goes to the long seat, walking self-consciously, and takes a seat. Unhappily, it is on the gun, and she gets up with a loud cry. The man, all nerves, gets to his feet with a jump which takes him to the other side of the room.

THE MAN [*angrily*]: Don't give me a shock like that. What is it?

RAINA: Your gun! It was looking that Russian in the face all the time. What a near thing!

THE MAN [*disgusted at his unnecessary fear*]: Oh, is that all?

RAINA [*looking at him without very much respect while forming a poorer and poorer opinion of him, and so feeling more and more herself in his company*]: I had no desire to give you any cause for fear. [*She takes up the gun, and gives it to him*]. Please take it to keep yourself safe from me.

THE MAN [*smiling in a tired way at these cutting words while he takes the gun*]: No use, dear madam, there's nothing in it. [*He makes a face at it, and puts it into its cover with an air of having a poor opinion of it*].

RAINA: You will quickly be able to put that right.

THE MAN: I haven't anything to put in it. What use is gunpowder in a fight? I make it a rule to take chocolate with me in place of it; and I came to the end of the last cake of that hours back.

RAINA [*shocked in her highest ideas of men*]: Chocolate! Do you have your pockets full of sweets—like a schoolboy—even when you are fighting?

THE MAN [*smiling*]: Yes: isn't it shocking? [*With feeling*] I'd give anything to have some now.

RAINA: Let me give you some. [*She goes to the chest-of-drawers with a look of disgust, and comes back with the box of sweets in her hand*]. Unhappily I have taken all but these. [*She puts the box before him*].

THE MAN [*his mouth watering*]: You're a dear! [*He puts the sweets quickly into his mouth*]. Soft ones! How good they are! [*He takes a good look, hoping there may be some more. There aren't any: he is only able to put his fingers round the box to get the last taste. When that is at an end he makes the best of it, and with sad good humor he says with feeling*] What a sweet girl you are! You may quickly see if a man has been in the army a long time by what he takes with him to the wars. The young ones take guns and gunpowder with them; the old ones, food. That was good of you. [*He gives back the box. She takes it from him quickly, hating him for what he has said, and gives it a push away. He gives another jump, as if she had been going to give him a blow*]. Ugh! Don't do things so suddenly, dear madam. It's unkind to give me this punishment for causing you a minute's fear a little earlier.

RAINA [*her nose in the air*]: Fear, did you say? Though I am only a woman, sir, I am certain that at heart I have as little fear of danger as you.

THE MAN: I would say so. You haven't been under fire for three days as I have. I am able to put up with two days without being much the worse for it; but no man is the same after three days: I'm all nerves, like a bird when the cat is after it. [*He takes a seat, and puts his head on his hands*] Would it give you any pleasure to see me crying?

RAINA [*shocked*]: No.

THE MAN: If it would, all you have to do is to get angry with me as if I was a little boy, and you were taking care of me. If I was under canvas now, they would be playing all sorts of tricks on me.

RAINA [*a little moved*]: Poor thing! I'll not be angry with you. [*Touched by the kind note in her voice, he puts up his head and gives her a happier look: she takes a step back quickly and says stiffly*] I had no thought of giving you pain. Our fighters are not like that. [*She goes away from the seat*].

THE MAN: Oh yes, they are. There are only two sorts of men in the army: Old ones and young ones. I have been at it fourteen years: half of your men haven't ever been in a fight before. Why, how is it that you have got the better of us? By having no idea at all of the art of war, simply that. [*Angrily*] I have never seen so little knowledge of the rules.

RAINA [*cuttingly*]: Oh! was that why they overcame you?

THE MAN: Well, come! Is it right to send a force of horsemen against a machine-gun position, when it is certain that if the guns go off not a horse or man will ever get nearer than fifty yards? I simply had no belief in my eyes when I saw it.

RAINA [*quickly turning to him, all her interest and all her hopes coming suddenly back to her*]. Did you see the great attack by the horsemen? Oh, give me an account of it. What was it like?

THE MAN: You have never seen an attack by horsemen, have you?

RAINA: What chance would I have had?

THE MAN: Ah, possibly not. No: naturally not! Well, it's a strange thing to see. It's like sending a hand-full of small stones against a window: first one comes, then two or three at the back of him; and then all the rest in a mass.

RAINA [*her eyes getting round, gripping her hands together and lifting them while she is talking*]: Yes, first One!—the greatest and best of them!

THE MAN [*quite unmoved*]: Hm! you have only to see the poor thing pulling at his horse.

RAINA: Why does he do that?

THE MAN [*angry at such a foolish question*]: Because it's running away with him, naturally: is it probable that the man has a desire to get there before the others and be put to death? Then they all come. It is clear which are the young ones by their violent behavior and the way they are waving their blades about. The old ones come all together in the safest possible position: they are conscious that they are simply being used in place of lead, and that it's no use attempting to put up a fight. The wounds are chiefly broken knees, from the horses getting pushed together.

RAINA: Ugh! But it doesn't seem to me that the first man has any fear. He is a great man!

THE MAN [*good-humoredly*]: That's what you would have said if you had seen the first man in the attack to-day.

RAINA [*out of breath, overlooking everything*]: Ah, I was certain of it. Give me an account of him.

THE MAN: He did it like an opera-actor—a very good-looking young man, with bright eyes and beautiful black hair on his lip, giving his war-cry and coming down on us like a Don Quixote. How we were laughing!

RAINA: What? You made sport of him!

THE MAN: Yes; but when the Sergeant came running up as white as death, and said we had been sent the wrong things, and that we would be unable to let off a machine-gun for ten minutes, we were laughing at the other side of our mouths. That was the worst experience I've ever had; though I have been in one or two tight places. And I hadn't even lead for my gun; only chocolate. We'd no other arms at all: nothing. Naturally, we were simply cut to bits. And there was Don Quixote waving his blade like a chief bandsman, quite certain that it was all his doing, though he might well have been turned out of the army for his behavior. Of all the foolish men ever let loose in a fight, that man is certainly the most feather-brained. He and his men were going straight to their death—but the gun didn't go off: that's all.

RAINA [deeply wounded, but still true to her high ideas]: So that's your opinion! If you saw him again, would you be able to say who he was?

THE MAN: His face is printed in my memory!

She again goes to the chest-of-drawers. He keeps his eyes on her half hoping that she may have some more food for him. She takes the picture down and goes back to him with it.

RAINA: That is a picture of the man—a great lover of his country and a great fighter—to whom I am going to be married.

THE MAN [seeing who it is with a shock]: Truly, I had no idea I was paining you. [Looking at her] Was it quite right to make me go on? [He takes another look at the picture]. Yes; that's Don Quixote. Not a doubt of it. [He keeps back a laugh].

RAINA [quickly]: Why are you laughing?

THE MAN [shamed, but still with a feeling of great amusement]: I wasn't laughing. At least, I had no desire to. But when I see him in my mind's eye acting the part of Don Quixote and quite certain he was doing the greatest thing— [*He is bursting with amusement*].

RAINA [*in a hard voice*]: Give me back the picture, sir.

THE MAN [*with true regret*]: Why, certainly. It was shocking of me. [*He gives her the picture. She slowly gives it a kiss, looking him straight in the face before going to the chest-of-drawers to put it back. He goes after her, still regretting his behavior*]. I may be quite wrong, you see: no doubt I am. Most probably he had got news of our condition somehow, and did it in the knowledge that it was safe.

RAINA: That is to say, he was not what he seemed, and was in fact in fear of danger! You had not the face to say that before.

THE MAN [*with the motion of one who gives up hope*]: It's no use, dear madam: I am unable to make you see it from the expert's point of view. [*While he is turning away to go back to the seat, the sound of gun-firing in the distance gives the suggestion of further trouble*].

RAINA [*in a hard voice, when she sees he is troubled by the firing*]: So much the better for you!

THE MAN [*turning*]: How?

RAINA: You are fighting against my country; and you are in my hands. What would I do if war was my trade?

THE MAN: Ah, true, dear madam; you're right every time. I am conscious how good you have been to me: to my last hour I will keep the memory of those three soft chocolates. It was a most unmilitary thing to do: but it was very, very sweet.

RAINA [*coldly*]: It is kind of you to say so. And now I will do a military thing. It is not possible for me to keep you here after what you have this minute said about the man to whom I am going to be married; but I will go outside the window and see if it is safe for you to get down into the street. [*She goes in the direction of the window*].

THE MAN [*his face changing*]: Down that waterpipe! Stop! One minute! It's impossible! I'm not strong enough! The very thought of it makes my head go round and round. I came up it quickly enough with death at the back of me. But to do it now, when there's nothing to make me—! [*Slowly taking a seat*]. It's no use; I give up; you have got the better of me! Let them take me. [*He puts his head down on his hands, at the end of everything*].

RAINA [*moved by his unhappy condition*]: Come: don't give up hope. [*She is acting to him almost like a mother: he gives his head a shake*]. Oh, you are a very poor fighter—you're only made of chocolate! Come, take heart. That journey is more readily faced than the danger of being made a prisoner: keep that in mind.

THE MAN [*softly, comforted by her voice*]: No; if they took me it would only be death; and death is sleep—oh, sleep, sleep, sleep, untroubled sleep! Getting down the pipe would be doing something—using my muscles—taking thought! Death ten times before that.

RAINA [*softly and with surprise, hearing the tired rhythm in his voice*]: Are you as much in need of sleep as that?

THE MAN: All the time I have been with this army I've not had two hours unbroken sleep. I haven't had my eyes shut for forty-eight hours.

RAINA [*at a loss*]: But what am I to do with you?

THE MAN [*getting up uncertainly, moved by her trouble of mind*]: Naturally, I will have to do something. [*He gives himself a shake; gets control of himself; and says with new force and a new air of facing danger*] You see, sleep or no sleep, desire for food or not, tired or not tired, you are able to do anything at any time if you are certain it has to be done. Well, I have to get down that pipe: [*he gives himself a blow on the chest*] is that clear to you, you man of chocolate? [*He gives a turn in the direction of the window*].

RAINA [*troubled*]: But if you have a fall?

THE MAN: I will go to sleep as if the stones were a feather bed. Good night. [*He goes with an air of decision in the direction of the window; and his hand is on the shutter when there is a loud burst of firing in the street under the window*].

RAINA [*running to him*]: Stop! [*She takes him by the arm

violently, pulling him quite round]. They'll put you to death.

THE MAN [*quietly, but with attention*]: Don't be troubled: this sort of thing is all in my day's work. I have to take my chance. [*With decision*] Now do what I say. Put out the light; so that they will not see it when I get the shutters open. And keep away from the window, whatever you do. If they see me, they are certain to let off a gun at me.

RAINA [*hanging on to him*]: They are certain to see you; it's bright moonlight. I'll keep you safe—oh, how is it possible for you to have so little feeling! Have you no desire to be kept safe?

THE MAN: It would be a shame to give you any more trouble. [*She gives him a shake in her desire to do something*]. I am not without feeling, dear young woman. But how is it to be done?

RAINA: Come away from the window. [*She takes him back to the middle of the room by force. The minute she takes her hands off him he goes automatically in the direction of the window again. She takes him by the arm again, and turning him back, says*] Please! [*She lets him go, and says kindly, but with authority*] Now give attention. You've got to put yourself in our hands. You have still no idea in whose house you are. I am a Petkoff.

THE MAN: A what?

RAINA [*somewhat angrily*]: I am saying that I am of the family of the Petkoff's, the most well-off and the most noted family in our country.

THE MAN: Oh, yes, I see. Do not be angry with me. The Petkoffs, naturally. How foolish of me!

RAINA: It is clear you had no knowledge of their existence till this minute. Why go to the trouble of acting as if you had?

THE MAN: Don't be angry with me: I am so tired that I am unable to give thought to anything; and what you said had so little connection with what had gone before that I was at a loss. Don't be angry with me.

RAINA: Oh, yes. I might have you crying in front of me. [*He makes a motion of agreement, quite seriously. She makes a little face at him, then puts on the same voice again*]. I may say that my father has the highest position of any Bulgarian in our army. He is [*very self-important*] a Major.

THE MAN [*seeming to be much surprised*]: A Major! I say, he is an important man!

RAINA: You made it clear that you had no idea who we were by acting as if it was necessary to get up the drain pipe to the railed walk, because ours is the only private house which has two lines of windows. There are steps inside to get up and down by.

THE MAN: Steps! I say! You are certainly living in great comfort, dear madam.

RAINA: Have you any idea what a library is?

THE MAN: A library? A room full of books?

RAINA: Yes. We have one, the only one in Bulgaria.

THE MAN: A library! It would give me great pleasure to see that.

RAINA [*putting on airs*]: I am saying these things to make it clear to you that you are not in the house of foolish country persons who would put you to death the minute they saw your Serbian dress, but among persons of education. We go to Bucharest every year for the opera; and I have been a complete month in Vienna.

THE MAN: I saw that, dear madam. I saw very quickly, that you were a person of wide experience.

RAINA: Have you ever seen the opera of Ernani?

THE MAN: Is that the one with Satan in it in red silk, and massed military voices?

RAINA [*making clear that she has a very poor opinion of him*]: No!

THE MAN [*very tired but keeping back the signs of it*]: Then I have not seen it.

RAINA: I had an idea you might have kept in mind the part where Ernani, with his attackers after him like you tonight, went into the house of a man by whom he was hated, an old Castilian of high birth. The Castilian will not give him up. The man under his roof is safe.

THE MAN [*quickly, becoming a little more awake*]: Have your father and mother got that idea?

RAINA [*very self-important*]: That idea, as you say, is not strange to my mother and me. And if, in place of pointing your gun at me as you did, you had simply come to us as a runaway, putting yourself in our hands, you would have been as safe as in your father's house.

THE MAN: Quite certain?

RAINA [*turning her back on him in disgust*]: Oh, it is no use attempting to make you see.

THE MAN: Don't be angry; you see what a tight place I would be in if there was any error. My father keeps open house: he has six hotels; but I wouldn't take that sort of chance with him. What about your father?

RAINA: He is away at Slivnitza fighting for his country. I make myself responsible for you. There is my hand on it. Will that make you happier? [*She puts out her hand to him*].

THE MAN [*looking in doubt at his hand*]: Better not take my hand, dear madam. I will have to have a wash first.

RAINA [*pleased*]: That is very touching of you. I see that you are a man of good family.

THE MAN [*in doubt*]: Eh?

RAINA: Don't get the idea that I am surprised. Bulgarians of good education—persons in our position—give their hands a wash almost every day. You see your delicate feelings are not wasted on me. You may take my hand. [*She puts it out again*].

THE MAN [*kissing it with his hands at the back of him*]: It is very good of you, dear madam: I have the feeling that I am safe at last. And now will you take the news to your mother? I had better not be here secretly longer than is necessary.

RAINA: If you will be so good as to keep quite quiet while I am away.

THE MAN: Certainly. [*He takes a seat*].

Raina goes to the bed and puts the coat round her. His eyes are shut. She goes to the door. Turning for a last look at him, she sees that he is going off to sleep.

RAINA [*at the door*]: You are not going to sleep, are you? [*He says something in a low voice: she goes quickly to him and gives him a shake*]. Are you giving attention? Get up: you are going to sleep.

THE MAN: What? Going to sl—? Oh no: not in the least: I was only going over things in my mind. It's all right: I'm quite awake.

RAINA [*sharply*]: Will you please keep on your feet while I am away. [*He gets up in a protesting sort of way*]. All the time, see?

THE MAN [*his balance very uncertain*]: Certainly—certainly: you may be quite happy about me.

Raina gives him a doubting look. He gives a feeble smile. She goes slowly, turning again at the door, almost in time to see his head dropping forward. She goes out.

THE MAN [*only half awake*]: Sleep, sleep, sleep, sleep, slee— [*The words come to an end in a low sound. He comes awake again with a shock, almost falling over*]. Where am I? That's what I've got to be clear about: where am I? Have to keep awake. Nothing keeps me awake but danger—keep that in mind —[*with interest*] danger, danger, danger, dan— [*going off again; another shock*] Where's danger? Have to see where it is. [*He goes uncertainly round the room looking for it*]. What am I looking for? Sleep, danger, no idea. [*He comes up against the bed*]. Ah, yes; now I've got it. All right now. I'm to go to bed, but not to sleep—be certain not to go to sleep—because of danger. Not to get inside it, only to take a seat on it. [*He takes a seat on the bed. A happy look comes into his face*]. Ah! [*With a happy sound he gets on to his back, lifting his boots onto the bed with the last bit of force he has, and goes to sleep straight away*].

Catherine comes in with Raina after her.

RAINA [*looking at the long seat*]: He's gone! He was here when
I went out.

CATHERINE: Here? Then without doubt he got down from
the—

RAINA [*seeing him*]: Oh! [*She makes a sign with her finger*].

CATHERINE [*shocked*]: Well! [*She goes quickly to the bed.
Raina comes after her and goes to the opposite side*]. He is in a
deep sleep. The pig!

RAINA [*hoping to make her keep quiet*]: Sh!

CATHERINE [*shaking him*]: Sir! [*Shaking him again, harder*].
Sir! [*Violently, shaking very hard*]: Sir!!

RAINA [*gripping her arm*]: Don't, mother: the poor dear is tired
out. Let him go on sleeping.

CATHERINE [*letting him go, and turning in great surprise to
Raina*]: The poor dear! Raina!!! [*She gives her daughter a cold
look*].

The man goes on sleeping deeply.

The start of our example from *Treasure Island* comes more than one third of the way through the story. By this time a number of non-Basic words have been made clear (in the same way as 'pine' and 'oar' are made clear in this part) and are being freely used. For any reader without a knowledge of full English we give here the senses of those used in the example, in the order in which they come in.

spy-glass	metal instrument through which things at a great distance away are seen more clearly and as if nearer
boom	rod of wood keeping the base of a sail stretched out
rudder	flat structure going down into the water at the back end of a ship or boat, which is turned from side to side for guiding it
treasure	store of gold, silver, jewels, money, and so on
anchorage	place where a ship may let down her anchor and keep at rest
skeleton	the dry bones of a dead man or animal
wheel	the wheel-like structure which is turned by hand for turning the rudder
anchor	great iron hook let down to sea-bed on a chain to keep a ship at rest
captain	man in authority over a ship
cabin	a room in a ship
rock	great mass of stone
doctor	medical man
wig	false hair for covering the head, a special form of which, made white with powder, was in general use among men in the days of the story
aboard	on(to) or in(to) a ship
deck	wood floor over all or part of one level of a ship
crutch	support put under arm and used in place of a leg when it has been damaged or taken off
squire	chief landowner in a country place
pistol	small firearm used with one hand
hill	small mountain
bow	the front end of a ship or boat
shipmates	men working together (for example in a ship) are one another's 'mates.' 'Mate' is frequently used by sailors and so on in the sense of 'friend'
pirate	outlaw of the sea, attacking ships transporting treasure

3. From *Treasure Island* by Robert Louis Stevenson

XIII

THE START OF MY LAND EXPERIENCES

The look of the island when I came on deck in the morning was completely changed. Though there was now no wind at all, we had got on well in the night, and were now stopped about half a mile to the south-east of the low land on the east side of the island. A great part of the island was covered by gray-colored woods. This unchanging color was, however, broken by long narrow stretches of yellow sand in the lower land, and by a great number of tall trees of the pine [1] family over-topping the others—some by themselves, some in groups; but the general color was sad, and the same everywhere. The hills were wooded only on their lower slopes. Higher up they came out as tall pointed structures of uncovered stone. All were strangely formed, and 'the Spy-glass,' which was by three or four hundred feet the tallest on the island, was the strangest in form as well, going up straight to a point on almost every side, and then suddenly cut off at the top like a table.

The 'Hispaniola' was rolling deeply in the lift and fall of the sea. The booms were pulling at the cords, the rudder was jumping from side to side, and every part of the ship was giving out troubled sounds, and shaking like a building full of machines.

[1] *pine:* sorts of evergreen tree with needle-like leaves in groups of two or more, much valued for wood.

I had to keep a tight grip on the cords, and the earth went turning round and round before my eyes; for, though I was a good enough sailor when we were moving, this stopping and letting ourselves be rolled about like a bottle was a thing I was never able to put up with without my stomach turning over, specially in the morning before a meal.

Possibly this was the reason—possibly it was the look of the island with its gray, sad woods and strange stone points, and the line of white water thundering onto the sharply sloping land— at any rate, though the sun was bright and warm, and the birds were fishing and crying all round us, and I had naturally been looking forward to getting to land after being so long at sea, my heart went down, as the saying is, into my boots; and from my first view of it I was unhappy at the very thought of Treasure Island.

We had a very uninteresting morning's work before us, for there was no sign of any wind, and the long boats had to be got out and manned, and the ship pulled three or four miles round the curve of the island, and up the narrow way to the anchorage at the back of Skeleton Island. I made an offer to go in one of the boats, where I had no business to be. The heat was overpowering, and the men were protesting violently at their work. Anderson was in control of my boat, and in place of keeping the hands in order, he was protesting as loudly as the worst.

"Well," he said, using bad language, "it's not for ever."

This was to me a very bad sign; for, till that day, the men had done their work quickly and readily; but their first look at the island had made them harder to keep under control.

All the way in, Long John was by the man at the wheel giving him directions for getting the ship into the anchorage. He had a very detailed knowledge of the narrow way in; and though the man with the measuring chains got deeper water everywhere than was marked on the map, John was never uncertain.

"There's a strong pull when the water goes out," he said, "and this way through has been hollowed out, one might say, as if with a spade."

We came to a stop in the very same place where the anchor was marked on the map, about a third of a mile from the two islands, Treasure Island on one side, and Skeleton Island on the other. The sea-bed was clean sand. The noise of our anchor dropping into the sea sent up clouds of birds circling and crying over the woods, but in less than a minute they were down again, and all was quiet as before.

The place was completely shut in, with woods all round, the trees coming down to high-water mark, the land at the sea-edge flat for the most part, and the hill-tops seen at a distance in a rough half-circle, one here, one there. Two little rivers, or, more truly, two stretches of wet land, sent their water down into this basin of sea, as you might say; and the leaves round that part of the island had a sort of unhealthily bright look. From the ship nothing was to be seen of the house or the stockade,[2] for they were deep among the trees; and but for the map in the Captain's cabin, we might have taken ourselves for the first who had ever been there from the time when the island came up out of the sea.

There was not a breath of air moving, and no sound but that of the waves half a mile away boiling onto the land and against the rocks outside. A strange smell was hanging over the anchorage—a smell of death, of dead leaves and long-dead trees gone soft on the wet earth. I saw the Doctor smelling at the air like someone tasting a bad egg.

"I'm not certain about treasure," he said, "but you may have my wig if there isn't disease here."

If the behavior of the men had given cause for fear in the boat, it gave very much more when they had come aboard. They were stretched about on the deck talking together in low, angry voices. The smallest order was taken with a black look,

---

[2] *stockade:* wall of upright sticks fixed very near together in earth, for keeping off attack and so on.

and done slowly and without care. Even the true men seemed to have got into the same humor, for there was not one hand aboard to give a good example to another. The danger of their taking up arms against us, it was clear, was hanging over us like a thundercloud.

And it was not only we of the cabin group who saw the danger. Long John was working hard, going from group to group, doing everything in his power to keep them in order by talk and argument, and, as for a good example, he was the best possible. He was readier than ever to do things, and full of respect; he was all smiles to everyone. If an order was given, John was on his crutch in a second, with the best-humored "Ay, ay, sir!" on earth; and when there was nothing further to do, he kept up one song after another, as if in an attempt at covering up the bad humor of the rest.

Of all the troubling things on that troubling day, the fact that Long John himself was clearly in fear of an outburst seemed to be the worst.

We had a meeting in the cabin.

"Sir," said the Captain, "if I give another order, all the ship will come at us, at a run. It'll not do to take the chance. You see, sir, here it is. I get a rough answer, do I not? Well, if I give one back, there will be a fight in less than no time; if I don't, Silver will see there's some reason for my not doing so, and that will be the end of us. Now, there's only one man in a position to be of any help to us."

"And who is that?" said the Squire.

"Silver, sir," was the Captain's answer; "he has as great a desire as you and I to keep it from coming to an open fight. There have been some angry words between them; he will quickly get them to see reason if he has the chance, and my suggestion is to give him the chance. Let's give the men half a day off to go on land. If they all go, we'll keep the ship against them all. If not one of them goes, well, then we'll keep the cabin, and may God be on the side of the right. If some go, take note of my words, sir, Silver will make them come aboard again as quiet as sheep."

That was the decision we came to; pistols were made ready and given out to all the men of whose support we were certain; Hunter, Joyce, and Redruth were let into the secret, and they took the news with less surprise and better heart than we had been ready for; and then the Captain went on deck to give his talk to the men.

"My boys," said he, "it has been like an oven today, and we're all tired and not feeling very pleased with things. A walk on land will do everyone good. The boats are still in the water; you may take the two long ones, and whoever has the desire may go on land for the rest of the day. A gun will be fired half an hour before sundown."

It's my belief the thickheads had the idea that they'd be falling over treasure the minute they put a foot on land; for straight away they came out of their bad humor, with a 'Hurrah' which was given back by a far-away hill, and sent the birds up into the air again, circling and crying round the anchorage.

The Captain had the sense to get out of the way. He quickly went off the deck, letting Silver see to getting the landing group ready; and in my opinion it was a good thing that he did so. If he had been there, it would have been impossible for him any longer to seem to be unconscious of the true position. It was as clear as day. Silver was the captain, and having hard work to keep his authority. The hands who were straight—and it was not long before it was clear that there were some such men aboard —were, it seemed, very slow in the uptake. Or it may be truer to say that all hands were to some degree turned against us by the example of the chief trouble-makers, but some more, some less; and one or two, being straight men for the most part, were not letting themselves be pulled or pushed any farther. It is one thing to do as little as possible, and that with black looks, and quite another to take a ship by force and put to death a number of men who have done no wrong.

At last, however, the group was complete. Six hands were to keep to the ship, and the other thirteen, with Silver, went to get into the boats.

Then it was that there came into my head the first of the unreasoning impulses which in the end did so much to keep us from death. If Silver was keeping six men on the ship, it was clear that our group would not be able to take control of it and keep the others off; but as there were only six of them, it was equally clear that the cabin group had no present need of my help. I straight away had the idea of going on land. In a second I had got quietly over the side, and made myself small in the forward part of the nearest boat, and almost at the same time she was pushed off.

No one gave any attention to me, only the man at the front oar [3] said, "Is that you, Jim? Keep your head down." But Silver, from the other boat, gave a sharp look over, crying out to see if it was me; and from that minute I wasn't very happy about what I had done.

The men had a competition to see who would get to land first; but the boat I was in, starting a little before the other, and being at the same time of less weight and better manned, got far in front, and the bow was among the trees on the water's edge, and I, gripping a branch, had got myself out and into the nearest undergrowth, while Silver and the rest were still a hundred yards off.

"Jim, Jim!" came his cry.

But naturally I gave no attention, and with bent body I went jumping and pushing my way through, running straight before my nose, till I was unable to go on running any longer.

[3] *oar:* long-bladed instrument of wood pulled by hand against support on side of boat and forcing it through water.

XIV

THE FIRST BLOW

I was so happy at having got away from Long John, that I let myself take some pleasure in the walk, looking about me with interest at the strange land I was in.

I had gone across a very wet part full of water-side trees, tall water-loving grasses, and strange, unnatural-looking plants; and I had now come out on the edge of an open stretch of waving, sand-covered country about a mile long, with one or two pines, and a great number of low, twisted trees, not unlike the oak[4] in form, but with light-colored leaves like water-side trees. On the far side of the open space was one of the hills, with two strange-looking tops formed of masses of rock, bright in the sun.

Now for the first time I became conscious of the pleasure of discovery. There was no one living on the island; my shipmates were far away; and before me the only living things were animals and birds. I went this way and that among the trees. Here and there were flowering plants which I had never seen before; here and there I saw snakes, and one, lifting its head from a narrow shelf of rock, made a strange noise at me. I had no idea till later that his bite was poisoned, and that I had been very near death at that minute.

Then I came to a long mass of these oak-like trees—evergreen oaks they were named, as came to my knowledge later—stretching low over the sand like blackberry plants, the barnches strangely twisted, the leaves forming a solid mass, like a roof. This growth went down from the top of one of the sand-hills, becoming wider and taller as it went, till it came to the edge of the wide, green stretch of low, wet land, through which the

[4] *oak:* great tree, common in England, valued for wood.

nearest of the little rivers went, as through a sponge, to the anchorage. The wet land was steaming in the strong sun, and the outline of the Spy-glass was dancing up and down through the heat mist.

Suddenly there came the sound of something moving among the tall grasses; a bird went into the air with a cry, another came after, and in almost no time, over all the wet land, a great cloud of birds was hanging, crying and circling in the air. I was straight away certain that some of my shipmates were coming near, on the edge of the wet waste. And I was not wrong; for not long after there came to my ears from a distance the low sound of a man's voice, which by degrees got louder and nearer.

This put me in great fear, and I went on my hands and knees under the cover of the nearest evergreen oak, and, seated there, with legs pulled up and back bent, I kept as quiet as possible, waiting for more sounds.

Another voice gave an answer; and then the first voice, which it was now clear was Silver's, again took up the story, and went on for a long time, stopping only when the other man put in an infrequent word. By the sound, they seemed to be talking very seriously, and almost angrily; but no word came clearly to my hearing.

At last the two men seemed to have come to a stop, and possibly to have taken a seat, for not only did they not come any nearer, but the birds themselves became more quiet, and went back again to their places.

And now the thought came to me that I was not doing my work; that, as I had done such a foolish thing as to come on land with these pirates, it was my business to make some use of it by at least overhearing their discussions; and that I clearly had to get as near to them as possible, under the helping cover of the twisted trees.

I was able to get a good idea of the direction of the men, not only from the sound of their voices, but from the behavior of the one or two birds which were still hanging about in fear over the heads of the unlooked-for company.

Making my way on my hands and knees, I went without stopping, but slowly, in this direction; till at last, lifting my head to an opening among the leaves, I was able to see straight down into a little green hollow near the wet land, thickly circled with trees, where Long John Silver and another of the ship's company were talking face to face.

The sun was coming down strongly on them. Silver's hat was near him on the grass, and his great, smooth, white face, all wet with the heat, was lifted to the other man's as if to a friend for help.

"Mate," he was saying, "it's because I've got such a high opinion of you, valuing you like gold dust—gold dust, and that's a fact! If I wasn't a friend to you from the first, would I be here giving you news of your danger? All's over—you've no power to do anything about it; it's to keep you yourself from death that I'm talking, and if it came to the ears of one of the bad ones, where would I be, Tom—now, in your opinion, where would I be?"

"Silver," said the other man—and I saw that he was not only red in the face, but talking from a dry throat, in a voice shaking like a tight cord—"Silver," says he, "you're old, and you're straight, or has the name for being so; and moreover you've money, which a number of poor sailors hasn't; and you're a good one in danger, if I'm not wrong. And will you say that you'll let yourself be pushed into this by that sort of low-down cut-throat? Not you! As certain as God sees me, I'd let my hand be cut off before I'd do it. If I'm false to——"

And then suddenly he was stopped by a noise. Before me was one of our supporters—well, here, at the very same minute, I had news of another. From far away out in the wet land there came, suddenly, a sound like an angry cry, then another on top of it; and then one shocking, very long, sharp cry of pain. The rocks of the Spy-glass gave back the sound time after time; all the birds were in the air again, with a great noise of wings, making the sky dark; and long after everything was at peace again, the warm quiet broken only by the sound of the birds as they came back to rest and the low *boom* of the sea in the distance, that cry of death was still sounding in my head.

Tom had given a jump at the sound, like a horse at a sharp touch of the whip; but Silver had not made the smallest move. He kept his place, resting quietly on his crutch, watching Tom like a snake about to make an attack.

"John!" said the sailor, stretching out his hand.

"Hands off!" was Silver's cry, jumping back a yard, as it seemed to me, as quick and certain as an expert trained to do tricks with his body.

"Hands off, if you say so, John Silver," said the other. "It's the knowledge that you've done wrong which puts you in fear of me. But, for the love of God, what was that?"

"That?" said Silver, smiling all the time, but more than ever on the watch, his eye nothing more than a pin-point in his great face, but bright as a bit of glass. "That? Oh, that was Alan, very probably."

At this poor Tom made answer like a man.

"Alan!" he said. "Then may God take care of him, for he's a true seaman! And as for you, John Silver, long you've been a mate o' mine, but you're mate o' mine no longer. If I'm to be put to death like a dog, I'll go to my death doing what's right. You've put an end to Alan have you? Do the same to me, if you're able. But you'll not make me give up."

And with that, this great-hearted man, turning his back to the cook without another word, went walking off in the direction of the sea. But he did not go far. With a cry, John took a grip of the branch of a tree, got the crutch quickly under his arm, and sent it with great force through the air after him.

It went straight into the middle of poor Tom's back, point first, giving him a violent blow. Up went his hands, he made a sound like letting out a long breath, then went flat on his face.

It was impossible to say if he was wounded much or little. Most probably, judging from the sound of the blow, his back was broken straight away. But he had no time given him to come round. Silver, quick as a monkey, even without leg or crutch, was on top of him in no time, and twice had sent the blade of his knife as deep as possible into that quiet body. In my secret place I was in hearing of his loud breathing when he gave the blows.

I'm not certain if I became truly unconscious, but what I am certain is that for a short time everything before me went swimming away from me in a circling mist; Silver and the birds, and the tall Spy-glass hill-top, going round and round and upside down before my eyes, and all sorts of bells sounding and far-away voices crying loudly in my ears.

When I came to my senses again, the unnatural devil had got himself in order, his crutch under his arm, his hat on his head. There in front of him was Tom, stretched unmoving on the grass; but the man who had put him to death took no note of him at all, turning his attention to cleaning the blood from his knife with a bit of grass. All the other things were unchanged, the sun still coming down cruelly on the steaming wet land and the tall point of the mountain, and it was almost outside my power of belief that a man had in fact been put to death, a man's existence cruelly cut short, only a minute earlier, before my eyes.

But now John put his hand into his pocket, took out a whistle, and sent out one or two notes with it, which went sounding far across the heated air. What this was a sign for was, naturally, not clear to me; but straight away my fears were awake. More men would be coming. I might be seen. They had by now put to death two of our supporters; after Tom and Alan, might it not be my turn?

Straight away I made a start at getting myself out and going back again on my hands and knees, as quickly and quietly as possible, to the more open part of the wood. While I was doing so, there were cries coming and going between the old pirate and his friends, and this sound of danger gave me wings. When I had got clear of the undergrowth, I went running off at a greater rate than ever before, almost not caring about the direction of my flight, so long as it took me away from those men of death; and as I went, my fear became greater and greater till I was almost off my head.

In fact, was it possible for anyone to be in a worse position than I? When the gun was fired, how was I to get myself to go down to the boats among those devils, whose hands were still red with blood? Would not the first of them who saw me give my neck a twist like a bird's? Would not the very fact of my not being there be a clear sign of my fear of them, and so of my knowledge of their crimes? It was all over for me, I said to myself. I would never again see the 'Hispaniola'; or the Squire, or the Doctor, or the Captain. There was nothing for me but death from being without food, or death by the hands of the pirates.

All this time, as I say, I was still running, and, without being conscious of the fact, I had come near to the foot of the hill with the two points, and had got into a part of the island where the evergreen oaks came up more thinly, and seemed more like normal trees in their growth and size. Mixed with these were pines here and there, some fifty, some nearer seventy feet high. The air, moreover, had a more healthy smell than down near the wet land.

And here a new shock made me come to a stop with a hammering heart.

Basic English Books

(A SELECTION)

From The Basic English Publishing Company, London

GENERAL

Basic English. A general account of the system, its history, and its purposes.

Basic English Versus the Artificial Languages.

Basic for Science. With the special word-list for general science and those for certain branches.

Basic for Geology. With a special word-list.

Basic for Economics. With a special word-list.

Basic English and Grammatical Reform. A discussion of the place of Basic English in general education.

'The Basic News," No. 10.

TEACHING BOOKS AND MATERIALS

The Basic Teacher. A full and detailed work chiefly for older European learners—and see *Phonograph Records* (2), further down in this part of the list. (May be had, in addition, in German and Italian.)

Basic Step by Step. A simple teaching-book giving the 850 words in 30 groups, with reading-material, notes, and pictures. (May be had, in addition, in Dutch, French, German, Italian, and Spanish.)

The ABC of Basic English. Gives an account of the structure of the language in an ordered way. (May be had, in addition, in Dutch, French, German, Italian, and Spanish.)

501

502 BASIC ENGLISH BOOKS

The Basic Words: a detailed account of their uses. All the different ways in which the 850 words may be used in Basic English made clear by very short examples and by French and German words. (Latest printing, 1964.)

Basic by Examples. One representative statement or question for every use, inside the limits of the system, of every one of the 850 words.

Basic Picture Talks. Pictures, with questions and answers about them, designed to make clear some representative expansions of sense—for schoolroom use.

Basic by Isotype. Isotype teaching-pictures for international use.

Everyday Basic. A wide range of everyday examples.

Word-Stress and Sentence-Stress. A guide for teachers of Basic English, together with a discussion from the point of view of "phonetics" (the science of language sounds).

Phonograph records. (1) A two-sided record giving a talk about the sounds and a reading of the Basic words by J. C. Catford; and (2) A two-sided record of readings from *The Basic Teacher.*

Wall Pictures. (1) Words of Direction and Position; (2) Operations; (3) Acts; (4) Country; (5) By the Sea; and (6)—two Pictures—Present, Past and Future.

The "Basic Way" Reading Cards. 45 cards for use with *"The Basic Way to English,* Book 1. See under *From Other Book Companies,* further down the list.

FOR THE YOUNG

Black Beauty, A. Sewell. With pictures.

Gulliver in Lilliput, Jonathan Swift. With pictures.

Jackanapes, Juliana Horatia Ewing.

Keäwe's Bottle ("The Bottle Imp"), R. L. Stevenson.

Pinocchio, C. Collodi. With pictures.

Robinson Crusoe, Daniel Defoe.

Stories for the Young, Leo Tolstoi.

Stories from France, Perrault.

Stories from Hans Andersen.

("Our Changing Times" books)

Across the Isthmus of Panama.	*Schoolboys of Early Times*
All About Motion Pictures.	(I and II).
Electric Power at Work.	*Ships of Yesterday.*
Fireside Stories.	*The Thunder Bird.*
The First Virginians.	*To Far Cathay.*
Great Discoveries.	*Traders of Santa Fe.*
How Men Have Kept Their	*The White Man Comes to*
Records.	*New York.*
Late Night Special.	*Wings Away.*
The Post Bag.	*Wires Round the Earth.*
The Potter's Wheel.	

FOR OLDER READERS

Arms and the Man, Bernard Shaw.

A Basic Astronomy, S. L. Salzedo.

The Basic St. John. This book of *The Bible* put into Basic English by the Rev. Edwin W. Smith.

Between the Lines, Old Greek Stories in New Dress, W. Repton.

Carl and Anna, Leonhard Frank.

The Chemical History of a Candle, Michael Faraday.

Death in High Society, Inez Holden. Short Stories.

Electricity and Magnetism, H. S. Hatfield.

European Science, H. S. Hatfield.

The Gold Insect ("The Gold Bug"), Edgar Allan Poe.

International Picture Language, Otto Neurath. An account of the Isotype system.

Japanese Stories, Lafcadio Hearn.

Julius Caesar, William Shakespeare. With Basic parallel and notes by A. P. Rossiter.

Mr. Midshipman Easy, Captain Marryat.

The Outlook of Science, J. B. S. Haldane.

The Potter's Art, W. Repton.

Science and Well-Being, J. B. S. Haldane.

The Three Signs, Hawthorne, Irving, and Poe. Three short stories.

The Time Machine, H. G. Wells.

The Two Friends, Ivan Tourgenieff.

Uncle Silas, J. Sheridan LeFanu.

From Other Book Companies

The Bible in Basic English (Cambridge University Press).

The New Testament in Basic English (Cambridge University Press).

The General Basic English Dictionary. Giving the sense in Basic English of over 20,000 English words (Evans Brothers Limited).

The Science Dictionary in Basic English. Giving the sense of over 25,000 words and word-groups taken from all branches of science. First put out in 1965, this work is an addition to the list of books in print at C. K. Ogden's death (Evans Brothers Limited). (Published in the United States under the title *The Basic Science Dictionary* by The Macmillan Company, New York, 1966.)

The Basic Way to English, Books 1–4, in ordered stages, with pictures, and separate Teachers' Books 1–4 (Evans Brothers Limited).

The Basic Way Reading Books, 1 and 2 (Evans Brothers Limited).

From Basic to Wider English, Books 1–6. Latest printing, with new pictures and other changes, 1968 (Evans Brothers Limited).

A Christmas Story ("A Christmas Carol"), Charles Dickens (Evans Brothers Limited).

The Roots of Science, J. A. Lauwerys (Evans Brothers Limited).

The Sea and Its Living Things, H. S. Hatfield (Evans Brothers Limited).

Stories from the Odyssey (Evans Brothers Limited).

Treasure Island, R. L. Stevenson (Evans Brothers Limited).

The Water-Babies, Charles Kingsley (Evans Brothers Limited).

A list giving the current prices of the books in print will be posted to anyone who sends a request for it, together with stamped posting directions on it, to:

Orthological Institute, c/o Evans Bros. Ltd.,
Montague House, Russell Square, London, W.C.1.

Index to the Basic Words

This word-list is a guide to the 850 words as they are put before the learner in *Basic English* (Section One of this book) and *The ABC of Basic English* (Section Two, Part 1 of this book). It might seem that, as we have in *The Basic Words* (Section Two, Part 2) a complete handbook of the words, giving in short form all directions for their senses, forms, behavior, and special uses, there would be little need for such a list. But it is in *The ABC*, and to a less degree in *Basic English,* that the separate words are talked about in relation to the system and to one another, and that light is given on the facts which are simply noted in *The Basic Words.* It will frequently be of help to take a look back at what has been said about a word in the detailed accounts of the system.

The most important of the complex words (see pages 156–58) are here listed in their places. A great number of others may be seen in *The Basic Words.* For the international words, see pages 35–36 and 235–36, and for a selection of onomatopoeic words, page 37, and page 151.

a (an), 19, 20, 23, 63, 128, 129, 150
able, 131, 209, 223, 231; *ably,* 147
about, 140, 201, 214, 219
account, 215, 223
acid, 190
across, 141, 214, 215
act, 125, 177, 180, 203; *-or,* 177, 230; *-ing,* 220, 230
addition, 152, 187, 209, 220, 232
adjustment, 152
advertisement, 187

after, 140, 141, 161, 201, 219, 229
again, 147, 229
against, 141, 195, 224
agreement, 152, 214
air, 125, 180, 208
all, 129, 205, 219, 220, 222, 228, 229
almost, 147, 164
am, see *be.*
among, 140, 141, 202
amount, 126, 204
amusement, 152, 187

his, 170, 172; *she*, 149, 170,
171; *her*, 170, 172; *hers*, 170;
it, 149, 170, 171–72, 173; *its*,
170, 172; *they*, 149, 170, 171,
172; *them*, 170, 172; *their*, 170,
172; *theirs*, 170
head, 124, 127, 181, 183, 202,
219, 231
healthy, 131; *healthily*, 147
hearing, 206, 207, 229
heart, 162, 183, 216
heat, 177, 180; -*ing*, 231; -*ed*, 231
help, 127, 180, 192
her, hers, see *he*
herself, 158
here, 134, 147, 194, 220
high, 130, 131, 148; -*er*, 227
him, see *he*
himself, 158, 216, 231
history, 152, 197, 205
hole, 127, 173
hollow, 131, 132, 190
hook, 124, 181
hope, 126, 180, 194, 206
horn, 144, 188
horse, 124, 127, 143
hospital, 124, 163
hour, 125
house, 124, 127, 181, 214, 230;
houses, 128; *housing*, 231
how, 161, 166
however, 159
humor, 152, 180, 190, 195

I, 149, 170, 171, 172, 173; *me*,
170; *my*, 170; *mine*, 170; *we*,
149, 170, 171, 173; *us*, 170,
172; *our*, 170, 172; *ours*, 170
ice, 125, 180
idea, 153, 227

if, 160, 161, 162, 219, 232
ill, 131, 208
important, 131, 163
impulse, 152, 220
in, 140, 141, 142, 191, 205–06,
207, 211, 213, 217, 220, 221,
222, 231, 232
income, 157
increase, 126, 152, 180; *increasing*, 227
industry, 152, 191
-*ing*, 168, 176–82, 189, 230–31
ink, 125, 177, 180
insect, 126, 132
inside, 157
instrument, 126, 152, 156
insurance, 152, 203
interest, 180, 200, 211, 218, 220;
-*ing*, 197
into, 140, 141, 157, 191, 195,
198, 214, 215
invention, 152, 206
iron, 125, 180
island, 163, 216
it, see *he*
itself, 158

jelly, 195
jewel, 181; -*er*, 230
join, 180; -*er*, 230; -*ed*, 209
journey, 180, 200, 218
judge, 125, 178, 180, 188–89
jump, 134, 180

keep, 134, 135, 136, 169, 172,
196, 207, 214–15, 222, 231;
keeper, 230; *keeps*, 172; *keeping*, 169, 171; *kept*, 169, 171,
172
kettle, 147
key, 127

General Index

abstracts, science, 81, 108
ABC of Basic English, 7, 31, 39, 43, 89
acts, names of simple, 134
Addison, 17
adjectives, 23–24, 37, 129–33, 157–58; used as nouns, 189–90
adverbs, 32, 57, 146–47; position of, 164–65; and see *relative*
ambiguity, 72
America, 91
American Association for the Advancement of Science, 13, 14
American influence on English, 17
analytic tendency, 11, 15–17
Anglo-Saxon, 15
Annales Guébhard Séverine, 80–81
Argentine, 50
articles, 128–29
artificial languages, 8, 99
Athens, 91
Australia, 90
auxiliary language, international, 5, 50

Basic by Examples, 43
Basic Dictionary, The, 138
Basic English Foundation, 89–92, 101–02

Basic English Word List and System, copyright in the, 101
Basic English, the future of, 92–95, 107–08
Basic English word-list, 6, 7, 56–58, 73, 99
Basic Mathematics Dictionary, 107
Basic Parallel Library, 93–94
Basic Picture Talks, 19
Basic Step by Step, 6, 39, 43
Basic Way to English, The, 39, 74
Basic Words, The, 38, 39
Bengali, 49
Bentham's Theory of Fictions, 11, 20, 98
Bible in Basic English, The, 88, 441–42
Biology, 9, 393
Boston, Mass., 91
British Association, 81
British Council, 101
British Government and Basic English, 99–103, 376–80
Burma, 90
business, Basic for, 82–87

calendar, 14
Canada, 91
Catford, Professor J. C., 40
case inflections, 32
chemical formulae, 14

521